HISTORICAL SURVEY

OF

PRE-CHRISTIAN EDUCATION

HISTORICAL SURVEY

OF

PRE-CHRISTIAN EDUCATION

BY

S. S. LAURIE, A.M., LL.D.

PROFESSOR OF THE INSTITUTES AND HISTORY OF EDUCATION IN THE UNIVERSITY
OF EDINBURGH; AUTHOR OF 'INSTITUTES OF EDUCATION,' 'LANGUAGE
AND LINGUISTIC METHOD IN THE SCHOOL,' 'LIFE AND EDUCA-
TIONAL WRITINGS OF COMENIUS,' ETC.

FOURTH IMPRESSION

LONGMANS, GREEN, AND CO.
91 AND 93 FIFTH AVENUE, NEW YORK
LONDON, BOMBAY, AND CALCUTTA

1907

Republished, 1970
Scholarly Press, 22929 Industrial Drive East, St. Clair Shores, Michigan 48080

Standard Book Number 403-00214-1
Library of Congress Catalog Card Number: 76-108504

COPYRIGHT, 1900, BY

LONGMANS, GREEN, AND CO.

First Edition, June, 1900.
Reprinted, November, 1902.
October, 1904.
August, 1907.

This edition is printed on a high-quality,
acid-free paper that meets specification
requirements for fine book paper referred
to as "300-year" paper

PREFACE

THIS book is a historical survey, not a history. At the same time I believe that nothing essential to the understanding of pre-Christian education has been omitted.

In traversing so wide a field, I cannot expect to have escaped errors: I hope these are of a minor kind and that they will be pointed out. Certain opinions may be considered erroneous by some of the experts in the various departments of historical inquiry in which I have involved myself: but until experts are themselves at one, I may be allowed to form my own judgment.

The greatest difficulty that presented itself was the giving expression, within the limits of a few pages, to the religious and ethical attitude of the various nations of antiquity to life and its duties. Brief statements on so all-important a matter cannot fail to be inadequate, and this all the more because the gradual historical development of religious beliefs has, for our purposes, to be ignored.

My aim has been to seize the leading religious and social characteristics of pre-Christian societies as these were actually found *operative in the life of the people* of each nation taken as a whole. For example, the purified and abstract religious conceptions of the Greek dramatists and philosophers are in the history of thought of surpassing value, but they had little to do with the religious and moral forces which governed the actual life of the Hellenic races. The general current of religious belief and emotion on which Greece was carried forward to the manifestation of a supreme activity in arts and arms is what chiefly concerns the educational historian. For it was on this broad current alone that the life, and consequently the education, of the people was borne along.

So with the Hindus. The doctrines of Brahmanical philosophical sects are part of the history of thought, but it is only the governing idea of Brahmanism and the moral sentiments and convictions flowing from this, that are reflected in the life, character, and education of the race. I hope that the reader will bear these things in mind and not expect from me more than I profess to give.

Further, in estimating the civilisation of a people, I have had to confine myself to that point of time at which they were approaching the highest expression of the national idea.

As regards Egypt, Babylon, and Assyria, I have formed my own judgment on the materials at present available. Every reader will understand that the history of these countries is now in the process of reconstruction. Professor Flinders Petrie's History, now being published, when followed by a history and estimate of Egyptian civilisation, will doubtless place Egyptology on a firmer basis.

S. S. LAURIE.

NOTE.

THE various chapters are based on the authorities enumerated, with references to many others not named (including Encyclopædias). In the final revision before printing, I kept before me, and took occasional assistance from, Schmidt's *Geschichte der Pädagogik*, 1870, and Schmid's *Geschichte der Erziehung*, &c., 1885, chiefly in the chapters on Greek education.

UNIVERSITY OF EDINBURGH, *April*, 1895.

NOTE TO SECOND EDITION

IN this second edition I have made corrections — these, however, verbal except in the chapter on the Jews.

S. S. L.

EDINBURGH, 1900.

CONTENTS

THE ARYAN OR INDO-EUROPEAN RACES

Hindus, Medo-Persians, Hellenes, Italians (Romans)

HISTORICAL SURVEY

OF

PRE-CHRISTIAN EDUCATION

INTRODUCTION

THE PLACE OF THE HISTORY OF EDUCATION IN UNIVERSAL HISTORY

THE history of education is involved in the general history of the world. No adequate survey of it is possible which does not presume a considerable acquaintance with the history of the leading races which have occupied and subdued the earth and formed themselves into civilised societies.

At what successive periods did these races enter on a progressive civilisation ; what were the leading intellectual and moral characteristics of each ; under what circumstances of climate, soil, and contention with other nascent or dying nations were these native characteristics developed and moulded; and what was the issue of all to the wealth, the life, the thought, the art of humanity ? — these are questions which concern us intimately as students of the history of education. For the history of the education of a people is not the history of its schools, but the history of its civilisation; and its civilisation finds its record mainly in its intellectual, moral, and æsthetic products, and only in a subordinate way in its material successes, and its achievements in war.

To treat of the education of the human race in this its broadest conception would be to attempt a philosophy of

1

history. We have accordingly to narrow our view, and this we can do only by first narrowing the scope of the word education. The education of the ancient Egyptians, for example, is not precisely synonymous with the history of the civilisation of that race as a factor in the universal history of man. At the same time, it certainly embraces an estimate of the civilising forces at work among that remarkable people, and involves our forming a pretty clear conception of their social organisation and of the ideal of life and character to which they unconsciously attained, or after which they consciously strove. For by education, even in the narrow sense in which the word must be employed here, I understand the means which a nation, with more or less consciousness, takes for bringing up its citizens to maintain the tradition of national character, and for promoting the welfare of the whole as an organised ethical community. It is essential, therefore, that we should understand the objects which the nation, as such, desired to secure; in brief, its own more or less conscious ideal of national and civic life, of personal character, and of ideal political justice. If we can ascertain this by the study of its highest products in men, deeds, thought and arts, we have made a great step towards interpreting the course of training to which it would naturally endeavour to subject its youth by means of its laws and institutions.

In a historical survey we can afford to ignore the vast variety of tribes which are still in a savage state, and which, either by innate incapacity for development, or by the force of irresistible external circumstances, have risen little above the beasts that perish. The human possibilities of such tribes may be, in germ, as high as those of many more favoured races; but this is doubtful. They labour to acquire skill in getting food by the exercise either of bodily vigour or successful cunning, and they cherish the virtue of bravery in warding off the attacks of others like themselves. As they have, however, no political or ethical ideal, they can have no education in the sense in which we use the term in this book. They can teach us nothing. For, training to expertness in the use of the weapons of the chase or of war is not education, except in a narrow technical sense. It is only when the *ideas* of bodily vigour, of bravery, of strength, bodily beauty, or personal morality, become desired for themselves, or as the necessary conditions of political life and national conservation, that education begins. The training which the national idea gives has then an ideal aim more or less conscious. An education which contemplates an ideal of life for each man, as distinct from the state organism as a whole, is, necessarily, of later growth.

It is only, then, with those nations which, by virtue of their ordered civilisation, had an idea of individual or of national life, and which, by virtue of their having this idea, possessed a civilisation, that we have to do. The races which chiefly interest us are the Indo-European or Aryan, to which we ourselves belong, and it might be sufficient to trace the history of education among the peoples who bear the Aryan character as that has developed itself west of the Caucasus. But we should feel the survey of educational history to be imperfect if we did so. It is desirable, therefore, to comprehend other races, such as the Hamitic, the Semitic, and Uro-Altaic; and not wholly to omit the Aryan element south-east of the Caucasus. We are, of course, compelled to confine ourselves, in dealing with the education of almost all these races, to the highest and most generalised expression of their national life; and this, frequently, for want of materials to do anything else.

As the ideal of life grows in a nation, its idea of education grows and it begins to ask more and more in a self-conscious way, How can we attain this ideal in the persons of our children ? Thus arise *systems* of education in civilised countries. Such systems or customs as may have existed prior to the asking of this question are not consciously constructed with a view to a specific result. Nations feel their way, by slow degrees, to the highest expression of their corporate life and to the best machinery for sustaining and promoting it, taught by the results of experience and their ever-growing thought on the nature and destiny of man and the conditions of national permanence. Thus it is that the education of a nation has always been determined mainly by its moral and spiritual leaders. These, as the historians of its experience and the conservators of its thought, rightfully govern. They have in all ages, till recent times, been more or less identified with a church or priesthood in one form or other; and if there be no distinctive organised priesthood as among the Chinese, Greeks, and Romans, then by that which takes its place — a political aristocracy which always embodies in its scheme of civil life, moral and religious, if not also theological, conceptions. In such cases the State is the church.

The educational aim, we shall find, is always practical in the large sense of that word; for, even in its highest aspects, it has always to do with life in some form or other, and indeed presumes a certain philosophy of life. Even philosophy, religion and poetry have a practical aim — the nobler life of a man as an individual and as a citizen; and, when they forget this aim, they degenerate into verbal frivolities or empty forms. This higher form of the practical aim is 'liberal' education.

But not only in this larger sense is the educational aim always practical, but till the time of the Athenians it was always practical in the narrower sense of the word. Indeed, in every form of national education, the 'practical' in the restricted sense of the term, in other words, the professional and technical, always occupied (and must always occupy) the greater part of the field, thwarting or promoting the larger general aim. It is this narrower aim, which statesmen and politicians generally contemplate in their public acts; for all civilised societies demand services of a specific kind, which can fitly be discharged only by those who are trained to discharge them. The division of occupations, all of which

are in their degree serviceable to the community, makes
specific training necessary, if service is to be efficiently rendered. Thus we have classes of the population trained and
devoted to the various industrial arts; to the fine arts; to the
service of man's body—the medical art; to the service of
mutual rights — the legal art; to the service of man's spirit —
the priestly art, of which last the teaching art, in the highest
conception of it, is a branch; to the military art; and so forth.

The education of a man as a member of a nation and for
manhood simply, is what we mean by 'liberal' education,
and this, I have said, is to be identified with the 'practical'
in its highest sense, which may be summed up in the word
'ethical': the training for specific services, again, is technical,
whether we dignify some of these services by calling them
professions or not. The stress of competition among individuals and nations compels us, unhappily, more and more
to give a specific character to our training, and to ignore the
larger national and human aims. It is clear, however, that
in so far as we lose sight of the latter in the interest of the
former we err: because it is the broad human and national
element in education that gives character and power and
makes itself felt in every department of work. If we fail in
giving this, all specific activities of mind will be weakened
by the weakening of their foundation in the man as a man.
In the systematisation of education accordingly, the real
problem amounts in these days to this: How shall we rear
specific aptitudes on the basis of a common instruction and
discipline which shall contemplate the man and the citizen,
and only in the second place the worker? 'This (ideal perfection of citizenship) is,' says Plato,[1] 'the only education
which in our view deserves the name; that other sort of
training which aims at the acquisition of wealth or bodily
strength or mere cleverness, apart from intelligence and justice, is mean and illiberal and not worthy to be called education at all.'

[1] *Laws*, i. 465, as rendered by Jowett.

The modern educational problem may, perhaps, be put thus: — How shall we conserve the national type, tradition, and ideal, and, while training for specific arts, educate all to such manhood as their racial possibilities and historical tradition admit of?

In the historical evolution of the educational idea we may note at least three stages. First of all, we have the unpremeditated education of national character and institutions, and of instinctive ideals of personal and community life in contact with definite external conditions, and moulding or being moulded by these. Secondly, we find that the education of the citizen becomes a matter of public concern, and means, often inadequate, are taken by individuals or societies within the State for handing down the national tradition by the agency of the family and the school, and by public institutions and ceremonials; but there is no systematised purpose. Thirdly: Education passes out of the hands of irregular agencies, and, from being a merely public and voluntary, becomes a political or State interest. We then have a more or less conscious ideal of national life, determining the organisation of educational agencies and reducing these to an elaborate system designed to meet the wants of the citizen at every age from infancy to manhood.

Education, in the third stage of development, is to a large extent taken out of the hands of the family. But at all stages of educational history (and notwithstanding the action of the State) the family is the chief agency in the education of the young, and as such, it ought never to be superseded. The State is made up of families rather than of individuals: the family is the true moral unit. We are what our fathers have made us, and future generations are what we are even now making our children. There is a continuity in the life of a nation, and the individual, here and now, is a mere transition point from the past to the future. It is in truth the family tradition, along with civil and religious institutions, which chiefly educates. Whatever tradition there may be of opinion and conduct, whatever may be the laws and institutions by which the State protects itself as an organised body, it must rely on the family to hand down and perpetuate these and to give them the support of the affections and sentiments of our nature. And where, owing to the social necessities of a complex civilisation, it is found necessary to set apart a class to help in the work which it is the primary duty of parents to discharge, that class should regard itself as, in every sense, *in loco parentis :* that is to say, the aims, instruments, and methods of the school should always be those of a humane and enlightened parent. The moral and religious influence of the school ought to be, for example, as far as possible, a mere continuation and extension of the family conception of education, and not an alien substitute for it. If this be understood and accepted, the deductions from it will be found to be numerous and significant.

As we survey the annals of education we see that it is the national tradition through the family that constitutes the earliest form. The Romans had thus moulded themselves and their State and were already marked for empire, before they had any schools. So the Persians were a brilliant and imperial nation, though destitute of schools in any modern sense of the word. Hellenic education, again, for probably two centuries before Socrates, was an illustration of the second period of national education in which State tradition and institutions combined with schools (existing but as yet undeveloped) to form the Greek mind and body. In post-Socratic times the Greek became self-conscious in his educational aims — he had a type of man whom he aimed at producing. The Romans towards the end of the Republic followed, with some differences, the leading of Greece ; but it cannot be said that education was ever systematised by either people.

The only nations in pre-Christian times, who had attained to the third stage of national education before the Christian era, were the Chinese and the Doric Greeks as represented by the Spartans. The former had, and have, a definite ideal of human excellence, such as it is ; but always with a view to the service of a bureaucratic State. So with the Spartans, where the whole organisation (but the Spartans were, after all, a mere tribe) was educational, and where every freeborn citizen was deliberately formed to a certain ideal — also (as in China) in the interests of civic continuity.

The Hellenic races, however, much as we owe them, had no conception of education as a *human* need and a *human* right; they thought only of the free, pure Greeks who formed an aristocracy among a body of servile inferiors. This characteristic of the Greeks was specially emphasised in Sparta. The Romans, also, thought chiefly of the upper half of society. In Egypt, Judæa, Persia, and China, on the other hand, nothing stood, *theoretically at least*, between the lowest member of the community and the best the State could offer in the way of education, except poverty. It was the Stoics in the earlier imperial times who first rose to the conception of humanity and of human, as distinct from local and national rights ; and Christianity about the same time proclaimed these. The Stoic and Christian were the first humanitarians, and consequently the first to believe in the inherent right of each citizen to claim education for himself.

In taking a survey of educational history we have to bear in mind the distinctions I have made in these introductory remarks (and which might with advantage be even further elaborated) and carry them always with us. If we do not, we shall certainly fail to interpret facts aright and to learn the lessons which the past has to teach.

THE HAMITIC RACES

THE HAMITIC RACES

UNDER the designation Hamites are generally included Egyptians, Ethiopians to the south of Egypt, Libyans to the west and north-west, the inhabitants of south-eastern Arabia, and the Hittites (extending from the Taurus range to Canaan). In the Egyptians this race of mankind found the highest expression of its capacity for civilised life, as did the Hebrews among the Semites, the Chinese among the Uro-Altaic (Turanian) and the Greeks among the Aryans. And quite apart from their superiority to other nations of their own blood, we find the Egyptians to be by far the most interesting of ancient peoples, in respect, at least, of the antiquity and detailed organisation of their complex civilisation.

EGYPT

IT is now generally believed that the original immigrants who formed the Egyptian nation did not come from Ethiopia or Libya, but from the interior of Asia.[1]

Egypt proper is a country made, and it may be almost said annually re-made, by a single river — the Nile, which, rising in the equatorial regions, falls into the Mediterranean. The water and mud deposited by the river in its annual

---

[1] Professor Petrie, in vol. i. of his History, says that the Egyptians came from the land of Pun or Punt, which seems to have been on both sides of the southern part of the Red Sea, having reached this region from the vicinity of the Persian Gulf, moving south and west. He connects them with the Phœnicians, who would then have to be classed under the Hamitic, and not the Semitic, race. The history of Egypt is usually given under thirty dynasties, beginning, according to Mariette, with Ména, 4400 B.C., and ending with Alexander the Great, B.C. 332. These do not include that of the foreign (and doubtless Semitic) Hyksos, which lasted about 500 years prior to 2226 B.C.

inundations have made Egypt probably the most fertile tract of country in the world. When we consider that it is enclosed on all sides by desert or mountains or seas, and thus shut off from contact with other countries, we can understand that it should early become the home of a settled people who would develop their life and civilisation from within. It is this exclusion from external influences that gives to Egypt, a unique position in the history of civilisation.[1] The fertility of the soil, and we may add the easy conditions of life caused by an almost uniform climate, enabled the Nile basin to support a large population. The tradition is that there were 20,000 cities, but doubtless among cities were included what we should call villages.

The conquering race which occupied Egypt (already inhabited by a primitive barbarian population) had three leading characteristics — a natural capacity for equity and government, a shrewd practical intelligence, and a deep religious sense in which the feeling of awe predominated. Their religious sentiment revolved round two points, (1) A feeling of wonder as they contemplated the forces of nature and the regular and beneficent recurrence of natural events. This was forced on the Egyptians, above all other races, by the peculiarities of their physical conditions. (2) The fact and mystery of death which always lay close to the Egyptian mind. The Pyramids alone, were there no other records, would testify to all time the profound sense of the seriousness of life and the majesty of death which characterised the ancient Egyptians.

Political constitution. — At a very early period we find the country divided into forty-two nomes or districts, each with its own captain or governor. It would seem that the chieftainship was originally hereditary, and that Egypt was a feudal monarchy; but as the monarchy gained strength these heads of nomes were either appointed by the sovereign

---

[1] The same remark applies to China. I do not mean to say that Egypt and China had no external relations, but merely that they were as nothing compared with those of other races.

or had to be confirmed in their authority by him. Egypt was a monarchy from very early times (probably 5000 years B.C.), but the relation of the monarch to the nomes and their chiefs fluctuated, and the heads of principalities frequently quarrelled with each other and with the central government. The monarchy, when finally supreme, was despotic in its character, and supported by a strong and wealthy priesthood. Ranke points out that a despotic monarchy was a necessity of the situation, not only because of the need of a central authority for civil and military purposes, but also because of the annual inundations which had to be regulated throughout the length and breadth of Egypt and made local autonomy impossible. One river made Egypt, and there was consequent need for a central administration to watch and regulate the waters and settle questions of ever-shifting boundaries as the waters retired. The monarch was centre of all government, and, as symbol of the unity of the life of the nation in a material as well as moral sense, he was likened to god, and called the son of god; and not only *called* the son, but *believed* to be the son of the god (RA), and treated as such during his lifetime. He was, in a real and practical sense, regarded as god on earth and intermediary with the gods in heaven.

The administrators of justice, after a certain date, may have been men of legal training; but speaking of Egypt generally, we find that the decision of civil suits and the trial of criminal cases was a part of the general executive functions of the chiefs of nomes and the governors of towns or villages. ' For a certain number of days in the month they sat at the gate of the town or of the building which served as their residence, and all those possessed of any title, position, or property, the superior priesthood of the temples, scribes who had advanced or grown old in office, those in command of the militia or police, the heads of divisions or corporations, might, if they thought fit, take their position beside them and help to decide ordinary lawsuits.'[1] The

[1] Maspero's *Dawn of Civilisation in the East*, p. 336.

poor man, we may presume, had little chance of obtaining a just decision before a tribunal so constituted, if his claim conflicted with that of his social superiors. The monarch was fountain of law and justice. The system, on the whole, of law or usage seems to have been mild, and to have been administered with equity and clemency.

The government really governed, and the consequence of this was infinite bureaucratic detail and an army of officials of all kinds.

Religion and Ethics. — It is exceedingly difficult to give an account which shall be at once brief and intelligible, and at the same time fairly accurate, of the religion of Egypt, the land of the 'thousand gods.' Our desire to attain to a unity of view and to discover some central-principle is almost baffled, and we can, at best, only partially succeed.

There can be little doubt that the earliest gods worshipped by the Egyptians were, as was natural, the Sun (Ra) and the Nile. But some confusion arises from the fact that the same gods were worshipped under different names in the various cities.

It would appear, however, that a very simple idea lay at the root of the Egyptian religion. The elements were not merely objects of sense, they were living gods; they had their doubles. 'The sky,' says M. Maspero,[1] 'the earth, the stars, the sun, the Nile, were so many breathing and thinking beings whose lives were daily manifest in the life of the universe. They were worshipped from one end of the valley to the other, and the whole nation agreed in proclaiming their sovereign power. But when they began to name them, to define their powers and attributes, to particularise their forms or the relationship which subsisted among them, this unanimity was at an end. Each principality, each nome, each city, almost every village, conceived and represented these differently.'

Animals and statues were not merely symbolic of the gods; but the gods dwelt in them. Other objects of nature

---

[1] Maspero's *Dawn of Civilisation in the East*, p. 85.

which evoked surprise were worshipped, *e. g.* sycamore trees growing where no tree should be. It is evident that on these lines of religious thought, there would be no end to the number of gods. 'Each family and almost every individual possessed gods and fetishes which had been pointed out for their worship by some fortuitous meeting with an animal or an object, or indicated by a dream or a sudden intuition' (p. 122).

The worship was a worship by sacrifice and offerings and invocations, wholly with the purpose of securing the help of the god or gods in the affairs of life. I cannot find that it had any ethical or spiritual significance, save thus far, that it was an expression of reverential awe and not of craven fear. The ordinary Hebrew also looked for material blessings, but there was much more than this in his case: his worship was essentially the fulfilling of a contract or covenant — on his side the fulfilment of the moral law, and on the other side, the favour of God as God. The detail of sacrifice in the Egyptian temples was most minute, affecting the purification and dress of the priest, and the qualifications and slaughter of the animals. It was necessary also that the priest should repeat the traditionary formulas and prayers with absolute exactness and with the authorised intonations and rhythm ; otherwise they lost altogether their efficacy.

The chief of the nome or principality acted as priest in the earlier centuries : the high priest of all was the Pharaoh. It being vain, however, to expect ritualistic perfection in men occupied with other affairs, the custom grew up of associating officials as priests with the civil authorities. Thus each temple had its staff of priests and a high priest set over them, and gradually there grew up a graded hierarchy. These temples received numerous gifts and legacies from worshippers seeking favour in this life from the gods, or wishing to buy the prayers of the priests when they, the worshippers, were dead. The temples thus became wealthy corporations.

The sacerdotal temple or college had each not only its own hierarchy, but its own theology. The god of each nome temple was addressed as the chief god among all the gods and as the maker of the world. To Heliopolis, where there was a strong priestly college, is due the attempt to arrange the chief gods in a hierarchy with one supreme over all the rest. The other temples of Egypt accepted this substantially; but they naturally reserved the supreme position for their own local god. The idea, however, was the same — a supreme god working through subordinate agencies in the creation of the world. It may be, as M. Maspero says, that Egypt, as a whole, never accepted the idea of a one sole god;[1] but in the elevation of the various nomic gods to supremacy, the idea of a one supreme god was unquestionably operative.

The belief in immortality was universal; but the life beyond the grave suggests to us, in the earlier stages of doctrine, nothing better than the Accadian underworld or the Homeric Hades. The soul kept the distinctive character and appearance which pertained to it ' upon the earth '; as it had been a ' double ' before death, so it remained a double after it, able to perform all functions of man-life after its own fashion. It moved, went, came, spoke, breathed, accepted pious homage, but without pleasure, and as it were mechanically; rather from an instinctive horror of annihilation than from any rational desire for immortality. Unceasing regret for the bright world which it had left disturbed its mournful and inert existence. ' O my brother,' are the words of a hymn, ' withhold not thyself from drinking and from eating, from drunkenness, from love, from all enjoyment, from following thy desire by night and by day; put not sorrow within thy heart, for what are the years of a man upon earth ? The West is a land of sleep and of heavy shadow, a place wherein its inhabitants when once installed slumber on in their mummy forms, never more waking to see their brethren; never more to recognise their fathers or their mothers; with hearts forgetful of their wives and children. The living water which earth giveth to all who dwell upon it is for me

[1] It does not follow from this that the more cultured few did not recognise a One Supreme Being.

but stagnant and dead; that water floweth to all who are on
earth, while for me it is but liquid putrefaction, this water
that is mine. Since I came into this funereal valley I know
not where nor what I am. Give me to drink of running
water! Let me be placed by the edge of the water with my
face to the North, that the breeze may caress me and my
heart be refreshed from its sorrow.' [1] This is a very ancient
hymn. The conception of the life beyond the grave, however, subsequently took a more elevated form, and to secure
eternal felicity good works had to be done on earth.

The Book of the Dead (more correctly translated, 'The
Book of the goings forth to Day'), the sacred Scripture of
the Egyptians, is in truth a guide book for departed spirits in
the underworld where they find their way through many
difficulties, by the help of texts, prayers, and incantations, to
the presence of OSIRIS, god of the dead and of the underworld,
and his jury,[2] the forty-two judges who are ' Lords of Truth.'
The confession which the soul is represented as making before the god and jury is the most interesting of Egyptian
theological remains, indicating a marked advance on earlier
ideas. The soul which is acquitted of evil escapes the misery of the underworld as described above, and it does so
on moral grounds. Having found its way to the halls of
OSIRIS in Hades it makes an appeal to OSIRIS and the jury
of gods.[3] This appeal is of the nature of a confession which,
however, is chiefly negative. The appellant spirit says
that he has *not* been guilty of the oppression of the poor
and the slave, of assassination, treason, cheating by false
balances, refusing temple offerings, disregard for temple
property, lying, stealing, fornication, adultery, blasphemy,
false witness, and generally that he has not committed any
crime. The positive part of the confession says that he has
spread joy on all sides, given bread to the hungry, water
to the thirsty, clothing to the naked. We have here the

[1] *The Dawn of Civilisation*, p. 113.
[2] The translations I have read are that of Birch in Bunsen, and that in
Dr. Davis' recent *Book of the Dead*. This is sufficient for my purpose.
[3] Chap. 125 in Davis' edition.

ethical creed of the ancient Egyptian, a good working commonplace creed, but nothing more. If we add the proverbs
and prudential precepts of Ptah-hetep (3600 B.C., the oldest
book in the world), we probably exhaust the thought of
the Egyptian on moral and social relations. His relation
to the gods was, and could be, nothing but abstract adoration or service in the interests of his own material felicity.
It has further to be noted that the bliss which a favourable
sentence secured to the soul was, in the earlier stages of
religious development, simply the enjoyment of life in its
old haunts, somewhat heightened and permanently secured.
A further advance was manifest when the highest bliss was
held to be sharing the life of the sun-god, but with power
to leave the bark of the sun when the soul chose, and enjoy
earthly life once more. We may, if we choose, call this a
'blessed immortality.' It certainly was as high a conception
of the future as any pre-christian nation attained to.

The question is, was there behind all this polytheistic confusion any esoteric religious doctrine reserved for the inner
circle of the priesthood? If there had been, should we not
have had some record of it? One comes across suggestions
of a mystic esotericism, but in the books I have read I find
no evidence of it. This much, however, seems fully worthy
of acceptance, that the myth of Osiris, which embodied the
idea of the triumph of Light over Darkness, was interpreted
by the more thoughtful in an ethical sense. Further, that
the more thoughtful believed in a One God the Source of
All, Himself the 'Hidden One,' 'Self-begetting'; and not to
be represented by any symbol. The other gods, even when
addressed as supreme, were so only as operative gods. Many
of the hymns that survive place beyond all question the
existence of a belief among the more cultured in a one
Supreme Being not to be represented by any symbol. I
give in a footnote Professor Sayce's view,[1] which seems to
me highly probable.

[1] Professor Sayce says (*Ancient Empires of the East*, p. 60): ' The kernel
of the Egyptian state religion was solar.' At the head of the hierarchies of
gods we have ' a form of the sun-god.' The priesthood could have no diffi-

The popular religion was on a much lower plane of thought than that which we have been endeavouring briefly to describe. The worship of animals, on the assumption that they were, not merely the visible symbols of gods, but their abode, was highly characteristic of the people. It was a genuine worship and encouraged by the priests. But this animal worship seems, as the nation advanced, to have been regarded by all the more educated as merely symbolic. It clearly mattered little to the priests of a religion which had no special religious moral sanction derived from the essential attributes of the 'Hidden God,' what the masses worshipped, so long as they were reverent and devotional and obedient.[1] And this they certainly were. The belief in amulets, charms, and incantations was universal.

Along with the animal worship, and taking universal precedence of it, the visible objects of worship were always the Sun and the Nile. The following, which I quote from the ' Records of the Past,' vol. iv. (including the notes), is as late as the 19th Dynasty (1400 B.C.). It will be noted that the names of gods are frequently interchangeable, and fur-

culty in accepting this physical symbol of the creative and life-giving source of all. It was to Ptah, the ' personal ' creator, that the sacred bull was dedicated, in which he was incarnate. Nor is the above central conception inconsistent with the cosmogonic system, as given by Professor Sayce, which seems to be prior to the Theban Dynasty. ' In the philosophic system of the priesthood,' he says, ' Nun, or Chaos, was the first cause from which all proceed — unshaped, eternal, and immutable matter. Kheper, the scarabæus with the sun's disk, was the creative principle of life, which implanted in matter the seeds of life and light. Ptah, " the opener," was the personal creator or demiurge, who, along with the seven knumu, or architects, gave form to these seeds, and was at once the creator and opener of the primæval egg of the universe (the ball of earth rolled along by Kheper), out of which came the sun and moon according to the older myth, the elements and forms of heaven and earth, according to the later philosophy. Nut, the sky, with the star and boat of the sun on her back ; Seb, the earth, symbol of time and eternity, and Amenti, or Hades, now took their several shapes and places. Over this threefold world, the gods and other divine beings presided.'

[1] Almost all nations which have attained to civilisation have entered on the possession of lands already inhabited by inferior races. It is not improbable that animal worship was a continuation of the Totemism of the original occupants of the Nile Valley.

ther, that the devotional writer frequently passes from the particular god to the Universal Source of Order and Life — a natural transition common enough in all poetry, and constantly to be met with in Egyptian writings.

HYMN TO THE NILE

STROPHE I

Adoration of the Nile

1 Hail to thee, O Nile!
2 Thou showest thyself in this land,
3 Coming in peace, giving life to Egypt:
4 O AMMON, (thou) leadest night unto day,[1]
5 A leading that rejoices the heart!
6 Overflowing the gardens created by RA.[2]
7 Giving life to all animals;
8 Watering the land without ceasing:
9 The way of heaven descending:[3]
10 Lover of food, bestower of corn,
11 Giving light to every home, O PTAH!

II

1 Lord of fishes, when the inundation returns
2 No fowls fall on the cultures.[4]
3 Maker of spelt; creator of wheat:
4 Who maintaineth the temples!

---

[1] If this rendering is correct the meaning must be that the god of the Nile is the secret source of light; see sec. iii. 1. 5, and sec. viii. 1. 1. The attributes of Egyptian gods, who represent the unknown under various aspects, are interchangeable to a great extent; here the Nile is AMMON, doing also the work of RA. Dr. Birch suggests that the rendering may be 'hiding his course night and day.'

[2] RA, the sun-god, who is represented as delighting in flowers, see *Ritual of the Dead*, lxxxvi.: 'I am the pure lily which comes out of the fields of Ra.'

[3] The Nile-god traverses heaven; his course there corresponds to that of the river on earth.

[4] See x. 6. This is obscure, but it may mean that the Nile-god protects the newly-sown fields from the birds.

5 Idle hands he loathes [1]
6 For myriads, for all the wretched.
7 If the gods in heaven are grieved,[2]
8 Then sorrow cometh on men.

III

1 He maketh the whole land open to the oxen,[3]
2 And the great and the small are rejoicing,
3 The response of men at his coming![4]
4 His likeness is NUM![5]
5 He shineth, and then the land exulteth!
6 All bellies are in joy!
7 Every creature receives nourishment!
8 All teeth get food.

IV

1 Bringer of food! Great Lord of provisions!
2 Creator of all good things!
3 Lord of terrors [6] and of choicest joys!
4 All are combined in him.
5 He produceth grass for the oxen;
6 Providing victims for every god.
7 The choice incense is that which he supplies.
8 Lord in both regions,
9 He filleth the granaries, enricheth the storehouses,
10 He careth for the state of the poor.

V

1 He causes growth to fulfil all desires,
2 He never wearies of it.

[1] *I. e.* he sets them at work. Thus, *Ritual*, xv. 20: 'Ra, the giver of food, destroys all place for idleness, cuts off all excuse.
[2] As they are by idleness; see *Ritual*, cxxv. p. 255, Birch.
[3] *I. e.* he makes it ready for cultivation.
[4] Their joy and gratitude respond to his advance.
[5] Num is the Nile-god regarded as giving life.
[6] The Egyptian word corresponds to Ἀρσαφης, which, according to Plutarch, signifies τὸ ἀνδρεῖον, *Isis et Osiris*, c. 37. The Egyptians, like all ancient people, identify terror with strength or greatness.

3 He maketh his might a buckler.[1]
4 He is not graven in marble,[2]
5 As an image bearing the double crown.
6 He is not beheld :
7 He hath neither ministrants nor offerings :
8 He is not adored in sanctuaries :
9 His abode is not known :
10 No shrine is found with painted figures.[3]

VI

1 There is no building that can contain him ![4]
2 There is no councillor in thy heart!
3 Thy youth delight in thee, thy children :
4 Thou directest[5] them as King,
5 Thy law is established in the whole land,
6 In the presence of thy servants of the North :[6]
7 Every eye is satisfied with him :[7]
8 He careth for the abundance of his blessings.

VII

1 The inundation comes (then), cometh rejoicing :
2 Every heart exulteth :

[1] This scriptural phrase comes in abruptly. It is probably drawn from some older source.

[2] The true deity [*i.e.* the supreme god of gods], is not represented by any image. This is a relic of primæval monotheism, out of place as referring to the Nile, but pointing to a deeper and sounder faith. Compare the laws of Manu, i. 5–7.

[3] See last line of sec. xiii. There are no shrines covered, as usual, with coloured hieroglyphics. The whole of this passage is of extreme importance, showing that, apart from all objects of idolatrous worship, the old Egyptian recognised the existence of a Supreme God, unknown and inconceivable, the true source of all power and goodness. Compare the oldest forms of the 17th chapter of the funeral ritual in Lepsius, *Aelteste Texte.*

[4] 1 Kings viii. 27.

[5] Or, 'thou givest them counsels, orderest all their goings.'

[6] *I. e.* 'all magistrates are the servants of the deity, and administer his law from south to north.'

[7] Maspero, 'par lui est bue l'eau (les pleurs) de tous les yeux,' *i. e.* 'wipes away tears from all eyes.'

3 The tooth of the crocodiles, the children of NEITH [1]
4 (Even) the circle of the gods who are counted with thee.
5 Doth not its outburst water the fields,
6 Overcoming mortals (with joy) ;
7 Watering one to produce another? [2]
8 There is none who worketh with him ;
9 He produces food without the aid of NEITH. [3]
10 Mortals he causes to rejoice.

VIII

1 He giveth light on his coming from darkness : [4]
2 In the pastures of his cattle
3 His might produceth all :
4 What was not, his moisture bringeth to life.
5 Men are clothed to fill his gardens :
6 He careth for his labourers.
7 He maketh even and noontide,
8 He is the infinite PTAH and KABES. [5]
9 He createth all works therein,
10 All writings, all sacred words,
11 All his implements in the North. [6]

IX

1 He enters with words the interior of his house, [7]
2 When he willeth he goeth forth from his mystic fane.
3 Thy wrath is destruction of fishes. [8]

---

[1] Dr. Birch, to whom I am indebted for this rendering, observes that the goddess Neith is often represented with two crocodiles sucking her breasts.

[2] *I. e.* 'The Nile fills all mortals with the languor of desire, and gives fecundity.'

[3] *I. e.* 'without needing rain, the gift of the goddess of heaven.' Such seems to be the meaning of a very obscure passage.

[4] See note on section i.

[5] The meaning is evidently that he combines the attributes of Ptah, the Demiurge, and Kabes, an unknown god.

[6] All things serviceable to man — arms, implements, &c.

[7] This seems to mean, he gives oracles at his shrine. Observe the inconsistency of this with section 5.

[8] Causing scarcity of food in the land. See Exodus viii. 18, 21.

4 Then men implore thee for the waters of the season,[1]
5 That the Thebaid may be seen like the Delta,
6 That every man be seen bearing his tools,
7 No-man left behind his comrade!
8 Let the clothed be unclothed,
9 No adornments for the sons of nobles,
10 No circle of gods in the night!
11 The response (of the god) is refreshing water,
12 Filling all men with fatness.

X

1 Establisher of justice! men rejoice
2 With flattering words to worship [2] thee,
3 Worshipped together with the mighty water!
4 Men present offerings of corn,
5 Adoring all the gods:
6 No fowls fall on the land.[3]
7 Thy hand is adorned with gold,[4]
8 As moulded of an ingot of gold,
9 Precious as pure lapis lazuli; [5]
10 Corn in its state of germination is not eaten.

XI

1 The hymn is addressed to thee with the harp;
2 It is played with a (skilful) hand to thee!
3 The youths rejoice at thee!
4 Thy own children.
5 Thou hast rewarded their labour.
6 There is a great one adorning the land;

---

[1] In a season of scarcity prayers are offered for supply of water. The following lines seem to describe great haste when the inundation comes on; none wait for their clothing, even when valuable, and the nightly solemnities are broken up. But the passage is obscure.

[2] Literally answer, *i. e.* ' with thanks and prayers, when thou bringest the water in abundance.'

[3] See ii. 2.

[4] The gold represents the preciousness of the gift of food.

[5] This is often mentioned in the inscriptions amongst the most precious stones.

7 An enlightener, a buckler in front of men.
8 Quickening the heart in depression,
9 Loving the increase of all his cattle.

XII

1 Thou shinest in the city of the King;
2 Then the householders are satiated with good things,
3 The poor man laughs at the lotus.[1]
4 All things are perfectly ordered,
5 Every kind of herb for thy children.
6 If food should fail,
7 All enjoyment is cast on the ground,
8 The land falls in weariness.

XIII

1 O inundation of Nile, offerings are made to thee:
2 Oxen are slain to thee:
3 Great festivals are kept for thee;
4 Fowls are sacrificed to thee;
5 Beasts of the field are caught for thee;
6 Pure flames are offered to thee;
7 Offerings are made to every god,
8 As they are made unto Nile.
9 Incense ascends unto heaven,
10 Oxen, bulls, fowls are burnt!
11 Nile makes for himself chasms in the Thebaid;[2]
12 Unknown is his name in heaven,
13 He doth not manifest his forms!
14 Vain are all representations![3]

XIV

1 Mortals extol (him), and the cycle of gods!
2 Awe is felt by the terrible ones;
3 His son[4] is made Lord of all,

---

[1] Which he ate when he could get nothing else.
[2] An allusion to the legend that the Nile comes forth from two openings in the south.
[3] See v. last line.   [4] The Pharaoh.

4 To enlighten all Egypt.[1]
5 Shine forth, shine forth, O Nile ! shine forth !
6 Giving life to men by his oxen :
7 Giving life to his oxen by the pastures !
8 Shine forth in glory, O Nile !

But while the Nile and the Sun were always the supreme visible gods to the Egyptian, from a very early date the symbol of supreme divine power, as manifested in nature, did not restrict itself to these deities, but extended to animals as symbolic of various gods; and, in the course of time, there can be little doubt that with the masses nothing remained but the symbol, with a vague sense of some divine power behind it.[2] This vague sense was, however, undoubtedly there, and its existence could alone justify Ranke's view that there was nothing secular to the ancient Egyptian; 'properly speaking, there was nothing profane in the land.'[3] What most struck Herodotus, when, in the middle of the fifth century before the Christian era, he visited the country, was the extreme religiosity of its inhabitants. 'The Egyptians,' he says, 'are religious to excess, far beyond any other race of men. They themselves speak of the "thousand gods."' The greater portion of the description of Egypt by the Greek historian is occupied with an account of the priests, the temples, and the religious ceremonies. In the architectural remains, we see that the temple dominates the palace, and is

[1] The two regions.

[2] 'Who does not know,' says Juvenal (xv. 1), 'what kinds of monsters demented Egypt worships ?'

[3] The animal worship reached its culmination at Memphis in the worship of the sacred bull, known as Hapi, or Apis, an incarnation of the god PHTHAH. He had a temple, priestly attendants, and a harem of cows. He was brought out on the occasion of great processions and was worshipped by the people. When he died he was embalmed and buried in a polished granite sarcophagus.* It is a remarkable spectacle the mixture which Egypt presents of 'high spiritual conceptions with debased animal worship' (to borrow Professor Sayce's expression). I cannot identify the 'high spiritual conceptions' to which Professor Sayce refers, at least as far as the commonalty was concerned.

---

* The cost of his funeral is said to have been about 20,000*l.*

itself dominated by the tomb, both the temple and the tomb being the expression of religious ideas. Everywhere in Egypt gigantic. structures upreared themselves into the air, enriched with all that Egyptian art could supply of painted and sculptured decoration, dedicated to the honour, and bearing the sacred name, of some divinity. The great temple of each city was the centre of its life. A perpetual ceremonial of the richest kind went on within its walls; along its shady corridors, or through its sunlit courts, long processions made their way up or down its avenues of sphinxes. The calendar was crowded with festivals, and a week rarely passed without the performance of some special religious ceremony possessing its own peculiar attractions.[1]

The sentiment of religious awe in the contemplation of the facts of life and death, did not interfere with practical activity or the enjoyment of life. The mental attitude of the Egyptian is, in part at least, well expressed in the festal song which was so universally popular among them.

FESTAL DIRGE

1 Wanting

2 The song of the house of king ANTUF, deceased, which is (written) in front of

3 The player on the harp.[2]
   All hail to the good Prince,
   the worthy good (man)!
   The body is fated (?) to pass away,
   the atoms

4 remain, ever since the time of the ancestors.
   The gods who were beforetime rest in their tombs,
   the mummies

5 of the saints likewise are enwrapped in their tombs.
   They who build houses, and they who have no houses, see!

---

[1] The above sentences seem to be a quotation from some one — probably Rawlinson or Wilkinson, I forget which.

[2] *The Song of the Harper* in the tomb of Nefer-hotep bears a great resemblance to this composition; see Dumichen, *Historische Inschriften*, ii. pl. 40.

6 what becomes of them.
   I have heard the words of IMHOTEP [1] and HARTATEF.[2]
   It is said in their sayings,
7 After all, what is prosperity ?
   Their fenced walls are dilapidated.
   Their houses are as that which has never existed.
8 No man comes from thence
   who tells of their savings,
   who tells of their affairs,
   who encourages our hearts.
   Ye go
9 to the place whence they return not.[3]
   Strengthen thy heart to forget how thou hast enjoyed thyself,
   fulfil thy desire whilst thou livest.
10 Put oils upon thy head,
   clothe thyself with fine linen adorned with precious metals,
11 with the *gifts* of God
   multiply thy good things,
   yield to thy desire,
   fulfil thy desire with thy good things
12 (whilst thou art) upon earth
   according to the dictation of thy heart.
   The day will come to thee,
   when one hears not the voice
   when the one who is at rest hears not
13 their voices.[4]
   Lamentations deliver not him who is in the tomb.
14 Feast in tranquillity,[5]
   seeing that there is no one who carries away his goods with
   him.
   Yea, behold, none who goes thither comes back again.[6]

---

[1] Imhotep, the son of the primæval deity Ptah, was the mythical author of various arts and sciences. The Greeks spelt the name Imepth, but more frequently substituted the name Asclepios.

[2] Hartatef was the son of King Menkera (Mycerinus), to whom the discovery of part of the *Ritual* (cap. lxiv.) is attributed, and who was the author of a mystical work.

[3] Compare the Assyrian phrase 'The land men cannot return from.' 'Descent of Ishtar,' *Records of the Past*, vol. i. p. 143; ii. p. 5.

[4] *I.e.* ' of the mourners.'   [5] Here follows a lacuna.

[6] From *Records of the Past*, iv. 117.

The beliefs and worship of the Egyptians, while giving expression to a sombre religious sentiment and a feeling of profound awe in contemplating Nature, the life of man and above all the stern fact of Death, exercised great influence in teaching reverence generally, and consequently submissiveness and obedience. But they had little moral significance. The only potent ethical force in the system of religious thought was the belief in immortality. When this had fully emerged from its cruder form of ancestor worship, it assumed a character which places it on a high level, and far above the conceptions of the Greeks and Romans. A great and godlike future life was secured by a good life on earth. The human spirit which had been weighed in the balances of the Hall of Osiris returned to the God of Light, but yet retained its individuality. There arose in connection with this an ideal of conduct. That this ideal was understood or fully realised by the masses it is absurd to suppose. Indeed, among all classes the morality seems to have been often as low in practice as it was elevated in theory. But what shall we say of Christianity itself after 1900 years of existence? The following dirge well expresses the higher thought on life and immortality and reveals the undercurrent of melancholy in the Egyptian mind.

THE SONG OF THE HARPER

Chanted by the singer to the harp who is in the chapel of the Osirian, the Patriarch of Amen, the blessed Nefer-hotep.

He says:
The great one is truly at rest,
the good charge is fulfilled.
Men pass away since the time of RA,[1]
and the youths come in their stead.
Like as RA reappears every morning,
and TUM [2] sets in the horizon,
men are begetting,

[1] The sun.
[2] A form of the sun god of the west, the chief god of Heliopolis.

and women are conceiving.
Every nostril inhaleth once the breezes of dawn.
but all born of women go down to their places.

Make a good day, O holy father!
Let odours and oils stand before thy nostril.
Wreaths of lotus are on the arms and the bosom of thy sister,
dwelling in thy heart, sitting beside thee.
Let song and music be before thy face,
and leave behind thee all evil cares!
Mind thee of joy, till cometh the day of pilgrimage,
when we draw near the land which loveth silence.
Not . . . . [1] peace of heart . . . . [2] his loving son.

Make a good day, O blessed NEFERHOTEP,
thou Patriarch perfect and pure of hands!
He finished his existence . . (the common fate of men).
Their abodes pass away,
and their place is not;
they are as they had never been born
since the time of RA.
(They in the shades) are sitting on the bank of the river,
thy soul is among them, drinking its sacred water,
following thy heart, at peace . . . .
Give bread to him whose field is barren,
thy name will be glorious in posterity for evermore;
they will look upon thee . . . .
(The Priest clad in the skin) [3] of a panther will pour to the ground
and bread will be given as offerings;
the singing women . . . .
Their forms are standing before RA,
their persons are protected . . . .
RANNU [4] will come at her hour,

---

[1] Lacuna.   [2] Lacuna.

[3] The panther's skin was the special characteristic of the dress of the priest of Khem, the vivifier.

[4] Rannu, an Egyptian goddess who presided over the harvest.

Some one, I think, has suggested that the esoteric doctrine of the priesthood was this: The self-begetting Hidden One gives birth to Osiris the animating principle (Light of God and of life after death), and Isis as Nature — the manifestation of this principle in conflict with *Set* — darkness and evil.

and SHU will calculate his day,
thou shalt awake . . . . (woe to the bad one !)
He shall sit miserable in the heat of infernal fires.

Make a good day, O holy father,
NEFERHOTEP, pure of hands.
No works of buildings in Egypt could avail,
his resting place is all his wealth . . . .
Let me return to know what remaineth of him !
Not the least moment could be added to his life,
(when he went to) the realm of eternity.
Those who have magazines full of bread to spend
even they shall encounter the hour of a last end.
The moment of that day will diminish the valour of the
rich . . . .

Mind thee of the day, when thou too shalt start for the land,
to which one goeth to return not thence.
Good for thee then will have been (an honest life),
therefore be just and hate transgressions,
for he who loveth justice (will be blessed),
The coward and the bold, neither can fly, (the grave)
the friendless and proud are alike . . . .
Then let thy bounty give abundantly as is fit,
(love) truth, and ISIS shall bless the good,
(and thou shalt attain a happy) old age.[1]

Literature and Art. — Intellectually, the Egyptians must
take high rank, though they cannot for a moment compare
with the great European races whose rise was later — the
Greeks and Romans. Their minds possessed much subtlety
and acuteness; they were fond of literary composition; they
made great advances in most of the arts and sciences and
were in every department of life intelligent and ingenious.
It is astonishing what an extensive literature they possessed
at a very early date — books on religion, on morals, law,
rhetoric, arithmetic, mensuration, geometry, medicine, books
of travels, and, above all, novels ! There were many poems

[1] From *Records of the Past*, vi. 129.

also, and some of the love-stories, it is said, are fairly good.[1] As early as the 6th Dynasty (3500 B.C.) an official bears the title of 'Governor of the House of Books.' But the literary merit of the Egyptian works is slight. The novels, we are informed by Egyptologists, are vapid and often licentious, the medical treatises interlarded with charms and exorcisms, the travels devoid of interest, the general style of all the books forced and stilted. Egypt is said to have stimulated Greek speculation by some of its doctrines; but otherwise it cannot be said that the world owes much of its purely intellectual progress to this people, about whose literary productions, it is said by experts, there is always something that is weak, if not childish. The rhythmically constructed book of practical precepts by Ptah-hetep[2] already referred to as the oldest book in the world is, however, valuable for its counsels, as well as its practical sagacity. Philosophic speculation seems to have received no contribution from the higher doctrines of the priesthood.

In Art, the power which the Egyptians exhibited was greater than in thought; but the very highest qualities of art were wanting, although there was a period when it attained to great excellence in bas-reliefs and colour. That it did not make greater progress is a matter for surprise to anyone who will look at the wooden head to which the date 3700 B.C. is assigned and a drawing of which will be found in Brugsch's 'History' and Maspero's 'Egyptian Archæology.' In one department, however, it was art of a very high order, for the architecture produces its effect not only by its mass, according to Fergusson ('History of Architecture'), but also by its harmony of proportion. He says that the Hall in Karnak 'is the noblest effort of architectural magnificence ever produced by the hand of man.' The skill exhibited in overcoming difficulties in construction is also marvellous. In building, sculp-

---

[1] Professor Flinders Petrie has issued translations of stories from the papyri.

[2] Or Ptah-hotep, as in *Records of the Past*, in vol. iii. of which the Precepts are translated.

ture, and colour decoration generally, we find in Egypt the ' dawn of artistic development for the whole human race.' (Ranke.)

Social Condition. — The classes were so separated one from another that it was long believed that the caste system prevailed, as among the Hindus. It was not so, however; there was no rigid and compulsory system of division. In a general way, it would seem to be right to adopt the classification of Strabo, and to say that the entire free population of Egypt which did not belong to the sacerdotal or the military order, formed a sort of third estate, which admitted of subdivisions, but is properly to be regarded as politically a single body. The soldiers and the priests were privileged: the rest of the community was without privilege of any kind; but the recognised usages and customs, as well as law, gave them protection.

Of all the classes, that of the priests was the most powerful, and the most carefully organised. Priests often held important political offices; they served in the army also, and received rich gifts for their services. Many of them accumulated great wealth through these secular employments, and their residences were of a luxurious kind. But they were only partially hereditary and grew up into an established Order slowly. They were divided into several classes; and next to them came four orders of prophets, and below them again the ' divine fathers.' Sacred scribes and servitors were attached to the temples. In the precincts, monks occupied cells. There were also priestesses, and prophetesses (among whom were to be found women of the highest rank), the singing women, and the sistrum players of the ' Hidden One.' The priests and their families and subordinate ministers were maintained out of the revenues of the temple and formed a corporation.

Besides agriculture and the trades and handicrafts in which so many of the Egyptians found occupation for their time and talents, a considerable portion of the population pursued employments of a more elevated and intellectual character.

3

Sculpture, painting, and music had their respective votaries, and engaged the services of a large number of artists. If dancing is to be viewed as a 'fine art,' we may add to these the paid dancers, who were numerous, but were not held in very high estimation.

Of learned professions in Egypt outside the priesthood, the most important was that of the Scribe, which might be called the literary profession, though not in the sense of authorship. Though writing (at least the cursive or demotic in later times, about 900 B.C.) was an ordinary accomplishment of the industrial classes, and scribes were not, therefore, so absolutely necessary as in most Eastern countries for general correspondence, yet there was still a large number of occupations for which professional penmanship was a pre-requisite, and others that demanded legal knowledge, and skill in forms of transfer and of business and in the due recording of ceremonials and contracts. Moreover, a scribe would often profess not only the demotic cursive script, but also the ideographic [1] and hieratic, and then his prospects of promotion were considerable. The Egyptian religion necessitated the multiplication of copies of the ' Ritual of the Dead,' and the employment of numerous clerks in the registration of the sacred treasures and the management of the sacred estates : also librarians for the care and multiplication of MSS. The civil administration also depended largely upon a system of registration and of official reports which were perpetually being made to the court by the superintendents in all departments of the public service, which was a highly organised bureaucracy. Most private persons of large means, also, kept bailiffs or secretaries who made up their accounts, paid their labourers, and otherwise acted as managers of their property. In commerce of all kinds scribes were indispensable. There were thus numerous lucrative posts which could be properly filled only by persons who were ready with the pen, familiar with the different kinds of writing, and good at figures. The

---

[1] The ideographic or hieroglyphic was picture-writing, but even in early times the hieratic which represented the sounds of words was invented.

occupation of scribe was regarded as one befitting men from the middle ranks of society, who might otherwise have been blacksmiths, carpenters, small farmers, or the like. If scribes failed to obtain government appointments, they might still hope to have their services engaged by the rich corporations which had the management of the Temples, or by private individuals of good means, or in business houses. Hence the scribe readily persuaded himself that his occupation was the first and best of all human employments. And assuming that Tiele and others are correct in saying that the priesthood was only partially hereditary, the scribes would naturally look to the priestly profession as a possible occupation bringing both money and influence.

The great number of persons who practised Medicine in Egypt is mentioned by Herodotus, who further notices the remarkable fact that, besides general practitioners, there were many who devoted themselves to special branches of medical science, some being oculists, some dentists, some skilled in treating diseases of the brain, some those of the intestines, and so on. According to a modern authority, the physicians constituted a special subdivision of the sacerdotal order; but this statement is open to question, though physicians may have belonged for the most part to the priest class.

The profession of Architect in some respects took precedence over any other. The chief court architect was a functionary of the highest importance, ranking among the most exalted officials. Considering the character of the duties entrusted to him, this was only natural, since the kings generally set more store upon their buildings than upon any other matter. Religion and architecture were closely associated. ' At the time when the construction of the pyramids and other tombs,' says Brugsch, ' demanded artists of the first order, we find the place of architect entrusted to the highest dignitaries of the court of the Pharaohs. The royal architects recruited their ranks not unfrequently from the class of princes; and the inscriptions engraved upon the walls of their tombs inform us that, almost without exception, they married either the daughters or the grand-daughters of the reigning sovereigns, who did not refuse the architect this honour.' Schools of architects had to be formed in order to secure a succession of competent persons, and the chief architect of the king was only the most successful out of many aspirants, who were educationally and socially upon a par. Practical builders and the ordinary sculptors constituted a lower class. It has been well said that the Egyptians might be classed apart as a nation of monumental builders. We can understand the importance assigned to the profession of architect.

Finally, Engineering must have been an important profession in a land of irrigation and embankments.

Women. — The relations of the sexes were decidedly on a better footing in Egypt than at Athens or in Greece generally, save perhaps in Sparta. Not only was polygamy rare among the inhabitants of the Nile Valley (although permitted by law), but woman even took her proper rank as the friend and companion of man. She was never secluded in a harem, but constantly made her appearance alike in private company and in the ceremonies of religion, possessed equal rights with man in the eye of the law, shared equally with her brothers in her father's estate, was attached to temples in a quasi-sacerdotal character, and might ascend the throne and administer the government. Even among the poorest classes the rights of the women were respected. She shared equally with her brothers in any inheritance there might be, and was left free to manage and direct the household. Her occupations were water-carrying, grinding the grain, and making bread for the daily consumption. She span, wove, and made and mended the few clothes required in the Egyptian climate. If she was the wife of an agriculturist, she went to market to sell poultry and eggs and the butter she had made, or the linen she had woven. A large family was regarded as a blessing ; and it may be easily understood, consequently, that the wife and mother had a hard life and grew prematurely old. But she had freedom to come and go as she pleased, with uncovered face, and talk with whom she pleased. Among the labouring classes, however, the woman who lived with a man was not always married to him; and among the well-to-do, concubinage was not uncommon.

Meanwhile the mass of the people — the fellahîn — were as poor, oppressed, and miserable as in modern times. They lived from day to day and hand to mouth. Their chief virtue was obedience to their superiors, and they were well inured to the ' stick.' Forced labour was common. The craftsmen formed corporations and depended on their ' masters ' or presidents for the recognition of their rights and for justice. The monuments, it seems, bear witness to the fact that both peasants and artisans were, notwithstanding their poverty and oppression, a cheerful race and fond of merriment. This is quite possible; for we often find a ' happy-go-lucky ' spirit and an enjoyment of the passing hour among people who are quite at the bottom of the social scale. They have been trained by circumstances to improvidence; they cannot fall lower, and to rise higher is almost impossible.

To sum up: Taken as a whole we may say that the ancient Egyptians, or, let us say, the ' average man ' among them was, intellectually, eminently practical. His religion was not a reasoned or philosophic religion even in its highest forms. It was, in its highest form, the fruit of a dreamy meditation on the broad aspects of life and death rather than of speculative analysis; in its vulgar form a mixture of animal worship and debased superstitions. In ethics his morality was preceptive and dogmatic — not a subject of philosophic investigation. His artistic tastes were limited to the symbolic and realistic and did not embrace ideal forms, save in architecture; and even in architecture the grandeur is due to its symbolic character. Personally, he was grave and serious, industrious, orderly, kindly, peaceable, and submissive. And, with all his gravity and seriousness he (as we now learn from Egyptologists) seems to have enjoyed life and to have been fond of merriment.

The preceding synopsis of Egyptian life (as accurate as I can make it in so short a space) shows that in this Nile Valley a highly civilised people, among whom the art of government was organised down to the minutest bureaucratic detail, existed as a community under monarchs for more than 4,000 years before Christ. 'With the 4th Dynasty' (4235 B.C.), says M. Mariette, 'Egypt emerges from the obscurity with which it is, till then, surrounded, and we are enabled to date facts by the help of the monuments. . . . The 4th Dynasty marks a culminating point in the history of the kingdom. By an extraordinary movement forward, Egypt threw off all trammels and emerged in the full glory of a fully developed civilisation. From this moment class distinctions were recognised in Egyptian society, and art attained a breadth and dignity that even in later and more brilliant days were hardly surpassed.'[1]

Even Chinese civilisation is a thing of yesterday as compared with the Egyptian. Here we see what a nation, practically excluded from alien influences, could accomplish for its own indigenous growth in political life, in social justice, in the arts and sciences, and in education. It was overrun, rather than conquered, by the Hyksos, Assyrians, Persians, Greeks, and Romans. The country seems to have gone on its way very little influenced by foreign interference with its native dynasties. It is this that makes Egypt so interesting a study in world-history. Its geographical position secured its originality. Doubtless it had to pay a price for its exclusiveness, for it suffered from the absence of the stimulus which almost all civilised nations have received from imported ideas.

EDUCATION IN EGYPT

THE Education of a nation is to be found in the characteristics of its civilisation. It has educated itself by every progressive step it takes in religion, politics, justice, arts, and

[1] Mariette's *Outlines*, translated by Miss Brodrick.

thought. The ever-accumulating tradition of the people is passed on from parents to children and made permanent in institutions. The present has been created by the past. In the above endeavour, then, to estimate the character, life, and institutions of ancient Egypt, we have been virtually giving an account of its national education.

The education of the young Egyptian, in brief, was through the religion, morality, law, and social customs of his native land. The general influences of the inherited civilisation would of course be felt in different ways according to the social position and opportunities of the children. Compared with the youth of other nations the Egyptian of the lower classes grew up, we may think, too patient of toil and the stick; but, spite of the oppressive conditions of life, there seem to have been prevalent a mildness, kindness, and equity of disposition and a simplicity of life and domestic relations which an organised educational system might have failed to secure. I should say that they compared very favourably as regards their moral training and their sentiments of religious reverence with the lowest stratum in Great Britain now. All, however, lacked the education which free political life gives, and we find that, where this is the case, it operates to deprive men of initiative, reacting on the whole intellectual life, making it torpid and content with the *status quo*, whatever that may be. Doubtless, the political constitution was, to begin with, itself an expression of a certain racial temperament, but it reacted on the popular mind so as to confirm natural predisposition. If we may make a distinction between individuality and that personality which comes into life along with the free exercise of self-conscious reason, we should say that there was in the ancient Egyptian a marked individuality exhibiting itself in a keen practical intelligence, but that personality as we find it in European nations was absent. Nor do we find this sense of personality, with which is always associated the idea of self-direction and self-government, in any of the Oriental races, except the Persians (and that empire was a short-lived phenomenon) and the

Jews; and it is interesting to note that this strong sense of personality existed, in both cases, side by side with an intense monotheism. This fact suggests many thoughts which would be here out of place.

The practical intelligence of the Egyptian race had an immense field for its activity. They had to devise the engineering works which enabled them to utilise the Nile; and every year they had a recurring struggle to maintain their supremacy over it. With comparatively little foreign trade they had themselves to produce the articles of necessity and luxury which a growing nation requires. Thus all the industrial arts flourished, and, apart from the professions, every boy had an industrial or technical education from his own father. We are told in these days that manual work is educative, but how much more educative the prolonged and careful training required for the acquisition of a skilled trade with all its traditions! The Egyptian boy had this.

On the spiritual side he was under powerful influences, he breathed an atmosphere of mystery and awe, and lived in the constant presence of gods, and in expectation of immortality. His crude conceptions of the unseen were, it is true, associated with magic and sorcery;[1] but has modern Europe no superstitions equally absurd? We boast ourselves of our religion, but it is difficult for us with all our affected superiority to realise the extent to which the constant presence of unseen powers pressed on the daily life of a race like the Egyptians. We look back with a feeling akin to contempt on their faith in magic, sorcery and incantations, forgetting that the more educated classes have merely to give the word and one half of Christendom would, even now, be plunged to the neck in similar beliefs.

In the bringing up of children there seems to have been

---

[1] Mr. Flinders Petrie, in *Ten Years' Digging*, says that the modern fellahîn are a prey to gross superstition and worshippers of innumerable local saints, and full of faith in magic and charms. This was equally true of their ancestors 6,000 years ago, under a totally different religious system.

much kindliness. They had their toys and games and nursery stories like other children all the world over.

Instruction of the People. — It is possible that the facilities for obtaining school instruction in ancient Egypt have been much exaggerated.[1] But, theoretically at least, all that was known or knowable was open to all except such esoteric doctrines (if any) as the higher priesthood may have possessed. There is evidence that if there were not numerous elementary schools scattered over the country, yet teachers might always be had, and that reading and writing and the elements of arithmetic were accessible to those who desired instruction. There is no evidence, however, it seems to me, that the labouring class received any benefit from these schools save in exceptional cases; but there was nothing to prevent a clever boy, whose parents were well-disposed, receiving elementary instruction. On the whole, I cannot see that on this point modern exploration has added much to the information given by Diodorus Siculus, i. 81, who says, 'A little reading and writing are taught, but not to all; but to those engaged with the industrial arts.' At the chief provincial cities (in connection with the Temple which was the centre of the civic life) more advanced instruction was obtainable, including the writing and reading of the hieratic and hieroglyphic character and mathematics. These higher schools doubtless supplied the professions.

The Professions. — I have been speaking of the masses generally; but outside and above the masses were the professions. And the vital question connected with Egyptian education is this. Were the professions open to all? It is now generally held that they were open; but the fact that for long the caste-organisation was believed to be the chief characteristic of the Egyptian social system must satisfy us that, in all save exceptional cases, children fol-

---

[1] The inferences drawn from incidental phrases by philo-Egyptians are often more than questionable.

lowed the occupation of their parents. Still I say the
way was open for clever boys, and this is the important
point.

The higher and professional education had for its chief
aim the Scribe. A young man who was a scribe would hold
in Egyptian society the position assigned to an university
graduate now, or to a literate in China. A scribe was not
necessarily also an architect or a physician or a priest,
although these professional men had of course the accomplishment of scribes. I would refer back to what I have
already said as to the function of the scribe, and the numerous lucrative openings, conferring a certain social standing,
that awaited him. An accomplished scribe would have
acquired the cursive or demotic script in which the ordinary
affairs of life were transacted and also the hieratic in which
the records and traditions of all professions were written, and
finally, the ideographic or hieroglyphic. He would also be
an arithmetician, as then understood, and have an adequate
knowledge of the law as affecting ordinary affairs and business contracts. What else he might study or acquire
depended on his aims and ambitions. I would point out
(subject to the correction of Egyptologists) that there must
have been two classes of scribes: first, there was a large
class, which, after a certain amount of preliminary education, entered as apprentices the service of those scribes who
conducted commercial and family affairs. A boy displaying
some intelligence would be sent to the village school at six
or seven, where some old pedagogue would teach him the
rudiments of the three R's. If he did not find his way next
to a provincial school, he would enter an office that he
might become a 'learned scribe.' Occupied there in copying
letters, circulars, and legal documents, his master supervising his work and correcting it while the boy rewrites it, he
gradually acquires a competent acquaintance with writing
and with business and legal forms of all kinds. If he aims
at a knowledge of the hieratic script he will have to copy
from books which contain examples. Having gone through

this apprenticeship, he applies for a better post.[1] The commercial or notarial scribe is described in the above passage: and we also see indicated the higher class of scribe, who studied at the central temple schools and became an expert in all kinds of script and a student of law and administration. The latter might attain to a very high social position. 'Neither descent nor family,' says Brugsch, 'hampered the rising career of the clever.' The higher scribe schools were connected with the royal court and also with the provincial courts, and were conducted by a high official. Rawlinson says, 'Egypt provided an open career for talent such as scarcely existed elsewhere in the old world, and such as few modern communities can be said even yet to furnish. It was always possible, under despotic governments, that the capricious favour of a sovereign should raise to a high, or even to the highest position, the lowest person in the kingdom. But in Egypt alone, of all ancient states, does a system seem to have been established whereby persons of all ranks, even the lowest, were invited to compete for the royal favour, and, by distinguishing themselves in the public schools, to establish a claim for employment in the public service. That employment once obtained, their future depended on themselves. Merit secured promotion; and it would seem that the efficient scribe had only to show himself superior to his fellows in order to rise to the highest position but one in the empire.' This is too rose-coloured a view, but it has a considerable basis of fact. Maspero (chapter i.) says, 'There is no sacrifice which the smaller folk deem too great if it enables them to give their sons the acquirements which may raise them above the common people, or at least ensure a less miserable fate.'

In addition to the profession of scribe, there was the profession of architect, as distinct from builder. Here, again, I must refer to what I have already said a few pages back. The education of the architect in the Temple schools of architects doubtless embraced much sacred as well as

[1] Maspero's *Ancient Egypt and Assyria*, p. 11.

historical learning, a knowledge of writing and mathematics, and that part of engineering which concerns itself with the strength of materials and practical dynamics. The architects were often priests, but not necessarily members of that order.

The profession of physician demanded all the usual learning of the upper class as well as special knowledge of a vast tradition of curative agencies with their related magic charms and incantations. I do not suppose it can be doubted that this knowledge could be obtained only at great Temple centres where the manuscripts could be read; but it is rash to conclude that there were medical 'schools.' It is much more probable that young men became physicians by apprenticeship to established practitioners. Those who desired to be fully accomplished had to master the original treatises ascribed to Thoth and Imhotpou with their subsequent interpretations and glosses.

There were professional singers, as well as dancers, musicians, and jugglers, for all of whom a certain training must have been provided.

The soldiers lived on the lands assigned to them and were called out for regular training in military exercises and gymnastics. Generally speaking, the privileges of the army were such that the lower classes were glad to belong to it. Music also is said to have been taught in connection with the army, but it does not follow that it was taught to all even of those who aimed at the position of officer. It is more probable that there was a regimental band. The music was of a primitive and stereotyped kind and had descended from remote antiquity. Plato in his 'Laws' (ii. 63, 7) praises the Egyptian music because it was of a kind not to soften the manners, but grave and serious. It was largely composed of sacred chants. At the best period, education of a general kind was essential to promotion in the army. There were 'scribes' of the army. These educated officers were employed in connection with the engineering works of the country.

The priesthood was the highest order in the state, and along with the monarch governed Egypt; the alliance of state and church seems to have been in the main harmonious. All the learning of the Egyptians was to be found in the higher orders of the priesthood, and their education embraced an elaborate study of ancient religious documents, a complicated ritual and ceremonial, the various kinds of script, ethics, mathematics, astronomy, and astrology. The royal family, and we may presume the children of court dignitaries, shared to a certain extent in the education of the young priests. The priesthood was not till comparatively recent times wholly hereditary, and learned scribes might find their way into it ; but it is said that the more profound doctrines (and therefore the highest education) were reserved for those who were hereditary priests.[1] The chief priest colleges were situated at the great cities of Memphis, Thebes, and Heliopolis. In these the highest instruction obtainable in Egypt was given.[2]

We have mentioned mathematics as entering into the higher education of the Egyptians ; but we are not to imagine that mathematics was with the Egyptians a science in the Greek sense. It was chiefly practical ; but for that very reason it must have been a study of a countless number of practical rules and much more laborious than a study of rational principles which carry practical rules with them as deductions.

Women of the upper classes received a certain education — probably from private tutors.

Let it be noted that there was no deliberate effort made by state or church to raise the standard of intellectual life and culture among the people generally. In so far as instruction went beyond the acquisition of reading and writing, it had always a technical or professional purpose — except

[1] Clement of Alexandria partially enumerates the books that had to be studied by the Egyptian priesthood in his time.
[2] I avoid using the word 'University' and generally I have exercised my judgment in moderating the tone of some philo-Egyptians.

perhaps in the highest Temple-schools of the priests. What we call 'liberal' education was not dreamt of even for the few. The idea of liberal education did not exist; on the other hand, the course of instruction for the higher priesthood comprehended the whole range of knowledge as then understood, and as this was pursued for its own sake, and in the interests of learning, it may, perhaps, be called liberal education.

With these facts before us, I think we must admit that it was not the want of education which restricted the continued advance of Egypt, for it had an educational system as widespread and as effective, relatively to the then state of knowledge, as Europe had up to the earlier decades of this present century. Even the masses, spite of the poverty and monotonous character of their lives, had the means of obtaining from some scribe-pedagogue the elements of literature. They were, however, chiefly educated by the family and national tradition, by their training to technical arts, by the laws, and the festivals and ceremonials of their religious system. It cannot be said that they were educated by their *political constitution* to anything but submission. Personal interest in civic and political life, and personal responsibility for the welfare of the state, were things alien to the Egyptian as to the Oriental mind generally. It was left to Greece and Rome, to modern Europe and America, to find, in a free community of political interests and responsibilities, a potent element in the education of individual citizens better than many schools.

Method and Discipline. — The methods pursued we know little of. That dictation was largely resorted to we can rightly infer from the school copies in the British and French museums, as well as from the necessity of devoting a large portion of time to learning the Egyptian character. The copies were traced on wooden tablets or bits of stone, and the pupil imitated them with a style on wooden tablets covered with a layer of red or white stucco. The more advanced were promoted to write extracts from good authors on papyrus, both by transcription and from dictation. The master corrected the exercises by putting the true forms on the margin wherever the pupil had made a mistake.

By giving passages to the boys to copy, caligraphy and orthography were taught, and at the same time the rudiments of composition. These passages were sometimes tales, and extracts from religious or magical books. More frequently the pupil had to copy an 'instruction.' These 'instructions' contained rules for wise conduct and good manners, ascribed mostly to Ptah-hetep, the ancient writer of moral precepts. The 'instructions' were often in the form of letters between tutor and pupil, 'in which the former is supposed to impart wisdom as well as to form an epistolary style.' This accomplishment was of great importance to the scribe, as much of the work of public administration seems to have been done in writing.

The difficulties of teaching must have been great, and, as we know, the discipline was severe. 'The hawk is taught to fly and the pigeon to nest; I shall teach you your letters, you idle villain!' is the utterance of an irate Egyptian schoolmaster. There was also a pedagogic saying, ' A young fellow has a back; he hears when we strike it.' A scholar writing to his master, after having left school, says that ' his bones had been broken like those of an ass.'

Egypt was so long the land of wonder and mystery, that there were men who dreamed that its records might yield secrets of thought which might throw light on many of the problems of life and destiny. As a matter of fact, it seems to me, the race was incapable of great exploits in the region of philosophy and religion. Practical sagacity and a profound religious awe were curiously combined in them; but the analytic labour by which alone truth yields itself to the earnest pursuit of man was alien to the Egyptian mind. Their religion, moreover, held no idealising principle: their morality was preceptive, not reasoned. Even their history is only bald registration. Authority and antiquity governed the thought of each successive generation in every department of human inquiry. This gave stability and continuity to the kingdom ; but the stability was gained at the cost of true intellectual progress. Hence, so far from contemplating with astonishment the achievements of Egypt, we are rather filled with wonder that 5,000 years of opportunity produced so little. It is precisely its surprising failures as well as its astonishing successes, which make Egypt so interesting and instructive a chapter in the history of the human race.

Authorities : Herodotus ; Diodorus Siculus ; Ranke's *History of the World ;* Rawlinson's *Five Monarchies of the Ancient Eastern World ;* Professor Ebers' appendices to novels ; Strabo ; Maspero's *Ancient Egypt and Assyria,* also his *Histoire Ancienne* and *L'Archéologie Egyptienne ;* Brugsch's *Egypt under the Pharaohs ;* Bunsen's *Egypt's Place in History ;* Duncker's *History of Antiquity ;* Dr. Birch's *Egypt ;* Professor Sayce's *Ancient Empires of the East ;* Le Page Renouf's *Hibbert Lectures on Egyptian·Religion ;* Wilkinson's *Manners and Customs of the Ancient Egyptians ;* The Story of the Nations ('Egypt,' by Rawlinson) ; Mariette's *Outlines of the History of Egypt,* by Miss Brodrick ; Professor Tiele's *Outlines of the History of Religions : Records of the Past ;* Erman's *Life in Ancient Egypt,* translated by Tirard ; *The Dawn of Civilisation in the East,* by Professor Maspero ; *The Book of the Dead,* by Dr. Davis ; Professor Menzies' *History of Religion.*

Professor Flinders Petrie has issued a History of Egypt, and this will be followed, I believe, by a book on its civilisation. These will doubtless be the authoritative books when they are completed. Meanwhile I have had to form my own conclusions from the evidence before me, the witnesses being by no means always in agreement with each other or themselves.

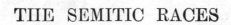
THE SEMITIC RACES

THE SEMITIC RACES

A. — ARABS — BABYLONIANS — ASSYRIANS — PHŒNICIANS

THE Semitic races inhabited that central region of the old world which extends from the Arabian and Persian Gulfs and the Zagros Mountains to the Mediterranean and the Taurus range. All the nations named at the head of this chapter were Semitic ; but, as was the case with every other race we encounter in historic times, they were mixed with prior populations or fresh immigrants. The greatest of these races, from the point of view of general culture and art, were the Babylonians, or, as they are sometimes called, Chaldæo-Babylonians : the most warlike and energetic were the Assyrians : among the Jews or Hebrews, again, the Oriental religious spirit found its highest and purest expression. The Semitic races generally were like the Egyptians of a serious, prosaic, practical, matter of fact character. The Hebrews alone exhibit a certain loftiness of genius, but this within a narrow field. It is this portion of the Semitic race that has influenced the education of the world and is consequently of chief interest to us. But before speaking of the Hebrews, we must advert for a moment to the Arabs, and give some attention to the older Semitic communities which grew up in the Mesopotamian plains and highlands.

(1) THE ARABS

OWING to their geographical position the Arabs preserved the Semitic character and blood in its purest form, and their religious beliefs may probably be regarded as the primitive Semitic religion. This religion was fetichistic, and varied among different tribes. All worshipped the sun and moon and certain constellations, but the god of each of the numerous clans was the chief object of devotion. He was the captain and master of the clan. Idolatry was of late introduction. Sacred stones and mountains were objects of adoration, especially the Black Stone of the Kaaba which was at the national centre, Mecca. They were essentially a nomadic race, but there were settled kingdoms. The most recent explorations speak of two kingdoms which probably in succession to each other extended their power, or at least suzerainty over the most of Arabia, viz. Saba (Sheba) and Ma'in. The kingdom of Saba was flourishing before the time of Solomon and there are inscriptions ascribed to that period showing that writing was known. But as we know nothing about the constitution of these kingdoms, no materials exist for a history of education. Among the Arabs generally, however, there existed from a very remote period a considerable body of poetry of a lyric kind, chiefly warlike and elegiac. These were handed down by rhapsodists who recited them at tribal meetings. Tradition gives the name of Lokmân, a contemporary of King David, as that of a celebrated poet, and 'round his name,' says Duncker, 'is gathered a number of proverbs, gnomes, and fables.' The oral poetic literature was, however, floating and unorganised. Even of the Arabs in the century preceding the rise of Mahomet, Ibn Khallikân (who wrote his biographical dictionary in the thirteenth century) says, 'the people consisted of Arabs wholly ignorant of the mode by which learning is taught, of the art of composing works and of the means by which knowledge is enregistered.' (Introd. to vol. ii.) While this was so, we must still allow a certain educative effect to the floating unwritten literature. In speaking of Oriental nations, we must always remember that their memories were facile and retentive to an extent which to the modern European is almost incredible. When Mahomet arose, for example, the Koran was learnt by heart and recited, and those who had acquired this power were held in great respect as ' Readers.'

There can be no doubt that writing (on palm-leaves, leather, and stone) was known long before the Christian era. The writing introduced into Mecca A.D. 560 was a reformed script.[1]

But very few could write, and even these few seemed to make little use of it.

(2) THE BABYLONIANS

THE Babylonians were the primary centre of the Mesopotamian culture and religion, they themselves, however, as we shall see, resting on a still earlier civilisation. The true greatness of Babylon as a city began about the eighteenth century B.C.

It was from the southern Chaldæo-Babylonian district that the Assyrians of Nineveh in the north migrated. It was only in the thirteenth century B.C. (about the time of the death of Moses) that the Assyrians began to extend their power over other races. In 1100 B.C. they were the acknowledged masters north, south, and east of Nineveh. The empire rapidly grew in the ninth century B.C., extending even to the Mediterranean. Nineveh was always more warlike than the great centre of culture, Babylon;[2] and after the middle of the thirteenth century B.C., the latter was virtually in subjection to the Assyrians. In the middle of the seventh century B.C., the loosely-jointed Assyrian empire began suddenly to collapse, after it had extended itself to Media in the East and Egypt and Arabia on the South. It was an empire of violence; but it concentrated in itself and raised to a historical world-importance, as Ranke says, the martial vigour of the Semitic race. Nor were the Assyrians only warriors: the ruins of Nineveh to this day testify to its

---

[1] Sir W. Muir's *Life of Mahomet*, p. 8. Caussin de Perceval does not deny this, as Sir W. Muir seems to think.

[2] The revival of letters and of the sciences and arts under the Mohammedan conquerors in the eighth and subsequent centuries A.D. belongs to the mediæval period. The eminent men during this period were probably not genuine Arabs at all.

greatness and challenge the public works of Babylon and Susa. It fell before the Medes (towards the end of the seventh century) assisted by the Babylonians, who thus avenged their own prior subjection. It had enjoyed an imperial existence of 250 years, and was the first conquering power founding an empire which we meet with in the history of the world.

Babylon was now the head of all the Western portion of the former Assyrian empire, but only for a brief period. It fell before the Medo-Persians (also including Elamites) in 538 B. C.

But though the Assyrian and Babylonian empires were shortlived, Nineveh, and above all Babylon, had been for a very long period the centres of Mesopotamian civilisation. They had attained to political constitutions, religious systems, and laws, and to the highest degree of material wealth. We may date the importance of Nineveh as a civilised centre and a rising military power from 1400 B. C.; but Babylon and the civilisation of the Babylonian and Chaldæan country (the southern portion of Mesopotamia) have a much more ancient record.[1]

The Babylonian culture, *in all its forms*, rested on that of the early occupants of the alluvial plains between the two rivers — known as Accadians or Sumir-Accadians.[2]

The Accadians had, it is commonly held, come from the plains south of the Caspian Sea and entered the southern Mesopotamian valley probably through Elam east of the Tigris. After they had developed a certain civilisation here, the wandering Semites took possession and were amalgamated with the resident population — entering probably about 2200 B. C. Tiele ('Die Assyriologie, eine Rede') says that

---

[1] As a help in taking a chronological and comparative view, it is of importance to note that Solomon, who raised the power of the Israelites to its highest point, died in 975 B. C., and that the date of the foundation of Rome was 753 B. C.

[2] The most recent information points to inhabitants of a Cushite type prior to the Accadians.

the Semitic civilisation in the Mesopotamian plains cannot be put further back than 2000 B.C., but we know that the Accadian civilisation, including religion and science, was developed long before that date. It would not now, indeed, be considered an exaggeration to date the *beginnings* of Sumir-Accadian civilisation in the lower Mesopotamian basin from nearly 4000 B.C.[1]

The Accadian religion was animistic and fetichistic. There was an organised priesthood and temples. They believed in multitudinous demons, good and evil, between whom there was continual warfare. But this contest had no ethical significance. Their priesthood, however (at least after a certain date), believed in a supreme God among the gods. The practice of magic and incantations, worked out into the most elaborate detail, flourished. Evil spirits had to be conciliated, and these were everywhere. But this relation to unseen powers had among the Accadians no moral meaning. As regards a future life, it was held that the spirits of the dead lived an unhappy and dreary existence for ever in a gloomy Hades — a world of shadows — the underworld ; subsequently, it was taught that the gods received into pleasant regions all who served them well during life. The ethical importance of this advance is manifest.

A Semitic race, which seems to have entered the northern portions of the Mesopotamian basin, amalgamated with this primitive Accadian people, and the combined people are thereafter known to history as Babylonians or Chaldæans. Gradually the religious conceptions to which we have referred above, reached a still higher development under the influence, one would be disposed to say, of the specifically Semitic spirit. The nature-beings became gods, truly governing the natural order ; and the study of astron-

---

[1] I follow the leading authorities. Maspero is much less confident than many other writers, and would consider the above statement much too definite, and in fact the most recent explorations show that the history prior to 2200 B.C. has to be reconstructed.

omy and mathematics, by exalting men's minds, gave to the supreme deities a more refined and elevated character. Above all the numerous gods, one was now placed whose commands were absolute — the Lord of Lords. Without throwing off the magic and augury and elaborate system of incantations which they had adopted, they (*i. e.* the more advanced priesthood) exhibited in their worship 'a vivid sense of sin, a deep feeling of man's dependence, even of his nothingness before God, in prayers and hymns hardly less fervent than those of the pious souls of Israel' (Tiele). As evidence of this we may here cite an extract from one of the penitential psalms, merely premising that at the time it was written there had grown up a belief that each individual soul had his god — a belief which would easily be universalised and pass into that of a one God who was truly the god of all human spirits alike. The sense of a personal relation between God and the human soul, so characteristic of the Semitic race, here makes its appearance (but in a particular, not a universal form), and suggests that the remains we now have of this purer religion did not date prior to the amalgamation of Semitic immigrants, or, indeed, prior to 2000 years B.C.

From a Penitential Psalm.

The heart of my Lord was wrath, to his place may he return ;
From the man who sinned unknowingly, to his place may my God return !

And so on, frequently repeated in slightly altered forms; then :

The transgression that I committed, my God knew it.

Oh, my God, that knowest that I knew not, my transgressions are great, my sins are many.

God, who knew though I knew not, hath passed me.

I lay on the ground, and no one seized me by the hand.
I wept and my palms none took.

And so forth. This is evidently part of a liturgy, as appears from rubrical directions.[1]

The following Address to the Sun illustrates the stage of poetical culture which the higher type of Chaldæo-Babylonian mind had reached :

' O Sun ! thou hast stepped forth from the background of heaven, thou hast pushed back the bolts of the brilliant heaven — yea, the gate of heaven. O Sun ! above the land thou hast raised thy head ! O Sun ! thou hast covered the immeasurable space of heaven and countries ! '

There are also many passages of poetic vigour in the Epic of Izdhubar.

The Chaldæan priesthood, which was partly hereditary, partly selected, conserved and developed the religious system which we may call Accadian-Semitic, and maintained the ceremonies of the temples. They handed down the traditions of the race and had an oral as well as a written literature, which embodied their philosophy of life and poetic conceptions.

Education. — All the arts of life that minister to comfort and luxury attained great perfection : the Babylonian architecture was conceived and executed with a certain vastness of imagination, and their canals and embankments showed great engineering skill. All this implies a highly developed technical instruction. Of education, however, in any literary sense, or even of the ethical education of the family, there can have been little or none. This must always chiefly depend on the religious and ethical conceptions of a nation as a whole, and not of a restricted order in a nation. At the same time the people as a whole can, especially under a despotic political system, be sustained at a certain level by the convictions of the few. But, where the religion in its popular form was a crude polydæmonism accompanied by magic and incantation and the worship of arbitrary spirits good and evil, the people could receive no education from a spiritual ideal of life. Marriage was set about with great

---

[1] From *Records of the Past.*

formality and regarded as a social act of great importance; but the husband was not restricted to one wife. Although the wife in the middle and lower orders had great liberty of action allowed her, her life was not much better than that of a slave. It was impossible, accordingly, that domestic relations could furnish any moral basis for the family. Nor could citizens who had no political status receive education from the working of political institutions. Doubtless, had the later religious conceptions, to which I have referred above, been the possession of the people and not merely of a class, their educative influence might have moulded the Mesopotamian civilisation to a much higher form than it ever attained; but there is no evidence that this was so.

Education of the upper classes. — The education of the few, on the other hand, was by no means despicable. As time advanced, the higher minds held monotheistic views, the numerous gods being regarded as merely aspects of the supreme divine Being. In the course of time, the gods were resolved, under the influence of a speculative philosophy, into elements and abstractions; and a cosmogony arose like that given in the first chapter of Genesis, with this important difference, however, that the universe was regarded as a series of emanations from the Supreme Being. This speculative view passed even into Ionic Greece and neo-Platonism. Charms, amulets, sorcery, divination, incantations, all continued, however, to flourish side by side with these higher ideas, and the conception of man's life as haunted by devilish spirits (a survival apparently of the older Accadian religion), who had to be driven off or appeased, had not been superseded even among the priesthood.

The literature which constituted the material of education for the higher orders was extensive. Every great town had its library on brick tablets, which were thrown open to the public (Sayce). A great astronomical work, compiled for Sargon's library at Agade, is said to be of the early date of 3800 B. C. 'There were historical and mythological writings, religious compositions, legal, geographical, astronomical, and astrological treatises; magical formulæ and omen tablets; poems, fables, and proverbs; grammatical and lexical disquisitions, beside archives' (Sayce, p. 170). There were state observatories in the chief towns and astronomers-royal were appointed who had 'to send.fortnightly reports to the king.' The knowledge of arithmetic, mathematics, and mechanics also had made considerable progress, but only on the practical, not the scientific, side. We have to add the great Epic of Izdhubar, which belonged to the domain of literature.[1]

The interest of the Chaldæans in astronomy was not strictly scientific. They made numerous observations and had constructed many astronomical tables, but this not so much with a view to a knowledge of the heavens as to astrology. The position of the heavenly bodies indicated earthly destinies, and to foretell these was the function of the Chaldæan priest. Diodorus tells us (ii. 29) that the sons of the priestly class were carefully instructed from boyhood up, and this, indeed, was necessary to their acquisition of the detailed learning required of them. Astronomy and astrology alone demanded persevering study. Medicine was not a subject of serious pursuit. As diseases were caused by evil spirits, the medical art in Chaldæa confined itself to

---

[1] It was Shargena or Sargon I. who (coming from the north or north-east had conquered the Babylonian territories) flourished somewhere about 2200 B. C., to whom the institution or revival of libraries was due. A royal library was collected by him in the town of Ourouk, hence sometimes called the Town of Books, and the library contained the traditionary lore of the Chaldæo-Babylonian priesthood, among which were histories, theology, elaborate treatises on divination and magic, catalogues of beasts and minerals, medicine (incantations chiefly, accompanied by a materia medica), astronomy, astrology, and mathematics. Nor was this the only library ; there were several in the Babylonian territory. Sargon was himself a modern, and the literature he collected was the accumulation of probably 2000 years. There was another Shargena I., 3800 B. C., who seems to be legendary (?). About B. C. 628 Assurbani-pal, king of Assyria, had bilingual copies of the Babylonian library made and placed them in Nineveh, and a considerable portion are now in the British Museum. The authorities for the above quotations are numerous, but see Maspero's *Histoire Ancienne*, pp. 157–9. But doubtless all that has been said of the first Shargena or Sargon requires reconsideration.

the invention of magical formulæ which should exorcise the demons.

The higher education was not confined to the priestly class (which, however, was itself a large and powerful body), but extended to the body of scribes. These men were not held in such high social estimation as in Egypt. The working of the local and central administration was, however, largely in their hands. ' We continually meet with them in all grades of society, in the palace, in the temples, in the storehouses, in private dwellings. In fine, the scribe was ubiquitous at court, in the town, in the country, in the army, managing affairs both small and great, and seeing that they were carried on efficiently. His education differed but little from that given to the Egyptian scribe; he learned the routine of administrative and judicial affairs, the formularies of correspondence either with nobles or with ordinary people, the art of writing, of calculating quickly and making out bills correctly.'[1] They wrote on slabs of fine plastic clay with a stylus and then sent it to the potter to be baked or put it into an oven of their own. Besides these clay tablets, they sometimes used hollow cylinders on which they wrote public events of importance. Forms of judicial decisions and business contracts &c. are found written on these. The writing was originally ideographic as in Egypt. It is to the indestructible character of these baked tablets and cylinders that we owe what knowledge we have of those remote times.

Nor was the education confined even to priests and scribes. Many of the upper classes shared in it to a certain extent, while the public libraries afforded the means of study to all who had ambition to learn. That a portion of the upper classes received instruction there can be no doubt. Among Oriental races generally we find that young men, not of the priestly order, were brought up in the royal court for the service of the country; and there is no reason to doubt that Nebuchadnezzar's instructions as regards the Jewish children were only the continuation of an ancient Babylonian prac-

[1] Maspero, *Dawn of Civilisation*, p. 726.

tice. In the first chapter of Daniel the prophet, it is narrated:

'And the king spake unto Ashpenaz, the master of his eunuchs, that he should bring certain of the children of Israel, and of the king's seed, and of the princes; children in whom was no blemish, but well favoured, and skilful in all wisdom, and cunning in knowledge, and understanding science, and such as had ability in them, to stand in the king's palace, and whom they might teach the learning and the tongue of the Chaldeans. And the king appointed them a daily provision of the king's meat, and of the wine which he drank: so nourishing them three years, that at the end thereof they might stand before the king. Now among these were, of the children of Judah, Daniel, Hananiah, Mishael, and Azariah.'

It is difficult, indeed, to see how the government of any civilised country could have been carried on without a lay royal school as well as priestly and scribe schools. The palace school of Charlemagne in the eighth century was thus a much more ancient institution than he himself imagined. We may also conclude generally that, in a country which erected monuments with inscriptions for all to read, not a few of the population could read and write, outside the priesthood, the scribes, and the royal court.

Of the schools and teachers we know nothing. Tablets have been found in Babylon on which school-exercises are written. Where learning and teaching existed there must, of course, have been teachers, and we may conclude that pedagogues (priests and scribes) were numerous, who probably gave *individual*, not class, instruction. Priest and scribe would, of course, be careful to instruct their own children who were, after the Oriental fashion, to succeed them in their public functions.

(3) THE ASSYRIANS

THE Chaldæo-Babylonian priesthood had attained to the idea of one supreme God. The Assyrians accepted the religion of the race, but emphasised the *personal* character of the supreme God under the name of Asshur. As was natural in a warlike people, they recognised the military leadership and command of the God — the ' God of battles,' who was also king and father. The people as a whole were victims of a debased superstition ; religious, however, in the sense in which they understood religion.

But for our purposes here there is nothing to be said which has not already been said of the Babylonians, except that, as befitted men living in a more elevated country, the Assyrians exhibited many of the virtues of a vigorous and conquering people. Hunting was a favourite amusement ; the chase of the lion, buffalo, gazelle, horse, and wild ass. The Babylonian love of magnificence in architecture, sculpture, and decoration was even exceeded in Nineveh, and the Assyrians were famous for the art with which they adorned their palaces and temples. Their technical and military education must have been highly developed ; but education of the higher kind was restricted to the priesthood, the royal court, and to the scribes. It was Chaldæo-Babylonian in its character.

The priesthood seems to have inherited those conceptions regarding the personal relation of the soul of man to a, or the, divine Being which we have found among the Babylonians. I may cite, in illustration and evidence of this, the hymn quoted in ' Records of the Past ' by Mr. Talbot.

Oh, my Lord, my sins are many, my trespasses are great,
And the wrath of the gods has plagued me with disease
And with sickness and sorrow.
I fainted, but no one stretched forth his hand ;
I groaned, but no one drew nigh.
I cried aloud, but no one heard.
O Lord, do not abandon thy servant.
In the waters of the great storm seize his hand,
The sins which he has committed turn thou to righteousness.

The Assyrians, however, paid a tribute to learning in having, like the Egyptians, a 'god of letters.' It was to an Assyrian monarch also (Assur-bani-pal) (p. 59, footnote) that we owe the preservation of a great portion of Babylonian literature. He had copies of the Babylonian brick tablets made, both the Accadian text and a parallel Assyrian translation being given. These were placed in the great library at Nineveh. In that library also were preserved numerous government despatches, letters, astronomical and astrological treatises, and tables giving an account of the law, of legal decisions, contracts of sale, records of tributes and taxes, &c.

So far as national religion, literature, and the arts were concerned, there is no apparent reason why education should not have been as accessible and widely diffused in Babylonia and Assyria as in Egypt. But when we read of the constant wars, we can see how it was that certain forms of civilisation which could grow up and flourish in an isolated land like the Nile valley, did not take root in a country so disturbed as the Mesopotamian basin.

(4) THE PHŒNICIANS

THE narrow coast-line between Lebanon and the Mediterranean (little more than 120 miles long and 15 broad), was occupied by Semites famous in history for their commercial enterprise. Tyre and Sidon were the two chief cities.

The Phœnician government was a monarchy tempered by an oligarchy of wealth, the king being apparently only first among a body of ruling merchant princes. When the monarchy disappeared, the chief magistrate was called 'judge,' and he held office for shorter or longer periods.

With the Phœnicians we find material aims and luxurious living similar to those which marked the Assyrians and Babylonians, but in a grosser form. The former owed their wealth to trade, the latter found the basis of their material civilisation in the fertile alluvial tracts of the Euphrates and Tigris and in the well irrigated northern parts of the Mesopotamian basin. Phœnicia was the gate of communication between Europe and the Orient. With Phœnicia is associated the invention of symbols for numbers and the elements of sound in words; but these seem originally to have been drawn from Egypt where there was a large Phœnician settlement. The necessities as well as the opportunities of commerce would naturally lead to the adoption and development of what was derived from Egypt, with a' view to facilitate communication with foreign nations. Their buildings, their harbours and ships, and the works of art which they produced, all point to a high efficiency in their technical instruction. They were manufacturers, merchants, and colonisers. But commerce and money-making seem to have engrossed their minds, and there is no evidence of any moral idea in their civilisation.[1]

And yet Phœnicia, as intermediary between East and West, played an important part in the history of civilisation; but only as intermediaries. Greek art owed its early Assyrian character to it, and to it also the Greeks were indebted for the alphabet and for many Oriental elements in their religion and mythology. But it would have been better without them. On the Israelites their influence was even more marked. The Temple at Jerusalem was built by Phœnician artists and workmen. They were also the founders of Carthage, which contested the sovereignty of the Mediterranean with the rising power of Rome. Both as artists and craftsmen they originally borrowed from others; but they improved on their Egyptian and Assyrian masters.

Their chief gods were the sun and moon. But they degraded what they received of the spiritual element from the Mesopotamian priesthood, more than they improved on the arts which they received from them and the Egyptians. They were an impure and cruel people. They sought to win the favour of Heaven by lascivious practices on festal occasions. Destitute of literature, if we except historical archives, and destitute also of an initiating or progressive spirit in art, they were lost in a sensual materialism.

If it be true, as I think it is, that genuine progress in civ-

---

[1] For a brilliant description of the wealth and occupations of the Phœnicians, see Ezekiel xxvii. and xxviii.

ilisation is determined by the ethical and religious conceptions of a nation, we can understand that Phœnicia has little to teach us save by way of warning. Enterprising on the sea and highly intelligent they certainly were. But for all else they cannot arrest the attention of the historian.

B. — THE HEBREWS OR JEWS

OF the Semitic races by far the most famous was the Hebrew which emigrated from the west side of the Euphrates to Canaan or Palestine about 2000 B.C. Their centre of origin was Ur of the Chaldees, where the Abrahamic religion is understood to have arisen. Whether dissatisfaction with the mixed character of the Chaldæo-Babylonian religion instigated the migration or not it is impossible to say.[1]

The history of this remarkable people, however, properly dates from the emigration from Egypt under Moses about 1490 B. C.[2] After a period of wandering and many petty wars, in which they exhibited no small violence and cruelty, the land acquired on the east and west side of Jordan was divided among the twelve tribes. The tribe of Levi, however, which represented the sacerdotal class, was scattered throughout the country — the object of this being, it may be presumed, the maintenance of religious life and historical tradition among the people. For, Jewish history begins and ends with a great historical deliverance and an exalted religious idea.

' It was the aim of Moses,' says Ranke, ' that the idea by the power of which he had led them out of Egypt should continue to form the central point of their spiritual and political life. Moses is the most exalted figure in all primitive history. The thought of God as an intellectual Being independent of all material existence was seized by him and, so to speak, incorporated in the nation which he led. Not that the nation and the idea were simply co-extensive; the idea of the most High God as He revealed Himself on

[1] The name Jew is strictly applicable only to the Hebrews of Judæa.
[2] The date assigned varies from the above to 1320.

5

Horeb is one for all times and all nations : — an idea of a
pure and infinite Being, which admits of no limitation, but
which nevertheless inspires every decree of the legislator,
every undertaking of the captain of the host.'

The religion of the Hebrews was Abrahamic : and by
this I mean that it was an outgrowth of certain Chaldæan
religious conceptions brought from Ur by the nomadic tribe
of which Terah, the father of Abraham, was the chief. But
when we have granted this we must recognise that a fresh departure was made under Moses. It matters not to us what the
date of the various books of the Pentateuch may have been :
there can be no reasonable doubt, it seems to me, that the
Mosaic tradition was preserved by a priesthood, although
this priesthood was not fully organised till the time of David.
The tradition took its departure from the idea of God and
the Law as delivered by the new founder of the nation ;
and amid all the narrowness and the aberrations of tribes
and parties, the tradition survived, and grew by logical development till it reached its full expression in the prophets
— from Amos in the eighth century B.C. till after the Exile.
Moses was a remarkable man, and of a transcendent personality ; for, cognisant as he was of the religion of Egypt, he
was yet able in his spiritual strength to set it aside, and to
bring a nation to the foot of Sinai. Neither Osiris, nor Isis,
nor Ptah, nor Ammon, was allowed to influence, much less
to dominate, his religious thought. God was One — the sole
creator of heaven and earth — ultimate Being. The powers
of nature, and animals and men, were His work, and could
not be deified. He was a Spirit, and had to be worshipped
as a spirit, and in spirit. But above all, He was a God
supremely ethical, and demanded of men the service of
obedience to the moral law. It is impossible to exaggerate
the importance of this thought in the history of mankind.
It furnished a fresh point of departure for the whole human
race. Moses was the greatest of schoolmasters. Strange to
say, though familiar in Egypt with the idea of life after
death, he does not embody this idea in his teaching.

Where the ark of God was, there too was the centre of
Jewish faith and ritual. It was a golden-plated chest which
was said to contain (and why should it not contain?) the
Mosaic tables of stone; but there were necessarily, especially
in pre-Davidic times, many local altars and open-air sanctuaries — 'worship of the high places and under green trees'
(by which is meant worship of stones or monoliths placed on
eminences and symbolic of Baal and frequently also the trunk
of a tree as representing the female deity) — where vows were
made and sacrifices offered; and these for the most part, of
an idolatrous kind. Round the central sanctuary, however,
whether at Shiloh or afterwards at Jerusalem, the best tradition gathered, and there seems to be no sufficient reason to
doubt that it was orally handed down by the priesthood
before writing was common. The ark along with the Tabernacle (subsequently represented by the Holy of Holies in the
Temple at Jerusalem) was the centre of national unity, as
well as of the national faith, in a much more real sense than
Delphi was the centre of Hellenic unity. That writing was
used much earlier than the 'higher criticism' admits is so
highly probable as to be almost certain. Why should we
imagine that the art of writing universal in Egypt and Babylon was forgotten, especially when the Jews were in constant
intercourse with surrounding nations who all possessed the
art?

For two or three centuries, the Hebrews held their own as
what might be called a loosely federated tribal republic (with
industries which were chiefly pastoral) under the occasional
guidance of local chiefs or judges, some of whom received
national, and not merely tribal, recognition, and the last and
greatest of whom was the prophet Samuel. It became necessary to organise themselves as a monarchy in order to defend
their country against their enemies. Saul, the Benjamite,
was chosen 1095 B.C. and David succeeded him in 1055 B.C.
The incessant attacks of the Philistines were doing much,
while making a monarchy essential, to weld the Jewish
tribes into the unity of a nation, and the national idea natu-

rally led David to organise the Priesthood. Under the long reign of David's magnificent successor Solomon, the Hebrews reached their highest eminence as a secular polity, and extended their dominions to the Euphrates and the Red Sea. After his death differences, partly political, partly religious, brought about a civil war, led on the one side by Rehoboam, Solomon's son, and on the other by Jeroboam. The former party represented the interests of Judah and Benjamin in the south, while the latter represented Ephraim in the north. Many of the original tribes, it is necessary to note, had by this time become amalgamated with the more powerful ones, and were largely mixed with Canaanitish elements. The issue of this strife was two kingdoms — the southern, that of Judah (including Benjamin) with its capital Jerusalem, and the northern, Israel, with its capital Samaria.

This internal dissension led ultimately to the overthrow of both kingdoms. First of all, the Israelites of the north, attacked by the Assyrians, were subdued and carried off and planted in Media, Assyrian colonists taking their place (720 B.C.). The Israelites of the northern kingdom, thus crushed by the Assyrian king, are spoken of as the ' lost ten tribes.' Those who remained (the larger number of the commonalty), became mixed with immigrants, and in their religious life seem to have differed little, for a time at least, from that of other Semitic races round about, being especially influenced by Canaanite conceptions. They ultimately organised a Mosaic religion of their own based on the Law, but they seem to have ignored the prophets.

The centre of Hebrew nationality was now Judah, Jerusalem, and the Temple — the symbolic centre of the Hebrew faith; there the true Mosaic tradition was preserved. But Judah did not for long escape the misfortunes of her northern brethren. The Babylonian king, Nebuchadnezzar, took Jerusalem, burned the Temple, and carried off the leading inhabitants to Babylon (588 B.C.). Cyrus gave the Jews permission to return (538), but only the lower section of the people and the priests and scribes took advantage of the permission. The Temple was rebuilt 516 B.C. and the priesthood began to reconstitute the doctrine and practice of the law. But it was not till the second migration from Babylon under Ezra (458 B.C.), who was soon followed by Nehemiah, that the Mosaic tradition became fully formulated and an elaborate ritual constituted.

The monarchy now gave way to the rule of the hereditary priesthood. The real government of the Jews, accordingly, was now in the hands of a senate of priests, scribes, and elders called the Great Synagogue,[1] which as time went on took more and more definite shape, and developed into the famous Sanhedrin. The form of government was a natural development of the governing idea of the Hebrew race, which was a strictly religious idea.

It is a question whether any portion of the Pentateuchal books was committed to writing before the time of Josiah (640 B.C.), and certain critics maintain that the Law as a whole was written under the direction of Ezra and Nehemiah. I think we may safely conclude that the Law could not have been invented and suddenly sprung upon the people. Its root ideas had been orally handed down from Moses, and doubtless grew and expanded, partly as oral tradition, partly as written documents, as generations succeeded each other until the time of the Exile.

The written as well as the oral law was now enforced, and the beginning laid of an organised system of legal formalism and of ecclesiastical ceremonial which in the course of time became oppressive. All religious ideas when reduced to a system by an official body have a tendency to become formal and external. The formulation, however, preserves the substance of the living doctrine ; and so we find in the case of the Jews. The legal and ceremonial system was not only conservative of past history and religious tradition, but it secured the unity of the Jewish race, and made that unity independent of a political nationality. The Jews long before the Christian era were an

---

[1] Probably not formally organised under this name.

emigrating people and were dispersed over the cities of the East and of the Mediterranean.[1] The body of doctrine and ritual sustained them in their existence among the nations as a 'peculiar people.'

Mosaism and the Priesthood, Prophets, and Scribes, as educational forces. — Whatever other gods might have been worshipped by the Hebrews at local altars ('high places and under green trees') during the nomadic, and even during the more settled agricultural period after Samuel (and these gods were various, and increased in number under the influence of neighbouring and immigrant populations), they yet, as a nation, preserved a distinctive religious belief and character which marked them off from other branches of the Semites. From the time of Moses they had unquestionably a theology and a law. Deep in the traditional life of the people, though often doubtless confined in its outward manifestations to the conservative priestly order or the reforming prophets, was the idea of Jahveh — Sole God. Not merely a God *above* other gods within the nation (for within the nation he was alone God and a 'jealous' God), but above all gods recognised among the superstitious and idolatrous cotemporary peoples. This God was One and Sole — Being universal and yet personal — 'I am that I am'; and he was a God moreover of ethical attributes, comprehending in Himself the idea of moral law and proclaiming the duty of the believer to the law. The Infinite God was thus in *personal* relation to man as a moral finite being; — and, accordingly, we may say with truth that it was among the Jews that God first began to dwell with man. To Moses and the development of his teaching the world owes, not perhaps the idea of God as One and Sole Supreme Spirit (for the Zoroastrians independently attained to this), but the more practical conception of God as a self-subsistent moral personality in

---

[1] Alexander the Great and one of his generals who became king of Egypt carried off many to people Alexandria Cyrene ; and these spread through Egypt and along the northern coast of Africa.

direct relation with the finite spirit of the rational creature. For this and the sublime expression of exalted spirituality which by natural development arose out of it, the world owes a permanent debt to the Hebrews. They had little art and no science. The energy of the race was concentrated on a great central thought and its logical issues; and with this remarkable result, that the pure literature contained in the Old Testament is as true an expression of the relation of the devout soul to God to-day as it was 2500 years ago: and, as such, it can never be superseded. The Mosaic idea was a protest against idolatry and nature-worship on the one hand, and Pantheism on the other. To trace the gradual growth of the primary Mosaic conception is not our business. Enough, from the point of view of the education of the human race and specially of the Jews themselves, that at the date of the canon of Ezra we not only have the final formulation of the priestly tradition of the Law, but, above all, the completed spiritual interpretation of the prophets.

The priesthood in the earlier times discharged the public function of sacrificing (I say 'public' because private offerings and sacrifices were common among the Israelites, as among all nations, and did not require the official presence of a priest). It is not to be alleged against them, as in any way detracting from the sacredness of their office, as intermediaries for the ascertainment of the will of Jahveh, that they shared the belief in magic and incantations common to all races of mankind, and that, by lending themselves to the interpretation of dreams and the prediction of events, they often prostituted their true function. Perhaps the most important characteristic of the priesthood as educator of the nation, was its relation to civil affairs. The priests gave advice to the people, they issued judicial decisions on questions brought before them, and gave shelter against oppression. The unwritten Law (Torah) was gradually built up by them. I am here summarising their functions, while of course recognising to the full its irregular action and gradual development. 'They shall teach Jacob thy judgments and Israel

thy Law' (Deut. xxxiii. 10) may have been written down,
for all I know, on parchment for the first time in the days
of Josiah or Ezra, but it was an *ex post facto* writing. Mr.
Montefiore quotes from Professor Stade as follows: 'No one
in old Israel was more capable of protecting the unfortunate
from oppression, of punishing the injustice of the mighty,
and thus of strengthening the moral conscience, softening
public manners, and educating society, than the priests. . . .
Their importance for the development of religion, justice,
and public morality cannot be too highly estimated.' That
their full organisation did not take place till the time of
David does not affect the truth of this. Thus the close connection between religion, morality, and civil polity gave a position of power to the priesthood much greater than that found
among other nations. At the same time it saved the priesthood from exclusive and esoteric beliefs, and from the proud
isolation of a class. Civil law and social practices were mere
deductions from the Divine law. The banal distinction between sacred and secular, from which modern Europe suffers,
did not exist. The Levites were ministers to the Aaronic
priests, but could not themselves perform the highest functions.

In the Mosaic idea of God we have the Semitic mind on
its highest plane of religious possibility; however restricted
by national limits that God might be, it was still an ever-
potent educative force of a progressive kind. And we are
not surprised to find that, ere long, the higher minds of the
nation began to recognise its full significance. The masses
of the people accepted Jahveh as a great self-subsistent
moral being with whom they had a covenant of works very
much of the nature of a business contract. He was doubtless to the people, till post-exilic times, a mere God of the
Hebrews whose seat was Sinai, and the worship of Him
did not preclude the worship of other gods. But the more
thoughtful spirits evolved out of the whole a nobler and freer
spiritual life than any mere official priesthood could have
conceived. These men were called the prophets; they began
to prophesy a purely spiritual faith as early as the eighth

century B. C., although we are justified in holding that from Samuel downwards the larger conceptions were steadily growing, though probably confined to a restricted class. The prophets, until post-exilic times, represent in their teaching the highest education — an education which, in its highest as in its lowest form, was always religious. They maintained the idea of Jahveh in all its purity. They did not disdain the ritual and ceremonials of the Law, but they represented the spirit and not the mere outward form of Hebraism, and were distinguished by profound thought, theological and ethical. They thus exercised a powerful influence on the life and polity of the Jews, recalling princes and people alike to the worship of the true God, and that 'in spirit and in truth.' They held, even more than the priestly order, the principles of the theocratic constitution of society, but in a broader and more liberal sense. The gradually increasing psalter was meanwhile giving lyrical expression to intense religious emotion, and supporting the high prophetic teaching.

During this prophetic period down to the Exile, the class of scribes (*bookmen* is the translation of the Hebrew), mostly, doubtless, belonging to the priestly, or at least Levitical, order, were growing in importance. Priests and scribes do not seem, however, to have been strictly differentiated till after the Exile. The chief function of the former was the Temple services, of the latter the preservation and teaching of the Law. Temple and Law, it has been said, imply priest and scribe. The scribe always comprised many members of the priest class, but the function was one which was during the prophetic period, no less than in the post-exilic, open to laymen as in Egypt. Their precise function before the exile is not ascertained; but we may infer from the word itself and from the early traditional influence of Egypt, that they were engaged in such transcriptions of sacred and historical literature as were required.[1] They also

[1] I have read much, merely as a layman desirous to get at the truth as regards the Israelites, and it appears to me that to the historian it matters little whether the Hexateuch was formulated after the Captivity or not. In

acted as notaries among the people. After the exile, however, and the cessation of the Great Synagogue, those who followed this function were the recognised Masters of the 'law and the prophets' and continuators of tradition. They thus constituted a learned and progressive lay order of students and teachers, apart from, but not necessarily in opposition to, the sacrificial priesthood. I write of these things in general terms because I cannot find that there is a consensus of opinion as to the details of the organisation of priest and scribe and their mutual relations after the Exile. The fact of the rise of the scribes to importance as an academic class is enough for the purposes of a student of education.[1]

We thus find among the Jews three classes of men, all of whom were engaged in the preservation and gradual develop-

---

countries like Egypt, where the people had a mania for recording all contemporary events on stone or papyrus, oral tradition was superseded; but in the rise of other civilisations we find that the handing down orally of sacred doctrines with their ever-growing accretions, was common. Even in post-exilic times we find this practice in Judæa when writing might have been alone resorted to. It is only ignorance of the origins of the religious scriptures of other nations which would make us doubt the possibility of the *substantial* truth of a Jewish pre-exilic tradition of the Law. The formulation may have begun in the reign of Josiah, say about 630 B. C., and have been completed by Ezra; but it was the formulation of what already existed and had been preserved by the priesthood, partly at least in writing. No one, I suppose, asserts that all the details of the ceremonial law are Mosaic. It is enough that we recognise a growth out of a central idea and see the fruitful beginnings of the Law carried out by the priesthood, and illuminated by the prophets, and at a certain date (post-exilic) taking systematic written form. This is the common history of national religions; and I do not see why we should be so unhistorical, and therefore so unscientific, as to treat the organised Jewish system very much as if it were an invention of Ezra and Nehemiah. In the case of a tradition chiefly oral and only partly written and wholly edited with a purpose, one would expect composite books. Of course, I cannot speak as an expert, but the 'intelligent layman' has his rights. I would, in this connection, direct special attention to Professor Robertson's *Early Religion of Israel*.

[1] With scribes on one side of them in Egypt, and on the other in Babylon and Assyria, it is surely quite in accordance with recognised historical principles to regard the scribe organisation after the Exile as merely a development of an order which had existed in some form or other from the time of Samuel at least.

ment of the Mosaic monotheism, the Sinaitic moral law [1] and the civil law based on it. The literature of the country, lyrical, historical, and theological, all gathered round the one central thought of Jahveh. The 'masses' were continually falling into idolatry and forgetting the best tradition of their fathers; but under the influence of the 'classes,' of whom we have been speaking, the great tradition was always living and gradually developing (especially from 800 B. C. onwards) from a tribal religion with its tribal god who, though supreme, admitted of the worship of other gods, into a religion of genuine monotheism and of universal characteristics. The God of the Jews, as conceived by the prophets and psalmists, a God of justice, truth, and compassion, might indeed have become the recognised God of the whole earth but for the over-elaboration of religious observances and legal technicalities by the post-exilic scribes.

The tribe of Semites out of whom came Genesis, the Book of Job, the Psalms, the eloquent utterances of the Prophets, the Proverbs, and the post-exilic Book of Wisdom, stands apart from all other ancient races, and was manifestly destined for a special mission to the world. When we bear in mind too, the concentrated intensity of the Jewish personal character, and of their family life, we see in the very narrowness which accompanied that intensity, the possibility of going far. The 'I am that I am' of Moses, whether promulgated in these abstract terms by him or not, and, though to the masses for centuries little more than a tribal God, as was the case with the primitive gods of all nations, was yet a *spiritual* God who brooked no equal. The idea had a powerful formative influence; and this all the more because it was possible for the primary conception to be identified in the course of time with an Universal Unseen self-conscious Spirit. Moreover, this God Jahveh, as I have pointed out, was not

---

[1] I am quite well aware that the Decalogue, as we have it, is ascribed to the reign of Josiah; but I cannot but conclude that the elements of the Decalogue were contained in the Law imposed by Moses. Much of it may be found in the Egyptian religion (Confession before Osiris).

only a spiritual but an ethical Being, concerned in the moral order and having personal relations to all His creatures. It is true that the observances of thanksgiving and sacrifice and of formal obedience to the law which this God demanded of all had very much the air of a business contract, as I have indicated above, in which each side was expected to fulfil his respective obligations; but none the less was the idea moralising, and itself sufficient to educate a primitive race, while in the hands of the prophets it expanded into a pure spiritualism. And are we not sane historians when we add that, whatever might be the defections of the Israelites, however gradual their religious growth, what may be called the Mosaic idea of Jahveh must have contained the germ of such possibilities, and, consequently, have been from the first a God unlike the other gods of the Canaanites?

EDUCATION OF THE YOUNG AMONG THE JEWS GENERALLY

IF we take a general, and at the same time, it is to be admitted, a somewhat ideal, view of the education of the Jewish race, we shall find its beginnings and its specific character expressed in the sixth chapter of Deuteronomy:—

'Hear, O Israel: The Lord our God is one Lord: And thou shalt love the Lord thy God with all thine heart, and with all thy soul, and with all thy might. And these words, which I command thee this day, shall be in thine heart: and thou shalt teach them diligently unto thy children, and shalt talk of them when thou sittest in thine house, and when thou walkest by the way, and when thou liest down, and when thou risest up.'

The father and mother were thus the divinely appointed teachers. As has been said, 'The dwellings of Abraham, Isaac, and Jacob were at once house, school, state, and church.' The family life was intense, and the more so that the Law thus directly addressed parents and placed on them the responsibility for the moral and spiritual well-being of their children. To the Jews more than to any other race we may apply the words of Shakespeare:

Let never day nor night unhallowed pass,
But still remember what the Lord hath done.
                                        2 *Henry VI.* ii.

As might be expected, respect for parents and elders was rigidly enforced.

Thou shalt honour thy father and thy mother, &c.
Thou shalt rise up before the hoary head.

The family bond, so potent among the Jews, embraced God Himself, demanding, as Father of the race, implicit obedience from His children.

If we may infer from the Proverbs of Solomon that maxims and reflections such as are collected in that book were in general currency, we may further conclude that the domestic education was powerfully reinforced by traditions of practical wisdom. The Book of Ruth also could have emanated only from a people sensitive to the finer and more spiritual significance of domestic relations, while the post-exilic Book of Wisdom gives us a religious philosophy of life. Accordingly, we may say that a present God, whom to fear was 'the beginning of wisdom,' the honouring of parents and elders, a sacred family life, the memory of a great history, the practical wisdom of proverbs, and a gradually growing lyric psalmody, constituted the elements of the education of the masses down to the time of the Exile. 'My son, hear the instruction of thy father, and forsake not the law of thy mother' (Prov. i. 7). No special *public* means, however, were taken by the Jews any more than by other nations to give education to the people, so that the fundamental conception of the equality of all before God, a thoroughly Jewish idea, remained a barren conception so far as organised action to raise all to a certain level of intelligence and moral life was concerned. In post-exilic times it was otherwise.

Such, *speaking generally*, were the life and education of the Jewish people; but to understand them more fully we must look at them in their historical development. The domestic tradition varied, and, as generation succeeded generation, grew richer and fuller. It is true that among the Jews, as among all other nations in pre-christian times, the culture of the period, whatever it might be, was confined to the upper classes of priest, scribe, prophet, and the lay aristocracy. On the other hand, every nation, *as a whole*, lives in a certain atmosphere of religion and morality, and all participate, in part at least, in the life and thought of the more educated. All are borne along in the main current. I think we may say that this was the case among the Jews more than in any other ancient nation. Their literature was of a grave, thoughtful, and earnest type, and it might be said that it was above the understanding of the mass; but none the less was it the expression of the true life and character of the people, permanent and enduring amidst all their deviations from the path pointed out to them by Moses and the prophets.

In truth, from Moses downwards even to this day, the central religious conception of the Jewish mind was the great educative force, both in its early rudimentary, and later universalised, form. But in the case of a people which had so long a history and encountered such varying fortunes, it is necessary to look at their education as it existed at different periods of their civilisation.

EPOCHS OF JEWISH EDUCATION

We may distinguish four epochs of Jewish education.

The First Period

The first period extends from the emigration from Egypt down to Samuel and Saul. Samuel died 1043 B.C. During this period the Hebrews were still largely a pastoral and wandering race, and were fighting for the conservation of such permanent settlements as they had made. The different tribes were very loosely connected. The centre of the

Mosaic teaching was to be found with the ark and the Tabernacle, which were in the keeping of the Aaronic priestly family. Local altars were erected by the people in various places and sacrifices offered, not always to Jahveh alone; for in very many cases the tribes had lapsed into idolatries. And yet in the domestic teaching of the rising generation the Mosaic ideas of "God and Lord" could not have been anywhere wholly lost. The effect of this tradition in moulding the character of the Hebrews must have been great. The existence and recognition of leaders or tribal captains, under the name of judges, in whose hands lay the application to the ordinary affairs of life of the Mosaic teaching, concurred with the one central Tabernacle and its priesthood to maintain a certain unity of belief and life, spite of constant lapses into idolatries. The movement favoured by Samuel which led to the anointing of a king is itself evidence that notwithstanding many backslidings, the national unity, as constituted by the idea of Jahveh, was profoundly felt. The education of the people by this idea was going on. National songs were handed down along with the national history and religious festivals. Writing in the form of inscriptions on stone was known, and writing, it is said also, on parchment or paper; but this only as the accomplishment of a few.

Even the education of the priesthood must have been entirely confined to preserving and extending the Mosaic tradition. We must remember, however, that in the case of the Jews this tradition, as I have shown, meant a great deal. For the religious and civil polity were not dissociated. Morality, civil law, and religion were one; and these, too, were bound up with a great history. We find during this period the existence of what survived even after the destruction of the Jewish nationality — the interweaving of religious feeling with the moral law and the civil law. The distribution of the Levites among the tribes must have helped to maintain the tradition of the law among the whole body of the people. Some learned Jews who write on the education of their race would claim a knowledge of mathematics, geography, and history for the Levitic scribes during this early period. But there is no evidence of this.

The Second Period

The second period extends from Samuel till 538 B.C. — the return from the Babylonian Captivity. The Hebrews had now become an agricultural, as well as pastoral, people, living for the most part in villages and cities, from which they went out to their daily work. They were consequently in closer communication with each other. But as regards the mass of the people there is not yet evidence of any instruction save that which oral tradition afforded. Sacrifices at local altars (though often taking the form of idolatrous services) doubtless helped to maintain this. Boys accompanied their fathers to their daily labour at the field or workshop, girls were trained at home in domestic arts, cooking, weaving, and the making of garments. Music, dancing, and song were practised, and there can be no reasonable doubt that during this period many of the psalms were composed, and influenced, while expressing, the life of a considerable portion at least among the population. The erection of the Temple, to which all citizens were required to repair at certain periods, helped to give unity to religious belief, and intensify the national feeling.

Education of the higher section of Society. — The priesthood, as the depositary of the growing historical and judicial literature, was daily extending the moral and civil law which was studied as part of its function, while scribes (generally Levites, if not priests of the higher order) seem to have been employed to make transcriptions. The scribes also acquired a certain knowledge of the law and acted as notaries among the people and helpers in the adjusting of difficulties. (For the early existence of scribes, *vide* Joshua xviii. 9.)

But the most interesting fact during this period was the rise of the prophets, who are mentioned as early as Samuel. There can be little doubt, I think, that these bands of men had, to begin with, a very loose organisation, and might be regarded as religious revivalists — many of them wild, uneducated, and fanatical. But from·among them came the greatest Jewish intellects. From the eighth century to the fifth century B.C. we have such of their writings as have survived, and they constitute a permanent part of world-literature. The prophets were, as I have already said, quite outside the ceremonial priesthood, and as a body they had for their aim the maintenance and purifying of the idea of Jahveh in its monotheistic and ethical sense. Their text was, 'I desire mercy and not sacrifice, and the knowledge of God more than burnt offerings.' That there were fortune-tellers and hypocrites among those who assumed the name is not to be doubted; that most of them believed in divination and magic, is only to say that they belonged to their own period of world-history; that many of them used their supposed magical powers for their own pecuniary profit is only to say that they were men. Take them as a whole, however, the formative principle which entered into this new organisation was a spiritual one. They generally lived in community, and tradition says that they occupied rude huts of their own erection, and wore a characteristic dress. Confraternities (sometimes called schools) arose in connection with this movement; we find them (though not as contemporary institutions) at Gibea, Rama, Bethel, Jericho, and Gilgal.[1] Let us specially note that the students in these schools were not necessarily Levites. Prophets were essentially a lay order, and it may almost be said that they stood to the religious and social life of the time very much in the relation in which some of the monastic orders stood to European society in the eleventh and twelfth centuries. These prophets and 'sons of the prophets' as (the aspirants were called) constituted (according to Rabbinical tradition) colleges numbering from fifty to four hundred which were somewhat of the nature of

[1] I follow in all this the Jewish tradition. 'The higher criticism' rejects much of what I say. In the pages that precede there is nothing inconsistent with the best results of the 'higher criticism.'

theological institutions, and were presided over by a senior member formally elected. Music and sacred poetry were studied as well as the profounder aspects of theology. Out of these 'schools,' or at least out of this class, came the national poets and historians. As preachers, the prophets promulgated the righteous government of the world; they inculcated morals and taught a spiritual life far transcending the religion of mere Temple services, protesting also against the idolatries and immorality often associated with worship in the 'high places.' The existence of this class is the most interesting fact in the higher education of the Jews. Whether the tradition as given above is to be accepted or not in all its details, it is substantially true. The actual organisation of colleges may be more than questionable.

During this period, writing became customary, and priestly decisions on questions of law were thus preserved while cotemporary historical records were made, or added to. The accumulation of legal decisions added to the learning and importance of the sacerdotal class, many of whom were also scribes.

While it cannot be said that the education of the people, as a whole, had altered its domestic and traditionary form, this is not true of the higher section of society from David onwards. It is not to be supposed that the prophets spoke to empty air: they had an audience, and such of their lofty spiritual conceptions as found expression in lyrics would easily find their way even among the masses. We are, indeed, quite justified in dating the fact and influence of the prophets from Samuel onwards. For it is in direct contradiction of all the principles applied to historical investigation to imagine that men like Amos and Hosea had no predecessors. 'The condition we find prevailing at the time of the first admitted literary compositions implies an antecedent period of literary activity and religious education' (Professor Robertson, p. 70). And the words of Amos and Hosea themselves (see the passages quoted by Professor Robertson) fully justify our conclusions, if it be the truth we seek and not the cheap reputation of the man who is up to the fashion of the, hour in criticism. The existence of the prophets, I have said, implies an audience and numerous sympathisers, while the existence of written prophecies presumes that there were people who can read them. That writing and reading were pretty widely spread during the latter half of the period of which I am speaking there can be no reasonable doubt. It does not follow that there were 'schools' in our modern sense of the word. Priests and scribes would, according to the universal Oriental custom, be taught at the Temple, or wherever there were priests; and it is probable that the teaching was individual teaching.

While it is doubtless correct to say that reading of MS. rolls and writing were confined to the upper section of society, we are not to conclude that the teaching of the growing literature of the nation did not reach the masses of the people, and influence, if not mould, their lives. Amos himself was one of the people. It is only the other day that the arts of reading and writing were unknown to the masses in England.

The Third Period

PERIOD OF THE SCRIBE AND THE SYNAGOGUE

(*Decree of Cyrus* 537 B. C.   *Ezra* 458 B. C.)

After the rebuilding of the Temple (the dedication was 516 B. C.) and the return of Ezra (458 B. C.), we have a new development. For a time, the Judaic organisation, never fully expressed or stringently enforced owing to the constant lapse of kings and people into Canaanitish and Phœnician idolatries, had been broken in pieces. Semitic immigrants had found their way into the southern as they had formerly done into the northern kingdom, and the memory of the Mosaic tradition and all that so signally differentiated the Hebrews from other Semites had been imperilled. The most strenuous efforts were now made to restore what had been lost and to formulate the whole Jewish conception of theocratic tradition. More than ever before, we now find a polity organised on the basis of a common religious idea and administered by religious functionaries. The high priest was now the true king, and the council or senate of which he was president, composed of elders and scribes as well as priests, governed all things both civil and ecclesiastical.

The prophets now disappear, but they had left behind a rich inheritance to the people. Their lofty utterances were now, as written documents, accessible to all who could read or listen intelligently to reading, and must have been in the highest degree educative. For what had been their aim from the time of Amos and Hosea in the eighth century B. C.? To abolish all idolatry and to purify and exalt the popular conceptions of the national God, as the God of the human race, who cared less even for Israel than for righteousness. They taught that the right, the just, the good were the attributes of Jehovah, and thus gave him an universal character. All nations were to be brought to Him. He was no longer the mere ' Hearer' of Israel. Priestly sacrifices were as nothing in the eyes of the universal God of heaven and earth, compared with integrity of heart and purity of conduct. In truth, religious faith and philosophic contemplation of the graver aspects of human life had reached in the writings of the prophets and in the psalter to the highest expression which the world had ever seen or, probably, ever will see. These writings were now the possession of the nation, although for want of schools they could influence them only through the priestly and higher classes. Their teaching, however, would receive confirmation and an ever-fresh impulse from the prescribed periodical visits to the Temple.

Higher Education. — Meanwhile there was arising a class of learned men side by side with the priesthood. The scribes, who had been coming more into prominence even before the Exile, had, before 300 B.C., become an important order. As the name and function of scribe was open to all, it is to be regarded as a lay order like the schools of the prophets. A priest or Levite might be a scribe, but the profession was not confined to any order. Men of various occupations were also scribes. Ezra, fifth century B.C., was both priest and scribe. After the return from the Captivity the scribe class gradually increased in number. They became in fact the learned and legal class, and as such the more eminent of them were teachers — expounders of the law. They also extended the law by their glosses and interpretations. The prophets were thus practically superseded by a written law and an authoritative oral interpretation, out of which came the Talmud.

The legal tradition of the scribes, based on the law, was oral, and the amount of memory work demanded of those who would excel in this profession as teachers or advisers was very great. They taught chiefly in the porches of the Temple (the headquarters being Jerusalem) and in synagogues, and gradually the whole law and its application to the affairs of life fell into their hands. Unless they had private means they did not always devote themselves exclusively to study and teaching, but followed also some special industry. These schools of the scribes were also headquarters of disputation by which difficult points were settled. Their teaching was for all, there being nothing esoteric in Judaism. They came to be known in the beginning of the Christian era as the 'Rabbinical' schools, and acquired gradually an influence with the people greater than that of the priests. The heads of these schools were first technically called 'Rabbins' (Masters) about the time of Christ.

It was a great fall, certainly, from the schools of the prophets to the schools of the scribes — from the spiritual life to the formal, legal, and external; but unquestionably the gradual multiplication of legal dicta and prescriptions and of ritual observances tended to preserve the Jewish nation in its exclusiveness and in 'soundness of faith.' The instruction of youth formed one of the chief functions of the order. 'Every eminent teacher of the law . . . collected round him a larger or smaller number of young men,' says Schürer, 'who desired to be educated by him so as to become capable scribes. With this purpose in view there existed school-houses in which the law was methodically taught. In Jerusalem they assembled in the outer porch of the Temple. Teachers and scholars sat, the teacher being generally raised a little above the level of his pupils. The instruction was oral and disputatory. The teacher asked, how must it be done (or determined) in this or that case.. And the scholars had to answer. They were also at liberty to put questions to the teacher.' The great aim was to receive in the memory, and to reproduce, what was taught; and this latter in identical terms. The pupil, as was the general Oriental practice, hung on the lips of his master. All this presumed a prior elementary instruction, but this must have been, largely at least, domestic, for there is no evidence of the existence of elementary schools.

During the centuries immediately preceding the birth of Christ, the growing power of the scribe (or Rabbinical) schools threw the priesthood more and more into the shade, confining them to functions of sacrifice, ceremonial, and government. After the destruction of the Temple by the Romans, A.D. 70, the teaching scribes called Rabbins finally superseded the priesthood. This development of a learned order is the leading fact of this period of Jewish educational history. Besides the interpretation of written statutes by common sense, these teachers and expounders of the law believed that they alone were the vehicles of the development of the Mosaic law outside the Torah or Pentateuch. This unwritten and ever-growing tradition (Massorah and Kabbala) gave them great power.

In these schools of the scribes all learning was concentrated, but the priesthood and the higher laity generally shared in the educational advance. The learning of the time entered into the higher course of study — not only mathematics and astronomy, but, from the third century B. C., Hellenic literature and philosophy.

Popular Education. — But while the higher classes of the community shared in the progressive movement which was in the hands of the scribes, an educational change had begun among the masses of the people of still greater significance than the schools of the scribes. This was the gradual institution, from the time of Ezra, of synagogues throughout the land, where the law might be weekly read and expounded to the people, and prayer and praise offered. We can easily see that the influence of these local schools of religion must have been incalculable. Young and old benefited by them. It was, doubtless, to the Central Council at Jerusalem constituted in the time of Ezra and Nehemiah that the Jews owed these institutions — the prototype of the Christian parochial system. Scribes read and taught in the synagogues; but it was competent for the elders of the people to conduct service, so that here again as in the case of the prophets, we have cropping out the essentially lay and unsacerdotal character of the most theocratic of races. All the people might now be regarded as students of the law and the prophets. In the fourth century B. C. there were synagogues in all towns, and in the second century in villages also.

Dean Milman says, speaking of this movement: 'In addition to the central Temple and its ceremonial the Jew now had his synagogue — where, in a smaller community, he assembled, with a few of his neighbours, for divine worship, for prayer, and for instruction in the law. The latter more immediately, and gradually the former, fell entirely under the regulation of the regular interpreter of the law, who, we may say, united the professions of the clergy and the law — the clergy considered as public instructors; for the lawschool and the synagogue were always closely connected, if they did not form parts of the same building. Thus there arose in the state the curious phenomenon of a spiritual supremacy distinct from the priesthood, for though many of these teachers were actually priests and Levites, they were not necessarily so — a supremacy which exercised the most unlimited dominion, not formally recognised by the constitution, but not the less real and substantial, for it was grounded in the general belief, ruled by the willing obedience of its subjects, and was rooted in the very minds and hearts of the people, till at length the maxim was openly promulgated, "the voice of the Rabbi the voice of God." Thus, though the high priest was still the formal and ac-

knowledged head of the state, the real influence passed away
to these recognised interpreters of the divine word.' (Milman, ii. 410). The attendant or beadle of the synagogue, it is
said, taught the children during the week, and thus the synagogues gradually became schools for the young as well as
the adult. But it is not to be inferred from this that even
so late as three centuries B.C., instruction in reading, writing,
and arithmetic reached any, save a small proportion of the
general population, except in so far as it was home teaching. [1]
This proportion, however, went on increasing, and, it would
appear, with considerable rapidity, after the Maccabean revolt, 167 B.C. Still I think we may fairly conclude that for
about four centuries before Christ, elementary instruction
was generally accessible through individual public teaching
or parental teaching, and that clever and energetic boys
could thus raise themselves above the humbler ranks of
poverty. Popular education was, however, *education by the
synagogue*, which brought home to every small community
of Jews the central idea of their faith and the system of
morality, law, and ritual based on it. Speaking of the
synagogue Wellhausen says (p. 159), ' The Bible became the
spelling-book, the community a school, religion an affair of
teaching and learning. Piety and education were inseparable.
Whoever could not read was no true Jew.'

The services of the synagogue were : 1. The recital of
what was substantially a Creed. 2. Prayer. 3. Reading
and expounding of Scripture. 4. The Blessing. And the
whole was under the general control of a Board of Elders
with a chief or president. Nor did the Reader merely read:
he expounded, following the example of Ezra and his friends,
of whom Nehemiah (viii.) says, ' They read in the book in
the law of God, distinctly : and they gave the sense, so that
they understood the reading.'

Quite apart, then, from the educational and formative
influence of the great stream of religious tradition supported

[1] There is no actual *evidence* of the existence of schools for children before
200 B.C.

by sacrificial acts and solemn festivals at Jerusalem,[1] we must fix attention on the pre-exilic schools of the prophets and the post-exilic organisation of the scribes as truly representing the higher education of the Jews. As to the former, I have already said that many who attached themselves to the prophetic communities had a low enough moral standard and looked to divination and soothsaying as the source of their power over the people and of profit to themselves. But in all religious and academic orders, we find men who fail to rise to the idea which first constituted the order and continues to maintain it in existence. With all their defects they were all members of a voluntary religious community out of which from time to time rose men of light and leading — many doubtless whose names have perished. The prophetic studies apart from theology were (tradition says, and as I have already mentioned) music and verse, mathematics and Chaldæan astronomy, as well as the law and its spiritual interpretation. I do not mean to say that all this was thoroughly organised, but it was an operative reality. Nor could these communities have existed without finding a response in the minds of (at least) the higher classes of the community, and influencing the tone of thought among the common people. To enter into this field of religious and intellectual activity it was not, let me again point out, necessary to be a priest or Levite, and this is an important fact to the historian of education. The prophets were a lay order, though not excluding Levites.

After the rebuilding of the Temple (516 B.C.) although we still have one or two prophets, the intellectual life of the Jews passed, as we have seen, into the keeping of the organised scribes. (They were frequently organised into Guilds.) This organisation furnished men to read and interpret the law and the prophets in every part of the kingdom and also among the dispersed colonies ; while public worship

[1] Doubtless this kind of education was common to all nations, but it is the *kind and quality* of the tradition that is all-important as a formative power. (Compare the Aztecs.)

and sacrifice and the offering of incense were still çentralised
at Jerusalem with a view to the preservation of their purity
(although the ark of the covenant was now lost).   The
scribes were literary men, learned in the law, and not only
teachers of the law but alive to all the educational influences of their time.   Hellenic speculation and literature
gradually found their way among them.   It is not to be
supposed that all of this order had wide intellectual interests;
but among them were many who studied the Greek language
and literature, mathematics, foreign tongues, geography, and
such science as was current, including astronomy.   There also
grew up among them a belief in immortality and the resur-
rection of the body.[1]   They were, moreover, as far as the law
was concerned, progressive; for they assumed the authority
of continuous oral tradition which enabled them, by interpretations and glosses and artificial constructions, to adapt the
law to changing circumstances.   A bad use unfortunately
was made of this freedom to multiply forms and ceremonies,
and to confound the petty with the important in morality and
religion.   Prescription and proscription of certain outward
acts characterised these teachings — acts which in themselves
had no spiritual significance.   The burden which they gradually imposed on the people (as did the Brahmans in India)
was greater than they could bear; although the more zealous
delighted in it.   The point of interest for us, however, is
that they were an educated and studious and learned body
of men.   They had to translate the Hebrew scriptures into
the Aramaic dialect, for the majority had by this time ceased
to understand the ancient Hebrew tongue.   They also formed
the literature of the people ; for out of their schools came
the Talmud.   The Talmud began in the production of the
Mishnah, a paraphrase of the law.   Then followed in future
generations commentaries, homilies, &c., which, with a large
mass of oral tradition, constituted the Talmudic literature,

----

[1] The bulk of the nation were Pharisees accepting the doctrine of the
scribes.   The small Essenic party were an offshoot of the Pharisees with
mystical and ascetic beliefs.   The Sadducees were chiefly a political party.

all centring round the law and its interpretation and practical application.

As tradition accumulated, the schools of the scribes, as depositaries of all learning, bearing alike on the great and small affairs of life, became a dominating force in the life of the nation. They made their power felt as guides in the whole business of life and as deciders of cases among the whole population, and exercised an intellectual despotism. After the fall of Jerusalem, A.D. 70, they succeeded as Rabbins to the position and privileges of priesthood. So great was the mass of oral and written tradition that to be a worthy Rabbi demanded very great learning. [It was 190 A.D. before a critical edition of the Mishnah was issued, and 270 A.D. before a critically edited authoritative commentary appeared.]

I have said that, in addition to the law and the prophets and the mass of oral traditions and interpretations, the Greek language, Greek philosophy, and mathematics were prosecuted by many at least from the third century B.C. Greek was esteemed more highly than all other foreign tongues, and next to Hebrew was considered the most beautiful of all. 'The Torah (Law) may be translated only into Greek, because only by this language can it be faithfully rendered.' It is further said, 'the Greek language may in every respect be used.' It is true that Greek philosophy was suspected and denounced by the Rabbinical doctors for manifest reasons; but not more earnestly than by the Christian church after the third century A.D. The sages say of the tongue of Hellas, that the words 'there is no blemish in her,' may be applied to it, for 'it distinguishes itself by a keen sense of that which is perfectly noble.' 'There are four languages,' observes Rabbi Nathan, 'which are distinguished by superior and special qualities. The Greek sounds beautifully in poetry on account of its rhythm; the Roman in war, on account of its sonorous masculine power; the Syriac in mournful songs, on account of its numerous dull, hollow vowel-sounds : the Hebrew for its clear and articulate utterance in speech.'

Instruction in Greek, indeed, became quite general before the birth of Christ, and a knowledge of the language formed an essential part of a good higher education.[1] But the national literature, *i. e.* the Scriptures, the Talmudic Mishnah, Gemara, &c., continued to furnish the principal material for teaching in the schools. The religious aim was always dominant, if not exclusive.[2]

Fourth Period

PERIOD OF THE RABBIN AND THE ELEMENTARY SCHOOL

(*From the Birth of Christ onwards*)

Notwithstanding the great advance in general education in the upper half of society, the majority of Jews, it is said, could neither read nor write in the generation preceding the birth of Christ; but this fact is comparatively unimportant. It was true of England less than 100 years ago.

The chief educational feature of the period after the birth of Christ is the further extension and consolidation of the Scribe schools now called Rabbinical schools ; and, along with this, the extension of the Rabbinical power. As the body of law increased in bulk, the people became more and more dependent on Rabbinical experts for advice and direction in their social and business relations, as well as for instruction in the 'acts' of religion. An order which was at once preacher, teacher, and legal adviser could not fail to exercise supreme power; and, as I have already said, it became, after the cessation of the Temple sacrifice (A.D. 70), the sole authority.

It was not till a few years before the destruction of Jerusalem that primary schools became general, and these do not concern us so closely as the pre-christian education, for nothing later than the second century before Christ can

---

[1] It is probable that schools of the Hellenic type existed at Jerusalem 200 years B.C.

[2] The vessels of the Temple were marked with Greek letters.

be regarded as of *purely* Israelitish growth. Hellenic influences had been long felt and acknowledged at the headquarters of Judaism. The settlements scattered round the Mediterranean coasts had, moreover, reacted powerfully even on the hierarchy at Jerusalem, as well as on the schools of the scribes and had probably led to schools of the Hellenic type at Jerusalem nearly 200 years B. C.

In A.D. 64 elementary schools were first made obligatory by the high priest Josué ben Gamala. One teacher was to be employed where there were 25 children, an assistant when the number exceeded 25, and two teachers where the number of pupils exceeded 40. These schools were now everywhere diffused in the countries inhabited by Jews — indeed wherever there was a synagogue. The instruction was gratuitous. The introduction of alien races and religions among the Jews, and the dispersion of the Jews themselves, made schools for children, as well as synagogues for adults, essential to the protection and preservation of the true faith. It was this necessity, and the example of the Greeks, which led to the general diffusion of instruction among the people. Without the synagogue and its school the national tradition and law would have gradually disappeared under foreign influences.

It is interesting to note, however, that the Jews were the first to insist on the education of the *whole people*. All were equal before God: the law was laid on each man and was not the secret of a class.

The course of instruction was as follows. From the sixth to the tenth year the law (Pentateuch) was the only study, along with writing and arithmetic. From the tenth to the fifteenth year, the pupil was instructed in that part of the Talmud called Mishnah, substantially a paraphrastic development of the law. After the fifteenth year the Gemara was taught. Learning by rote was an inevitable and leading characteristic of such teachings. We can easily understand that instruction of this kind must have inflicted a grievous burden on young minds and crushed out all spontaneity of life. Doubtless this was quite understood and intended by the authorities: all were to be cast in one mould. Up to the age of thirteen the boy was not expected to either know or fulfil the whole law. He then, at the presumed age of puberty, entered on the rights and duties of a full-grown Israelite.

The pupils wrote on waxen tablets with a style, and when advanced, on paper or parchment with a pen, like the children of the Romano-Greek world generally.

In the higher schools Greek, mathematics, and such science as was known were taught.

The sole aim of female education was the making of the accomplished housewife, of whom we have a description in the Book of Proverbs.

That the discipline, domestic and other, was in pre-christian times severe might be inferred from the intolerable nature of the instruction given and from the material rewards and punishments which were so prominent a characteristic of the Jewish religion. It is in perfect consonance with the Judaic code that pain of a bodily kind should be the only correction which suggested itself to the early Jewish writers when they touched on education. ' He that spareth his rod hateth his son, but he that loveth him, chasteneth him betimes.' — Prov. xiii. 24. ' Chasten thy son, seeing there is hope, and set not thy heart on his destruction.' — Prov. xix. 18. ' Foolishness is bound up in the heart of the child; but the rod of correction shall drive it far from him.' — Prov. xxii. 15. ' Withhold not correction from the child; for if thou beat him with the rod, he shall not die. Thou shalt beat him with the rod and shalt deliver his soul from Sheol.' — Prov. xxiii. 13. In Deuteronomy xxi. 18, we find that if the rod fail, the son is to be stoned to death ' at sight' of the elders of the city. This conception of discipline seems to have prevailed till about the time of Christ.

In so far as severity of discipline was modified after the birth of Christ, it was under the influence of the Talmudic writings, and not of the law in its purity.

The Talmud and Education

The Talmudic writings contain so much that bears on education as understood by the Jew when brought under humane Hellenic (and doubtless also Christian) influences, that I shall add a few remarks on this stage of Jewish educational history.[1]

The School and the Schoolmaster. — That the work of the school and the function of the teacher hold a high place in the Talmud could be shown by numerous quotations. But it would be to confound chronology to regard the Talmudic precepts as indications of opinion among the ancient Israelites. They are to be met with only after the Jews had been in contact with the Greek and Roman civilisations, while some of them belong to early mediæval history. 'It is the breath of school children that sustains society,' says R. Jehuda Hanassi. 'He who studies and does not teach others is like a myrtle in the desert.' The teachers had to be married men and not too young; for 'instruction by young teachers is like sour grapes and new wine; instruction by older teachers, however, is like ripe grapes and old wine.' 'Your teacher and your father have need of your assistance ; help your teacher before helping your father, for the latter has given you only the life of this world, while the former has secured for you the life of the world to come.'

Method. — As regards method, the following text is wise : 'If you attempt to grasp too much at once, you grasp nothing at all.'

The teachers, after the Oriental fashion, generally relied on memory and slavish reproduction. 'First learn by heart and then know' was the governing formula. On the subject of memory, it is well said : — ' Four dispositions are found among the disciples; he who comprehends quickly and quickly forgets; such an one loses more than he gains : he who with difficulty comprehends, but does not readily

[1] I base what I here say on Spiers, and on Gelder's *Die Volkschule des Jüd. Alt.*, 1872, as verified by reference to other writers, including Dr. Samuel Marcus.

forget, gains more than he loses : he who comprehends easily, but does not easily forget, has a good portion : he who slowly comprehends and forgets quickly has an evil portion.' One of the instructions for learning by heart deserves notice : — 'To speak out loudly the sentence which is being learned strengthens the same in the memory.' 'Open thy mouth in order that thou mayest retain the subject of thy study, and that it may remain alive within thee.' The wife of Rabbi Meir, on meeting a certain student who was learning his lessons in a low tone, rebuked him, saying that it was not the right way of learning. 'Rabbi Elieser had a pupil who studied without articulating the words of his lessons, and in consequence thereof he forgot everything in three years.'

With regard to the system of repetition Rabbi Akiba says : 'The teacher should strive to make the lesson agreeable to the pupils by clear reasons, as well as by frequent repetitions, until they thoroughly understand the matter, and are enabled to recite it with great fluency'; but this was a pious opinion, not the school practice. A certain Rabbi, it is stated, 'had a disciple with whom he repeated the subject four hundred times, until he became a thorough master of the same.'

Special regard should be had to the child at the beginning of his studies, it is said, because 'what is learned as a child remains in his memory as ink written on new paper.' Nevertheless, as the faculties of boys do not always expand with their advancing age, the Talmud advises in case the boy does not make progress in his studies, to exercise forbearance towards him up to his twelfth year, but that henceforth he should be dealt with more severely. Experience proves, it is said, that children do not begin to show much mental capacity as a rule until their twelfth year.

Further, it is recommended to the teacher to have pauses and periods in each subject. 'The Almighty Himself,' it is said, 'did not impart the law to Moses all at once, but in different divisions and pauses, so as to make it more intelligible. How much more then ought not this to be done by a human teacher?' Again: 'He who studies hastily and crams too much at once, his knowledge shall diminish; but he who studies by degrees or step by step, shall accumulate much wisdom and learning.'

Brevity in imparting was likewise held to be an indispensable qualification of the teacher. He should, as much as possible, be concise and make use of few words. Far-fetched digressions are to be avoided, and that which could be told the pupil in one word should not be imparted in three. 'One should instruct the pupils in the shortest manner possible.'

Discipline. — The discipline included in the Talmud, unlike that of the ancient Jews, is mild and was doubtless largely influenced by the teaching of Christ; but corporal chastisement is recognised. 'Although at first there should be shown indulgence to the child, yet further on, if it should prove stubborn and inattentive, a slight corporal punishment and some restrictions may be adopted.' The elder pupils, however, should not have to undergo corporal punishment for two reasons: first, lest it should wound their sense of honour; and secondly, lest it should arouse resistance. The Rabbins say, 'A man who strikes his grown-up son should be earnestly reprimanded, because he transgresses the commandment, "Thou shalt not put a stumbling block before the blind,"' which is thus explained by Rashi: 'Because being grown up he might rebel against his father, who would thus cause him to sin.' Again, it is enjoined that if it should be found necessary to apply corporal punishment, it must be inflicted very mildly and the master is not to use a cane, but a light strap, in order not to injure the pupils. In reference to this we read in the Talmud: 'If thou art compelled to punish a pupil, do it only with gentleness; encourage those who make progress, and let him who does not, still remain in the class with his schoolfellows, for he will ultimately become attentive and vie with them.' R. Samuel Edels, in his Commentary on the Agadoth, writes: 'Only those pupils should be punished in whom the master sees that there are good capacities for learning and who are

7

inattentive; but if they are dull and cannot learn, they should not be punished.' Just as punishment formed a part of school discipline, so also did rewards. For we are told in the Talmud that Rabba had in his school some dainties of which he would occasionally make a present to his young pupils. Again, there is a saying, 'Children should be punished with one hand and caressed with two.'

The school hours were long.

To conclude: the subjection of the human spirit to the conception of absolute Law and the prominence given to external observances in the conception of religion as a kind of contract between God and man, gave birth among the Jews to a barren formalism. The spiritual ideas which doubtless underlay the whole and preserved the spirit of the ancient prophets, were for the few.

The Jews were *par éminence* a race of theological genius as the Greeks were a race of æsthetic genius. In their writings, the personal relations of man to God as a god of moral law, found a language for themselves which had never been reached by any other nation. The universal conception of God as Creator, and Preserver, and Father of all His creatures, and as rejoicing in the work of His hands which in its turn praised Him, transcended all other human interpretations of the divine. But at this point all true progress of the intellect and imagination ended. The scientific and dramatic spirit were alike alien to the Jew. He imbibed both from other races. The Judaic theory of life required also that the past should be all in all. The spiritual unity of the race was doubtless thereby secured, but at an enormous sacrifice.

Christ opens out a wider vista to the eye of man, and at no point checks his onward advance. In Him we have a transition from the finite to the true infinite in the religious conception. The moral ideal supersedes the prosaic moralities of the understanding, and, seen in God, it becomes the spiritual life. With the genuine Jew the personality of God was too clearly defined, and His externality as a Law-giver too strongly emphasised, to admit of infinite ideas. Again, wHile the identification of religion and the moral law was in principle sound, the stereotyping of the latter in external observances emanating from an unquestioned authority, killed both. A free personal outlook on nature and life was, under such conditions, impossible. We must trust humanity as an ever-progressive reason, and take our chance of the incidental evils which may attend the practice of the humanistic free Christian faith.

Indeed, we can scarcely say that among the Jews religion and the moral law, as we now understand these, were one (as they boast it was and is), but rather the Sinaitic voice of God as despotic command and a corresponding legality— a system in which external prescriptions tended to choke the purely moral, and still more the spiritual, element of the life of mind. The prophets live for all mankind; to the Jew their spiritualism was lost in formalism. Externalities of technical obedience being rigidly attended to, the Jew performed his part of the covenant with God — a mere business transaction. God thereupon was bound to perform His part, which in early times was the granting of benefits in this life; at a later period, in this life and the next. There can be no spiritual or religious life save that which the voice of God penetrates and sanctions, but, with the ordinary Jew, this voice of God was, I repeat, an external voice; and, practically, in the hands especially of post-exilic priests and scribes, it became a detailed series of legal prescriptions and observances. God stood apart, and, like a schoolmaster, imposed rules, with rewards and penalties for observance and non-observance. This was the 'letter' that killeth. Christ swept it away and preached the 'Spirit' that giveth life, and thus transformed a national into an universal religion. On the other hand, it has to be observed that in all national religions, ancient and modern, we find two parties — those who, endowed with a deep religious sense, live in the spirit of the religion they profess, regarding all else as merely symbolic of the inner needs and history of the spiritual man, and those for whom the intellectual dogma and the sensuous symbol and the religious rite are all in all. In the case of the Jews, the former found a pure and noble expression of their inner life in the Psalms and the Prophets, the latter were represented by the scribes and Pharisees and the mass of the people.

It seems strange that a system of life so encumbered with ceremonial and externalities should have attracted converts in the heathen world. But, before and after the time of Christ, Greek, Roman, and Oriental had lost faith in their gods and were looking for God, and for a moral system sanctioned by Him. This the Jew could give; and allow the proselyte to accept as much or as little of the ceremonial as he pleased.

Authorities. — Many of the books mentioned under ' Egypt,' especially *Records of the Past.* Also *History of Babylonia,* by George Smith ; Professor Tiele's *Die Assyriologie, eine Rede ; Assyria,* by George Smith; Maspero's *Dawn of Civilisation in the East ; Essai sur l'histoire des Arabes,* par Caussin de Perceval   Sir W. Muir's *Life of Mahomet.*

Scripture which ends 442 B. C. ; Ranke's *History of the World ;* Milman's *History of the Jews ; The School System of the Talmud,* by Spiers; *L'éducation et l'instruction des enfants chez les anciens Juifs,* par J. Simon ; *Geschichte der Erz. u. des Unt. bei den Israeliten,* von B. Strassburger ; Van Gelder's *Die Volkschule des Jüd. Alt.* 1872 ; Schürer's *Jewish People in the Time of Christ ;* Tiele's *Outlines of the History of Ancient Religions ;* Duncker's *History of Antiquity ; Die Pädagogik des Israelitischen Volkes,* &c., von Dr. S. Marcus, 1877 ; Wellhausen's *Israel und Judah ;* Montefiore's *Hibbert Lectures ;* Graetz's *History of the Jews ;* Professor Robertson Smith's writings ; Professor Robertson (of Glasgow), *Early Religion of Israel : Lex Mosaica,* recently published ; Professor Menzies' *History of Religion.*

Note. — I have endeavoured, not without great difficulty, to steer my way among conflicting accounts. It is impossible to accept the rose-coloured views of Jews or those who seem to hold a brief for them, when alleged facts are not dated and guaranteed. On the other hand, the facts which are available, combined with necessary and irresistible inferences from Jewish history make it equally impossible to accept the views of those who would minimise the educational work among the Jews themselves, and its significance in the education of the whole race of mankind.

THE URO-ALTAIC OR TURANIAN RACES

THE URO–ALTAIC OR TURANIAN RACES

The races of mankind not Hamitic, Semitic, and Indo-European have been classed as Turanian, or Uro-Altaic; but this classification is so inadequate that it will doubtless be modified as ethnology progresses. In the meantime, for the Eastern Hemisphere it may be accepted. Omitting the merged Accadians of the Mesopotamian basin of whom we have already spoken, we have to go north and east to follow the migrations of the Turanian races.

The Turanian, or Uro-Altaic, races (so called from the Siberian range of mountains of this name) comprise the Mongolians, Chinese, Manchus, Japanese, Turks, and Tartars, the European Finns, and the original stock of the Hungarians. Longer than other races they retained nomadic habits, and in some districts of the East still retain them. The inhabitants who occupied Chaldæa before the arrival of the Semites in that region were called Accadians; and to these we have referred in speaking of the Babylonian Semites who absorbed them.[1] The Turanians generally have a mono-syllabic and agglutinative language, and have never exhib-ited a capacity for progress either in literature, arts, or science beyond a certain fixed point, except under post-christian influences. Their highest development is to be found in China, where as a civilised power they have existed for, certainly, 5,000 years; and what we have to say of the Turanians must be confined to this the highest specimen of their social organisation.

[1] The most recent explorations would point to the conclusion that the Turanian or Accadian civilisation itself also rested on a prior people. Dr. de Lacouperie connects closely the Accadians and Chinese.

As the education organised among this remarkable people affords a curious contrast to that both of the Semitic races and of the Asiatic Indo-Germans or Aryans, of whom we shall afterwards.speak, it is quite worth our while to endeavour to enter into some detail. The Chinese educational development is indeed highly instructive both to the educational politician and the schoolmaster.

EDUCATION IN CHINA

CHAP. I.   NATIONAL CHARACTERISTICS

CHINA had a consciously organised scheme of education long before any other Asiatic or European people. Egyptian education existed from an earlier date, but it was never an organised system. The Chinese system is instructive as well as interesting, because it suggests many considerations as to the organisation of education by the State and also as to authoritative modes of testing ability and learning which bear very directly on European and American education at the present day.

The Chinese empire embraces, besides China proper, Manchuria, Mongolia, Turkestan, and Tibet. It is China proper and a portion of the Burmese peninsula, however, with which we have to do. The dependencies are in no way so advanced in civilisation as China-proper. This portion of the empire is itself 1,600 miles long and averages in breadth 1,100 miles. The population is variously estimated at from 300 to 400 millions. A remarkable evidence of its early civilisation is to be found in the Great Wall which was constructed in the third century before the Christian era and extends up hill and down dale along the northern boundary for 1,250 miles, is 20 feet high including the parapet of 5 feet, 25 feet thick at the base, and strengthenéd at intervals of 100 yards by square towers from 37 to 50 feet high.

In the north the land is elevated; in the centre it is an alluvial plain through which the great rivers Hoang-ho and

Yang-tse-kiang flow. In the south the land is undulating and interspersed with valleys and mountains. The middle region is the centre of the rice, sugar, and silk culture; in the southern part of it the tea-shrub flourishes; in the north we find the usual food grains.

The accepted history of China dates from 2,500 years B.C., although it is far from trustworthy for long after this date. As early as 2205 B.C. we find the country organised as a feudal State, the system being somewhat similar to that which prevailed in Europe in mediæval times. In the eighteenth century B.C. there were seventy-two feudal States. In 403 B.C. the feudal princedoms had been reduced to seven great States, and in 220 B.C. the whole was organised into an Empire. There have been many changes of dynasties, but the imperial organisation has remained much the same for more than 2,000 years. The present dynasty is Manchu and dates from 1643 A.D. The native Chinese, however, are fully recognised in the highest councils of the emperor as well as in the whole administrative system. The imperial government in Peking supervises and controls the administration of all the provinces and exercises the power of removing all officials.

Language. — The speech of the Chinese is monosyllabic: out of the radical they form compounds. There are no inflections — nay, the same root is retained to denote noun, verb, preposition, adverb — the grammatical class to which it belongs being indicated by tone, accent, or position alone. The language is, in brief, inorganic, a mere aggregate of roots, not of letter-sounds. In all speech there must of course be organism, but in the case of the Chinese, I suppose we may say that the organism is *understood;* it is in the thought of the speaker and hearer, and not embodied in the forms of the language as in Latin or Greek. The speech of the Chinese has been aptly compared to that of a child, which utters words one after another without forming them organically into a sentence. The letters, or shapes to denote words, were originally hieroglyphic or ideographic, the symbols gradually losing their ideographic character; and this especially in compounds. ' When letters were invented,' the Chinese say, ' the heavens, earth, and the gods were all agitated. The inhabitants of Hades wept at night, and the heavens, as an expression of joy, rained down ripe grain.' (Preface to Morrison's Dictionary.) There is evidence that writing was practised 1,740 years B.C., and it is believed that it existed in some form 3,000 years B.C.

It is important to note, as bearing on the question of Chinese education, that the literary language, the language of books, is different from the spoken dialects, which are numerous; and that it differs to such an extent as to make its acquisition by a native almost as difficult as a foreign tongue.

If the unclassified elements of the language were indifferent to position ' the labour of arrangement would be nothing and style impossible. But most of them appear to be endowed with a kind of mysterious polarity, which controls their collocation and renders them incapable of companionship except with certain characters, the choice of which would seem to be altogether arbitrary. The origin of this peculiarity it is not difficult to discover. In this, as in other things among the Chinese, usage has become law. Combinations which were accidental or optional with the model writers of antiquity, and even their errors, have, to their imitative posterity, become the *jus et norma loquendi.* Free to move upon each other when the language was young and in a fluid state, its elements have now become crystallised into invariable forms. To master this pre-established harmony without the aid of rules is the fruit of practice and the labour of years.' [1]

General Character of the Chinese. — The impression made on a stranger by the character of the Chinese people is, that it is as a whole child-like, gentle, kindly, and peaceful, but it is equally apparent that these qualities are in union

[1] *Han Lin Papers.*

with much cunning, suspicion, trickery, and immorality. Their industry and contentment are marvellous, and their personal habits temperate. It does not appear that respect for self, and value for self as a personality, is a conception of the Chinese mind. The 'person' is not of the same account as among the Aryan races; the family is the governing conception. The personality of the individual is not only overshadowed by the family and the state-machinery, but is oppressed also by the spirits of the dead which are worshipped.

The Chinese have had their civil revolutions and modifications of belief like other people, but as a whole they have made little or no progress for more than 2,000 years; but grind on as their fathers did before them. Their enormous national self-conceit helps to prevent advance. Philosophic speculation and physical science are absent. *Literature* is in the ascendant, but it consists chiefly of a bald kind of history, the literature of the sacred books and endless commentaries on them. Lyric poetry is cultivated very extensively, and the power of writing elegant verses in good caligraphy is the highest proof of learning and culture. Art, in the higher sense, does not exist, although there is much skill and delicacy of execution, and considerable imitative power.[1] At one time the art of landscape painting flourished.

The broad fact for us Europeans to recognise is that in this portion of Asia we have a people of Mongolian extraction, including about a third of the population of the world, who, for at least 4,000 years, have had a settled system of life and government, and with whom education has always been a matter of national importance for nearly 3,000 years.

---

[1] There are some men (who may be called Sinophils) who speak in laudatory terms of the lyrical literature, just as they exaggerate the intellectual power of the Chinese, but the specimens given, even allowing for the difficulties of translation, do not justify their admiration. They read like the Latin verses of English schoolboys. See the collection of Romilly Allen.

CHAP. II. RELIGION AND PHILOSOPHY OF LIFE

Sacred Books. — To understand the Chinese attitude of mind we should have to understand Confucius, the great moral and political philosopher and reformer, who was born 551 years B.C. But the national life did not start with him. The record of his life would itself show, even were there no native historical treatises, that China was at the time of his birth a civilised country and an organised government with many subordinate governors. Confucius himself is most careful to insist that he merely revives the customs and beliefs of his ancestors. He led a life of noble example himself : at one time held high in honour, at another dishonoured and persecuted, always suffering grief and disappointment at the failure of his great scheme of social reform. But he professed no novelties; he rested all his teaching on the sacred books which he edited with annotations. He did not, however, alter them or digest them into their present form (Legge). His chief addition to the practical philosophy of preceding ages was his 'Doctrine of the Mean.' The first sentence of this work is as follows : 'What heaven has conferred is called the nature : an accordance with this nature is called the path of duty : the regulation of this path is called instruction.' (Legge, 'Religions of China,' p. 139.)

The earliest of the sacred books was attributed in its original form to the first introducer of letters and philosophy among the Chinese, Fû-hsî, to whom the date of 3,323 years (less or more) B.C. is assigned. (This, of course, is legendary.) The next continuator after Confucius of the philosophy of the sacred books was Mencius, who died 317 B.C. Printing from blocks of wood was invented in the tenth century of our era. The issue of the sacred books was, as a matter of course, then multiplied, and much intellectual activity was the result, as was the case in Europe after the invention of printing. But all this activity was still controlled by superstitious reverence for the past and merely took the form of a further explication and evolution of accepted doctrines The man who seems to have gathered into a focus all the intellectual activity of this time was Chow-Tsze. This truly eminent philosopher exhibited great ability as an administrator, thinker, and writer, and the books issued by him, for the most part as commentaries on, and introductions to, the sacred books, numbered 23. On them, without derogating from the primary authority of Confucius, the life of the people is modelled. He died 1200 A.D. His writings are held to contain the true interpretation of Chinese philosophy, but by no means on that account to supersede Confucius and the sacred books themselves. We must therefore, if we would understand the Chinese people and their education, form to ourselves some idea of the contents of these books. To attempt an account here, in any detail, would be out of place; but we may state, on the authority of Professors Legge, Douglas, Tiele and others, all that is necessary to our purpose as students of the educational system of China.[1]

The sacred books or scriptures of China consist of ' Five Classics' and 'Four Books.' The *five classics* are ('Encyc. Brit.'): 1. 'The Book of Changes' (Yî-King) — seemingly an effort at a kind of nature-system (obscure magic, says Tiele). To this book the date 1150 B.C. is assigned; 2. ' The Book of History' (Shû-King); 3. 'The Book of Odes' (Shîh-King). At the time of Confucius there was an official collection of 3,000 odes, which he reduced to 311, preserving chiefly those which had a moral and domestic tendency and classifying them under four heads: (*a*) National airs; (*b*) The lesser eulogies; (*c*) The greater eulogies; (*d*) The song of homage sung by or before the emperor when he sacrificed in the name of the State as its high priest. 4. 'The Book of Rites'; 5. 'Spring and Autumn Annals,' by Confucius.

The Four Books are of the nature of exposition and commentaries. (1) The Great Learning; (2) The doctrine of the Mean, these two being continuous treatises; (3) Con-

---

[1] I follow Legge where he differs from Tiele, and I have paid due attention to Martin's account.

fucian Analecta, or sayings of the master; (4) The works of Mencius, by a pupil of that philosopher.

Commentaries on the classics and books are very numerous ; but all have the same characteristics as the originals, that is to say, they are ' servile,' ' iterative,' ' cold,' ' formal.'

Philosophical Attitude of the Chinese Mind. — Like most moral reformers, Confucius was too intent on the renovation of the national life around him to concern himself deeply with those metaphysical questions which form so perennial an attraction for the Indo-European mind. It is a mistake, however, to say he was an atheist, unless we are to class as atheists men who, denying or doubting a personal God, yet believe in a great but mysterious power which governs all. That Confucius believed in a personal God is not apparent, and it is certain that he purposely declined to go far into the discussion of such questions. Morality, social order, and propriety of conduct alone interested him, and this so profoundly as to exclude from his system of practical ethics all other subjects. There can be no doubt, however, that he believed in the Supreme One. It is worthy of remark, and, indeed, full of interest, that, in the very sacred books edited by him, there is the recognition of a Supreme Being called ' Supreme Ruler,' ' Heaven,' and ' Supreme or Sovereign Heaven,' and Professor Legge has made it, I think, evident that the Chinese were in the earliest times — that is to say, the earliest *historic* times, Monotheists. Chow-tze did not profess to originate a philosophy, but to draw it from the ancient books by interpretation. But it cannot be said that even in his case the thought of a personal God ever occurred. At the beginning of all things is what is called the ' ultimate principle,' or ' grand extreme,' which is immaterial, which is spirit, which, in brief, is *mind*. It operates to produce the world of nature and man according to an invariable process. Dr. Martin gives this exposition : ' The Infinite [Great Extreme] produced the Finite, and the Finite produced Light and Darkness.' The ' ultimate principle,' or ' great extreme,' is, however, frequently spoken of as if it were an independent entity, and sometimes as punishing the evil and rewarding the good. But these are evidently figurative expressions, and the idea of the Supreme to be found in Chinese philosophy is that of a causal principle existing from all eternity *along with* the world or nature, also existing from all eternity, the latter exhibiting the mode of operation of the ultimate principle in accordance with fixed and unalterable laws.

Chinese philosophy does not affirm the great fact of Will as entering into the scheme of creation. Nor has the 'ultimate principle' ethical attributes.[1] Order is its chief characteristic, and this exhibits itself in the nature of man as well as in other creations, and the holy man is he who has a clear intuition of the ultimate principle and its ground-processes. Seeing these clearly, he cannot err; knowledge is virtue. The nature of man is, to begin with, good in itself, for it is the true product of the heavenly order. Chow-tze teaches that ' the bright principle of virtue man derives from his heavenly origin, and his pure spirit when undarkened comprehends all truth, and is adequate to every occasion. But it is obstructed by the physical constitution and be-clouded by the animal desires so that it becomes obscure.' The moral character, to begin with, is determined by the prevailing influence (primordial harmony or gross matter), and mankind are accordingly divided into three classes : ' those who are good without teaching, those who may be made good by teaching, and those who will remain bad in spite of teaching' (Martin, p. 129).

Absolute truth is simply the course or way of nature, and he who sees this has absolute truth. Virtue is the complete possession of absolute truth by man ; and it is by knowledge or study that man attains to truth, and so to virtue. Intellect is thus the basis of virtue and morality. Private and political morality are closely connected. The whole aim of the higher teaching of China is, in brief, morality — the conduct of life and the art of government. Though China

---

[1] I do not suppose Professor Legge would admit this.

has produced men differing in opinion as to the foundation of ethics, they have no speculative philosophy in the Aryan sense. A very interesting chart of Chinese ethics will be found in Dr. Martin's book on education in China. This shows considerable power of *orderly* tabular arrangement in the classification of the virtues, but the Chinese mind is not, even in this its own chosen sphere, analytic.

Religion. — There are three religions in China: 1. The official or state religion, already described in the previous section, viz. the ancient doctrine of China handed down from remote antiquity, revised by Confucius and commented on by him, by Mencius and by Chow-Tsze. It is essentially a moral and political system, resting ultimately, however, on a recognition of a Supreme God or Divine Order. It recognises this Being or Order as a fact simply, and there leaves it, lying outside daily life and remote from men. Connected with this official religion, however, there is an annual ceremonial of worship. It is the State not the individual, the emperor, not as priest but as representative of the nation, who then worships God. Provincial governors also perform the service in the name of the State. This ceremonial is in honour of the powers of nature and expresses the dependence of man on the order of nature, the productivity of the soil and the recurrence of the seasons. It is thus in perfect harmony with Chinese religious philosophy, and recognises the Supreme Spirit in the sense which I have already explained. The remarkable prayers cited by Professor Legge ('Religions of China,' p. 43 *et seq.*), which were offered up at the solstitial services of 1538 A.D., testify to a pure and exalted Deism in the mind of the then emperor, approximating even to Theistic language. But with this solstitial ceremonial the Deism as a factor in the life of the Chinese ends.[1]

---

[1] Professor Legge says, p. 114, that there are numerous passages in the ancient books speaking of Heaven as approving and disapproving the acts of man. But neither in the literature generally nor in the schoolbooks is account taken of this. Even the verses quoted by Legge do not necessarily convey anything save the general statement that Heaven is on the side of justice and

Confucian polity and the worship of ancestors constitute the genuine religion of the educated Chinaman.

The official religion is acquiesced in by all; but in addition, Tâoism and Buddhism are professed by the masses of the people. Buddhism practically occupies the field. It is an importation from India, and as it entered only in 76 A.D., it found the Chinese national character already formed. Tâoism, originally mystical and having affinities with primitive Buddhism, has degenerated into a religion of spells and incantations. The priests profess, like modern spiritualists, to hold communication with the spirits of the dead. Buddhism, again, seems to have degenerated into a system of idol-worship. Indeed very early, Gautama Buddha, the founder, was himself worshipped as a god. The doctrine of transmigration which connects itself with the more popular form of this religion would seem to exercise a powerful practical influence on the life of the Chinese. The doctrine of immortality is blank and undefined.

Alongside, then, of the intellectual and purely politico-moral and abstract deism of Confucius, we find the ceremonial periodical nature-worship by the emperor as representing the nation; the survival of primitive beliefs in various spirits among the people;[1] along with ancestor worship (which last is also an integral part of Confucianism) a widespread, debased, and idolatrous Buddhism, and the magical practices to which Tâoism has degenerated. These religions, satisfy-

---

truth. Von Strauss's description of Chinese Theism on p. xxvi of Allen's translation of the 'Book of Chinese Poetry' seems to me to be a devout imagination.

[1] These beliefs are probably a survival of the primitive and prehistoric religion of China, which, Tiele holds, was a purified and organised worship of spirits, including the spirits of the dead. The spirits to be worshipped were without number. They reside in visible objects, and also assume the form of animals. A popular religion of this sort might easily run parallel with the higher and better tradition represented by Confucianism, and, as a matter of fact, it does so. The popular necessities have also found satisfaction in Buddhism and Tâoism, neither of which excludes the State religion. Even in the State religion there is a curious mixture of pure Confucianism with nature-worship and the worship of certain recognised gods.

ing, as they do, by means of idols and communication with the unseen world, the need of man for an ever-present power interested and concerned in his destiny, are found to be compatible with a belief in the governing intellectual theory of life and society.

It is not to be supposed that the ordinary Chinaman is a Buddhist in the monastic sense. This philosophy of religious ecstatic atheism is reserved for a few in those sequestered monasteries and temples, where, in disdain of life, they endeavour, by endless repetitions of liturgical pieces and a strenuous thinking of Nothing, to realise a condition which is neither life nor death, in the hope of ultimately attaining the nothingness of Nirvana. The common man worships in the numerous temples the goddess of mercy and many idols besides, including the idols of the past and the present, hoping through their aid and by works of merit to secure for himself happy transmigrations, if nothing more.

The genuine Confucian Chinese believe that convulsions of nature, epidemics, &c., are indications of something wrong in the administration of government; but this not from any belief that providence interferes to punish but purely from the conviction that a disturbance of the natural order is indicative of a disturbance in the social order.[1]

Man, they hold, stands in the midst between heaven and earth to preserve the equipoise of the whole and to bear the burden of the moral world-order. By keeping the middle or mean himself, he can alone succeed in discharging his world functions. This religion of the more educated classes has formed the character of the people. To take care that this right mean is observed is the grand duty of the emperor, the great son of heaven, the god on earth who as father of his people, not as a despot, orders and governs all human institu-

---

[1] Although it is true that there is no State priesthood, there are yet ' professors of ceremonies ' appointed and paid by the State to regulate public ceremonial acts of worship, &c. Many such men also are employed by the people on all important ceremonial occasions, that everything may be done in order. They live by fees.

tions by means of laws which bear on every department and act of life; and he is aided by a graded and countless number of subordinate administrators.

We see in all races that the higher form of their religion is quite compatible with a worship of gods, demons, and spirits, also with what might be called subordinate religious beliefs which are considered not to conflict with the governing system. These are, doubtless, survivals of more barbarous times. This compatibility of the higher with the lower is specially characteristic of the Chinese. But whatever may be the private superstitions of the people, this is certain, that it is Confucianism which is the State church, and that the whole life of the Chinese is not only influenced but controlled by Confucian ideas. One result is that gods and ancestors are worshipped with a view to material security alone, and that there is no ideal of life possible higher than prosaic prudential Confucianism.

Let us now endeavour to bring together the governing conceptions which seem to constitute the motive-forces of Chinese life.

CHAP. III. THE DOMINANT IDEAS OF CHINESE LIFE

(1) THE brief survey which we have given justifies us, I think, in concluding that the idea of Order as established and maintained by a Supreme Principle or Mind, is the foundation of all Chinese thought and life; and if we realise to ourselves the influence which a conception so barren and cold must exercise on political doctrines and social customs, we have made one step towards the understanding of this remarkable people.

(2) The next idea animating these masses of men is that of reverence for the past, which exhibits itself in two forms, a superstitious regard for all past thought, and a reverence for ancestors which takes the form of worship. Antiquity is in fact the guarantee for truth — constitutes in itself an infallible guide. Even the members of the Han-lin or Im-

perial Academy, comprising the select men of the empire and residing at Peking, ' do nothing to extend the boundaries of human knowledge, simply because they are not aware that after the achievements of Confucius and the ancient sages any new world remains to be conquered.' (Martin, p. 24.)

(3) In a 'nation in which the idea of the world-order seems to have first found expression in the sanctity of the family relationship, family life, as the centre of all social order and civic union, is held in the highest veneration. The father has absolute power over his children, and the children must render unquestioning obedience. The family, indeed, is the centre of the moral, as well as the social and political, life of the nation. Out of it, all virtues grow, and on it the idea of the State is supposed to be modelled. The State is only a largely developed family. The emperor is the head of this large family of officials and of citizens, and having, like a father, the power of life and death, commands and receives absolute obedience. Marriage, as might readily be supposed, is held to be a sacred institution, and a civil duty imposed on every man. (Concubines are allowed, but their children have not the same family privileges as those of the legitimate wife.) The relation of the wife to the husband is that of practical slavery.[1] The family idea is, of course, sustained and intensified by the worship of ancestors. There seems, however, to be an element of fear in this quite as much as of respect or affection. The dead spirits may exercise a hurtful influence on their descendants if they are neglected. They are supposed to continue their interest in the affairs of their families, and may even be reborn into them. The Chinaman as a member of a family is thus in

---

[1] Even at birth the inferiority of the woman to the man is signalised. When a boy is born, a bow and arrow are hung before the door and he is wrapt in the finest clothes that can be had ; when a girl is born, the spindle and yarn are hung up, and any old rags are considered good enough for her. If a father is asked how many children he has, he counts only his sons.

close union with the past and future of his race, as well as with the present.[1]

(4) Prudential virtue usurps the place of the ideal and spiritual in the Chinese mind. The family idea, as may be easily understood, enters into and powerfully influences the system of morality. For, defective as some of the family relations are, the family bond is intensely strong, and the sentiment of the people gathers round the nearest and dearest relations of life, and does not much extend to spheres beyond. Thus it is said: ' If a man will attain to the completed perfection of his nature, he must begin with the five relations of human society — king and subject, father and son, elder and younger brother, husband, wife, friends — and practise the usual daily virtues. When the customary and easy virtues are neglected there is no possibility of attaining to the completed perfection of our nature.'

No exception can be taken to the moral teaching of the authoritative books. ' Heaven produces all men, and points out for them their duties, for the fulfilment of which also it gives them the means.' Again : ' He who renders obedience to heaven will be sustained : he, on the other hand, who resists heaven will perish.' Beasts have no spirit or mind we are also told : man alone has spirit. ' All men,' says Mencius, ' have a compassionate heart ; all men have a heart which is ashamed of vice ; all men have a heart naturally

---

[1] Tablets, almost always pieces of wood, four to seven by two to three inches, are fixed into niches in the wall of a room. The name of the father is carved or painted on them, and to this the assembled family offer incense, and on great occasions sacrifice food of various kinds. Other tablets of more remote ancestors are similarly preserved and worshipped. Wealthy families, who have large connections, erect ancestral halls, in which ancestral tablets are placed, and to which at stated times worship and sacrifice are offered. This illustrates well the intensity of the family idea. The worship of ancestors can only be conducted by the males (females may marry into other families and cannot be depended on). Hence, partly, the superiority of boys to girls. A man who has no boy adopts one rather than run the risk of having himself and his ancestors neglected — a fate which seems to involve absolute death or annihilation, and which is escaped as long as they are worshipped.

disposed to pay respect and reverence; all men have a heart which can distinguish between right and wrong: these virtues do not come from without, they are an essential part of our constitution.' 'If a man uses his understanding he will find the right way: if a man does not use his understanding he will not find it. Let no one be afflicted because of his want of strength; the fault lies in failure to practise.' These moral propositions and many others are not allowed to rest in the sacred books and the commentaries on them, and be read when and where the people choose; they are thoroughly mastered and, to a great extent, learnt by heart in all schools, and by all candidates for the public service. They constitute the national creed and the national conscience. They have been the means of creating, and sustaining for probably 4,000 years, a fairly efficient social system.

(5) A love of formalism is strong in the Chinese mind. This is very prominent in the mass of ritual ceremonies in which the moral and social life of the Chinese is enveloped. The Book of Rites is one of the sacred books, and contains directions for the acts of daily life in the family and in the State, and is also a manual of etiquette. All this is carefully mastered by those who affect to be educated. There can be little doubt that forms and ceremonies tend to give permanence to institutions, while they at the same time tend to deprive them of true vitality. Hence, partly, the stereotyped civilisation of China; practical virtue becomes almost identical with 'propriety' and convention.

As an explanation of the remarkable permanence of Chinese life and polity we may point to the conservative character of the dominant ideas and to the influence of an ideographic language in restricting the free play of mind. It may also be held that the longer the period during which the same 'set' of mind, the same habit of thought and action, continues in a nation, the more certain becomes the tendency to repetition, unless some very powerful force intervene. This doctrine of heredity in nations must never be lost sight of. Again, it may be said that a nation so large, if it once becomes the victim of a system, tends to perpetuate itself in the future as it has been in the past, because the dead weight of the whole is so great as to repress the parts. This specially happens where the political form of life is a highly centralised form: and a large empire is necessarily centralised where it is not a mere federation. Further, it is to be noted that the Chinese have been so placed geographically as to be cut off from intercommunication with the rest of the world. The wonderful variety of their climate and productions, moreover, has not made such communication necessary. In so far as they have had intercourse, it has been of a kind to drive them back on their own national life, to hug (so to speak) their own form of civilisation. It is on the west and north that they had in old times intercourse with others: this intercourse was of a very unpleasant kind, and led, in fact, to their building the Great Wall.

All these elements furnish, it seems to me, subsidiary explanations of the prosaic continuity of the Chinese life. However it may be, there can be no doubt that the supreme rule of life among the Chinese is ' Walk in the trodden paths,' that their philosophy of religion necessarily points to a first principle of world-order, and presumes a Deity to be invoked and thanked, but not propitiated and influenced — a cosmic machine remote from and indifferent to man; that their morality is a shrewd dogmatism, traditionary and preceptive, not reasoned; and that their complicated ceremonial is the outer garment of a fixed and imperious social and political system. Everything thus tends to fixedness and order, to a statical rather than a dynamical social and civil life.

I am perfectly well aware that, if we take a period of 4,000 years, China has passed through many changes and has not been unprogressive in politics or the arts. It is also true that in ethics one or two sages have reached a higher level than the traditionary creed. But one swallow does not make a summer; and, taking China from the time of Confucius onwards, I fail to see any signs of progress in the essential thought and life-standard of the nation. The gradual development of the educational machinery will be adverted to below. It appears to me, surveying the history of nations, that there is a vital connection between constitutional freedom and movement: whether that movement be progressive or retrogressive is another question.

It is quite conceivable, however, that, spite of the potent ideas which underlie and sustain the vast network of administration and its centralisation in an emperor, the unwieldy social system might break up under a heavy strain and perhaps revert to anarchy, were it not for two things: first, the universal self-centredness and self-government of the family and the consequent restricted view of life and its possibilities; and, secondly, the educational system which carefully trains the people in the way they should go, and which provides a governing aristocracy of intellect that commands the respect of the masses, while opening out a career to all who have the capacity to enter on it.

CHAP. IV. THE EDUCATIONAL SYSTEM

'Employ the able and promote the worthy.' — *Old Chinese Maxim*

1. *Its general character and aim*

LET us now summarise the chief governing principles of Chinese life. (1) The idea of order and static equilibrium. (2) The idea of the family as sacred and inviolable, and in connection with this of social duties as constituting the sum of morality — a system preceptive, prosaic, and destitute of all idealism. (3) The worship of ancestors, and, as inherent in this, a profound reverence for the past system of things. (4) An elaborate ceremonial (a kind of ritual of social life) as tending to confirm and perpetuate the first and second, and, in fact, essential to that end. The word 'propriety' seems to sum up the externalities of the moral relation and, in fact, to be almost synonymous with morality itself. All these governing principles, it is evident, are intensely conservative in their character and effect.

Now, the object of the Chinese government in constructing its educational machinery was, doubtless, to preserve all these characteristics: but they had also in view the welding together of the vast and varied mass of population in one common interest, thereby satisfying the democratic instinct under an absolute imperial system. While the chief object of all learning in China is, as I have said, the art of government and the art of life, it has to be admitted that a subordinate object with many of the emperors has also been the cultivation of literary attainment for its own sake.

To accomplish their educational purposes the Chinese did not institute schools. A State system of schools and colleges diffused among 400,000,000 (?) of people would have been a mighty administrative task. The governing authorities thought that enough was done if they encouraged education by confining the whole civil service of the country, and indeed all positions of honour, to those highly educated. The old feudalism had given place to the practical equality of each citizen under the emperor, and government henceforth was to be through literate, not hereditary, chiefs.

The state contented itself, accordingly, with instituting a board of examiners, the controllers of which were the Han-lin or Academicians of Peking — an order of distinction and power, into which only the most learned could hope for admission. The board organised periodical examinations of all who chose to present themselves; and only the sons of barbers and players, and one or two other classes, were to be excluded from competition.

The present system was *fully* organised only A.D. 700 (Morrison); but from the time of Confucius education was general throughout China. Nay, long before his time there were schools, and education held a high place in the esteem of all the thoughtful and governing men. (Plath, ' Ueber Schulunterricht und Erziehung bei den alten Chinesen,' 1868.) Biot gives an historical account of the fluctuations of the

educational system of China. From this account we learn
that the Chinese from the earliest times, certainly from nearly
2,000 years B.C., attached the highest value to school education. Colleges and schools were the care of the governing
powers; and to these (Professor Legge says) the sons of the
feudal lords were sent. It was at a period of degeneracy that
Confucius wrote. His aim, and that of his followers, was to
substitute personal merit for hereditary claims to office, and
to throw open all administrative positions to those who could
win them in open intellectual competition. This was a
democratic movement. The competitive system may be said
to date from the second century B.C. (p. 127, Biot), but it had
varying fortunes before it was finally organised 800 years
thereafter. It appears from old laws that the ruling dynasty
of Manchu was not at first favourable to the literary hierarchy.
So recently as 1726, indeed, the emperor stopped the examinations, because he said two of the literati had slandered
him; and in an edict passed on that occasion, he pointed out
that the object of government in supporting the literati was,
not to elicit 'skill in letters, but to teach the people to
recognise and obey their princes and fathers.'

The following brief survey of the history of examinations
in China is, I believe, substantially correct: — 'So early as at
the commencement of the Chow dynasty, B.C. 1115, the government was accustomed to examine candidates for offices;
and this time we are not left in doubt as to the nature of the
examination. The Chinese had become a cultivated people,
and we are informed that all candidates for office were required to give proof of their acquaintance with the fine arts,
viz. music, archery, horsemanship, writing and arithmetic,
and to be thoroughly versed in the rites and ceremonies of
public and social life, an accomplishment that ranked as a
sixth art. These six arts, expressed in the concise formula,
li, yo, shay, yu, shu, su, comprehended the sum total of a
liberal education at the period, and remind us of the *trivium*
and *quadrivium* of mediæval schools.

'Under the dynasty of Han, after the lapse of another thousand (900 ?) years, we find the range of subjects for the civil service examinations largely extended. The Confucian ethics had become current, and a moral standard was regarded in the selection of the competitors, the district magistrate being required to send up to the capital such men as had acquired a reputation for *hiaŏ* and *lien* — filial piety and integrity — the Chinese rightly considering that the faithful performance of domestic and social duties is the best guarantee for fidelity in public life. These *hiao-lien*, these "filial sons and honest subjects," whose moral characters had been sufficiently attested, were now subjected to trial in respect to their intellectual qualifications. The trial was twofold, first as to their skill in the six arts already mentioned, and secondly as to their familiarity with one or more of the following subjects, the civil law, military affairs, agriculture, the administration of the revenue, and the geography of the empire, with special reference to the state of the water communications. This was an immense advance on the meagre requirements of the more ancient dynasties.

'Passing over another thousand (900 ?) years, we come to the era of the Tangs and the Sungs, about 700 A.D., when we find the standard of literary attainment greatly elevated, the graduates arranged in three classes and officials in nine, a classification which is still retained.

'Arriving at the close of the fourth millennium, under the sway of the Mings and Tsings of the present day, we find the simple trials instituted by Shun expanded into a colossal system which may well claim to be the growth of four thousand years. It still exhibits the features that were prominent in its earlier stages, the "six arts," the "five studies" and the "three degrees" remaining as records of its progressive development.

. . . .

'Scholarship is a very different thing now from what it was in those ruder ages when books were few, and the harp, the bow, and the saddle divided the student's time with the oral instructions of some famous master. Each century has added to the weight of his burden, and to the "heir of all the ages" each passing generation has bequeathed a legacy of toil. Doomed to live among the deposits of a buried world, and contending with millions of competitors, the intending candidate can hardly hope for success without devoting himself to a life of unremitting study. True, he is not called upon to extend his researches beyond the limits of his national literature, but that is all but infinite. It costs him, at the outset, years of labour to get possession of the key that unlocks it, for the learned language is totally distinct from his vernacular dialect, and justly regarded as the most difficult of the languages of man. Then he must commit to memory the whole circle of the recognised classics and make himself familiar with the best writers of every age of a country which is no less prolific in books than in men. No doubt, his course of study is too purely literary and too exclusively Chinese, but it is not superficial. In a popular "Student's Guide" we lately met with a course of reading drawn up for thirty years!'[1]

The competition is so close that it is impossible for those under preparation to study any subject except that which the State prescribes.

While it is generally correct to say that all State offices are reserved for those who go through the complete Chinese curriculum and pass the examinations, it has to be noted that there is at Peking a State-supported college for the special instruction of the sons of high officials and of the Manchu governing and military class, and that the pupils of this institution are afterwards employed in the public service. Dr. Morrison says that the examination of members of the imperial dynasty is a mockery.

It sometimes happens also that for eminent social position or public services, a high degree and corresponding rank may

---

[1] From Han Lin Papers; or, Essays on the Intellectual Life of the Chinese, pp. 56-9, by W. A. P. Martin, D.D., LL.D., President of the Sungwen College, Peking.

be conferred, although the recipient is not a literate. Professor Douglas says that there is a large number of mandarins of different grades who have received their titles for public services.

Mr. Wells Williams [1] maintains that the examinations are not always purely conducted, and that bribes are frequently conveyed by wealthy candidates to the examiners. The lowest degree, especially, is frequently obtained by influence. There can be no doubt of this. Even the second degree is sometimes obtained by bribery, and the smuggling of essays into the examination halls connived at. Indeed, there is a regular scale of charges for successful fraudulent assistance or personation.[2]

For the examinations which are graded, and which I shall immediately describe, the people prepare themselves. It would appear, however, that government public schools existed nearly 4,000 years ago, for in the Book of Rites it is said that 'for the purposes of education among the ancients, villages had their schools, districts their academies, departments their colleges, and principalities their universities.' [3] Schools are set up by adventure teachers in every part of China proper, many families, however, preferring to employ private tutors. M. Simon, in a recent book, tells us that colleges under the direction of the central academy still exist, but the people do not seem to take advantage of them. The Chinese young man prefers coaching establishments to educational institutions; and, where a master has gained a reputation for skill in teaching, many pupils gather round him to prepare for examination. Such private colleges are numerous. Nor are the public colleges so deserted as M. Simon represents, if we are to believe others. The teachers of these are paid by the State, and admission to training is by competitive examination. Thus men and boys who are too poor to pay for their education have a chance afforded them (Doolittle).

---

[1] *The Middle Kingdom.*   [2] Doolittle.
[3] Quoted by Mr. Williams, i. 421.

Education in any form whatsoever cannot be said to reach the lowest stratum of the population. But, on the other hand, it is certain that all have the opportunity (if they have the pecuniary means) of acquiring the knowledge requisite for the State examinations.

Given the stimulus in the shape of the wealth and rank of official station, the practical results in China appear to be, that the people find they can educate themselves better than the government can educate them. Mr. Meadows holds that the institution of public service examinations (which have been always strictly competitive) is the cause of the continued duration of the Chinese nation; it is that which preserves the other causes and gives efficacy to their operation. By it all parents throughout the country who can compass the means of imparting to their sons a knowledge of their country's literature do so. A most important result is this, that the poorest man in China is constrained to say, if his lot in life be lowly, that it is so by the 'will of heaven,' and not through any unjust barriers or disqualifications erected by his fellow-men.

2. *The external organisation of the examination-system*

The so-called districts of China are about the size of an average English county. These are presided over by a civil mandarin. He is assisted by subordinate mandarins, among whom are two educational mandarins.

Several districts together are grouped as departments (the average being six districts to a department), at the head of which is the departmental judge or prefect, and his residence is known as the departmental city. These departments again are grouped — usually three of them — into circuits, at the head of which is a high officer called intendant (Taou-tae) — the lowest official who has power over the action of the military.

The officials above-named are all distributed through the provinces, and at the head of each province is a viceroy.

The viceroy is not only at the head of the civil administration of the province, but also controls the military, and has a general supervision. In fact, the provinces are virtually self-governing, but subject to the supreme imperial authority.[1] The viceroy is empowered to communicate with the emperor and the cabinet council direct, and he has the power of suspending all the mandarins in the circuits, departments, and districts of his province. Under this powerful viceroy there are three high officials: the finance superintendent, the judicial head or chief justice, and the provincial educational examiner. There are thus (1), districts; (2), departments; (3), circuits; (4), provinces; all under the emperor and his cabinet council.

The system of examination runs parallel, to a large extent, with the civil divisions of the country; and at the head of the whole educational administration is the Academy of Han-lin at Peking, to which I have already adverted. ' It numbers,' says M. Simon, ' 232 members recruited by themselves from among the literati. The State guarantees to each of them the use of a house and garden, with a small money allowance.' There are also ancient endowments. ' It is entirely independent of the government, in spite of the assistance rendered, which cannot be withdrawn.' Not only does this Academy control the educational examinations of the country, but it is virtually a kind of privy council advising the emperor. Forty of their number constitute a court of censors and supervise (Simon) both the public and private life of the emperor. Fifty-six censors also are distributed through the country, says Douglas. They are understood to expose all cases of maladministration. Members of the court are also sent on special missions to inquire into grievances, &c. Others have the charge of the public records.

---

[1] The provincial cities may have a population of from 500,000 to 3,000,000 people.

3. *The examinations* [1]

(1) Preliminary examinations are conducted in the districts or counties by the educational mandarins. These 'preliminaries' are two in number (Plath).

(2) Those who pass the preliminary examinations then go forward to an examination held twice every three years in the departmental city. This departmental examination is conducted by the *provincial* examiner, who goes to the departmental city for that purpose and is aided by the departmental prefect. The candidates make their appearance twice or oftener for examination, and those who stand a fair chance of the degree are then required to appear and write out from memory the whole of the Sacred Edict, a treatise prepared by one of the emperors for the instruction of his subjects in their moral duties (Doolittle). Failure in this is fatal to a candidate's chance, however high he may stand in the other exercises. This departmental examination is the last of the primary examinations and confers on those who pass it the designation of Sew-tzai,[2] 'flowering talent,' which Europeans have translated as the degree of Bachelor.[3] The successful Bachelor can wear a button on his cap and is raised above the common citizen. In fact he is now subject, even in the case of criminal offences, to the literary chief of the graduates of his district (Doolittle). This might be regarded as being admitted 'to the benefit of clergy.' He now belongs to the lowest grade of Chinese aristocracy. But only a fixed number receive the degree at each examination, and consequently youths often go back to their homes without public recognition of their attainments, although in reality standing high. It is thus in the strictest

---

[1] I have carefully read at least seven or eight accounts of the examinations, and all differ in their details somewhat. I give the result of a careful collation.

[2] Spelt sometimes siu-ts-ai.

[3] According to Doolittle, there are also certain intermediate or supplementary examinations of Bachelors, to weed out those who are not fit to go forward to the second degree.

sense a competition. Those who pass the examination are received with great rejoicings by their friends. I have already said that this B.A. is sometimes purchased, and often obtained by bribery. Of this there can be no doubt. According to Doolittle, it can be bought from the Imperial authority itself. The purchaser can then compete for the next higher degree. In any case, he has received a distinction of great social value.

(3) Every three years the Bachelors of each province have an opportunity of being examined at the provincial city at a great gathering presided over by two examiners sent from Peking, who are assisted by a large local staff. These examinations extend over three sittings. Although the average number allowed to pass in each province is only seventy (Martin gives one in a hundred), the competitions are frequently attended by from 7,000 to 8,000 Bachelors. There may be in a provincial hall as many as 10,000 examination cells: small and uncomfortable recesses. The candidates take in their own provisions (the State allowance being bad), and there are servants appointed to cook for them. Two days and nights seems to be the minimum amount of time spent in the examination hall. Martin gives three sessions of nearly three days each. Compositions in prose and verse are prescribed, and themes to test the extent and depth of scholarship. Those who pass are designated 'promoted men,' Chü-jin, which in Europe has been translated 'Licentiates,' or 'Masters.' They can now adorn their caps with a gilt button of a higher grade.

(4) The Licentiates or Masters are now entitled to compete for the metropolitan title of 'entered scholars,' or (as we have translated the degree) Doctor (Chin-tze) which is conferred after a severe examination at Peking, the capital, held triennially and conducted by the metropolitan Academicians, members of the Han-lin. It lasts thirteen days (Plath); but the percentage of elected men is now larger than in the lower examinations.

The mere details of working so huge an examination

machine are enough to overwhelm the ordinary European mind — officers to marshal the students before entering the examination hall; officers to paste down the corners of the themes on which is the number corresponding to the candidate's name ; servitors to wait on the candidates ; examiners and their numerous assistants.

The *Bachelor's* examination occupies only one day, the candidates assembling before dawn, and being provided with slate and paper. Though searched before entering they not unfrequently, it is said, find means of eluding their searchers, and instead of having the 'Four Books' at their fingers' ends have them, in the form of diamond editions, concealed up their flowing sleeves. As soon as it is light enough, two themes for prose essays and one for a poem are carried round on long poles and are copied down by all.[1] Then ensues a struggle as to who shall finish first, a certain proportion of marks being allowed for speed in composition, and by degrees all the papers are handed in and the candidates disperse. Some few days afterwards the list is issued.

Dr. Morrison summarises thus, in speaking of the *Licentiate's* examination. First day : three themes from the Four Books, one for a verse composition. Second day: one theme from each of the Five Classics ; one of these, according to most writers, being a verse composition. Third day: five questions on the history and economics of China. The theme-paper is printed with perpendicular and horizontal lines, dividing it into squares, one square for each character. Characters blotted out or altered must be numbered and noted down by the student according to a prescribed form. The number of characters for each essay is prescribed. It will not be accepted if there are any heterodox opinions.

In a great centre like Canton there will be found as many as 10,000 persons within the enclosure of the examination building, and the public interest is intense.

For the military service a very small knowledge of liter-

---

[1] Bishop Gray gives several days to this examination.

ature is needed. The special examination consists of physical exercises — the lifting of heavy weights, drawing the long bow, and drill with the sword.

4. *Rewards of success in the examinations*

It is a joyful moment for those who find themselves in possession of the first literary degree — a degree which launches its owner fairly in a recognised career, entitles him to wear official dress with a gilt button of the lowest grade, and exempts him, as a prisoner or as a witness, from the indignity of the bamboo — at any rate, until his case shall have been reported to the higher authorities and his diploma cancelled. From this moment he is nominally an officer of the State, though doomed to remain for some time, and possibly for ever, in the position of an unemployed and unpaid attaché. He is, however, whatever may happen, a member of the Chinese aristocracy. His own energy and abilities must determine the rest. He may now either obtain by purchase (not from the State but from the mandarin in whose office the particular patronage is vested) or by influence, subordinate employment as secretary, clerk, &c. in some department of the provincial administration, and trust to chance to work his way in the world : or he may become a scribe or a teacher.

While Bachelors have no right to expect office, the Licentiate may expect a post after waiting for one or two years ; but much depends on personal influence at this stage. The Doctor has, however, claim to a district magistracy at once, and the career of civilian in all its grades is opened up to him. Mr. Williams says (ed. 1857) that in his time, partly in consequence of the extensive sale of offices, 5,000 Doctors and 27,000 Licentiates were waiting for employment. In any other country save China these men would be a serious element of danger to the State.

'Hard and successful study,' says Mr. Meadows, 'alone enables a Chinese to set foot on the lowest step of the official ladder, and a long and unusually successful career is necessary to enable him to reach the higher rounds and we may add, in the words of this same author, that 'the administrative system into which learning thus secures an access is the most gigantic and the most minutely organised which the world has ever seen.'

It has to be noted that the specialised liberal professions as we understand them, do not exist in China, 'and a youth in determining his calling in life has to choose between becoming a scholar and a possible mandarin or teacher, and taking to trade. This narrowing of future possibilities induces almost every lad who possesses any talent whatever to throw in his lot with the students. And this point being decided, he devotes himself with all the industry of his race to preparing for the public examinations by perfecting his knowledge of the classics and by practising· the art of writing essays and penning verses.' (Douglas, p. 165.)

The few more distinguished Doctors may go forward to still another and final examination which makes them members of the Imperial Academy attached to the court at Peking, which is entrusted with the function of poets and historians of the empire, and the supervision of the State examinations. At each triennial examination the emperor designates the one consummate flower of the triennium, the 'Senior Wrangler' (as they would say at Cambridge) of the empire, and the city which has produced him becomes noted in the eyes of all China.

To what end all this? Not to promote philosophical speculation, scientific investigation, or even literary excellence, but merely with a view to ascertain fitness for the public service by testing the acquisitive, retentive, and reproductive powers of the candidates. Any originality would be fatal to the aspirant. We cannot shut our eyes to the barren result of all this hard study and excessive examination. The exclusiveness with which the Chinese minds are fed on the facts and bald precepts of history, on the poetical literature (mostly lyric and artificial) of the past, and the demand made on them for an exact reproduction of the words of their sacred books and the classical writers and commentators on them, has a tendency to confirm and perpetuate the Chinese peculiarities of mind, and to repress all true progressive intellectual life.

At the same time such a system manifestly has high political significance. The intellect of the whole empire is, so to speak, captured and enslaved not merely to the learning of the past but to the existing constitution of things. A system which gives every man, who can attain even to the lowest degree, a social status and the prospect of professional work of some kind, can be upset only by some extraordinary social upheaval. An aristocracy of intellect is in its essence a democratic institution, and from the point of view of the emperor and his cabinet, a very safe one. The system, moreover, while producing men attached to the institutions by which they have risen, acts as a check on the arbitrariness of despotism. The emperor must so conduct himself as to satisfy the conceptions of moral conduct and political justice which the highest intellect of the country has formed and formulated.

Great are the privileges, we see, belonging to those who have an opportunity of obtaining education, but it is impossible that education in any sense can reach the masses of the people. Time and money are needed to take advantage of the education offered. Nor, indeed, would it seem possible to give what we in the West call popular education save through the local dialects, in which there is little or no native literature. The literary language is as far removed from these dialects as Latin is from broad Scots.

5. *Subjects of examination*

To these I have already adverted. They are clearly defined, and it is impossible for any one who means to succeed, to allow his attention to be for a moment directed from the prescribed path. And yet, from the Chinese point of view the course of study is comprehensive. Biot correctly says that the competitive examinations are on principle founded on the reading and explanation of a limited number of ancient texts, and so far it is rightly called 'literary.' But it has also an intellectual character resulting from the fact that these texts contain all the essential documents of morality, philosophy, politics and history — the *ensemble* of rights and duties. The Five Classics and Four Books do not amount in bulk to more than our Old and New Testaments together.

But commentators have also to be studied, and these have produced works of inordinate dimensions. ' Century after century,' says Professor Douglas,[1] ' has produced scholars who have devoted their lives to the production of exegetical treatises which since, as every grain of wheat has been long well threshed out of the texts, have degenerated into trivial and verbal technicalities.'

6. *Teachers: Schools: Course of Study: Methods*

(*a*) **Teachers and Schools.** — The schoolmaster has not to pass an examination and requires no permit from the authorities, but I believe that the educational inspectors are empowered, if they see fit, to close bad schools. Parents choose for their children the teacher in whom they have confidence and they exercise the greatest care in doing so. The teachers are mostly Bachelors in arts who have not proceeded to a higher degree, frequently men who have failed in the competition for their bachelorship. But in the higher grades of teaching, even Doctors will be often found to prefer school-work to the public service. All instructors are much respected; no function is more highly esteemed, save that of an administrator. They are engaged by the year. Their remuneration varies. In ' private ' schools they receive from 35*l.* to 80*l.* per annum; in country schools they are paid by the fees of the scholars, usually from 2*s.* to 4*s.* per month, besides presents and provisions.

---

[1] *Society in China*, p. 164.

The children of the towns and villages meet in some dependence of a pagoda or temple or of some large commercial establishment. Frequently mere sheds are used. It is rarely that a building specially designed for a schoolhouse is to be seen.[1] The rooms are generally hired by the teacher : sometimes he may have himself a house suitable for a school and receive the children there. Private schools got up by a few well-to-do families for their own children, are kept in the halls dedicated to ancestors and are better provided than the public schools. It is private interest, not zeal for the elevation of the people, that leads to the institution of schools ; but here and there schools have been set on foot by the personal benefactions of some rich man who looks for his reward in some literary title.

In village schools, the number of pupils under one teacher may be from 20 to 40. The school hours are usually from sunrise to 10 o'clock, when the children go home to dinner, and then from 11 to 5. The arrangements of the school are very simple. The teacher has a table and arm-chair for himself, and every scholar has to bring with him a writing-table and chair. Every one has to provide himself, also, with books, paper, Indian-ink and pencil.

The boy enters school about the age of seven. The first going to school is a great occasion in the family. Admission into the school is accompanied by a formal ceremony under the name of Koi-hok, i.e., opening of studies. On first going to school the scholar pays his devotions (which consist in burning of incense and genuflexions) before the altar of Confucius. If there is no altar, a bit of paper with Confucius's name on it will suffice (Doolittle). He next salutes his teacher with great reverence. The boy is now a disciple of Confucius and remains so till the day on which he takes his final degree. Every day, when the pupils come to school, they bow and offer incense to the picture of a god of knowledge,[2] then bow to the teacher and take their places. Educa-

---

[1] Wells Williams's *Middle Kingdom.*
[2] One of these I possess, and it is a hideous object.

tion as well as instruction is understood to be comprised in the teacher's duties. Accordingly, he is required to train the pupils in good behaviour and convey to them the rules of decency and politeness, and, all through the school period, moral instruction and becoming conduct according to the rules of etiquette which regulate the relations of persons to each other in China are understood to be kept in view. In such matters nothing seems to be too minute for the Chinese mind.

(*b*) **The Course of Study.**—The course of study is rigid and the same for all: nothing in the whole of the long curriculum is optional.

Speaking generally, there are three grades of instruction — sometimes all within the same school. The primary, in which mere memory work is done, and script acquired; the middle, in which a translation is given of the canonical books; and the higher, in which composition and commentaries are the leading studies.

The first schoolbook is described as the 'Pass to the regions of classical and historical literature,' but this is not its name. It is sometimes called the 'three-character classic' — also the ' trimetrical classic.' [1] It begins with the necessity of education. Then the importance of their duties to children and brothers is impressed upon the pupils by precept and example. Then follows a survey of the various branches of knowledge in an ascending series: the three great powers (heaven, earth, and man); the four seasons and quarters of heaven; the five elements (metals, wood, fire, earth); the five cardinal virtues (love, justice, propriety, wisdom, truth — faithfulness); the six species of grain (rice, barley, wheat, beans, millet, and another kind of grain); the six domestic animals (horse, ox, sheep, fowl, dog, swine); the seven passions (love, hatred, joy, sadness, pleasure, anger, and fear);

---

[1] Quoting from the Abbé Huc, the *Dictionnaire Pédagogique* gives San-tze-king as the Chinese title of this book. A copy before me, printed in Hong Kong, reads *Sam-tsz-King*.

the eight notes of music; the nine degrees of relationship; the social duties as between ruler and subject, father and son, husband and wife, elder and younger brother, and friends. After this survey come rules for a course of academic studies with a list of the books to be used, and a general summary of the History of China with an enumeration of the successive dynasties of the empire.[1] The material is too compressed and too generalised for the youthful mind to assimilate; but at this age no regard is paid to the development of the thinking powers. The pupils are to receive quite mechanically a store of valuable information, till the time comes when their intelligence will be awakened by the explanations of the teacher, and this happens only in the case of those who propose to go forward to the public degree examinations. The Primer — the contents of which I have just summarised — begins thus (Eitel's translation):

Man's commencement of life is such that his nature is radically good.
But as to nature, men are mutually near each other
　Whilst in practice they are mutually far apart.
Suppose, however, that no education were given to a man,
His nature would then be diverted.
　Education's rationale is such in its tendency
　That the highest value is set on application.

The next five lines are from Bridgman's translation:

To educate without rigour shows a teacher's indolence.
That boys should not learn is an improper thing;
For if they do not learn in youth, what will they do when old?
Gems unwrought can form nothing useful;
So men untaught can never know the proprieties.

Another extract, having reference to the books to be studied, may be given:

Now in all cases when instruction is given to the ignorant,
Although it is well to explain characters orally and exhaustively,
Yet detailed moral instruction in the sayings of the ancients

[1] See Eitel's translation, published at Hong Kong, 1892.

Is just as necessary as precision regarding syntactic punctuation.
But as to [successful] practice of study, or rather that which con-
stitutes it,
It is indispensable to have a rational basis to begin with.
Starting therefore from a study of the filial piety classic,
We proceed to the study of the so-called Four Books.

And so on.

The concluding words of the book are these:

Whilst men leave behind them their sons,
And with gold fill their coffers,
I, Wong Poh-hen give an education to my sons,
Leaving behind nought but this one little book.

But diligence in the use of it will have its sure merits,
Whilst play is of no benefit at all.
Beware of that, do !
It is of imperative importance for you to exert all your strength.

Observe the generalised and abstract character of the instruction given to mere infants.   When we note further that
each notion is represented either by a distinct symbol, or a
symbol with more than one interpretation, we shall be able
to conceive the vast memory task which the Chinese child
has to face on the very threshold of learning.   M. Genähr (a
missionary) affirms that a great many even of the teachers
do not understand the meaning of what they teach children
to read.

The boy now knows the shapes and sounds of upwards of
400 separate characters, representing upwards of 1,000 words,
and is considered sufficiently advanced to take the second
step upon the road to knowledge and to proceed to commit
to memory in like manner the 'Thousand Character Book'
— Ts'in-Tsz-man.   This singular piece of composition is said
to have been the production of a man who was supplied in
prison with 1,000 different characters jumbled together and
to have been ordered to make out of them a poem.[1]   He
accomplished the feat in a single night, but his hair turned

[1] Giles' *Historic China.*

white with the effort. This is legendary, of course. The poem consists of 250 columns of four characters to each. The subjects are varied, and rather inconsequent, as witness the following specimen which I take from the beginning of the book, as being the best part from a literary point of view and also the most consecutive:

There is [father] Heaven above me and [mother] Earth below : how dusky the former, how tawny the latter !

And so there is the universe all around, with its æons all along : how vast the former, how limitless the latter !

Then there is sun and moon : even as the latter goes on to fulness, the former declines.

And so there are the other planets, with all the stars : how scattered they are, and yet how orderly the display !

[Hence it is that nature makes] the cold to come on, even as the heat begins to depart,

And as autumn gathers things up [into maturity], so winter again hides them all away.

[And hence also] men forming into intercalary months the surplus [of their reckoning of days] have perfected [their calculations] of the year.

And likewise in music, having discovered the sharps and flats, they have reproduced [in melodies] in harmonies of nature's expanding [and reverting] breath.

The book then goes on to treat of the beauty of natural objects, the origin and progress of Chinese civilisation, inherited physical and mental constitution, moral self-culture, moral reputation, filial piety, political loyalty, value of literary studies, deportment, founders of Chinese polity, topography, value of agriculture, advice and warning, natural gifts and organised study, the flight of time, and concludes with a warning against isolation.

Here again the chief object is to store the pupil's memory with the shapes and sounds of a large number of written symbols ; and by the time that the Thousand Character Essay (or poem) has been mastered, it follows that 1,000 [1]

---

[1] Unless the same characters frequently recur, which is probable.

new characters will have been added to the boy's stock-in-trade; besides which he ought to have acquired a knowledge of a very useful cardinal series of numbers from 1 to 1,000. But besides this, as the work is methodically constructed (a fact which puts out of court the legend of the prisoner), the children ought to have acquired a large amount of information on history, geography, morality, and the domestic virtues. I say 'ought to have acquired' advisedly; but they acquire nothing save the utterance of the literary words by rote, and the formation of the literary characters. No attempt is made to bring the intelligence to bear on the work done. The object is simply to give the children a rote-knowledge of the words and forms of the literary language. Still a certain intellectual result must follow.

If any one doubts the effect of school education on the character and life of a nation, let him consider with himself the respective influence of these Chinese classical primers so acquired, and the Shorter Catechism used as a school text-book and as constituting the rule of faith and life in Scotland.

One writer says, with manifest truth, that the Chinese child is in a position similar to that in which an English child would be who had to learn by heart Latin Grammar and several Latin books without understanding a single word. Rote-work, and this in what is practically a foreign tongue, governs all.[1]

The next step is an important one, analogous to the old Grammar-school transition in learning Latin, viz. from the 'Delectus' to Cæsar and Virgil — from the elementary to the more advanced. The budding student now opens the first page of the Four Books, which are of vital importance in the great competitive tests to which he will hereafter be subjected. These Four Books, to which are added the Five Classics, are now committed, one by one, to memory, in precisely the same way as the two foregoing schoolbooks, anything like explanation or consultation of the author-

[1] I have also seen a short book of poetry sometimes used in schools.

ised commentaries being postponed until some progress has been made in the arduous task of learning by heart. (Giles.) The master, it is true, now translates and the boys imitate him; but there is no independent effort to get at the meaning.

Then come the commentaries, as I have before explained. 'The memory work is prodigious, and is abnormally developed at the expense of all the higher mental faculties.' (Douglas, p. 165.) ' It is always easier to remember than to think, and according to the current Chinese system, it is also more profitable.'

(c) **Method of Instruction. Earlier stages.** — There are several highly esteemed books on the subject of education in China, and they contain admirable maxims, but there has been no attempt to discover a method of training. The most celebrated perhaps is one called ' Complete Collection of Family Jewels,' in which there are also rules for school management (Morrison). There is no class system. It is all individual teaching.

The method of learning to read is the following. The book is opened and the teacher begins to read. The pupils, each of whom has his book, repeat the words after the master, with their eyes fixed on the page, and following the words with their fore-finger. Only one line is read, and this is repeated by the pupils simultaneously in a loud voice till the pupils have acquired the pronunciation of every symbol and can read the line without the master. Then they go to their seats and learn the line by heart; this they also do with a loud voice, each one shouting out his task (the noise proceeding from a Chinese school is frightful), till he has imprinted it on his memory. When he is ready he goes to the master, puts his book on the table before him, turns his back and so repeats the lesson. Hence the phrase ' to back the book ' is equivalent to ' saying by heart.' Then the teacher proceeds to the next line, and goes on in the same way till the whole book is committed to memory. The book is rhythmically constructed, so that three symbols always form one sentence, and hence the name *Sam-tz-King*, or 'the trimetrical or three-character classic.' We have here developed to its fullest extent the universal Oriental custom of learning by heart — a survival from the time when oral tradition was the only possible way of learning and teaching. Before books or rolls existed the teacher recited what the pupils were to learn, and they repeated it after him till they knew it. The understanding of what was acquired was not thought of, nor indeed was the instruction graduated so as to fit the intelligence of the young. The understanding of what was learned was allowed to take care of itself. China, although it has the printed page, is no exception to the crude Oriental conception of instructing the young.

Besides the reading of the symbols, the only other subject taught in the elementary school is writing. The scholars receive a copy from the master, which contains in the first instance the simplest symbols, and they gradually learn to write those of more complex form. These copies are laid under the paper on which the pupil is to write, and are traced by him with the pencil. When he has obtained some facility in tracing he begins to copy.

Many boys who go to school never learn more than to read and write, and do not attain to an understanding of the characters ; so that even if one of them were capable of reading and saying by heart a whole book fluently, he would not be therefore able to give any account of what he had read. Although regular instruction in arithmetic, geography, history, natural history, or foreign languages is never thought of, and no religious instruction is given, it has to be remarked that the first and second books contain a great deal of geographical, historical, and naturalistic information of an elementary and crude kind. These things are set down, however, in a highly abstract preceptive way, and are not understood. But how long is it since in England Mangnall's 'Questions' and Pinnock's 'Catechisms' were almost universal, and how long since maps were considered essential to the teaching of geography ?

Method of Instruction. Higher stages. — For the mass, even of the educated, three or four years is the extent of the school period. Those who wish to devote themselves permanently to studies begin only after this to understand what they read, and receive in the course of time a thorough explanation of the classical authors. They are also exercised in making verses according to prescribed rules, and in writing themes in imitation of models. This higher training is conducted by masters who have passed an examination, and have graduated.

In the public and private colleges lectures are delivered on the Four Books and the Five Classics. Four times in the month compositions are written and verses made on themes which have been previously discussed under the guidance of the master. 'The first step in composition is the yoking together of double characters. The second is the reduplication of these binary compounds, and the construction of parallels — an idea which runs so completely through the whole of Chinese literature, that the mind of the student has to be imbued with it at the very outset. This is the way he begins: the teacher writes, "wind blows," the pupil adds, "rain falls;" the teacher writes, "rivers are long," the pupil adds, "seas are deep" or "mountains are high,"'[1] &c. To acquire fluency and elegance in composition, the Chinese students learn by heart a considerable number of essays which have been written by distinguished scholars in a masterly style; and these collections in considerable numbers are sold in the shops.

It is on his literary proficiency, reproductive powers, and attention to unalterable rules that the student's ultimate success wholly depends. A candidate receiving a given theme, is not at liberty to sit down and write an essay in the terms or sequence which unassisted fancy may dictate. There must be no originality of either thought or style. He must abide by fixed rules, introducing the subject in so many balanced sentences, developing it in so many more, sum-

[1] *Education in China*, p. 89. Martin.

ming up his arguments, and finally reaching the conclusion according to received principles of composition. The very number of sentences is prescribed, frequently the number of words. And so also with poems. These are invariably on the same model — a stated number of characters to each line, arbitrary rules of rhyme, trite similes and forced allusions to the past. The book-shops of Chinese cities are flooded with collections of essays and poems by famous authors of all ages, and these are carefully studied by intending competitors in the hope of borrowing therefrom something of their vigour and refinement (Giles).

.The most highly esteemed book on composition is called 'The Learner's Bright Mirror.' The steps of an essay as prescribed in this book are:

1. The breaking open of the theme.
2. Receiving the theme.
3. Beginning to discuss the theme.
4. Raising a branch or division.
5. The passing vein (passing from one idea to another).
6. The middle division (amplification, &c.).
7. The closing division (containing further elucidation).
8. The winding-up division (Morrison).[1]

As regards school-discipline need I say that, with such aims and such methods, the rod is freely and unsparingly used?

It is, of course, impossible that there can be in China any principles and methods of instruction and education in the sense in which Europe uses these words, because there is no scientific spirit and no psychology. But as I have said, they are not without their books on the art of education which contain very sagacious remarks and sound judgments. Of these the most important is a 'Treatise on the Education of Young Children,' written in the twelfth century by a philosopher named Tchow-hi or Chow-tsze; I suppose the

---

[1] Professor Douglas, in *Society in China*, expresses the rules differently, but they are substantially the same.

eminent thinker referred to before ('Dict. Péd.'). In this treatise we find such maxims as these: 'In teaching, a master should not go too quickly from one subject to another, and never explain several things at a time. If he observe this rule, ideas will arrange themselves and combine of themselves in the mind of the pupil. He ought to incite, animate, and urge his pupils, but never press them, still less force them.' 'If a master teaches clearly he will make himself understood without dealing in vain and long discoursing.' He also says that the grand art of teaching is to get the pupil to ask questions, and that he ought to correct the fault of a pupil without letting him suspect it. Another collection of educational precepts goes into great detail as to the duties of teacher and scholar. But in China, as elsewhere, what is axiomatic with the educationalist for the most part remains with him, and is not part of the practice of the teacher, because there is no school of didactics, and therefore no rational tradition.[1]

Women remain uneducated except among the wealthy. Among these, an educated woman is highly respected for her attainments. Her instruction has, of course, been private.

Conclusion. — I have spoken in a previous part of this lecture of the barren results intellectually of the elaborate educational curriculum of the Chinese, and this, indeed, is one of the causes of the stereotyped continuity of life. The poverty of results is due partly to the narrow range of the studies, but much more to the purpose, character, and method of them.

The highest intellectual employment of Chinese men of culture, apart from the work of administration, is the repeating of passages from the Books, and exercising themselves in the making of verses, in which perfect exactness in metre and conformity to classical usage are all-important, but not

[1] Bishop Gray says (p. 174, vol. i.) that *bachelors* become members of universities, of which there is one in every walled city! He must refer to the Provincial State Colleges, if, indeed, he is not altogether wrong.

more so than beauty of caligraphy. The celebrated novel called Yu-Kiao-li, or 'The Two Cousins,' admits us to the inner life of the Chinese, and gives us some idea of the intellectual condition of its cultured men, and their most elevated occupations. Intellectually there is great ability and great acuteness, but no originality — nay, a distrust of all originating power. The study of poetry, which is so largely encouraged, might be expected to exalt the imagination and stimulate thought among the Chinese, but even where it is not highly artificial and hampered by ridiculous rules, it is prosaic and preceptive. The following extracts illustrate what I mean:

> The cricket is in the hall,
> And the year is drawing to a close.
> If we do not enjoy ourselves now
> The days and months will have fled.
> But let us not go to excess;
> Let us think of the duties of our position;
> Let us not go beyond bounds in our love of pleasure.
> The virtuous man is ever on his guard.   (Legge.)

As a favourable specimen of the domestic odes I may cite the following:

> 'Get up, husband, here's the day.'
> 'Not yet, wife, the dawn's still grey.'
> 'Get up, sir, and on the night
> See the morning star shines bright.
> Shake off slumber, and prepare
> Ducks and geese to shoot and snare.
> All your darts and line may kill
> I will dress for you with skill.
> Thus a blithesome hour we'll pass,
> Brightened by a cheerful glass;
> While your lute its aid imparts
> To gratify and soothe our hearts.
>
> On all whom you may wish to know
> I'll girdle ornaments bestow,

And girdle ornaments I'll send
To anyone who calls you friend;
With him whose love for you's abiding
My girdle ornaments dividing.'

Again, as a specimen of another class of poetic imagery, the following may be taken:

A Solitary Carouse on a Day in Spring

The east wind fans a gentle breeze,
The streams and trees glory in the brightness of the spring,
The bright sun illuminates the green shrubs
And the falling flowers are scattered and fly away.
The solitary cloud retreats to the hollow hill,
The birds return to their leafy haunts,
Every being has a refuge whither he may turn,
I alone have nothing to which to cling,
So, seated opposite the moon shining o'er the cliff,
I drink and sing to the fragrant blossoms.

There is not much of the 'poet's eye in a fine frenzy rolling' in all this.[1]

As of poetry, so of literature generally: in our European sense we may say confidently that it does not flourish: this partly because it is taught, not for its own sake, but for ulterior ends, and subject throughout to strict examination tests, and to antiquarian fixed forms. The tendency of competitive examinations, even among ourselves, is to crush out originality and real interest in the very subjects in which a student distinguishes himself. The Chinese drama is realistic and photographic, and wanting in all the higher qualities.

In the department of encyclopædias and topographical work the Chinese are strong. Their characteristic qualities of mind have full scope in productions which demand chiefly industry, detailed accuracy, and discriminating judgment.

[1] I have read the whole of Romilly Allen's ' Book of Chinese Poetry,' and the above (taken from the *Encyc. Brit.*) are very favourable specimens indeed.

As to *moral* results, these unquestionably are very far indeed from being so high as might be expected from a nation whose whole energies are presumed to be set in the direction of moral and political training and the supreme virtue of propriety, while allowing the people to follow their own fancies in religion. After all, is it reasonable to expect a high moral result where instruction takes the place of training and discipline?[1] The supreme product in China, if we found it, would be a supreme moral pedant, just as the supreme product in the sphere of intellect is an intellectual pedant. The surrounding of religion with rites and ceremonies I have already remarked, while it tends to give it permanence, tends also to deprive it of vitality. This, indeed, is a trite saying. It is interesting to note, however, that the same remark may be made with equal truth when an attempt is made by means of an elaborate and complicated social ritual to regulate the moral and civil relations of men, and dogmatically to prescribe rules of conduct. The result is a vast appearance of ceremonious politeness, which, as it is enjoined and yet cannot possibly be always felt, is necessarily accompanied with a consciousness of its own hollowness. Hence the disappearance of those very virtues which the Chinese sages desired to cultivate — simplicity and truthfulness. Hence also trickery and wiliness. Honesty is not a conspicuous virtue in China, and what Europeans call honour does not, it seems to me, exist. The whole social fabric would seem to depend for its easy working and for the absence of violence between individuals, on the maintenance of a false and elaborate show of mutual respect. Professor Douglas, in the preface to 'Society in China,' says: 'There is no country in the world where practice and profession are more widely separated than in China. The empire is pre-eminently one of make-believe. From the emperor to the meanest of his subjects, a system of high-

---

[1] Theognis, the old Greek, said this: διδάσκων οὔποτε ποιήσεις τὸν κακὸν ἄνδρ᾽ ἀγαθόν.

sounding pretensions to lofty principles of morality holds sway, while the life of the nation is in direct contradiction to these assumptions. No imperial edict is complete, and no official proclamation finds currency, without protestations in favour of all the virtues. And yet few courts are more devoid of truth and uprightness, and no magistracies are more corrupt than those of the celestial empire.'

We must admit, however, that the political aim of the educational system is, to a large extent, attained; and also the social aim, for the Chinaman is, generally speaking, a good son, and a good subject, an industrious labourer, a man of gentle manners, contented and peaceable. On the other hand, we cannot shut our eyes to the fact that morally, as well as intellectually, as measured by Aryan standards, the education given leads, at best, to mediocrity. By crushing out all initiative it prevents the growth of a free personality. Where this is wanting, we may expect to find, not only the absence of all independent inquiry into new fields of thought, but also the absence of the more *manly* virtues.

Perhaps we may say that the secret of failure lies in the want of an ideal human aim, as opposed to a narrow political or social aim. Man has to be trained ever in the light of a type of manhood. All practical aims ought to be subordinated to this. It cannot be said that the course of education in China is illiberal or anti-humanistic; but restriction of aim and intense personal competition can deprive even liberal studies of their liberalising influence. The human ideal which we desiderate as educational end is not possible except where the spirit of man — of the individual man — is nurtured in freedom. God has in all history affirmed this, that the highest is conceivable and attainable only through freedom. Many errors, many calamities even, may flow from the untrammelled play of human reason; but these too are of God. Changes, and the freedom of mind which is their cause, are always hateful to the organising mind, which is a tyrannous and levelling mind, whether it clothe itself in the garb of a hard cold system like that of the Chinese, or of a

Catholic Church, a secular imperial bureaucracy, or a communistic police. No such organisation can rest content until it has achieved the enslavement of personality, whose essence is always freedom.

There are among us who are enamoured of state-systems which regulate education down to its minutest detail, and leave no room for the free play of mind: in China we have this indirectly accomplished and see it in all its necessary rigidity, uniformity, and pedantry. There are who advocate a secular system of education: in China we see this in full operation. There are who think that all success in the education of mind should be measured by external competitive tests: in China we have this elaborated into an iron system. There are who cling by the dogmatic and preceptive, and regard with suspicion the habituating of the mind of schoolboys to ideals æsthetic and spiritual, including even the simple elements of humanity: in China they will find what they desire to see. There are who hold that teachers and school-inspectors are heaven-born, and are above the study of educational principles and methods (as the Emperor Sigismund was *supra Grammaticam*) : so China thinks.

I am not going to elaborate didactic parallels and comparisons, tempting as the field may be; but this I may say by way of retrospect. I think we may find a similarity between the ancient Egyptian and the Chinese mind. Both are essentially creatures of the practical understanding, and of merely preceptive morality,unfit or indisposed (unlike the Aryan) to find the reason in things, and, consequently, essentially unspeculative and unscientific. And yet how different in some respects! The Egyptian had a profound sense of the mystery of life, and of infinite possibilities hereafter. The Chinese are essentially prosaic, and of the earth earthy. The Egyptian was saved by having, like the Semite, a divine standard and sanction, such as it was, and a corresponding responsibility to the Unseen. The Chinese seem to have no standard save the fit and the prudential and the 'proper,' and cannot, therefore, I venture to say, be deterred from unworthy action towards either their fellow-citizens or others by a sense of responsibility to ideal aims which connect them with the gods or with God.

It is the intelligence with which we permeate all school studies — that is to say, the free movement of mind which we evoke in the young — that alone truly instructs: it is the life of personality and personal responsibility which we infuse into ethical training and discipline, and the infinite relations with which we sanctify it, that can alone rear a people who are to be vigorous, virile, and progressive. Mere memory work in the sphere of intelligence, mere preceptive and dogmatic teaching in the ethical sphere, can produce at best the mere semblance of a true man or woman — the sterile convention of outer obedience.

We pass now from the highest and most organised expression of Turanian or Uro-Altaic civilisation to the Aryan races, to which we ourselves belong.

Note on Early Forms of Religion

Primitive religion (if it can be called religion) is known as Animism, that is to say belief in the existence of numerous souls or spirits. Those spirits on which man imagines himself dependent for material felicity and personal security naturally become objects of worship as divine beings. But the worship is the offspring of slavish fear, and takes all sorts of forms with a view to appease the reluctant spirits. Magic and various incantations are also resorted to, with a view to control them. There may be also good spirits, and among these the spirits of ancestors: to these offerings are also made. When spirits enter into an object of nature as a permanent residence, and these objects are worshipped, we have fetichism. The first priests are those who have or pretend to have the power of ingratiating men with spirits or demons by means of magical incantations and spells and sacrifices. 'In the animistic religions,' says Tiele, 'fear is more powerful than any other feeling; the evil spirits receive more homage than the good, the lower more than the higher, the local more than the more remote, the special more than the general.' There is nothing moral in the relations between men and such beings, since their favour or disfavour depends entirely on the gifts offered or withheld. The doctrine of immortality is, at this early stage, simply the doctrine of continuance, compensation for good or evil deeds being a late development and probably concurrent with a belief in a Supreme Spirit above all other spirits. Where this idea of compensation enters, we have the beginnings of the worship of a Being who takes note of moral conduct, though not necessarily himself moral according to man's notions. The next step is a God who is Himself an ethical Being with human relations.

We are not to depreciate the religion of a nation because we find animistic and fetichistic practices existing side by side with a higher doctrine, for we have to remember that a conquering race may occupy a country with a religion higher than that of its first inhabitants, while yet the lower form of religion continues to operate — nay even may infect the conquerors.

Authorities : Encyclopædias (especially *Encyc. Brit.*), English, French, and German; Dr. Morrison's *Dictionary;* Doolittle's *Social Life of the Chinese,* 1866 ; Giles's *Historic China* Meadows's *China;* Bishop Gray's *China;* Legge's *Religions of China;* Williams's *Middle Kingdom ;* Martin's *China, Political, Commercial, and Social,* 1847 ; *Ueber Schule-Unterricht und Erziehung bei den alten Chinesen,* von Dr. J. H. Plath, 1868 ; *Essai sur l'histoire de l'instruction publique en Chine,* &c., par E. Biot, 1847 ; *China,* by G. Eug. Simon, 1887 ; Tiele's *Outlines of the History of Ancient Religions ;* Dr. W. A. P. Martin's *Han Lin Papers,* London and New York, 1880; *Society in China,* by Professor Douglas, 1894. *Book of Chinese Poetry* (the Shi-King) translated by Mr. Romilly Allen, 1891. *Chinese School-books.* Many other books have been consulted.

Those who wish to read the Chinese sacred literature must, of course, betake themselves to Legge's monumental work entitled *The Chinese Classics,* in seven volumes, 1861.

Note. — There are the remains of an old university at Peking, founded in the fourteenth century, but now practically deserted. This institution sells the lowest degree, thus giving a qualification to compete for the higher. Mr. Martin says that there is a ' formal ' examination for the degree, and that prior to the holding of the examination numerous students fill the old halls. It is a great abuse.

THE ARYAN OR INDO–EUROPEAN RACES

THE ARYAN OR INDO-EUROPEAN RACES

HINDUS: MEDO-PERSIANS: HELLENES: ITALIANS (ROMANS)

'IT was not only,' says Duncker (vol. iv.), 'in the lower valley of the Nile, on the banks of the Euphrates and Tigris, and along the coast and on the heights of Syria, that independent forms of intellectual and civic life grew up in the ancient world.' By the side of the early civilisations of Egypt, the Semitic races, and the Chinese, we find forms of culture developed among races very different in their nature and temperament. The Medo-Persian civilisation is much later, it is true, than the Egyptian or the Semitic, but the branch of the Aryan race which crossed into India may claim an antiquity for civilised forms of life second only to that of Egypt and Babylonia.

The common characteristic of the Egyptian and Semitic and Chinese religions, in so far as they touched the people, was their externalism. In some of the highest utterances of Egypt, it is true, we find ethical conceptions characterised by sanity and humanity, but these did not emanate from the acknowledged relation of man to God, but rather arose, I think, out of the doctrine of immortality. The externalism of the Jewish religion was far in advance of that of other nations, because it was an externalism of moral acts, and not merely of ceremonies. The Semitic family generally have, it is true, through prophets and hymn-writers, admitted all who choose to follow them to great theologico-ethical ideas. But the *popular* religion of all these races was an external system; and, in the case of all save the Israelites, it was a superstition. The spirituality of religion was lost in ceremonial, and the practical ethics which the religions might have yielded were choked by external observances. All externalism tends to superstition, it matters not what form the externalism takes. Even in its very highest Christian form, it tends towards what is little better than an elevated and æsthetic fetichism. With superstition is always associated fear, and that awe of arbitrary unseen powers which produces slavish minds. In their political relations, Egyptian and Semite and Mongolian were all alike slaves rather than subjects. Further development was impossible save by the introduction of a new principle — the personal and free relation of the human spirit to an ethical God. This, wherever it exists, moulds political forms and social relations. It is in truth, the living unity, or rather identity, of the religious idea with moral ideas which alone can permanently lift religion out of the category of superstitions. God must dwell with men and in each man as a self-conscious person. Thus it is that Christ alone makes nations free by making each man a son of God.

When we pass from the Egyptian and Semitic territories to the home of the Aryan races, we feel like travellers ascending from monotonous and oppressive plains to a cool and invigorating table-land. The region east of the Caspian, which is still, spite of recent scepticism, regarded as the original seat of the Aryan or Indo-European race, sent its Persian and Hindu emigrants to the south-east, and successive waves of Kelt, Sclave, Teuton, and Hellene (including Italian) to the north and west.

It is a striking fact, however, that the fresh and virile spirit of this vigorous race could not sustain itself on the plains of India. The Hindus succumbed to the influences of nature, which were too great and overwhelming to admit of the free growth of the self-conscious personality so conspicuous in their brethren. These influences, and the habits of thought and life of the pre-Aryan races who formed a large proportion of the population, developed characteristics in the Hindus somewhat akin to much that we find in the Egyptian and Semite; and for this reason, as well as because of their greater antiquity, we shall speak of them before we ascend to the clearer atmosphere of the Medo-Persian hills, where the true Aryan spirit which we inherit first clearly declared itself.

(A) INDIA AND THE HINDUS

It is apparent enough from the preceding chapters on educational history, that it is quite impossible to give anything approaching to a correct view of what constitutes the education of a people, without first putting before the reader an outline of that people's civilisation. And civilisation resolves itself, for educational purposes at least, into the religious and moral conceptions of a nation and its consequent political (or at least social) organisation. At the same time, as I have already said, to treat of the characteristics of a nation's life and civilisation in detail is to forget the precise object of the educational historian, and even to obscure it. Such a brief account of a people and their special characteristics as is essential to the understanding of the education which tradition and environment unconsciously gave to all the members of it, is sufficient. This must always be followed by a statement of the means which the State, more or less consciously, took to bring up its children with a view to maintain and perpetuate the national life, if any record of this remain.[1]

When we approach the education of a country like ancient India, or rather that portion of it which was Hindu, we are at once met by the great and all-influencing social fact of caste. Of this we may be certain, that wherever in ancient

---

[1] I may be allowed here to repeat the words of the Preface, that any attempt to generalise in short compass the characteristics of a civilisation, must always be inadequate; and though not necessarily erroneous it must want balance because of the absence of historical development and of many qualifying considerations.

times there was a distinct sacerdotal hereditary caste, the higher education of the country was practically the education of that caste. Even in Europe this was the case up to the twelfth century, although the priestly order was open to all. With the rise of the universities rose the differentiation of the professions as lay spheres of intellectual activity ; and it was only in so far as it destroyed sacerdotalism as an exclusive representative of the Divine, that Protestantism in the sixteenth century gained the kingdom of knowledge and culture for the people as a whole. ' All are priests, all are equal in the sight of God,' is. of the essence of Reformed Christianity : this was the new, or rather the revived, doctrine. In Egypt largely, and in Mesopotamia and India wholly, the priestly order included what in modern times we call the faculties of law and medicine, nay even sometimes also the departments of architecture and music. It thus comprehended all the learning of the time. , In so far as instruction outside this circle may be met with in a caste society, it must inevitably be, so far as the great mass of the people is concerned, of a very slight and perfunctory character, and aim chiefly at putting in the hands of a limited portion of the people the necessary mercantile arts of reading, writing, and elementary arithmetic. All else is the education of apprenticeship to arts : a training in itself, however, of no mean character, although not aiming at the education of mind as mind.

The earliest civilisation of India may be embraced within 2000 to 1400 B.C. — the period of plastic traditions and of primitive Aryan survivals.

The books which embody the intellectual and moral faith of the Hindus are the Veda, the six systems of philosophy, the laws of Manu, and Buddhism. The Veda consists of three parts, (1) prayer and praise, (2) ritualistic precept with prose illustrations, (3) Upanishad or mystical and secret doctrine, written in prose, with occasional verse. The Code of Manu is a collection of traditionary usages and customs of a social and domestic kind, of practices of government and legal procedure, penitential exercises and 'consequences of acts.' It abounds in excellent moral precepts. The other treatises mentioned above are religious, theological, and metaphysical, but even the code itself contemplated a religious end — the transmigration of the individual soul and final beatitude. All these books spring from ancient oral tradition, gradually accumulating and receiving as time went on additions and critical expansion. The Vedic hymns of praise and thanksgiving and adoration of gods we may place as early as 1200 B.C. The recension of the law-book of Manu dates only about 500 B.C., but, like all literature in Oriental countries, it existed, in its essential parts at least long before as a tradition.

I do not propose to enter into the question of Hindu faith and practice generally, but merely to bring into relief the governing idea of the fundamental faith of the nation, whatever subordinate polytheistic forms the doctrine may have taken. I accept this governing idea as moulding the true life of the people, and also as itself primarily an expression of their way of looking at life.

The Brahmanical caste-system gradually grew up between 1200 B.C. and 1000 B.C. The Buddhistic reformation began about 500 B.C., but it was only from about 242 B.C. that Buddhism formulated itself as a rival of Brahmanism. Brahmanical religion had again gained ascendency in 500 A.D., and Buddhism was exiled to Ceylon, some portions of the north of India, Burmah, Thibet, China and Japan.

The caste system, I have said, determined the area, as well as the character, of the education. By caste we mean that kind of social organisation by which the natural divisions of the people are authoritatively fixed and made hereditary. These divisions were into priests, including scholars and legislators; warriors, including executive administrators; merchants, including all industrial members of the community who employed labour; and labourers. One of the Hindu legends (invented by the priests) is that the supreme caste of Brahmans proceeded out of the mouth of Brahma the creator the warrior (military executive caste) Kshatriyas, out of the arms; the industrial and mercantile Vaisyas, from the thigh; and the servile class or Sudras, from the foot. Besides these, there is a still lower class, standing outside the pale of the Brahmanical social organisation, called Pariah in Southern India, and Chandalas in other districts. The Sudras and the other lowest caste are understood to have been the aboriginal inhabitants of India prior to the Aryan Hindu invasion and conquest.

Mixture of castes was not absolutely forbidden, except as regards the marriage of men with women of a higher caste; but it entailed (and still entails) disadvantages, especially on the children. Indeed, it would appear that the caste organisation was never quite so iron as has been sometimes represented, although the Brahmans naturally did all they could to perpetuate it. In the post-Buddhistic reformed Brahmanism a more liberal doctrine was recognised; for it is held that the humblest member of the lowest caste might attain to union with Brahma, the supreme all-embracing Spirit, and this fact must have largely influenced the way in which the castes gradually came to regard each other. The following verses from the great Sanskrit epic, the Mahabharata, are in this relation interesting.

THE PATH OF SALVATION

A spirit (Yaksha) asks:

> What is it makes a Brahman? Birth,
> Deep study, sacred lore, or worth?

King Yudhishthira answers:

> Nor study, sacred lore, nor birth
> The Brahman makes; 't is only worth.

> All men — a Brahman most of all —
> Should virtue guard with care and pains.
> Who virtue rescues, all retains;
> But all is gone with virtue's fall.

The men in books who take delight,
Frequenters all of learning's schools,
Are nothing more than zealous fools ;
The learn'd are those who act aright.

More vile than one of Sudra race
That Brahman deem whose learned store
Embraces all the Vedic lore,
If evil deeds his life disgrace.

That man deserves the Brahman's name,
Who offerings throws on Agni's flame
And knows his senses how to tame.[1]

In the earlier Vedic thought we find characteristics which connect the primitive religion of the Hindus with the Medo-Persian, which found finally its highest expression in Zoroastrianism. The worship of Mithra the Sun and of fire was universal among the Aryans, and the recognition of three powerful gods along with an innumerable number of good and evil spirits. The climatic influence of India, however, so different from that of Medo-Persia, told on the primitive genius of the people, and as Brahmanism developed (1200 B.C. onwards), we find in it elements wholly antagonistic to the Zoroastrian individualism and the continual personal contest between light and darkness, good and evil, which that religion teaches. The old Vedic gods were retained by the Hindus, and sacrificial services to them, both domestic and public, were numerous. In all the Vedic hymns there is a pure worship of several gods — worship of nature and the spirit of nature. They are also highly ethical and personal. In the course of time this simple religion, influenced doubtless by the aboriginal tribes, who were by no means savages, degenerated into idolatry, and a religion of rites and ceremonies divorced from ethics. At the same time there gradually emerged among the more intelligent, the idea of the supreme god Brahma, who was universal, not merely national. In

[1] Translated by the late Dr. Muir.

connection with this theological conception arose a mystic philosophy; but philosophy and religion had in India their history and development as well as elsewhere, which here we cannot attempt to follow.

After a certain date, however, we find that through the whole system of thought there runs one general governing idea as the reflection of the mind of the race. Except in so far as it is atheistic, that idea is pantheistic — forms of belief which tend to the same ethical results. The practical effects of the pantheistic temperament are conspicuous; for the highest moral aim of the Hindu is not self-sacrifice in the sense of the sacrifice of all desires to the duties of this life, which is the true Christian idea, but it is rather the abnegation of life itself with a view to the absorption of the individual into the ' All.' The dominating idea in the conception of God is that of Absolute Being; inmost essence of all things. Being is quiescent: it is the negation of activity. The personal immortality of some of the Vedic hymns ceased under the influence of this mystic theology to be an operative faith. Transmigration was only a step in the process of absorption. It is manifest that the idea of perfect repose, a repose amounting to the death of personality, could not but largely influence daily conduct. Before the All-One, the particular and the individual are in truth of no moment, mere passing shows, and all that fills the senses is essentially illusory (Maya). What a contrast to the Hebrews! Such an idea, if rooted in the nature of a people, is an effective check to all self-reliant activity, weakens all sense of individual responsibility, and destroys what may be called the ambition of excellence. Even the daily duties of life are not done as the act of a free individual, seeking thereby the good of others and the growth of himself in virtue; and moral conduct, though it may be in itself unexceptionable, finds itself placed on the same level as sacerdotal prescriptions and sacrificial acts. Withdrawal from life and an ascetic contemplation become the supreme virtues. The idea of fatalism, also, though it may not find formal expression, inevitably

underlies the lives of men whose abstract conceptions of the
end of life are such as we have indicated. Wuttke very well
says that people of a strong personality pray, ' Thy kingdom
come; ' the Chinese pray, ' May thy kingdom remain; ' the
Hindus, ' May that which thou has created perish : ' that is
to say, ' May all existence be swallowed up in Being.'

It may be said that the above is, strictly speaking, the
Buddhistic conception ; but in truth the highest form of
Brahmanism which contemplates ultimate absorption in
Brahma has the same essential characteristics as Buddhism.
The latter was in antagonism to the former, inasmuch as it
preached salvation through the efforts of the individual soul
after perfection in Nirvana, the futility of prayers and sacrifices and ceremonials, and ignored the divisions of caste.
But it was itself a Brahmanical development ; ethical and
universal instead of national, doctrinal, and ceremonial. The
Buddhistic return of the imperfect soul to other visible forms
was similar to the Brahmanical transmigration, though not
identical with it. The goal of Brahmanism again was a
union with Absolute Being not to be distinguished from
absorption, while the goal of Buddhism was the extinction of
the empirical self or individual,[1] and a state of Nirvana from
which non-existence is not to be distinguished, because individuality is gone. Nothing, in fact, is left but an atom of
soul-stuff; at best, the continuity of the evolution of ' Truth '
towards which as a cosmic process the soul which has
attained Nirvana may be said in some way to contribute.
At the same time the increasing mass of followers could not
do without a god and Buddha became exalted to that position and the usual degradation of religion followed.

The educational significance of the mystic doctrine of the
highest state of the man-spirit on this earth and its ultimate
goal hereafter, lies not so much in the effect such a system
of thought would have on the Hindus, but in the fact that it

---

[1] I say ' empirical self' because Gautama seems to me never to have
properly distinguished between the empirical self of individuality and the
self-conscious ego of personality.

was a natural and full expression of the genuine Hindu mind which was at once religious, dreamy, and metaphysical. Not only the Brahman and Gautama-Buddha, but the rationalist philosopher Kapila, were all equally impressed with the nothingness of the world of sense and the misery of human life; and all alike contemplated escape from the conditions of earthly existence. With the two latter there was no God; and this gave the Brahman his advantage when Buddhism had to be fought and crushed. At the same time the epics show that the Hindu mind was not insensible to the charm of nature and life; but this in a passive way. Natural forms filled them with wonder and yielded a mass of legendary fable. And yet, as Duncker says, nature was essentially a ' magical illusion.' The general sentiment of the thoughtful Hindu, irrespective of sect and party, may perhaps be fairly summed up in the following verses:

THE PRIEST OF BRAHMA TO HIS DYING DISCIPLE

' Boy ! to fear death which only means
That body and soul, twin life in bonds,
Part and go forth their several ways ! '

' But I no longer am ; my individual self dissolved.'

' That may be so : and yet, if so it be,
What then ?   Thy soul goes gladly forth
To mix with God, sole Being, and live in Him,
Yielding its tribute to Universal Mind —
A spirit atom in the Eternal One —
Serving the more (high destiny !) to swell
The bliss of Being, which alone can be.'

' This pleasing body to the grave so grim ? '
' Not so.   Say rather to the arms, the kindly arms
Of gracious mother earth from whence it sprang,
Who turns it quick into her vital sap
That it may pass into a million forms

Of unreality that mock the sense,
Yet constitute the beauty of this world ;
No longer but a part, as now ; but interfused,
And dwelling in the life of grass and trees,
Made glorious in the budding flowers of spring,
Melting into the green of tidal caves,
Rolling in thunder and the ocean storm,
Gracious and tender in the light of eve,
And splendid in the rise and set of suns.

For soul and body such the rapturous end.'

It is worthy of note that the Hindu religion was not in its essence and Vedic origin a religion of externalism. It was the inner life of the soul that was of moment, and when this was lost sight of, Buddhism arose as a Brahmanical sect. It was because sacrifice, ceremonial, and penance began at a certain period to supersede the intellectual and ethical elements of Brahmanism that reform was inevitable.

Into the popular form of Brahmanism, both prior and subsequently to Buddhism, all sorts of corruptions entered. Superstitions and idolatries always abounded, and numerous sects arose. The uneducated mind must always have gods that are accessible, and pantheism can yield thousands of these. New gods, moreover, were authoritatively recognised from time to time to meet the wants of the people. The post-Buddhistic doctrine of a 'Trinity' of gods (as it is incorrectly called) who were emanations of Absolute Being had no national and popular influence in pre-christian times.

Concurrently with this popular degradation of religion the abstract and metaphysical development went on in the hands of the intellectual few. And, in addition to a metaphysical religion, with its hymns and prayers, active philosophical schools, and a school of singularly acute grammarians, we also find a literature in the modern sense. The tales of heroes, which were traditional, reach a literary consummation in the great epics — the Ramayana, which presents in a continuous story a high type of human life ;

and the Mahabharata, which has been called an 'encyclopædia of tradition,' and is of great length.[1]   These epics are the highest literary expression of the Hindu mind and have exercised a great influence on the life of the people.   They have reference to an early state of society; but they took their present form only about 200 B.C.   These epics (probably to meet the Buddhistic heresy) teach transitory incarnations of the Divine Being.

The ethical virtues of a race whose deepest convictions were pantheistic and whose highest hope was personal absorption in the Universal, were, as we might expect, temperance, peaceableness, patience, docility, gentleness, and resignation.   These virtues are naturally accompanied by politeness, respect for parents and elders, and obedience to the civil and ecclesiastical powers.   But duty in our commanding sense of the word, and the virtues flowing from a strong personality that controls circumstances and shapes the life of each man, were not to be expected.   Contrast the Hindu conception and its effects on national character with the Medo-Persian: the former stands as far above the latter in metaphysical profundity as the latter over the former in its ethical simplicity and truth and in its virile acceptance of life and its duties as a privilege.   And yet both alike are developments of the same Aryan primitive religious conceptions.

EDUCATION AMONG THE HINDUS

Aim, organisation and materials of education. — The end of the higher education is thus expressed in Manu's 'Book of Laws': 'To learn and to understand the Vedas, to practise pious mortifications, to acquire divine knowledge of the law and of philosophy, to treat with veneration his natural and his spiritual father [*i.e.* the priest] these are the chief duties by means of which endless felicity is attained.'   And endless felicity is absorption.

The brief summary we have given of the Hindu philosophy

---

[1] Seven times the length of the combined *Iliad* and *Odyssey*.   See Monier Williams's *Indian Wisdom* for an account of these poems.

of life would have led us to expect such words as these.[1] We may with advantage here contrast the Chinese and Hindu educational end. ' The Chinese,' says Wuttke, ' educate for practical life, the Indians for the ideal : those for earth, these for heaven [individual blessedness or absorption] ; those educate their sons for entering the world, these for going out of it. Those educate for citizenship, these for the priesthood [*i.e.* as the ideal of life]. Those for industrial activity, these for knowledge. Those teach their sons the laws of the state, these teach them the essence of the godhead. Those lead their sons into the world, these lead them out of the world into themselves. Those teach their children to earn and to enjoy, these to beg and to renunciate.' This may be a strong way of stating the case, but it has in it a large element of truth. The writer has, however, omitted to note the prominence given to certain kinds of virtue, and to social obligations generally, in the ancient tradition of the Hindus and the code of Manu. The ethical teaching of the Vedic hymns was as pure, though by no means so exalted, as that of the Jewish prophets. Although not enforced by a like definite divine sanction, yet, on the other hand, there was perhaps greater inner moral freedom in the Vedic system in its purity than in the Jewish, and less of mere externalism, until the development into Brahmanism. It taught a doctrine of personal immortality. Morality and religion were closely connected, and the doctrine of transmigration had not yet been thought of. In this respect, as in his more profound philosophy, the Hindu vindicated his Aryan ancestry. This is substantially true, spite of the multitude of ceremonial acts which the Brahman ultimately imposed on the people, the reaction against which so powerfully aided the new teaching of Buddha in the fifth century B.C.

Only the other day we found in a philosophical treatise an

---

[1] I use the past tense in speaking of India ; until it was modified by the British power, native education seemed to remain essentially unchanged in its main characteristics till this century. It has to be noted that the Mohammedans who preceded the British in India have their own schools and colleges.

interesting evidence of the persistent continuity of the Hindu point of view,[1] spite of European influences. ' The knowledge of the supreme soul is the ultimate aim of science. The supreme soul is one Infinite Lord of All, and is the dispenser of reward and retribution.' The ethical conception finds expression thus : ' Right knowledge is calculated to give an insight into the motives of human conduct, teach the exercise of sound discretion in all matters, and lead to the attainment of final beatitude.'

If we may trust Dutt's ' Civilisation in Ancient India,' there early arose (probably 1,000 years B.C.) Brahmanic settlements called Parishads, which approximated closely to what we should call collegiate institutions of learning. These Parishads were in later times understood to consist of twenty-one Brahmans well-versed in philosophy, theology, and law ; but, in their beginnings, three able Brahmans in a village, learned in the Vedas and competent to maintain the sacrificial fire, constituted a Parishad. (Dutt, i. 249.) To these centres men who wished to devote their lives to learning and who belonged to the caste might go and receive instruction in the Vedas, and in such traditionary law and astronomy and philosophy as was current. Private schools also existed, conducted by scholarly men at their own venture, and to these many boys were sent for training, giving personal and menial service in return for instruction. These boys did not necessarily belong to the Brahmanical caste.

Prior to the above rudimentary form of educational organisation it would appear that at the period of transition from the Vedic to the Brahmanic stage of religious development (say about 1200 B.C.), the courts of the kings were the centres of such culture as existed. Priests, of course, were attached to these courts, and in connection with them there grew up what may be called ' schools ' for the study and handing down of the sacred hymns and sacrificial practices.

---

[1] *Kalyana Majusha, or the Casket of Blessings,* an exposition of the principles of Hindu logic, by B. Swami (Calcutta, 1893).

Megasthenes, the Greek, who lived in North India three centuries before the Christian era, and indeed all the Greeks, spoke of the Brahmanical priests as the 'caste of philosophers;' and with truth, for metaphysics played as large a part in the forming of the Hindu religion as the Vedic hymns did. We are not, consequently, to look on the Brahmans as if they were, in the narrow sense, a priestly order. They were a caste, and men of Brahmanical descent constituted the aristocracy of India — an aristocracy with which learning and character were closely associated. The Chinese aristocracy, after the abolition of feudalism, was, as we found, not only associated with, but founded on, intellect, and renewed itself in every successive generation. This large Brahmanical body was, on the contrary, hereditary, but the members of it always received the highest education which India could afford. Among them were the recognised chiefs of all learning as well as òf religion, and they discharged many important functions in the State. In every Brahmanic family it still is, we are told, the custom to study and learn by heart a particular Veda. Those who desired to prosecute the higher studies were attached to particular Brahmans who devoted themselves to the work of instruction. A thoroughly equipped Brahman was understood to acquire by heart all the sacred books mentioned a few pages back. And when we consider that the Brahmanic colleges taught all the astronomy and mathematics known, and frequently carried their pupils into the elaborate linguistic treatise of Panini, we must recognise in the substance of the highest Hindu education a fully adequate course of liberal study, embracing as it did theology, philosophy, language, and science, while including the whole of the national literature as that gradually took shape.[1]

I think it desirable to emphasise the fact that while the memorial acquisition of the sacred writings, and this with scrupulous fidelity, was the chief object of Brahmanical

---

[1] The Brahmanical schools existing from the earliest times developed into important colleges, such as that at Benares.

instruction, the minds of the young Brahmans were brought into contact with philosophical systems and the general literature of the country. In such a course of study there was both discipline and culture. A similar system of instruction we found in China, but with this difference, that the young Chinese had the printed book to help them. The distinction between the education of the Chinese and the Hindus lies in the matter of their sacred works, their philosophical and literary tradition, and the prescribed goal of their studies.

We are told[1] that there was a scheme of life laid down for the higher castes which involved continuous study, and was divided into four stages, viz. studentship, married life, retirement, and forest life. But it is impossible that the scheme could be carried out by any save the very devoted Brahman. It is chiefly to the concluding period that the words in the Manu Code apply, ' Let him not desire to die; Let him not desire to live; let him wait for his time, as a servant for the payment of his wages.'

As to the rest of the nation, it would seem certain that the teaching and schools of the Brahmans were not only open to the caste of warriors and the industrial caste, but that they were expected to take advantage of them. There was no esoteric doctrine. The only exclusive privilege of the Brahmans was, not doctrine but, the functions of priest and teacher. Advantage was taken by many in the two castes next in order of this freedom to learn. The warriors, moreover, had a course of discipline in martial exercises.

Of the industrial caste, while some of these studied portions of the ancient books, we do not find that as a class they had any special instruction in reading, writing, and arithmetic. Boys followed the occupations of their parents, and received domestic training in these. Megasthenes, the Greek, speaks about 300 B.C. of the absence of the art of writing among the Indians. The art of writing certainly existed long before the time of Alexander's raid into India, but the

[1] Max Müller, *Lectures on the Origin of Religion*, p. 343.

habit of relying on oral teaching and memory was inveterate, and the writing down of traditionary literature was even looked upon with some suspicion.[1] In the transactions of ordinary life, as well as in learning, there can be no doubt that great reliance was placed on the memory. The remark of Megasthenes, however, puts it beyond doubt that among the population generally, writing was little known.

I can find no evidence of arithmetic being taught to the industrial class, but we have to remember that the very elementary arithmetic required in each occupation would be acquired under his master as part of the apprentice work of every boy.

The lowest caste did the menial work of the nation, and learned nothing.

Speaking generally, then, we may say that for 1,000 years B.C. the Brahmanical education was extensive and thorough, and that it was shared in to a certain extent by a considerable number in the second and third castes. It was, however, entirely oral in the earlier centuries; but later, it embraced reading and writing, and an introduction to the epic literature as well as to the sacred books: probably also to mathematics.[2]

Apart from such literary and religious education as the more ambitious might gain for themselves by the help of the Brahmanic teachers, the members of the second and third castes received their education from the laws, tradition, and customs of their country as handed down through the family. It seems to me, however, that it was to the village commune, so universal a feature of Indian social organisation, that the young chiefly owed the education which is elsewhere chiefly

---

[1] Virgil (*Æn.* vi. 74) expresses well this objection to the written word common to all the Oriental races :

'Foliis tantum ne carmina manda,
Ne turbata volent rapidis ludibria ventis :
Ipsa canas, oro.'

[2] I think that to say more than this is to infer more than the actual facts justify.

given by family tradition. These communes have always exercised a potent influence: and I am the more disposed to substitute the commune for the family as the vehicle and organ of the education of tradition, because of the position of woman among the Hindus, of which I shall shortly speak. But what was the nature of this traditionary oral village teaching? Apart from religious and ceremonial acts and the settlement of questions moral and legal arising among themselves, we may safely say that the teaching was of a kind that naturally would find acceptance among a religious, contemplative, and ethically disposed people — the teaching of fables, allegories, and parables. These fireside tales seem to have been numerous. And that this must have been so we find from two works published in post-christian times which contain popular stories embodying the moral faith of the people. Their oldest collection of fables and proverbs is called the 'Pantschatantra;' it dates from the fifth century after Christ, and was translated in the sixth century into Persian under the name of 'The Friend of Knowledge;' then from Persian into the Arabic, from the Arabic into the Greek, Turkish, Syrian, Hebrew, Spanish, Italian, English, French, and German. In that book we find such utterances as the following; and when we consider that the book is full of fable and allegory, and consider further its poetic feeling, we become alive to the spirit that animates Hindu life and education among the masses of the people.

'As the tree shades the man who is about to cut it down, and as the moon shines in the hut even of the lowliest Chandala, so must a man love those who hate him.'

'Be humble, for the tender grass bows itself unhurt before the storm, while mighty trees are shattered to pieces by it.'

'Virtue, after which man ought to strive, needs a mighty effort, for a cocoanut falls not through the shaking of a crow.'

'A knowledge of arms and of learning are both equally very famous, but the first is in an old man folly, the second is worthy of honour at every period of life.'

'A man without knowledge, though he possess youth and

beauty and high birth, does not excel, like the odourless Kinchuka flower.'

'Education is higher than beauty and concealed treasures. It accompanies us on our journey through strange places and gives us inexhaustible strength.'

'The wise man must strive to gain knowledge and wealth as if he were not subject to death, but the duties of religion he must fulfil as if death were hovering already on his lips.'

'Like as figures on a new vase are not easily washed out, so is it with wisdom of youth, through the charm of fable.'

Such are some of the sentiments on which the Indian youth was reared — all conveyed through a mass of fable and allegory. The Hitopadeça is a subsequent collection (see Fritze's German translation) of a similar kind. What a contrast they present to the popular literary inheritance of the Egyptians and Chinese![1]

Woman

The position of the woman among the Hindus was always that of subordination and subjection to the man. The estimate of female character and possibilities was low. 'A female child, a young girl, a wife, shall never do anything according to their own will, not even in their own house. While a child she shall depend on her father; during her youth on her husband; and, when a widow, on her sons.' (Manu, v. 147.) Women were regarded as essentially inferior to man, and having for the sole purpose of their existence the bearing of children and the tending of the husband. As might be expected from this view of the place of woman, she was excluded from all instruction. So strong, indeed, was the prejudice against the education of women, that the power to read and write was regarded as a reproach to them. The only exception was in the case of the dancing girls — these being daughters of various castes devoted, when yet children,

[1] I see just advertised (1895) a series of translations of Hindu tales which formed part, and probably a large part, of the educational material of the people.

to the services of the temple. As servants of the temple and 'maidens of the god,' the dancing girls had to cultivate their intelligence; mothers of households, on the contrary, their heart only, lest they should be drawn away by intellectual cultivation from domestic duties. The female servants of the temple were instructed in reading, writing, music, dancing, and singing. Their duties were to sing the praises of the god they served, and to dance on festive occasions. They were divided into two classes — the better class being confined within the temple, and restricted to temple services; the second and lower class being allowed greater freedom, and permission to perform at marriage festivities and the banquets of the nobility.

It is because of the position occupied by women that I have assigned more influence to the commune than to the family in the education of the young Hindu. It has to be noted, however, that in early Vedic times, the authorship of hymns and songs was ascribed to women, as in the case of the Israelites.

Method and Discipline. Teachers. — We are told that the teacher must himself have passed through the recognised curriculum, and have fulfilled all the duties of a Brahmanical student (*brahmâkarin*) before he is allowed to become a teacher, and he must teach such students only as submit to all requirements imposed by usage. The method of instruction was, as I have said, oral tradition, and the memory was consequently called upon to bear a burden which to a European would be intolerable. The rote character of the teaching began from the beginning; for the boy learned the alphabet by heart and some ten or twenty pages of Sanskrit before he could understand a word. Thereafter, explanation came (more or less); but the main object was to learn the sacred books accurately by heart, not from a printed page but from the mouth of a teacher. The following is from Max Müller's 'Lectures on the Origin of Religion,' p. 159, and are the directions given in an authoritative Sanskrit book. The teacher, we are told, should settle down in a proper place. If he has only one pupil or two, they should sit on his right side : if more, they must sit as there is room for them. At the beginning of each lecture the pupils embrace the feet of their teacher and say : 'Read, sir.' The teacher answers : '*Om*' (yes), and then pronounces two words, or, if it is a compound, one. When the teacher has pronounced one word or two, the first pupil repeats the first word, but if there is anything that requires explanation the pupil says 'Sir'; and after it has been explained to him '*Om* (yes), sir.'

'In this manner they go on till they have finished a *prasna* (question), which consists of three verses, or, if they are verses of more than forty to forty-two syllables, of two verses. If they are pankti-verses of forty to forty-two syllables each, a *prasna* may comprise either two or three; and if a hymn consists of one verse only, that is supposed to form a *prasna*. After the *prasna* is finished they have all to repeat it once more and then to go on learning it by heart, pronouncing every syllable with the high accent. After the teacher has first told a *prasna* to his pupil on the right, the others go round him to the right and this goes on till the whole lecture is finished; a lecture consisting generally of sixty (?) *prasnas*. At the end of the last half verse the teacher says " Sir," and the pupil replies " *Om* (yes), sir," repeating also the verses required at the end of a lecture. The pupils then embrace the feet of their teacher and are dismissed.'

' Only those, it is said, whose heart and speech are ever pure and attentive, can enjoy the full fruit of the study of the Vedas : ' and it was considered a great offence to study them without an authorised instructor. We thus see that before the introduction of writing, and for centuries after, the pupil learned by rote from the recitation of the master, a laborious and prolonged process. And when they had MSS. they were read aloud until they were known by heart, without being necessarily understood. Thus, the receiving of tradition from the lips of a master was necessarily the form of all teaching, and the attitude of the learner was servile acceptance. This notion of instruction both as regards method and the relation of pupil to teacher was, as I have frequently said, characteristic of the Oriental generally, and still is so, spite of printing and books.

The discipline among the Hindus generally seems to have been gentle, and only in the extremest cases was there any severity. Manu says : 'Good instruction must be given to pupils without unpleasant sensations, and the teacher who reverences virtue must use sweet and gentle words. If a scholar is guilty of a fault, his instructor may punish him with severe words, and threaten that on the next offence he will give him blows ; and, if the fault is committed in cold weather, the teacher may dowse him with cold water.'

The elementary schools (adventure schools) of post-christian times, were, like many in ancient Greece and Italy, held in the open air, the pupils sitting round the teacher under trees in front of a house ; and when the weather was bad, in a covered shed. In arithmetic, only the merest elements were taught. Writing, with which instruction in reading was closely connected, was first practised in the sand, then with an iron style on palm leaves ; and finally on plane-tree leaves with a kind of ink. But all this elementary education (as far as I can ascertain) belongs to the period after the birth of Christ. In the school, it was a common practice for a more advanced pupil to point out the letters to a beginner. They also heard each other their lessons. It was thus largely a system of mutual instruction. Dr. Bell took his monitorial system from what he saw at Madras.

Note.— The education of India by Great Britain can of course teach us little which is not better taught by the system of instruction in our own country. It is simply a attempt to plant British education in a foreign soil. It is an exotic. The native dialects are taught and natives largely employed. This British system is based on a despatch of Sir Charles Wood, dated July 19, 1854. The main principle of the despatch was that European knowledge should be diffused through the languages understood by the great mass of the people, but that the teaching of English should always be combined with careful attention to the study of the vernacular languages. With regard to the wealthier classes, it was declared that the time had arrived for the establishment of universities in India, conferring degrees, and based on the model of the University of London. They were not to be places of education, but to test the value of education obtained elsewhere, and to confer degrees in arts, law, medicine, and civil engineering. Such universities have accordingly been established in Calcutta, Madras, and Bombay ; and since 1859 Government schools have been opened for the instruction of all classes of the Indian people. In each Presidency there is now a director of public instruction, assisted by school inspectors, one of whom has under his care one circle or subdivision of the province. There are also colleges (both government and missionary) which prepare for the university examinations. Normal schools for the training of teachers have also been established, and attempts are being made to spread female education.

It is stated in Chambers' ' Cyclopædia ' (1892) that there are now in all 134,000 educational institutions of one kind or another in India.

Authorities : In addition to encyclopædias and references to various authors, I have relied largely on Dutt's *History of Civilisation in Ancient India ;* Hegel's *Philosophy of History;* Duncker's *History of Antiquity ;* Monier Williams's *Indian Wisdom;* Max Müller, *On the Origin of Religion,* and references to his other writings ; Tiele's *Outlines of Ancient Religions ; The Gospel of Buddha,* by Paul Carus ; *References to the writings of Rhys Davids.*

(B) THE MEDO-PERSIANS

IN dealing with ancient Persia, we have to include as part of the same nationality — Media to the north-west and Bactria to the north-east of Persia proper or Iran, both of which after a period of independence formed part of the Persian empire. As the word Iran denotes, the race was Aryan; and indeed it is this fact which gives the Medo-Persians special interest to us.[1] They are called Eranians to distinguish them from the Hindu branch of the primitive Aryans.

Speaking without minute regard to geographical limits, this branch of the Aryan race occupied the country lying between the Caspian Sea on the north and the Persian Gulf on the south, and they were bounded on the east and south-east by modern Afghanistan and Beloochistan, while on the west the mountain range of Zagros separated them from the Mesopotamian valley within which the Babylonian and Assyrian empires had their seats. The country is a table-land intersected with beautiful and rich valleys. Where it descends to the sea on the south it is desert; on the north, where it descends towards the Caspian, it is moist and warm and abounding in vegetation. Rich and various as are the products of much of Medo-Persia, a great part of it is barren. Its rivers are rapid and many of them pour down a great volume of water, but scarcely one can be said to be navigable. Physically, then, we find here a home for a race in which there are necessarily — owing to the existence of a high table-land and numerous deep valleys and the decline towards seas on the north and south — much variety of climate, production, and scenery, and at the same

---

[1] Media was the leading power up to 558 B.C., when it was conquered by Persia, of which it long remained the most important province.

time not of so large an area as to exclude any portion of the inhabitants from the various influences of the whole and from that sense of unity which is essential to all successful polities.

If the physical characteristics of a home can influence the character of a people we may safely say that irregularity of surface and climatic variation will have a potent effect. In a country, too, much of which called on man for a struggle with nature — a struggle, however, by no means hopeless — the seeds of an originally vigorous and vivacious character would be nurtured. Nature was not so large and oppressive as in India where man lived in a moist, torrid, and relaxing climate, and was overpowered by the mass and prodigality of natural forms. Although the physical circumstances of a nation are powerless to *make* it, they must largely modify its natural racial predisposition, while they profoundly influence the character of its industrial activities and much of its political history.

But it is the *breed* of men which occupies any portion of the earth's surface that determines the historical drama which is to be there enacted far more, probably, than any other fact. The Medo-Persians belonged to our own blood : that is to say, they were Aryans, and gave this name to what are otherwise called the ' Indo-European ' races. On the north-west the Medes, and on the north-east their fellow-Aryans of Bactria constituted, with the Persai of the table-land and the rich valleys, the Persian [1] people ethnologically : these three must be regarded as racially one ; but all were mixed with prior Turanian or Uro-Altaic tribes.[2]

' The first great wave of Aryan emigration,' says Professor Sayce,[3] ' which had resulted in the establishment of the European nations, had been followed by another wave which first carried the Hindus into the Punjab, and then the

---

[1] I use the word Persian to include all these.

[2] To what extent the Aryan element had overpowered the Uro-Altaic element in Media is as yet uncertain.

[3] *Ancient Empires of the East.*

Iranian populations into the vast districts of Bactria and
Ariana. Mountains and deserts checked for a time their
further 'progress, but at length a number of tribes, each under
its own chiefs, crept along the southern shores of the Caspian
to the northern coast of the Persian Gulf, and these tribes
were known in later history as the Aryan Medes and
Persians.'

The Persai spoke an Aryan tongue — called Zend, philo-
logically connected with the tongues of Europe. The sacred
writings were in this tongue and are known as the Zend-
Avesta. What remains of these is only part of a large body
of sacred literature. When the Persian empire, as distinct
from the kingdom of Persia, rose into power, on the ruins of
the Assyrian empire in the sixth century B.C., the pure
original language was already greatly modified.[1]

The accounts of the rise of the Persian empire are very
difficult to understand, especially since the discovery of the
inscription by Cyrus, the founder. It would appear, however, that Persia had been gradually consolidating itself while
yet under the suzerainty of Media, and that a portion of
Elam on the west, called Anshan, had been incorporated with
Persia. When Cyrus arose, and as king of Elam, but himself of Persian descent, conquered Media, he with singular
rapidity reduced not only Media but Bactria, and also the
ancient seats of the Assyrian and Babylonian empires. He
then carried his conquests to the west of Asia Minor, and
even to the Scythian country of the Oxus where, it is said,
he met his death.[2]

---

[1] A further stage of degeneration dated from the conquest of Alexander
the Great in 331 B.C. onwards ; and now we have modern Persian so powerfully influenced by the Mohammedan conquest in 651 A.D. as to consist largely
— to the extent, it is said, of nearly one-half — of Arabic vocables. We have
to do only with ancient Persia.

[2] The rapid rise of the Medo-Persian empire is one of the most remarkable
facts in Oriental history. But it can be partially understood if we bear in
mind that the Medes had been long growing into a commanding position as
a military power. They had united with the Babylonians to overthrow
Nineveh and break the Assyrian power for ever. Meanwhile they had been

During the absence of Cambyses confirming his father's conquests, the non-Aryan element in Media rebelled. After the suicide (?) of the king in Egypt, Darius Hystaspes and the leading Aryan nobles extinguished the revolt, re-established the reformed Aryan religion — Mazdeism or Zoroastrianism, B.C. 521, and rebuilt the temples of Ormazd. After putting down numerous revolts of the people that had been conquered by Cyrus, Darius was able to establish the headquarters of his empire at Susa and to organise it. Meanwhile the extension of the empire went on rapidly till it touched the Punjab on the east and Macedonia on the west. At the latter point and on the shores of Asia Minor, the Persian and Greek met in conflict with ultimate results known to all. The empire, however, sustained itself in full vigour till its subjugation by Alexander in 331 B.C. It was a despotism governed by means of satraps ; but local autonomy was everywhere conceded — the satraps merely *representing* the Great King, and having a military colleague and a council with an army. Centralisation of government was an almost unmixed blessing in those times, because it was only under one supreme sovereign that nations could live in peace and civilisation advance. So regarded, the Medo-Persian empire was a boon to the nations from the Mediterranean to Afghanistan, and from the Oxus to the Persian Gulf, and an important factor in the general history of the world. It was an immense advance as a humane and moralising agency on the barbarous empire of the Assyrians.

One of the most suggestive indications of the Persian natural disposition was to be found in that characteristic of their imperial administration to which I have adverted above — the recognition of local autonomy. They did not

extending their own influence to the west, and were virtually masters of the country as far as Asia Minor. Then Nebuchadnezzar had revived the ancient Babylonian greatness, and had subdued the south and west as far as Egypt and the Mediterranean. Accordingly, when Cyrus, at the head of the Elamites and Persians, came on the field, the subduing of Media and Babylon carried with it, as a consequence, a large empire already reduced to subjection.

impose themselves unduly on subject nations. They organised a fixed tribute, and forbore to make arbitrary exactions. They had great toleration of foreign customs and of other religious systems than their own. This characteristic of the Persian imperial sway is worthy of notice as contributing to a true estimate of the character of the governing race. In repressing rebellions they were severe, but not so in other circumstances.

Among themselves there were seven tribal princes under the king, and next to them seven supreme judges and a large staff of officials. The government was essentially bureaucratic, and all were subject to the despotic authority of the Great King.[1]

Social and Civil Relations. — Passing from the political to the social system, note first that here in Persia caste, if we except the hereditary Magian priesthood, was not recognised as it was among the fellow-Aryans of India. All may move freely, and, subject always to the absolute authority of the Great King, work out their own lives. The policy of the king was, it is said, to gather the great nobles round his court and to reward generously all who did service to the State. Every one, even the meanest, was kept conscious of the national unity and felt himself to have a share in the national activity. This community of feeling was strong; for example, in their prayers when offering sacrifices the Persian asked blessings on the Persian people generally, and on himself only as included in the nation. The Persians were, as compared with other Oriental races, virtually a free people, though under a despotic form of government.[2]

---

[1] I rely (not wholly, but largely) on the Greek writers, because there are no other sources. Have not some contemporary Orientalists occasionally shown a want of discriminating judgment in discrediting the Greeks?

[2] Doubtless Herodotus is not always to be trusted, but his description of the Persians seems to me, with all due respect to Professor Sayce, to ring true. We may discredit his history of Persia without doubting the impression the people and their customs made on him, even although he never reached as far as the Persian capital.

Persian Character. — The disposition of the Persian was towards equity, mercifulness of administration, and mildness of character. 'The king,' says Herodotus, 'shall not put anyone to death for a single fault; and none of the Persians shall visit a single fault in a slave with any extreme penalty; but in every case the services of the offender shall be set against his misdoings, and if the latter be found to outweigh the former, the aggrieved party shall then proceed to punishment.' They were also a kindly and domestic people. Children had to yield absolute obedience to their parents, just as citizens had to their rulers, it is true; but so convinced were they of the sacredness of the family tie as founded in love and reverence that they maintained 'that never yet did anyone kill his father or his mother, but in all such cases they are quite sure that, if matters were sifted to the bottom, it would be found that the child was either a changeling or else the fruit of adultery, for it is not likely, they say, that the real father should perish by the hands of the child.' (Herod.) We see here a strong family feeling resting on humane conceptions.

Further, when we contemplate the Persian at his best (including, as we here may, under that designation, the Medes and Bactrians), we cannot but be impressed with a certain freshness and nobility of mind among them. A high spirit and a pleasant and affable temper are conspicuous: in these respects they form a marked contrast to the Egyptian, Semitic, and Chinese races, and even to their cognates the Hindus. We seem suddenly, at a point not more than a few hundred miles west from the basin of the Indus, and as we reach the bracing table-land, to encounter a new phase of humanity altogether — surpassingly interesting to us because we recognise in it a distinctive European type. The air we breathe is no longer stagnant as in China, no longer heavy with moisture and warmth as in India, nor so dry, stimulating, and exciting as among the Semitic races, but breezy and healthful. We already feel half way to Greece; for along with their greater freshness of mind, nobility of nature, and equity

of disposition, we find in the Persian a friendliness and a
Hellenic grace of courtesy which charm us, and of which
Herodotus thus speaks: 'When they meet each other in the
streets, you may know if the persons meeting are of equal
rank by the following token. If they are of equal rank, then,
instead of speaking, they kiss each other on the lips. In the
case where one is inferior to the other, the kiss is given on
the cheek; where the difference of rank is great, the inferior
prostrates himself on the ground.' A mark of their openness
of mind is to be found in the readiness with which they
accepted foreign customs. 'There is no nation which so
readily adopts foreign customs. Thus they have taken the
dress of the Medes, considering it superior to their own, and
in war they wear the Egyptian breastplate. As soon as they
hear of any luxury they immediately make it their own.'
'Of the family of mankind,' says a historian,[1] 'which claimed,
not unjustly, the distinctive name of "noble" (Arya),[2] the
Persians formed one of the finest types. When we first meet
with them in history they are a race of hardy mountaineers,
brave in war, rude in manners, simple in their habits, abstain-
ing from wine, and despising all the luxuries of food and
dress. Though uncultivated in art and science, they, at a
more advanced period of their national life, were distinguished
for an intellectual ability, a lively wit, a generous, passionate,
and poetical temperament — qualities, however, which easily
degenerated into vanity and want of perseverance. Their
military spirit was kept in full vigour by their hardy mountain life, their simple and temperate habits, and the strict
discipline in which they were trained from their youth up.'
'In the reign of Cyrus,' says Plato ('Laws,' iii. 694) 'the
Persians were freemen and also lords of many others: the
rulers gave a share of freedom to the subjects, and being
treated as equals, the soldiers were on better terms with their
generals, and showed themselves more ready in the hour of

---

[1] Philip Smith in his *History of the Ancient World.*

[2] Derived from the ancient name of the territory Ariana. I am not aware
that nobility has anything to do with it.

danger. And if there was any wise counsellor among them, he imparted his wisdom to the public, for the king was not jealous, but allowed him full liberty of speech, and gave honour to those who were able to be his counsellors in anything, and allowed all men equally to participate in wisdom. And the nation waxed in all respects because there was freedom, and friendship, and communion of soul among them.' (Jowett's trans.)

Religion and Ethics. — The religion of the Persians when they first appear in history in connection with the conquests of Cyrus probably differed little from the Vedic form of Hinduism. The elements were worshipped as spirits. The specific North Aryan development which is called Mazdeism or Zoroastrianism came from Media, according to Darmesteter (more probably Bactria, according to Ticle) and was in the hands of a sacerdotal tribe called the Magi. The conquest of Media led to the adoption of Mazdeism by the ruling family or families in Persia. It may be said with truth that the mass of the people never rose to a conception of the principles of Mazdeism — at least during the period which concerns us here. On the other hand, it was practically the belief of the leading families, and through these it influenced the people and determined the general current of religious faith among them. In autocratic societies the belief of the few dominates the mass much more than in countries possessing what we call a free constitution. We are entitled accordingly to speak of Mazdeism as a powerful educative force among the Medo-Persians long before 521 B.C. down to the fall of the Persian empire in 333 B.C., and as exhibiting the mental tendency of the Persian race.

The fundamental idea of the national and State religion of Medo-Persia was that a pure One Spirit was creator and sustainer of all. We see in this a resemblance to the higher and later form of Judaism. Ahura-Mazda or Lord all-knowing (Ormazd), was the name of the Supreme God.

But even after he was recognised as supreme, much of the
Aryan belief in spirits of the elements, and in other spirits
good and evil, remained active among the people. The good
spirits were now, however, regarded as subordinate agencies
of the Supreme God: the evil spirits were the offspring of
Ahriman, the evil one. Ahriman, the source of evil, was not
self-originated, but arose out of the conflict of forces when
Ormazd created the material world out of nothing. Ormazd
is all-wise, creator of the spiritual as well as the earthly life,
the lord of the whole universe who will ultimately van-
quish the evil that is incidental. to creation. He is knowledge, and the 'One that knows,' he is 'Weal' and the
'One that is beneficent.' This lofty religious conception was
attributed to a religious reformer, Zarathustra or Zoroaster,[1]
and handed down by the hereditary priesthood or tribe called
the Magi, already referred to. Among the good spirits were
the gods of light and fire, and the latter appeared in all Maz-
dean worship both in its priestly and popular form. The
sacred writings are known as the Zend-Avesta.[2]

'The Persian religion,' says Hegel,[3] 'is the religion of
light. The source of light is not identified with nature as
one with it, but is rather regarded as that which creates
and vitalises. In its human mental relations this light is
wisdom, goodness, virtue purity, truth — in its physical
relations it is that which vitalises and makes beautiful—

---

[1] It cannot be said that the ancient hymns which survive show that
Zoroaster taught the doctrine of Ahriman as a Being, but this was the natural
outcome of his cosmic view.

[2] 'Avesta' means the law ; 'Zend,' commentary or explanation. We
ought, strictly speaking, not to talk of the Zend language, but of the Avesta
language. The Zend-Avesta — the collection of fragments which we now
have — consists of the Vendidâd, a compilation of religious laws and mythical
tales ; the Visperâd, a collection of litanies for the sacrifice ; and the Yasna,
also composed of litanies and of five hymns or Gâ (written in a special
dialect older than the general language of the Avesta). As a whole, the
Zend-Avesta bears more likeness to a prayer-book than a Bible. It is
only fragments that remain to us of the old original text and of what was
added from time to time by the Magian priesthood. (From Darmesteter in
Max Müller's series.)

[3] In his *Philosophy of History.*

physical light — the light of the sun, which is still worshipped by the Parsees — the modern representatives of the Zend religion — as the symbol of intellectual, and the source of physical, light.' Ormazd, the lord of life and light, himself emerges as pure spirit from the ' unlimited all,' and with him there is also Ahriman, the spirit (or principle) of darkness, decay, and death, spirit of evil, source of all wrong as a necessary incident of the act of creation. Ahriman is not the equal of Ormazd — only for a time does he maintain a seemingly equal warfare, to be finally subdued. Men as individuals are engaged in this warfare, and have to fight for light against darkness, good against evil, truth against falsehood, purity against impurity; but not hopelessly. Ormazd was above all. We see in this religion an expression of the highest type of Persian thought which could not fail to react on the individual life powerfully.

The doctrine of personal immortality was taught. After death the wicked fall into the underworld, there to be tormented by evil spirits, the good are received into the Abode of Song, the dwelling place of Ormazd and the saints. But a day of renovation even for the wicked will come, when, by the discipline of fire, all creatures will be refined.

It is easy to understand that even a religion as pure as this in conception might degenerate into a worship of the elements, or rather retain an ancient element worship and spirit worship as a parallel and popular system. The Magi — a powerful hereditary class, represented, as priests in those ancient nationalities necessarily did, the philosophy, science, and wisdom of their nation. Among them, as interpreters of the ancient writings, there seem to have been schools of thought — some inclining to the concrete and elemental primitive religion, as opposed to the pure and Eranian spirit-doctrine. But even among the former was an absence of all that savoured of idolatry. Herodotus, who saw and understood only the popular side of the Persian religion which contained some old Aryan elements, says : ' The customs which I know the Persians to observe are the following.

They have no image of the gods, nor temples, nor altars, and consider the use of them a sign of folly. This comes, I think, from their not believing the gods to have the same nature with men, as the Greeks imagine. Their wont, however, is to ascend the summits of the loftiest mountains, and there offer sacrifice to Jupiter, which is the name they give to the whole circuit of the firmament. To these gods the Persians offer sacrifice in the following manner. They raise no altar, light no fire, pour no libations: there is no sound of the flute, no putting on of chaplets, no consecrated barley-cake; but the man who wishes to sacrifice brings his victim to a spot of ground which is pure from pollution and there calls upon the name of the god to whom he intends to offer.[1] It is usual to have the turban encircled with a wreath, most commonly of myrtle. The sacrificer is not allowed to pray for blessings on himself alone, but he prays for the welfare of the king and of the whole Persian people, among 'whom he is of necessity included. He cuts the victim in pieces, and having boiled the flesh, he lays it out upon the tenderest herbage he can find, trefoil especially. When all is ready one of the Magi comes forward and chants a hymn, which, they say, recounts the origin of the gods. It is not lawful to offer sacrifice unless there is a Magus present. After waiting a short time, the sacrificer carries the flesh of the victim away with him, and makes whatever use of it he pleases.'[2]

[1] There was a fire, but the victims were not burned in it but before it, and afterwards eaten.

[2] At what date Zoroastrianism reached its full development is uncertain. The gradually-growing writings and traditions were formulated, though still in a rudimentary form doubtless, probably about 521 B.C. Some would assign a more modern date: on the other hand, inscriptions have come to light only two or three months ago (1895) which bear the name of Ormazd and Ahriman and must have been cut out on stone about 480 B.C. The Zoroastrian reformation of the old Aryanism must have begun about 900 B.C. (some experts say 1400 B.C.) the sacred writings gradually growing in bulk till formulated at the date just given. The Zend-Avesta, as we *now* have it, dates from about the 4th century A.D. The Medes at the time of their conquest by Cyrus seem to have followed the primitive Aryan religion, mixed with Semitic and Turanian elements, the worshippers of Ormazd being only a party in the nation.

What chiefly concerns us, as students of the education of a people, especially where we have no specific educational institutions, is to bring into view the religious idea as the ultimate expression of the national life. That a religious system such as we have briefly described affords a marked contrast to that of other nations is evident. It was supremely ethical and also free from idolatry. It gave a distinct value to the individual personality, and this, though it might be but imperfectly apprehended by the masses. Absorption or annihilation of his personality in Brahma is the last idea of perfected bliss which would have occurred to a genuine Persian! Nor would the idea of stern divine law and a rigid moral contract with God oppress. him as it did the Jew, who realised in God an infinite personality meeting his own finite personality on certain definite legal terms. On the contrary, the Persian seems to have been a happy, easy-going mortal: his birthdays were days of festivity. His life was to be a struggle to extend the kingdom of Light, but withal, a cheerful and a hopeful struggle.

The supreme virtues were — as we might expect where the personality was strong and the religion was a religion of light and truth as opposed to darkness and error — truth-speaking, and courage. Not only were they required to practise these virtues, but they were enjoined to guard their tongues. In the words of Herodotus: 'They hold it unlawful to talk of anything that it is unlawful to do. The most disgraceful thing in the world, they think, is to tell a lie; the next worst to owe a debt, because, among other reasons, the debtor is obliged to tell lies.' Personal purity and the preservation of the purity of water were also incumbent on the Persian. 'They never defile a river, nor even wash their hands in one; nor will they allow others to do so, as they have a great reverence for rivers.'

We know so little of the educational methods of the Persians that it would be unjustifiable in me to dwell so long on their national characteristics were it not that in the education of the human race generally, and as marking a step in its progress, the Persians are to be regarded as a potent factor, and were it not also that the current beliefs, religious and ethical, constituted their education.

EDUCATION OF THE ANCIENT PERSIANS

There was no educational *system* in Persia ; but after what I have said above, we can easily conceive the national result at which the education of family life and public institutions aimed. This it is easy to infer from the sketch I have given of the manners, life, and ethical religion of the people. Perhaps the following view of the life of the boy may be accepted as substantially correct.[1]

The education of a Persian was considered to begin at his fifth (some say his seventh) year and continue till his twenty-fourth. To the seventh year the child was left entirely in the hands of the women of the household. ' Up to the fifth year,' Herodotus tells us, 'they are not allowed to come into the sight of their father, but pass their lives with the women. This is done that if the child die young, the father may not be afflicted with the loss.' Of good and bad the child was not supposed to be capable of knowing anything. Obedience was his sole duty. It was considered wrong to beat a child before his seventh year. The family upbringing seems to have been genial and kindly.

From the fifth year, Herodotus says, the public instruction of the boys began. There is no evidence that any class, save what would correspond to our upper or wealthier classes, had any education beyond that which national customs, institutions, and religious beliefs and rites would necessarily give to all citizens. We are not to accept what Xenophon tells us in his romance. We know, however, from Strabo and

---

[1] Some write with fluency and confidence on the ancient Persian education, having apparently in their eye Xenophon's *Cyropœdia* (especially i. 9), forgetting that it is a romance, to be accepted perhaps in its spirit but certainly not in any other respect. Much might be extracted from the Avesta as to the regulation of domestic life, but it is difficult to *date* what has survived, and we are concerned only with the pre-christian.

the general evidence of antiquity that the boys of the higher classes were brought up together under men of gravity and reputation at the court of the great king, and also at the lesser courts of the great nobles and provincial governors. In these central and departmental court-schools they were trained in shooting with the bow, riding, the use of the javelin, and other military exercises, and in the course of this instruction great attention was paid to their education in truthfulness and self-control. The story of noble deeds was conveyed through the national traditions. The young men were rendered hardy by the severity of their physical exercise. We may perhaps see in such schools an anticipation of the mediæval schools of chivalry. In the first book of the 'Anabasis' (which is not to be rejected because the 'Cyropædia' is a romance) Xenophon says of Cyrus the Younger, that 'when he was receiving his education with his brother and the other youths, he was considered to surpass them all in everything.' 'All the sons of the Persian nobles,' he adds, 'are educated at the Royal palace, where they have an opportunity of learning many a lesson of virtuous conduct, but can see or hear nothing disgraceful. Here the boys see some honoured by the king and others degraded, so that in their very childhood they learn to govern and to obey. Here Cyrus first of all showed himself most remarkable for modesty among those of his own age, and for paying more ready obedience to his elders than even those who were inferior to him in station, and next he was noted for his fondness for horses and for managing them in a superior manner. They found him, too, very desirous of learning and most assiduous in practising the warlike exercises of archery and hurling the javelin. When it suited his age he grew exceedingly fond of the chase and of braving dangers in encounters with wild beasts.' Plato, again, in his 'Alcibiades,' speaks of the instruction of the sons of the kings in the wisdom of Zoroaster as well as in justice, temperance, and courage.

Prayer and the holy doctrines of the priests were learned (doubtless from oral and personal teaching, not from writings); and somewhere about fifteen years of age the boys were invested with the holy girdle (made out of seventy-two threads of camel hair or wool, and never laid aside day or night, as a protection against the Devas or evil spirits) with many ceremonies. On this occasion the young Persian, after reciting portions of the Avesta which he had been carefully taught, took upon himself a vow to follow the law of Zoroaster. It was at the fifteenth year that the boy was held to enter youth, that the family bands were relaxed, and that he became a servant of the State. In his twenty-fifth year the youth was looked upon as a man and citizen, and was subject to all duties in peace and war, till his fiftieth.

The highest education was for the hereditary Magian priesthood alone, but it does not seem to have embraced much more (so far as we know) than the traditionary religious writings which were numerous. The Persians were not an intellectual people like the Egyptians, Chaldees, Hindus, and Chinese. Life, with all its activities, was dear to them. But it might be held that it was precisely this want of abstract intellectual interest that helped to make their imperial power so short-lived.

The Semitic and Hamitic races were religious and devout. Their religions were their political and social bonds. But they all were characterised by a subjection of the spirit of man to divine powers — powers, too, not always of very humane attributes. Being superstitious, these races were slaves to the unseen; and they were all, save the Jews, idolaters. It was otherwise with the Persian. Morality and virility were the governing ideas. Personality and the responsibility of each individual for the diffusion of good might not be national characteristics, but they underlay the national character. Their religion taught them reverence — a reverence extended to the great king who was governor under Auramazda; but this reverence, while unquestionably it was subjection, was not slavishness. The individual had to fight with and for Auramazda and the kingdom of Light. Truthfulness, justice, and courage were accordingly, as I have said, the cardinal virtues, and by these characteristics the Persians were, if we may believe history and tradition, generally distinguished: in these they educated their children. The distinctive characteristic of the Persian education is its devotion to physical and ethical training. Education in our modern sense did not exist, either as instruction or discipline, outside the physical and ethical elements. It does not appear that the women had any save domestic training, but it is important to note that they held a higher position in the family life than was usual in the East.

As to method. — Where there is no instruction in literature, &c., there is no room for method as applied to intellectual acquisition and discipline. The method of moral training was the mingling of the young with their seniors, on which Crete and Sparta and early Rome also mainly relied.

This is all that can be said, with even an approximation to accuracy, about the educational machinery of the Persians. It was manifestly only the well-to-do who participated fully in the national training — possibly only the leading tribe of the Pasargadæ. All others would be dependent on domestic life and the current of religious and ethical belief and tradition.

The significance of Persian life and education lies in the combination of a free personality with an intense national feeling. I am not at all disposed to accept the sweeping estimate of their character which approves itself to Professor Sayce, in face of the universal tradition regarding them, supported as that is by the doctrines of their religion and the statements of the Greeks. In the mere fact of personality we have the beginning of an ideal aim for the personal life. Individual courage, truthfulness, and purity were constituents of this ideal; and the ideal of man was based on the attributes of God. Man becomes, under the Persian conception, a personal factor in the world-order. Caste, with its depressing and restrictive influences and superstitions and their accompaniment of slavish fears, is not compatible with these conceptions. Accordingly, I am disposed to regard the Persian as the true starting-point of the specifically Aryan character, and as marking the transition from the Semitic-Oriental to the Hellenic type of life. With a sense of personality there comes into existence freedom and many consequent virtues. The Persian thus seems to bridge the gulf between the Oriental and the European. And yet he was an Oriental.

It is not our business to trace the brief history of the Medo-Persian empire. When one considers, however, the high military and healthy ethical characteristics of the Persian when he was an all-conquering force, it is permitted to us to wonder at his rapid degradation and fall. With so excellent an ethical basis of national life, how came it that the court, in less than one hundred years from the death of Cyrus, had developed all the vices which are popularly associated with Oriental despotisms ? The imperial organisation was perhaps too lax to be permanent, but the degradation of the Persian character wants explanation. Personal vanity and love of luxury do not seem to explain everything. May we not believe that had there been an organised education of a considerable section of the people on the basis of Mazdeism, the empire, if reduced to manageable limits, might have held its own even against Alexander, who gave it its final blow ? Or was it that the religion itself had become debased, and that the degeneracy was due to a light-hearted unbelief, generated by luxury, which prepared the way for political dissolution ?

To conclude : — The nation which was most nearly allied to the Persian in its religious conceptions was the Jewish, and it is not impossible that the tribes deported to Media in the first exile may have influenced Zoroastrianism. But spite of a certain community of belief, there was all the contrast which the Aryan and Semitic race-characters would lead us to expect. On the one hand we see slavery to a technical legalism, a sacred covenant ; on the other personal freedom and a freely discharged responsibility. We may even say that the Persian idea of God and his relation to the world and the life of man was purer, more universal, and more pleasing than the Jewish. God attracts and does not coerce with threatenings. On the other hand we have in the educated Jew a far more intense conception of the moral element in God and of the absoluteness of Duty to Law. With the Persian the actual personality of God is lost in a principle, and the moral relation of God to the world and man is more generalised and less definite, and yet quite capable of being appropriated by an intelligent community. In the Persian idea there was a possibility of progress, and it is difficult to understand why the nation did not advance.

The reader who has accompanied us thus far will see that new elements of life enter the world with the Aryan race. The two branches of that race of which we have been speaking exhibit the two leading characteristics of their European brethren; in the one we find a certain simplicity of faith and morals accompanied with freedom of spirit, freshness, and ' go '; in the other, profound philosophic contemplation and literary excellence. Both these characteristics we find united in the race which now compels our attention, and which must arrest it much longer than any other; for in it we find the genesis of all subsequent human activity in philosophy, literature, and the arts that adorn and elevate the life of man.

Authorities :—Anabasis and *Cyropædia* of Xenophon ; Herodotus ; Plato ; Strabo; Sir H. Rawlinson's appendices and discussions in his translation of Herodotus ; Ranke's *History of the World;* Rawlinson's *Five Eastern Monarchies;* Schmidt's *History of Education;* Hegel's *Philosophy of History ;* Sayce's *Ancient Empires of the East;* Vaux's *Persia ;* Tiele's *Outlines of Religions ;* Duncker's *History of Antiquity ;* with references to many other sources, such as Darmesteter—especially his introduction to the translation of the *Zend-Avesta.*

C. — THE HELLENIC RACE [1]

CHAPTER I

GENERAL HELLENIC CHARACTERISTICS

ASSUMING that the reader has already a fair acquaintance with Hellenic history, I here restrict myself to the exhibition of those great and leading characteristics of life, religion, and art, to which it is absolutely necessary to refer if we would understand the education of the Greeks.

I have in view the highest type of the Hellenic spirit — the Athenian.

Look first at the map of the Eastern Mediterranean. The physical characteristics of the home of the Hellenic races — the variety of scenery which was to be found in a land broken up, as theirs was, by mountain, stream, and sea, and the pure and hilarious influences of the atmosphere, were all of a kind to promote the development of a cheerful, bright, life-loving people. The early separation of the common stock into tribes speaking different dialects (Doric, Æolic, Ionic, and Attic), and the establishment on the shores of the Mediterranean of numerous autonomous little kingdoms tended to establish a difference, and in many cases a mutual antagonism, of interests. Hence, in consequence of the

---

[1] *Important Dates in the History of Greece.* — Trojan War, 1183 B.C. (?) ; Homer about 950 and Hesiod about 850 B.C. ; Spartan power dominant in the Peloponnesus, 650 B.C. Athens — Legislation of Solon, 590 B.C. ; Persian invasion and Battle of Marathon, 490 B.C. ; Invasion by Xerxes, burning of Athens, and battle of Salamis, 480 B.C. ; battle of Platæa, 479 B.C. Supremacy of Athens. Peloponnesian war, 431 to 404 B.C. ; Defeat of Athens and supremacy of Sparta, 404 B.C. ; Spartan wars with Persia and Darius : divisions of Greece : ascendency of Philip of Macedon over Greece, 338 B.C. ; Alexander the Great. Greece made a Roman province, 146 B.C.

numerous centres of civic life, that rapid growth of independence and of the spirit of freedom which characterised the Greek, and which was, in fact, the beginning of the idea of liberty for the whole human race. This tendency to civic and personal self-assertion was strengthened by the island character of many of the settlements and the activity and energy called forth by contest with the sea. It is true that freedom and the spirit of independence were innate in the Hellenic character; but they were undoubtedly fostered into an almost feverish activity by social, geographical, and political conditions. What a contrast do they present to the Egyptian, Chinese, and Semitic national communities, and to the dreamy and abstract Hindus, their cousins by race !

Here among the Greeks you have all the grace and humanity which are noted in their fellow-Aryans the Persians, their courage and manliness, their enjoyment of life and of moral freedom; but all these issuing from a deeper nature, instinct with a broader human sympathy and, above all, animated by an intense intellectuality. In Homer[1] — the first and greatest literary representative of the Hellenic spirit — you have all these characteristics so early as about 1000 years B.C.; for Homer seems to have sung somewhere about 180 years after the Trojan War, to which the date of 1183 B.C. is usually assigned. These poems (which, as has been truly said, form the end not the beginning of a poetical period), so rich in their humanity, so full of character, of simple and naïve, yet penetrating, reflection, so abounding in romance, so magnificent in their conceptions of the virility of man, so touching in their pathos and so overflowing with fulness of life and energy, give the key to the Hellenic character. They formed the basis of all Greek literature; nay, we may say of all European literature. They were committed to memory by the Hellenic boys and studied by the Hellenic youth, who

---

[1] It does not matter to us, of course, whether one man wrote the *Iliad* and *Odyssey* or not. But, I suppose no one now doubts that these poems were the product of many singers, and, if so, their interest and value as the expression of the life of a race are increased.

saw in Achilles a type of free and warlike Greece, learned
to revere age and experience in Nestor, to recognise, in the
portraiture of the great Agamemnon, the necessity of leadership even for free men and democrats, and to appreciate the
oratory and the astute policy of Ulysses — a foreshadowing of
a potent factor in the life of the interplotting Hellenic States.
A people with such a start in national life could not but be
great in arts, literature, and arms, if their racial genius was
truly represented by their great epos. The teaching fell, as
we know, on fruitful soil; and the poems were received and
cherished as divine, inspired utterances.

We take the Homeric epos then, as we took the Confucian
books in the case of China, the Rig-Veda and Code of Manu
in the case of the Hindu, and the Zend-Avesta in the case of
the Persian, to be the starting-point of the inner life of the
Greeks. A natural humanity broad and various, instead of
religious conceptions, lies at the heart of Greek genius.
Homer was the first expositor of this humanity, and through
all Greek and even Roman education, the Iliad and Odyssey
formed the minds of the young. 'Boys,' says Professor
Jebb,[1] 'learned Homer by heart at school, priests quoted him
touching the gods, moralists went to him for maxims, statesmen for arguments, cities for claims to territory or alliance,
noble houses for the title deeds of their fame.' Even so late
as Quintilian, in the first century of the Christian era, we
find the use of Homer and Vergil in the elementary schools
recommended by the most competent of all educational
authorities. 'It has accordingly been an excellent custom,'
he says (i. 8), 'that reading should commence with Homer
and Vergil, although to understand their merits there is need
of a maturer judgment; but for the acquisition of judgment
there is abundance of time, for they will not be read once
only. In the meantime let the mind of the pupil be exalted
with the sublimity of the heroic verse, conceive ardour from
the magnitude of the subjects, and be imbued with the
noblest sentiments.'

[1] *Primer of Greek Literature.*

It is in the Homeric epos also that we find the earliest indications of Hellenic education. In the 9th Book of the Iliad, Phœnix, when supplicating Achilles to lay aside his wrath, recalls that his father, Peleus, when he sent him to the war, committed him to his care.

I, whom thy royal father sent as orderer of thy force
When to Atrides from his court he left thee for this course,
Yet young, and when in skill of arms thou didst not so abound,
Nor hadst the habit of discourse that makes men so renowned.
In all which I was set by him t' instruct thee as my son,
That thou mightst speak when speech was fit, and do when deeds
    were done ;
Not sit as dumb for want of words ; idle, for skill to move.
               Iliad, ix. 443, Chapman's translation.

If we would understand Greece, then, we must start from Homer. If we do not read, and, while reading, are not quick to feel the charm of the great epics, we shall never know anything about the great Hellenic race, or the vital element in their lives whether in school or at home.

The most remarkable outcome of Greek genius in political and social institutions as well as in art and literature was to be found in Athens — 'the eye of Greece.' It is of Athens and the Athenians that Thucydides thus speaks through the mouth of Pericles, giving us a picture of an ideal civic community, which it is not difficult to connect with the Homeric conceptions of life :

'It is true that we are called a democracy, for the administration is in the hands of the many and not of the few. But while the law secures equal justice to all alike in their private disputes, the claim of excellence is also recognised ; and when a citizen is in any way distinguished, he is preferred to the public service, not as a matter of privilege, but as the reward of merit. Neither is poverty a bar, but a man may benefit his country whatever be the obscurity of his condition. There is no exclusiveness in our public life, and in our private intercourse we are not suspicious of one another, nor angry with our neighbour if he does what he likes; we do not put on sour looks at him which, though harmless, are not pleasant.   While we are thus unconstrained in our private intercourse, a spirit of reverence pervades our public acts; we are prevented from doing wrong by respect for authority and for the laws, having an especial regard to those which are ordained for the protection of the injured, as well as to those unwritten laws which bring upon the transgressor of them the reprobation of the general sentiment.

'And we have not forgotten to provide for our weary spirits many relaxations from toil; we have regular games and sacrifices throughout the year; at home the style of our life is refined; and the delight which we daily feel in all these things helps to banish melancholy.

'Because of the greatness of our city the fruits of the whole earth flow in upon us, so that we enjoy the goods of other countries as freely as of our own.

'Then, again, our military training is in many respects superior to that of our adversaries.   Our city is thrown open to the world, and we never expel a foreigner or prevent him from seeing or learning anything of which the secret, if revealed to an enemy, might profit him.   We rely not upon management or trickery, but upon our own hearts and hands.   And in the matter of education, whereas they (the Spartans) from early youth are always undergoing laborious exercises which are to make them brave, we live at ease, and yet are equally ready to face the perils which they face.

'Then, we are lovers of the beautiful, yet simple in our tastes, and we cultivate the mind without loss of manliness. Wealth we employ, not for talk and ostentation, but when there is a real use for it.   To avoid poverty with us is no disgrace; the true disgrace is in doing nothing to avoid it. An Athenian citizen does not neglect the State because he takes care of his own household; and even those of us who are engaged in business have a very fair idea of politics. We alone regard a man who takes no interest in public affairs not as a harmless but as a useless character; and if few of us are originators, we are all sound judges, of a policy. The great impediment to action is, in our opinion, not discussion, but the want of that knowledge which is gained by discussion preparatory to action. For we have a peculiar power of thinking before we act and of acting too, whereas other men are courageous from ignorance but hesitate upon reflection. And they are really to be esteemed the bravest spirits who, having the clearest sense, both of the pains and pleasures of life, do not on that account shrink from danger.

'I say that Athens is the school of Hellas, and that the individual Athenian in his own person seems to have the power of adapting himself to the most varied forms of action with the utmost versatility and grace. This is no passing and idle word, but truth and fact; and the assertion is verified by the position to which these qualities have raised the State. For in the hour of trial Athens alone among her contemporaries is greater than her fame.' (Jowett's translation.)

Contrast for a moment this picture of a State with that of the nations we have been passing under review! These words of Thucydides portray an almost ideal political community, towards which, indeed, we hope that our modern life is tending. Strange it may seem that a civic constitution even though falling short of this ideal, as Athens most certainly did, could not sustain itself for ever. The decline and fall of Greece, manifest as were the causes, yields probably as profound political lessons as the 'Decline and Fall of Rome' even in the hands of the stately and all-comprehending Gibbon.

In connection with the Greek polity, however, let us never forget that when we talk of the Greeks, we talk not of the whole of the inhabitants of Hellas who spoke Greek, but of the aristocracy of free citizens. These rested on a large body of slaves who performed all manual and menial work — captives in war, or persons purchased at slave markets or the descendants of slaves. Though well treated, they had no civic rights to speak of.

Religion. — The earliest Greeks brought with them the Aryan religion and there is nothing in the Vedic hymns which they would not have accepted. But how different was the evolution of the religious sentiment from that which we have seen in the Persian and Hindu! The sacerdotal element was in abeyance, and religion partook of the humanity of their civil life. There was here no Semitic fear, no Egyptian awe, no abasement of human personality before an unseen power of possibly sinister intentions. It was a worship of the beautiful — of Art, *i.e.* the ideal in nature and human life. Their gods did not symbolise the mere powers of nature, and the worship was not an element worship, though doubtless it rested on a primæval adoration of the forces and forms of nature — earth, sun, moon, dawn, spring, and so forth. The gods as we find them in their specific Hellenic development were the perfect expressions of *human thought* regarding the powers that worked in nature and in man. They were ideals; and in these ideals they truly worshipped the divine element in man; and so they may be, in a sense, said to have worshipped a glorified and superhuman, but not supernatural, humanity.

On this subject Hegel says in his 'Philosophy of History': 'It must be observed that the Greek gods are to be regarded as individualities, not abstractions, like Knowledge, Unity, Time, Heaven, Necessity. Such abstractions do not form the substance of these divinities: they are no allegories, no abstract beings to which various attributes are attached like the Horatian [e.g. *dira et sæva necessitas*]. As little are the divinities symbols, for a symbol is only a sign, an adumbration of something else. The Greek gods express of themselves what they are. The eternal repose and clear intelligence that dignify the head of Apollo is not a symbol, but the expression in which spirit manifests itself and shows

itself present. The gods are personalities, concrete individualities : an allegorical being has no qualities, but is itself one
quality and no more. The gods are moreover special characters, since in each of them one peculiarity predominates as
the characteristic one; but it would be vain to try to bring
this circle of characters into a system. Zeus perhaps may
be regarded as ruling the other gods, but not with substantial
power — so that they are left free to their own idiosyncrasies.
Since the whole range of spiritual and moral qualities was
appropriated by the gods, the Unity which stood above them
all necessarily remained abstract; it was therefore formless
and unmeaning Fate (the absolute constitution of things) —
Necessity, whose oppressive character arises from the absence
of the spiritual in it; whereas the gods hold a friendly relation to men, for they are spiritual natures. That higher
thought — the knowledge of unity as God the One Spirit —
lay beyond that grade of thought to which the Greeks
had attained.' (Hegel, 'The Greek World,' page 256.) The
only exception that can be taken to this statement is as to
the 'substantial' power of Zeus. See Iliad, viii. 1–27, &c.,
&c. Moreover, the tendency of the intellect of Greece was
ever more and more to assign supremacy to Zeus.

Mr. J. Brown Patterson [1] also well says : ' The distinguishing characteristic of the religion thus created by the free
operation of the human faculties was naturally the freedom
and the fulness of the display which it contained of human
nature. It sought the causes of all being and all change in
moving principles similar to those which operate in human
breasts, and in doing so it seems to have had no principle
of selection either metaphysical or moral. Whatever was
palpable in man it made ideal in the divinity. Accordingly
we find the fulness and richness of human nature in the
gods — the Hellenic worship was in truth the worship of
humanity. To the Hellenic conception everything beautiful
was holy ; everything pleasant to man was acceptable to the
gods.'

[1] *Essay on the Character of the Athenians.*

The pervading spirit of the Hellenic religion has been best expressed in Schiller's famous poem entitled 'The Gods of Greece,' of which I may quote a few verses:

> When o'er the form of naked Truth
>   The Muse had spread her magic veil,
> Creation throbbed with life and youth,
>   And feeling warmed the insensible.
> Then Nature, formed for love's embrace,
>   The earth in brighter glory trod;
> All was enchanted ground, each trace
>   The footstep of a god.

> But Nature now, undeified,
>   Unwitting of the joys she gives,
> Unconscious of her former pride
>   And of the soul that in her lives,
> Regardless of her Maker's praise
>   And dead to human sympathy,
> Like a dull pendulum obeys
>   The law of gravity.

> Your gay religions knew no sadness:
>   They banished each austere emotion;
> What bosom could but throb with gladness,
>   When gladness was the best devotion?
> Whate'er was sacred then was fair;
>   No pleasure feared the eye of God
> Where roamed the blushing Muses, where
>   The Graces still abode.

> Your temples smiled like palace-halls;
>   And there ye held your dazzling court
> On many-wreathed festivals,
>   Midst thundering cars and hero-sport;
> And oft the soft soul-breathing sound
>   Of dance begirt your altars fair,
> Each brow with bright love-garlands bound,
>   Deep-wreathed in dewy hair.[1]

[1] Translated by John Brown Patterson.

That there was a deeper vein of religious thought in the
Hellenic mind is, however, true. The Eleusinian mysteries,[1]
the lyrical poets, and the tragic drama, give sufficient evidence of this; but it does not seem to have touched the
popular heart deeply. Their instinctive apprehension of
ideal forms seemed to satisfy their religious needs. The
true and all-pervading God of the average Greek was, in
truth, neither Zeus nor Athena, but Apollo, whose chief
shrine was at Delphi, the centre of Hellenic religious unity.
He truly expressed their art-loving and ideal tendencies in
all forms of mental activity, and through his oracles connected them with the superhuman world. The recently-
discovered Delphian hymn to Apollo may be here quoted.

Fragment I. 'Thee, son of great Zeus, famous in minstrelsy,
I will celebrate, since by the side of this snow-capped hill
thou dost show forth divine oracles to all mortals, after thou
didst seize the prophetic tripod which the hateful dragon
guarded, when thou didst pierce with thy darts the sheeny
twisted shape.'

Fragment II. 'Ye fair-armed daughters of loud-thunder-
ing Zeus, who have had deep-wooded Helicon assigned to
you for an abode, come hither, that you may chant in song
the praises of your kinsman, golden-haired Phœbus, who, on
his twin-peaked abode of the Parnassian rock, along with the

---

[1] Doctrines of a mystico-religious kind, believed to have been introduced
from Egypt and preserved by a priestly family or families at Eleusis. The
chief temple was afterwards in Athens, but Eleusis never lost the distinction
which associated the mysteries specially with it. Any Greek might be
initiated who was prepared to go through all the necessary ceremonies. The
precise nature of the doctrine revealed is not known. I am not aware that
modern research has gone beyond Thirlwall's conclusion: 'They were the
remains of a worship which preceded the rise of the Hellenic mythology and
its attendant rites, grounded on a view of Nature less fanciful, more earnest,
and better fitted to awaken both philosophical thought and religious feeling.'
(*History of Greece*, ii. 140.) Some more recent inquirers seem to think that
there was little in the so-called 'mysteries.' On the other hand, it is not impossible that they had Semitic or Hamitic relations, and Thirlwall's judgment
on the matter is probably still the soundest. The Greeks seemed to be, in some
cases, becoming alive to the sense of sin and the consequent need of *personal*
salvation. To this the mysteries as well as the Orphic rites would appeal.

famous Delphic maids, visits the rills of the gushing Castalian spring, presiding over the oracular hill upon the Delphian headland. Come with thy prayers, O famous Attic race, blest with mighty cities, dwelling on the inviolate soil of panoplied Tritonis; on holy altars, fire wraps in a blaze the thigh-bones of young bulls, and therewith Arabian vapours spread through it upwards to the sky; the flute with thrilling notes pipes its lay in varied melodies; the golden, sweetly-sounding lyre wakes music for triumphal songs, and the whole swarm of spectators to whom the Attic land has been assigned as a dwelling-place.' [1]

The growing idealism and the essentially æsthetic and joyous character of the Hellenic religion is already visible little more than half way from Homer to Pindar and Æschylus, in the hymn to Apollo, referring to the Ionian festival there, and in existence as early, probably, as 730 B.C.:

'There, in thy honour, Apollo, the long-robed Ionians assemble with their children and their gracious dames. So often as they hold thy festival, they celebrate thee, for thy joy, with boxing and dancing and song. A man would say that they were strangers to death and old age evermore who should come on the Ionians thus gathered; for he would see the goodliness of all the people, and would rejoice in his soul, beholding the men and the fairly-cinctured women, and their swift ships and their great wealth, and, besides, that wonder of which the fame shall not perish, the maidens of Delos, handmaidens of Apollo the Far-darter. First they hymn Apollo, then Leto and Artemis delighting in arrows: and then they sing the praise of heroes of yore and of women, and throw their spell over the tribes of men.' (Jebb's translation.)

To quote again from Hegel. 'The essence of the Greek religion is the spiritual itself, and the natural is only the point of departure. But, on the other hand, it must be observed that the divinity of the Greeks is not yet the *absolute* free spirit, but spirit in a particular mode fettered by the

[1] Fragment translated by Dr. Dunn, H.M.I.S., Scotland.

limitations of humanity — still dependent as a determinate individuality on external conditions. Individualities objectively beautiful are the gods of the Greeks.' The Aryan nature-worship had here evidently fallen into the hands of an æsthetic and idealising race, and spite of the traditional tales of the gods, against which philosophy protested, the recognition of the gods reacted on the moral life of the Greeks by virtue of the mere fact of idealisation.

The earliest formulated conception of the Hellenic religion after the race had emerged from a primitive element-worship, is to be extracted from the Homeric poems supplemented by Hesiod's ' Theogony.' It was in the human attributes of their gods, and the rich legendary tales about them and the heroes, that the Hellenic race first separated itself from the religious and intellectual life of other races. As time went on, these primitive conceptions became more and more idealised and more and more ethical, till we find that even the profound mind of an Æschylus and a Sophocles has room for the more important of the subordinate gods alongside their unquestionable monotheism.

It is to the philosophers and dramatists of Greece that we owe those deeper thoughts as to the origin of things, the nature of man, and the moral order of the world, which elsewhere were a derivation from sacred books and the monopoly of a priestly order. In Greece the lay spirit always dominated — the sacerdotal was almost non-existent. But even from the time of Homer, as I have already indicated, the Greek recognised a supreme God among the gods — Zeus, the father of gods and men : the all-powerful. In his supreme hands lay the order of the world and absolute justice. Homer represents Zeus as executing vengeance by making the transgressions of men fall heavily on themselves or their children. Æschylus, rising to a lofty conception, calls him all-causing, all-sufficing, all-seeing, all-accomplishing, Lord of lords, most Holy of holies : and Sophocles gives utterance to similar thoughts. Certainly from the time of Homer monotheism, or at least henotheism, lay at the basis of the Greek religion :

this, however, among all races has been found compatible with a belief in gods. Blue-eyed Athena was a great goddess, but she was only the idealised expression of Jove's wisdom, and to her consequently he yields: 'She only of gods may know that chamber's keys where sleeps the sealed thunder of her sire.'[1] Bright-haired Apollo, again, was the expression of the oracular decrees of the father of gods and men — Apollo, who was the god of light, saviour, purifier, and redeemer, and 'whose cultus,' says Tiele, 'exercised on the religious, moral, and social life of the Greeks so profound and salutary an influence.'[2]

The fact of death inevitable and of human suffering, so often to all appearance unjust, was a deep problem for the Greeks, as it has been for the thoughtful of all races. Behind the awful throne of Jove himself the Greek recognised the dark and fateful form of destiny, working out, for gods as well as for men, their lives and fortunes — answerable to no other power, caring for none.[3] A thread of mystery and awe accordingly ran through the web of Greek life; the pathos of human existence was in their hearts (Iliad, xxiv. *passim*), but their joyous and active nature, their constant struggles in politics, war, literature, art, and philosophy, accompanied by an all-prevailing gymnastic, enabled them practically to ignore the thought of the essential evil in life; and to treat all ultimate questions, chiefly through the imagination, and not as supreme and urgent realities in the problem of existence. 'Forasmuch as men must die,' says Pindar, 'wherefore should one sit vainly in the dark through a dull and nameless age, and without lot in noble deeds?'[4] What a contrast to the Brahman and the Buddhist!

Sacerdotalism, I have said, was alien to the Hellenic cast

[1] Æsch. *Eum.* translated by E. Myers.

[2] 'Ne'er spake I yet, from my oracular throne, of man, of woman, or of commonwealth, answer unbidden of the Olympian sire.' — *Eum.* 616.

[3] And yet it sometimes appeared that Zeus was powerful enough to be himself a factor in fate.

[4] *Olymp.* i. 82, quoted by Professor Butcher, p. 105 of *Aspects of the Greek Genius.*

of thought and life. The temples were simply the house of the god to whom they were dedicated, and the priest (except in the case of some families that had hereditary rights) was elected and might be changed from time to time, returning, after he had served his period, to the civil life from which he had been taken. The priest's duty seems to have been, in fact, chiefly that of a caretaker and of a regulator of the manner of offering sacrifices on special occasions : he assisted also in the offerings and sacrifices which others came to make. The oracular utterances at certain temples like Dodona and Delphi (for centuries the centre of Greek religious thought and guide of its political life), revealing the will of the god or future events, and the magical cures in some Æsculapian temples would seem to be the only characteristics of religion which connect the Greeks with the magical in religion. The most recent inquiries, it is true, point to both a Semitic and Hamitic element in the religion of the Greeks, but these elements were themselves Hellenised.

But although there was no priesthood or church in the modern sense, to the Greek, nature was full of deity ; holy were the haunted forest boughs, holy the air, the water, and the fire ; but whereas other races accepted the belief of an animated nature in a prosaic, and generally suspicious, spirit, with the Greeks the belief was characterised by amity and joyousness. There was also a full recognition of the gods in the great incidents of domestic life — birth, marriage, and death ; and, even at banquets, the libations always connected the banqueters with present gods. All these ceremonies, however, seem to have had an artistic quite as much as a religious character, in the sense which other nations understood religion. The relation of the Greek to his gods was an easy, pleasant, and friendly one. Natures so bright, joyous, and high-spirited were not likely to dwell on the mysterious and awful in religion. ‘ Truth and self-control,’ says Tiele (p. 218), ‘ without self-mortification or renunciation of nature, a steady equilibrium between the sensible and the spiritual, moral earnestness combined with an open

14

eye for the happiness and beauty of life, such are the characteristic features of the Delphic Apollo worship in which the
Greek religion almost reached the climax of its development.'

As regards a future state, Tiele points out that it was a
mark of the· ethical character of the Delphic religion that it
spoke of a future state of retribution ; but this was never a
definite popular belief, though taught by the poets. That it
was an article of faith among the more thoughtful is established by many passages in Greek literature, although few
may have shared the conviction of Antigone when she says :
' When I come there into the other world, such is the hope
I cherish, I shall find love with my father, love with my
mother, and love with thee my brother' (Soph. 'Antig.'
897).

Art. — The religion of the beautiful, joyous, and ideal
received fit expression in the sacred houses, the remains of
which are still a wonder and joy to mankind because of their
severe charm and refined simplicity. It is easy to see that
Greek art and Greek religion were necessarily one : both
were the expression of the same ideal conceptions :

' How grand and chaste is the Greek temple !' says
Hettner, ' so simple in its beauty, so solemn in its repose,
so divine in its serenity ! It is not like our churches — a
place of assembly for the devout congregation ; it contains
only ·the statue of the god to whom it is consecrated, and his
sacred treasures and votive offerings. It stands, therefore,
quite apart from every profane environment. An encircling
wall guards a wide, sacred precinct ; and in the midst of this
rises, with far-seen splendour of marble and of gold, the
house of the god. Nor may it stand on the common earth,
trod by the feet of mortal man. Broad and mighty it is true,
the fair structure stretches along the ground as the natural
basis of existence : but three mighty strata of steps lift it
above the level of everyday reality, and bear it, like a great
votive gift, towards heaven. The god who dwells within the
cella is no dark forbidding deity ; he is a god of joy and

perpetual serenity — a god of light. To embrace the light and air, the portico throws itself wide ; and all round runs a colonnade, connecting the narrow dwelling of the god with the happy outer world. Joyous in their living, elastic strength, rise these pillars. The counterpressure of the superstructure which it is their purpose to support, receives and checks them as they ascend. Above them rest the superincumbent beams of the ceiling; and over these spreads the lofty roof drooping on both sides its broad overshadowing wings as if to warn and compel the soaring and aspiring pillars to remain contented with the solid sufficient earth, the fair divine Now, and seek no beyond. It is this solution of opposing forces, this aspiration which with glad and willing self-control returns within its natural limits, this living, satisfied, and harmonious repose which reflects on the mind of the beholder such a grateful calm. The enjoyment we have in the intelligent contemplation of a Greek temple is a homage to and a celebration of the divine, eternal Sophrosyne.' A speaker representing Egypt in one of Professor Ebers' novels, says: 'There is such a great difference between the Greek and Egyptian works of art. When I went into our own gigantic temples to pray I always felt as if I must prostrate myself in the dust before the greatness of the gods, and entreat them not to crush so insignificant a worm ; but in the temple of Hera at Samos I could only raise my hands to heaven in joyful thanksgiving that the gods had made the earth so beautiful. In Egypt I always believed as I had been taught: " Life is a sleep; we shall not awake to our true existence in the kingdom of Osiris till the hour of death :" but in Greece I thought : " I am born to live and to enjoy this cheerful, bright, and blooming world." '

In statuary also the religious idea found expression. Pheidias, the greatest of Greek artists, wrought statues designed to give a moral, lofty idea of deity. 'In the Athena of the Parthenon,' says Tiele,[1] ' and the Zeus of Olympia and the ancient tragedy, the religion of the Hellenes

[1] *Outlines of the History of Ancient Religions*, p. 224.

reached the climax of its development. The ideal humanisation of deity for which the way was prepared by the cultus of the Delphic Apollo was perfected at Athens by Æschylus, Sophocles, and Pheidias.' The great Pericles 'was led,' says Ranke,[1] 'in promoting art to strengthen religion.'

Such, concisely summed up, was the Greek religion as realised in architecture and the plastic arts — the natural and necessary expression of their religious sentiment.

Art in literature distinguished the Hellenic race no less than their work in marble and stone. They created a language subtle, far-reaching, and flexible, and fit to give expression to every form of literature. These forms, lyrical, epic, dramatic, historical, philosophical, they indeed created ; and they still are the teachers of mankind. Their attitude to all knowledge was open and receptive. Nothing was common or unclean. What a contrast to the nations we have spoken of in past chapters ! ' The Greeks,' says Professor Butcher of Edinburgh,[2] 'before any other people of antiquity, possessed the love of knowledge for its own sake. To see things as they really are, to discern their meanings and adjust their relations, was with them an instinct and a passion. Their methods in science and philosophy might be very faulty, and their conclusions often absurd, but they had that fearlessness of intellect which is the first condition of seeing truly. Poets and philosophers alike looked with unflinching eye on all that met them, on man and the world, on life and death. They interrogated Nature, and sought to wrest her secrets from her, without misgiving and without afterthought. They took no count of the consequences. " Let us follow the argument whithersoever it leads," may be taken not only as the motto of the Platonic philosophy, but as expressing one side of the Greek genius.' Ranke, again, says (' History of the World,' viii. 7): 'There is something almost miraculous in this simultaneous or nearly

[1] *History of the World*, p. 229.
[2] *Some Aspects of the Greek Genius.*

simultaneous appearance of such different types of genius accomplishing in poetry, philosophy, and history the greatest feats which the human mind has ever performed. Each is original and strikes out his own line, but all work in harmony. By one or the other of these masters are set forth all the greatest problems concerning things divine and human. Athens rejoiced in the possession of a theatre the like of which, for sport or earnest, has never been seen in any other city. The people lived in the constant enjoyment of the noblest dramatic productions. Sophocles was not dispossessed by Euripides : their works appeared at the same time on the stage. The history of Herodotus was read aloud in public meetings. Thucydides was reserved for more private study, but his works had a wide circulation in writing.'

Manhood. — Observe, next, how Hellenic idealism entered into their conception of man himself. If gods were human, men might be divine. A perfect body, the easy and unencumbered vehicle of a free and happy spirit, was the object of their admiration. The Olympic dust was the richest treasure which a young Greek could gather. Speaking of the harmonious athletic of the Greeks, Hettner says, ' Let us follow all Greece to the great centre of national unity, the plain of Olympia.' Here the victor was raised to the elevation of the gods themselves. 'Poets like Simonides and Pindar sang immortal songs of victory in his praise ; the best cities were anxious that he should be enrolled among their citizens ; and when he reached his home, the gate and part of the city wall were pulled down in token that a city which produced such men needed not the protection of walls. The conqueror entered in festive procession drawn by four white horses, proudly clad in purple and wearing on his head the olive wreath he had won. . . . Putting these wonderful facts in array before our minds, we cannot fail to feel deeply how wide is the difference between the moral basis on which Greek antiquity rests and our modes of life and thought in modern times. We men of to-day can hardly even see how the Greeks, the most intellectual nation the world has seen, could make their highest national festival a gymnastic one, far less can we sympathise with or imagine ourselves actually taking part in this truly Bacchic enthusiasm for the Olympic victor.'

And for what did they contend? Not for money rewards, but for glory alone — their success being signalised by a reward in itself worthless: 'at the Olympic games, an olive-crown or garland; at the Isthmian, one of pine; at the Nemean, one of parsley; at the Pythian, apples from the trees sacred to Apollo; and at the Panathenæa, olives from the tree of Minerva.' (Lucian, 'Anach.') 'If we look at the inner nature of these sports,' says Hegel, 'we shall first observe how sport itself is opposed to serious business, to dependence and need. This wrestling, running, contending, was no serious affair; bespoke no obligation of defence, no necessity of combat. Serious occupation is labour that has reference to some want. I or nature must succumb; if the one is to continue, the other must fall. In contrast with this kind of seriousness, however, sport presents the higher seriousness: for in it nature is wrought into spirit, and although in these contests the subject has not advanced to the highest grade of serious thought, yet, in this exercise of his physical powers, man shows his freedom, viz. that he has transformed his body to an organ of spirit.' Nor do these pertinent remarks exhaust the significance of the great games: for they were always accompanied with Temple services and were pleasing to the gods. They thus stood out as the great events of the year, which symbolised the religious as well as political unity of the Hellenic races.

The statues of the gods were themselves Greek men. It is a grave blunder to look on them as idols. Idols are mere symbols, and often hideous symbols, of the human fears and hopes of those races who believe that they live in a hostile world. The Greek gods on the contrary were the idealised and artistic expression of the Greek himself. Apollo and Hermes as well as the demigod heroes Achilles and Theseus

are simply glorified Greeks. ' The benign and simple lines
of the countenance, the large eyes, the short forehead, the
straight nose, the refined mouth, belonged to the race and
were their natural characteristics: their harmony of proportion was a marked feature of the Greek physique. . . . The
physical, however, was itself only an expression of the
spiritual. The innate love of freedom and independence, and
the living consciousness of human dignity shone forth in the
erect bearing which distinguished the Greek from the barbarian.' (Curtius, ' Griech. Gesch.' i. 25.)

The Greek exaltation of courage, their love of country,
their intense personality, their freedom of political life, prepared them for a great world-task which it fell to them to
perform in the interests of civilisation and human progress.
Even in the time of the great Cyrus they endeavoured to
throw their shield over their brothers on the Asiatic coast.
They subsequently drove back the whole Oriental power led
against them by Xerxes in person, and by so doing laid the
whole future of humanity under eternal obligations. Marathon, Thermopylæ, and Salamis are imperishable names.
' Thus was Greece freed,' says Hegel, ' from the pressure
which threatened to overwhelm it. Greater battles unquestionably have been fought, but these live immortal, not in
the historical records of nations only, but also of science and
art — of the noble and the moral generally. For these are
world-historical victories ; they were the salvation of culture
and spiritual vigour, and they rendered the Asiatic principle
powerless. How often, on other occasions, have not men
sacrificed everything for one grand object ! How often have
not warriors fallen for duty and country ! But here we are
called on to admire, not only valour, genius, and spirit, but
the purport of the contest — the effect, the result, which are
unique in their kind. In other battles a particular interest
is predominant; but the immortal fame of the Greeks is
none other than their due, in consideration of the noble
cause for which deliverance was achieved. In the history of

the world it is not the valour that has been displayed, nor the so-called merit of the combatants, but the importance of the cause itself, that must decide the fame of the achievement. In the case before us, the interest of the world's history hung trembling in the balance.[1] Oriental despotism — a world united under one lord and sovereign — on the one side, and separate states — insignificant in extent and resources, but animated by free individuality — on the other side, stood front to front in array of battle. Never in history has the superiority of spiritual power over material bulk — and that of no contemptible amount — been made so gloriously manifest. This war and the subsequent development of the states which took the lead in it, is the most brilliant period of Greece. Everything which the Greek principle involved then reached its perfect bloom and came into the light of day.' (Hegel, 'The Greek World,' p. 268.) It may be added that the contest was also one between the spirit of centralisation and that of decentralisation.

When we first come in contact with the Hellenic race in history, we at once recognise the loftiest, and deepest, and richest expression of the genuine Aryan spirit. A strong and joyous personality, and its free and beautiful development, meet us. We are not surprised to read Aristotle's words in which, speaking for all Greece, he tells us that the aim of life is 'living happily and beautifully.' ('Pol.' iii. 9. 14.) They believed in the essential beneficence of Nature and thought life well worth living. Adamantius, the physician, says, 'they were the most beautiful eyed of all races,' and we can well believe it. Above all other races before or since they seem to have *lived*. It was their intense sense of life and the joy in life that lay at the bottom of their 'zeal for activity,' as the German historian Curtius well says. Humanity, in short, in all its breadth and variety, was represented in this wonderful race, free from the overshadowing idea of God as eternal law and

[1] So with the battle of Châlons, when Aetius drove back the Huns in 455 A.D.

stern judge, as a being of exacting claims if not of hostile intent.

But, let us now for a moment try to get rid of the Hellenic glamour and contemplate the other side of the picture.

I think we must admit that the Greeks, and above all the Athenian Greeks, were light-minded and frivolous, easily swayed hither and thither, vain, of a shallow, because merely æsthetic, morality; talkative, untruthful, scheming, and pleasure-loving, with a strong tendency to licentiousness. Brilliant comrades, I should say they were doubtful friends.

Again, if we set aside the philosophers and dramatists who represented the highest religious thought of the Greeks, it can scarcely be said that the Greeks as a race were, in any sense in which we now use the term, a religious people. The tales of the gods which Plato would have banished from education were unquestionably an expression of the riotous and imaginative spirit of the Greeks, and could not possibly have influenced their lives to virtue. That religion consisted in a personal ethical relation to God and gods was certainly recognised by them but did not very profoundly influence them, although all were so far restrained by the fact that Zeus punished iniquity. The gods generally had to be honoured and offerings made to them; but that was substantially all. Wanting in a deep religious sense and not distinguished by any high conception of abstract duty, they were consequently deficient in reverence. Nor were they capable of that feeling of obligation to supreme law which marked the Roman. Their true religion was Art: the becoming, the fit, and the beautiful were truly their gods. The Greek conception in truth fell far short of the Judaic and Zoroastrian and Hindu conceptions of a Supreme Being and man's relations to him. The moral force which sustained the inner life of the Greek was his idealising tendency which found expression in art. This was quite compatible with their acceptance of the popular stories about those whom they idealised.

Further, the position of Athenian women was far from being what we should have expected to grow out of the well-known scene between Hector and Andromache, and many domestic incidents in the Iliad and the Odyssey. It fell short of the Doric conception, and seems utterly incompatible with the women of the great dramatists. The women spent their time in looking after their domestic concerns and sat in a room set apart for them — the gynæceum — which was half boudoir, half a day-nursery. They sewed, wove, and embroidered. There is something Oriental in the conception of the wife's position among the Ionic Greeks. The chief glory of an Athenian woman was that she should not be talked about. The husbands regarded their wives as quite inferior creatures, fit only to look after the house and bear children. They themselves spent their time in the streets, gymnasia, and places of public resort, or in banquetings at each other's houses, or visiting purchasable women (who seem to have been numerous in all Greek towns except Sparta), and some of whom, like Aspasia, were women of high accomplishments and held ' salons,' frequented by all the literary, artistic, and political men who could secure invitations.[1] The position of women in Sparta was much higher, and it is interesting to note that the Greek poetesses were for the most part of the Doric stem.

Finally, democratic equality, notwithstanding the over-shadowing influence of the Areopagus (powerful as a restraining influence even after the democratic reforms of that council by Pericles), and the presence of powerful hereditary families who endeavoured to lead the mass, led to quarrelsomeness and jobbery within their own cities and constant little wars with their fellow Greeks. They could not sacrifice their narrow civic interests even to the idea of Hellenic nationality, except for brief and uncertain periods. Delphi and the Olympic games were their only living points of unity — the former religious, the latter gymnastic. Their town and tribal

[1] They were always foreigners or freed women, never daughters of citizens, it is said.

confederacies were loose associations held together by the worship of a common tutelary deity, Demeter, Apollo, or Poseidon.

It would almost seem as if Lycurgus saw the kind of creatures he had to deal with, and resolved to discipline them tightly and to subject them at Sparta to a civic system which was at once school and camp, and thus to mould, out of the facile Greek nature, the stern and upright Spartan. And for a time he succeeded, but it was a moulding from without, not from within.

Let us not forget, however, that it was these very Hellenic characteristics, and above all the personal freedom in which they had their roots, which made it possible for the Greeks to be artists, historians, and bold, speculative inquirers into all things human and divine. It was probably only character of the versatile Greek type, and under Greek conditions, that was compatible with the work they did for humanity. They had all the faults of the artistic temperament, but then they had the latter with its virtues and vitality in all its fulness. They had to pay the price of their defects that they might gain Art and Philosophy for themselves and mankind. They were gifted with a genius for perception and expression, and this in every kind of human emotion and every department of intellectual activity, and whatever they attempted they succeeded in doing in the best possible form. To them we owe our logic and philosophy, the beginnings of science, the advancement of mathematics, and the finest forms of history, poetry, and the drama, as well as the arts of sculpture, architecture, and painting. It is when contemplating the vast and various contributions which the Hellenes made to the life of humanity that Shelley beautifully says:

> Within the circuit of this pendant orb
> There lies an antique region, on which fell
> The dews of thought, in the world's golden dawn,
> Earliest and most benign; and from it sprung
> Temples and cities and immortal forms,
> And harmonies of wisdom and of song,

And thoughts, and deeds worthy of thoughts so fair:
And when the sun of its dominion failed,
And when the winter of its glory came,
The winds that stript it bare blew on and swept
That dew into the utmost wildernesses,
In wandering clouds of sunny rain that thawed
The unmaternal bosom of the North.

From the Prologue to *Hellas.*

CHAPTER II

THE GREEK IDEAL OF MANHOOD AND THE CONSEQUENT CHARACTERISTICS OF HELLENIC EDUCATION GENERALLY

As a necessary introduction to the understanding of the Hellenic ideal let me point out what is little more than a logical deduction from what we have already said. The genuine Greek did not make any real distinction between a virtuous life and a beautiful and happy one. Virtue doubtless was the condition of happiness ; but virtue itself meant a nature in harmony with itself and its external relations. It was essentially æsthetic. Thus we may truly say that it was not the abstract good of Plato which governed the ethical conceptions of the Greeks, but the beautiful as another expression for harmony. Hence the compound word *kalokagathia.* But inasmuch as the Greek mind was essentially concrete, it included in the idea of human excellence the outer aspect and bearing of the individual man.

The oldest form of Greek life was the Dorian. (We may here omit the Æolic.) The chief representatives of the Doric tribes were the Cretans and Spartans, and consequently we are justified in looking among them for the primitive laws, customs, and beliefs of the Hellenic race. If the Dorians were the first to form civic communities, we can easily understand that whatever their national temperament and unconscious life-aims might be, these would be subordinated to the necessity of maintaining the existence of their rising communities in the midst of hostile races. Hence the pure Hellenic spirit would be subordinated in them to military requirements.

In the education of the Dorians it is Sparta with which we have chiefly to do. Unlovely as at first sight the Spartan character and constitution seem, we must never forget that the Spartans were yet Hellenes, and that the Greek spirit, which reached its finest expression in Athens, animated them also — only subdued in their case by a sterner sense of duty, by an arbitrary state-supremacy over the individual citizen, and a conservative attachment to the older and simpler conceptions of the Hellenic race. They were of the past, and in their political system it is doubtful if they possessed the possibility of progressive development. Among them we find supreme attachment to the state, as the central motive force in the individual life, much more strongly expressed than among the Athenians; but it is still held by them in union with a deep sense of personal freedom — achieved through the state and (so to speak) *contra mundum*. For the fundamental characteristics of the Hellenic mind were not here wanting. 'In the genuine Doric form of government,' says Müller ('Dorians,' ii. p. 6), 'there were certain predominant ideas, which were peculiar to that race, and were also expressed in the worship of Apollo, viz. those of becomingness or graceful expression (*eukosmia*); of self-control and moderation (*sophrosyne*); and of manly virtue (*arete*). Accordingly, the constitution was formed for the education as well of the old as of the young; and in a Doric state, education was, upon the whole, a subject of greater importance than government. And for this reason all attempts to explain the legislation of Lycurgus from partial views and considerations have necessarily failed. That external happiness and enjoyment were not the aim of these institutions was soon perceived.' Again he says (ii. 3. 1): 'We may say that the Doric state was a body of men, acknowledging one strict principle of order and one unalterable rule of manners ; and so subjecting themselves to this system that scarcely anything was unfettered by it; but every action was influenced and regulated by the recognised principles.' But in carrying out his scheme of discipline Lycurgus was not, Plutarch says, 'himself unduly austere; it was he who dedicated, says Sosibius, the little statue of Laughter or Mirth, which was introduced occasionally at their suppers and places of common entertainment, to serve as a sort of sweetmeat to accompany their strict and hard life.'[1] The ultimate *aim* of the state-regulations, however, was such as we have quoted from Müller, and had a conscious ideal of personal as well as civic manhood in view. Müller maintains that up to the time of the Persian Wars (let us say even up to 450 B.C.) all mental excellence flourished at Sparta, and it has to be remembered that it was to the Dorian branch of the Hellenic race that we owe some of the lyrical poets.

We must recognise the Cretan and Spartan education as the oldest to take shape among the Hellenic races, and we would, accordingly, fain find among them the ideas which lay at the *root* of all Hellenic life. I think we do find them as summed up in the three expressions I have already quoted from Müller, *arete, sophrosyne*, and *eukosmia*. Indeed, I seem to see in these the basis of all Greek life whatsoever, even in its finest forms; and, as the basis of their life, they must also have been, more or less consciously, the aim of their education. The Athenian τὸ καλὸν κἀγαθὸν simply summed up these characteristics in different words. This was the Greek ideal of conduct. But all was subservient to the state, and the Hellenic ideal of man, both as body and mind, was thus inseparable from his state-ideal.

The Greek child, speaking generally, was brought up for the service of the state. The individual existed for the state. The civic idea was dominant, just as in China the *family* idea was and is dominant, and in India the caste idea, in Egypt

[1] *Life of Lycurgus.*

the class idea, among the Jews the theological idea, and among the Persians the virile military idea. But we must remember that, whatever might be the local form of government the numerous separate states of Greece were free; and that if there was, among the Dorians, an apparently arbitrary moulding of the mind of youth, what was done was done by the citizens themselves, in a free Greek spirit. In Sparta, such was the instinctive capacity of the race for the ideal, that the conditions of qualification for citizenship were necessarily good, inasmuch as they were determined by the ideal. Even the importance of bodily training was recognised with a view to a true manly product apart from the relation of gymnastics to the national defence, although this latter object was necessarily more pronounced among the Dorian than among the Ionic races. But even among the Dorians we must not concentrate our attention so exclusively on the gymnastic side of their training as to lose sight of its moral element. The aim of the severe discipline under which they were brought up was to produce obedience, self-sacrifice, courage, promptitude, self-reliance, and a single-eyed concentration on the immediate purpose of all action.[1] Thus was produced a self-controlled and victorious man. Accordingly, I conclude that while the defensive requirements of the state among the Doric races dominated and controlled the processes of education; yet the requirements of the state, inasmuch as they could only be satisfied by the rearing of citizens who were virtuous, self-controlled, and possessed of the graces of manner and physically well-grown, were also the highest possible even in the interests of each man. Thus, free development of the individual and the service of the state were within certain limits harmonised.

Among the Athenians also, and, in truth, in all Hellenic communities, the citizens lived for the state which was supreme; but it is necessary here to emphasise a distinction between the races.

---

[1] This reads like a quotation.

Among the Doric races, and notably in Sparta, the state existed as a great educational institution, and citizens were deliberately formed after a certain pattern. Among the Ionic races, and especially the Attic branch, on the other hand, the education was not state-education in any proper sense: there was no state-system, and the idea and aims of the state consequently did not rigidly control the education given. The individual was educated in the first instance for himself — with a view to his own full and free development — and only secondarily for the state. The best possible product in manhood is better than a second-rate manufactured citizen, even from the point of view of public policy. In short, a development of body and mind, so that the one should serve the other, and both work in subjection to the ideas of 'self-control, moral excellence, and the becoming,' and thus give to the state a harmonious man, was the Attic idea of education. The Dorian thought, on the contrary, first of the state in its integrity, and only in the second place of the man. But, as I have pointed out, his requirements for the man were conceived in a true Hellenic spirit.

It would appear, then, that it is among the Hellenic races, above all in Attica, that we find arising, for the first time in the history of the world, a wholly new conception of human life, and, consequently, a new conception of the end of education. The Chinese was trained in obedience to precepts and customs with a view to civic order and the more common social and prudential virtues; the Persian was trained to be truthful, generous, and brave for himself as well as for the state, and with these virtues there was a spirit of free individualism, but it was boyish and unthoughtful: other races of antiquity were held down by despotic tradition and overawed by the dogmatism of a (presumably) divine teaching; the Ionian Greek, however, formed a conception of the ideal for each man, which ideal was to be freely sought — an ideal much higher than any that had preceded it, because it aimed at manly dignity and harmony of the whole nature — mind and body. All authority of the state proceeded from the individual citizen in his free development and activity. The very laws were a counterpart of the life.

Another distinction between the Dorian and Attic is worthy of mention. The laws of Lycurgus imposed the education of the free citizen as a duty on the state, just as the laws of Solon at Athens imposed it as a duty on each father of a family. The difference is significant.

The Hellenic races generally, both Dorian and Ionian, endeavoured to realise their ideal by means of two educational instruments — music and gymnastic. Under the head of music was included literature as well as music in its narrower sense; and I would further point out that music, even in its narrower sense, embraced (among the Dorians especially) religious training, because of its connection with choral singing and the worship of the gods.

Such being the general character and aim of Greek life and Greek education, let us now consider in detail the means that were taken to train the youth of the country, beginning with the oldest Greek system — the Doric, as exemplified in Crete and Sparta — a system towards which both Xenophon and Plato, weary of licentious democracies, were disposed to look back with some longing. And yet, spite of Plato and Xenophon, it is in the Ionic-Attic life and education that the modern world must ever recognise the true Hellenic spirit.

But before going further, it is necessary for us to bear in mind that national education did not mean in any part of Hellas what it means in Europe now. Those who were free citizens or burgesses were alone regarded as forming integral parts of the state, the larger number of the inhabitants — composed of foreign residents and slaves — being excluded. In Sparta, for example, at its best period, the subject residents, including the Helots, were three times as numerous as the true citizens. In Attica, again, the total population was about 500,000, and of these only 100,000 were citizens. It

15

has also to be premised that the education which was given, both at Sparta and Athens, was the instinctive product of the life of the people, not the deliberate result of educational discussion and theory.

To fix the date of the first schools in Greece is difficult, but we do not go too far back when we fix it at 600 B.C. in Athens. This was a period of intense Hellenic activity. According to Plutarch, almost every free citizen received at least elementary instruction so early as the time of Aristides, who died 467 B.C. The Spartan education, if organised along with the Spartan state, must have dated from about 850 B.C.

I would, however, here emphasise what I have already frequently indicated — that we must not measure the education of a nation by its schools. These arise only where there is a written literature. But long before their existencè, oral literature, religious and heroic, not to speak of customs and laws, were educating the people. And again, I would point out that we are not to conclude from the non-existence of schools that children were not, in a considerable number of cases at least, taught to read and write in their own homes in so far as these arts were necessary for the conduct of the ordinary business of life.

CHAPTER III

EDUCATION AMONG THE DORIAN GREEKS

I. CRETAN EDUCATION

THE manly vigour of the Dorian, his simplicity and natural-ness, were reproduced in the education to which he subjected the young. The Hellenic idea of the supremacy of the state was recognised more fully than among the Ionians, who (as pre-eminently in Athens) allowed more individual freedom, and were characterised by more variety, flexibility, and subtlety of nature — elements necessary to bring to fruition the artistic genius of the Hellenic mind. With the Dorians the state was the schoolmaster : the state itself was, in truth, an organised educational polity.

In Crete the boys were retained in the family till their eighteenth year. At this age they were required to enter themselves (some say these associations were voluntary) as members of bands or troops to be trained in a severe course of gymnastic including archery, hunting, and military exercises. At this age also they were admitted to the public meals and allowed to listen to the conversation of the grown men.

These bands, each with its own head, were under the general superintendence of an overseer appointed by the state. There was no gymnastic 'specialist' employed as teacher — at least in the earlier times. Their literary education, so far as reading, writing, &c., were concerned received little or no attention. But in connection with the Doric music, which all learnt, they became thoroughly versed in the laws. These they chantéd. They also sang hymns to the gods, and recited tales of heroes, and narratives of the great achievements of their ancestors. Their literary education thus really comprised music, religion, civic economy, history, and poetry in their rudimentary forms.

As to the Æolic stem of the Hellenic race, I may say in passing that it was more nearly allied in its educational practices to the Doric than to the Ionic-Attic. Thebes in Bœotia was the representative town of this Hellenic branch. In music, both the lyre and the flute were taught at Thebes, and the influence of Athens was so far felt that literary schools existed there before the time of Socrates. The slaughtering of the children of the school of Mycalessus by a band of Thracians is narrated by Thucydides (vii. 49). Plutarch also tells us that Epaminondas, the great Theban, occupied himself with philosophic studies, and it is well-known that rhetoricians and philosophers taught at Thebes when Philip of Macedon was a boy.[1]

[1] The various colonies of the different Hellenic races in Asia Minor and throughout the Mediterranean followed each the customs of their mother city.

SPARTAN EDUCATION

The Cretan principles of education received their full development in Sparta. 'This is one point,' says Aristotle, 'in which the Lacedæmonians deserve praise: they devote a great deal of attention to the educational needs of their children, and their attention takes the form of action on the part of the state.' ('Polit.' v. 1.)

The position of Sparta in the centre of a hostile population compelled its statesmen to give prominence to the gymnastic and military side of education. The state had to hold its own, and it could only do so through the vigour and prowess of its *individual* citizens. Sparta, accordingly, was little more than an organised camp.[1] We are not to suppose that Lycurgus invented the Spartan civic system. He gave form and definite purpose to those traditionary Doric customs and tendencies which we find partially operative in Crete. Nor, according to Plutarch (i. 125), was it his intention to rear a conquering race. ' He thought rather that the happiness of a state, as of a private citizen, consisted chiefly in the exercise of virtue and in the concord of the inhabitants. His aim in all his arrangements was to make and keep the people free-minded, self-dependent, and temperate.' The state rested

---

[1] The Dorians effected a settlement in the Peloponnesus in the eleventh century B.C. Sparta was, before the time of Lycurgus, a double monarchy. Lycurgus about 850 B.C. still further weakened the monarchical authority, so that the two kings became little more than presidents of the senate. The senate consisted of thirty members, including the kings. The free inhabitants of Sparta alone had political rights. With few exceptions, they were owners of the soil and lived on their rents. The Periœci — inhabitants of the surrounding country and towns | were free, but had no political rights. They were engaged in actual farming and in various industries and commerce. The Helots, again, were in the position of slaves or rather serfs, and were composed of captives taken in war, or rebels who had submitted. They did menial work in Sparta and cultivated the lands of the free citizens, paying a fixed rent of one-half the produce. Sparta was regarded as a leading power in Greece from 555 B.C. In B.C. 510 it began to interfere north of the Peloponnese and as the supporter of the oligarchy to incur the hatred of Attica. The Peloponnesian War was waged, B.C. 431-404, resulting in the triumph of Sparta and of oligarchic versus democratic principles. Macedonian domination of Greece dates from 335 B.C.

on the idea that each citizen must be prepared to sacrifice himself to the whole.

1. *Infancy*

The governing conception in education was the production of a hardy spirit in a hardy body. To ensure this, the discipline began from the day of birth. The babe was bathed in water mixed with wine, because (it is said) the Spartans believed that only strong and healthy children could endure such a bath, and that the sickly must die of it. After this, the council of the elders of the tribe (*gerousia*) decided in the public place of meeting as to whether the child should die or live. The healthy and strong boy was preserved, but the sickly and weak one was ' put away.' It used to be held that it was thrown down a precipice on Mount Taygetus; but the custom seems rather to have been to expose it in a defile of Taygetus or some outlying district round Sparta and allow it to grow up, if any one among the subject population chose to save it. All rights of citizenship were for ever denied to it. Healthy children alone could be of service to the state.

Up to the seventh year the child belonged to the mother, by whom it was brought up, the health of the body being her chief care. In early times the Spartan mother nursed her child herself. After the Persian wars, however (B.C. 479), in the houses of rank, we hear of wet-nurses and nursery maids (hired women of the class of the Pericci), who were noted in Sparta for special carefulness and ability. They were on that account much prized by the citizens of other Greek states. The child was not wrapped in swaddling-bands (*spargana*). The Spartans held that its limbs should be free, so that the natural growth might be unimpeded. It was made hardy by fasting, and trained (it is said) to overcome fear by being left alone in the dark. Screaming was prevented as much as possible, for the Spartan, as a rule, was not allowed to cry out. The discipline of self-control thus began very early.

2. *The Education of the Boys*

(*a*) *Gymnastic.* — In their seventh year the legitimate sons of citizens were entrusted by the ephors to a state official, who was responsible for their upbringing. He was called the *Pædonomus*. The cost of education for all free citizens was defrayed from the revenues of the public lands and from the taxes of the Periœci. The object of this public education was to promote a feeling of equality among citizens of all ranks, and to implant in the youth of the state the feeling of a common interest. The Spartan youth, accordingly, were brought up in school-rooms, dormitories, gymnasia, and music-rooms, shared by all. The heirs-apparent of the kings were alone exempted. No Spartan was allowed to be educated in a foreign state. The *pædonomus* was assisted by officers called *bidiæi*.

When received into the public boarding schools, the boys were formed into small companies (*agelai* or *ilai*) and these formed portions of larger companies, called *bouai*. The older and abler boys were set over the younger and weaker ones as superintendents and leaders in their gymnastic exercises, as captains of the *ilai* and *bouai* (*ilarchai* and *bouagores*). 'The governor,' says Plutarch, 'set over each of the bands, for their captains, the most temperate and boldest of those they called *Irens* (youths) who were usually twenty years old — two years out of the boys' (i. 107). These monitors and captains were responsible to the *pædonomus* alone.

The *pædonomus* (under whom were the *bidiæi*), who was supreme, punished the boys on the spot for any offence, superintended their moral training and their gymnastic exercises. He also regulated the stories which the children were allowed to hear. 'Lycurgus,' says Plutarch, 'would not have masters bought out of the market for his young Spartans, nor such as should sell their pains : nor was it lawful for the father himself to breed up the children after his own fancy; but as soon as they were seven years old they were to be enrolled in certain companies and classes, where they all lived under the same order and discipline, doing their exercises and taking their play together. Of these, he who showed the most conduct and courage was made captain; the others had their eyes always upon him; obeyed his orders, and underwent patiently whatsoever punishment he inflicted; so that the whole course of their education was one continued exercise of a ready and perfect obedience.' [1] (i. 106.)

The age of the boys regulated the classification into different groups and classes. Up to the period of youth there were three classes to be gone through, from the seventh to the twelfth year, from the twelfth to the fifteenth, from the fifteenth to the eighteenth; and there were probably as many more from the period of youth to that of full manhood — in the thirtieth year.

Immediately on his entrance the boy's hair was cut short. The beds consisted of hay and straw, without blankets; from the fifteenth year of rushes, which the boys were required to collect for themselves, without a knife, on the banks of the Eurotas. In summer and in winter they went without shoes and but slightly clad: till their twelfth year in petticoats (scanty woollen ones); after that age they had only one garment, a kind of plaid. This plaid was a square piece of cloth, which was laid upon the left shoulder, passed round the back, drawn under the right arm, and then again thrown back over the left shoulder.

To accustom them to endure hunger in war, food was supplied to them but sparingly, and that they might be trained to overreach the enemy and provide their own food when campaigning, they had permission to steal provisions, but with the reservation that they did not allow themselves to be caught in the act. Whoever caught a boy stealing was required to punish him or to inform the *pœdonomus*, who then ordered punishment to be inflicted by the whip-bearers (*mastigophori*) who always accompanied him. The disgrace of the boy lay essentially in the fact that he had shown so little cunning and foresight. The ignominy of being dis-

[1] I quote always from Clough's *Plutarch*.

covered was greater than that of the blows, for blows were looked on as a means of hardening the young for the bearing of pain. Indeed, the boys had on certain great occasions to pass what might be called 'whipping-examinations.' On the annual festival of Artemis-Orthia youths were whipped to the drawing of blood. 'Nor must one be offended,' says Solon to Anacharsis in Lucian, 'when you see their young men whipped at the altar and streaming with blood, whilst their fathers and mothers stand by entreating them to suffer it courageously and even proceed to threats if they do not bear it with patience and resolution. Many have died under this discipline rather than acknowledge themselves unequal to it before their friends and relations. Statues of them have frequently been erected at the public expense.' The custom is referred to by Pausanias, and Plutarch in his Life of Lycurgus says — 'I myself have seen several of the youths endure whipping to death at the foot of the altar of Diana surnamed Orthia' (i. 109).

Led by the *ilarchai* and *bouagores* the boys went through the gymnastic curriculum under the direction of the *pædonomus* and his subordinate *bidiœi*. Gymnastic exercises, indeed, formed the chief instrument of education in Sparta. The Dorians had cherished them from time immemorial, and Lycurgus, who is said to have been one of the founders of the Olympic games, had regulated them by law. It was an organised and graduated gymnastic system. The exercises were meant neither to form athletes, nor to promote acrobatic dexterity, or beauty of form, but solely to develop qualities serviceable in war. They were performed in the gymnasia (probably in the morning before breakfast and in the afternoon before the evening meal), and generally naked. The exercises consisted principally in running, leaping, fighting, riding, swimming, throwing the discus, and (as the boys grew older) hunting.

The little boys began with running and leaping. At the same time they practised playing at ball to strengthen the arms. In the advanced classes the principal exercises were military evolutions; also wrestling, throwing the quoit, and hurling the spear. Some say that the *pancratium* — a personal contest in which any means might be taken of defeating an opponent — was discouraged, because it might disfigure the face and cause such serious injuries of other kinds as to unfit for war. But there can, I think, be no doubt that it existed and was encouraged. Not to speak of other authorities, we find it referred to in Plato's 'Laws,' and even so late as Cicero it might be seen. In the 'Tusc. Disp.' v. 27, he says: —' Adolescentium greges Lacedæmone vidimus ipsi incredibili contentione certantes pugnis, calcibus, unguibus, morsu denique, quum exanimarentur priusquam victos se faterentur.' Pausanias also speaks of the personal contests which were carried on in the island of Platanistas. He tells of the eyes being torn from their sockets in these encounters.

With the gymnastic exercises were conjoined exercises in dancing. The chief kinds of dance in use in Sparta were war-dances. When the boys had learned to march to the time of the *cithara* and wind instruments, instruction in the rudiments of the war-dance soon followed. This *Pyrrhic* dance (which Thaletas had brought from Crete to Sparta), according to Plato, represented the cautious movements necessary for avoiding blows and assaults of an enemy, as well as all movements suited to attack, *e.g.* springing to the side, drawing back, bending down to the earth, and springing up again. The *Pyrrhic* was also danced in armour, and in companies, in which case the movements of attack and defence were gone through in whole masses to the rhythm of the music. In addition to war-dances there were also the choral dances, which formed part of divine worship, representing mythical events and giving expression to religious feelings. The *Caryatic* dance was danced annually by the maidens in honour of Diana, and the *Bibasis* by boys and girls together. In this dance they sprang into the air and struck themselves behind with the feet.

We must never forget, however, that even the Spartan Greek looked with contempt on athletic training for its own sake. He did not, as has been already remarked, aim at making athletes. Men trained simply to run, and others trained only to box, could give only a disproportionate development to the human frame. The Spartans, it is said, had no separate institutions called gymnasia; but in truth their whole system was gymnastic, and they pursued every kind of physical exercise which could give activity to the body and power of endurance.

There can be no doubt that the tendency of the excessive gymnastic training of the young Spartans, while hardening, must have been at the same time brutalising, unless powerfully counteracted by intellectual and moral influences, which, as we shall see, it was not. The Spartan was, indeed, always hard and cruel. Aristotle sums up this whole question in his 'Politics:' 'At the present day the states which enjoy the highest repute for care in the education of children generally produce in them an athletic condition whereby they mar their bodily presence and development; while the Lacedæmonians, although they avoided this mistake, render them brutal by the exertions required of them in the belief that this is the best means to produce a valorous disposition. Yet, as we have several times remarked, valour is neither the only virtue nor the virtue principally to be kept in view in the superintendence of children; and even if it were, the Lacedæmonians are not successful in devising the means to attain it. For neither in the animal world generally nor among uncivilised nations do we find valour associated with the most savage characters, but rather with such as are gentle, like the lions. There are many uncivilised nations who think very little of slaying and eating their fellow-creatures, e.g. the Achæans and Heniochans on the shores of the Black Sea, and other nations of the mainland *in those parts*, some of whom are as savage as these, and others more so; yet, although their existence is one of piracy, they are absolutely destitute of valour. Nay, if we look at the case of the Lacedæmonians 'themselves, it is well known that, although they maintained their superiority to all other peoples so long as they alone were assiduous in the careful endurance of laborious exercises, they are now surpassed by others in the contests both of the wrestling-school and of actual war. The fact is that their pre-eminence was due, not to their disciplining their youth in this severe manner, but solely to their giving them a course of training, while other nations *with whom they had to contend did not.* Now it is right that we should base our judgment not upon their achievements in the past but at the present day; for at present they have competitors in their educational system, whereas in past times they had none. We may conclude, then, that it is not the brutal element *in men* but the element of nobleness which should hold the first place — for the power of encountering noble perils must belong, not to a wolf nor to any other brute, but only to a brave man — and that to give up our children overmuch to bodily exercises and leave them uninstructed in the true essentials, i.e. *in the rudiments of education,* is in effect to degrade them to the level of mechanics by rendering them useless in a statesman's hands for any purpose except one, and, as our argument shows, not so useful as other people even for this.'[1] ('The Politics of Aristotle,' Book V. page 229.)

(*b*) *Intellectual and Moral Education.* — Intellectual, moral, and æsthetic education were all included by the Greeks under the general designation *music.* 'Gymnastic for the body, music for the mind,' says Plato. This term, however, was frequently used (I think, always by Aristotle) in the narrower sense in which it is now employed. *Grammata* and *mousike* (in its narrower acceptation) *together* constituted *Mousike* in its larger sense. Now the training of the mind was in Sparta, as we might expect, essentially and almost exclusively represented by the instruction in music in the narrower acceptation of the word. Music was practised in order by its means to rouse the mind to bravery and patriotism. But it was always married to words — poems celebrating the glory of the gods, and also the deeds

---

[1] In quoting from Aristotle I take Welldon's translation.

of heroes. It is generally said that the boys and youths learned to play the cithara, but I cannot reconcile this with Arist. 'Polit.' v. 5, where it is said that the Spartans took pleasure in music and could judge it, but did not themselves learn it. They certainly sang. The songs were chiefly choric and were national, rather than personal, in their sentiment. It was the custom, according to Plutarch, to call on the boys to sing after supper. The chants that were approved by the ephors, sung in the manly and grave Doric style, were meant to instil into the hearts of the young citizens the moral elements of the Spartan life, viz. courage and discipline, a noble pride, contempt of cowardly and servile ways, the seriousness of existence, and the worthiness of effort. The laws of Lycurgus also, which Thaletas had set to music, were committed to memory and chanted, just as the Cretan laws were chanted in Crete. But the music had ever to remain grave and measured. Plutarch says: 'Their songs had a life and spirit in them that inflamed and possessed men's minds with an enthusiasm and ardour for action; the style of them was plain and without affectation; the subject always serious and moral; most usually it was in praise of such men as had died in defence of the country, or in derision of those that had been cowards: the former they declared happy and glorified; the life of the latter they described as most miserable and abject. Indeed, if we will take the pains to consider their compositions, some of which were still extant in our days, and the airs on the flute to which they marched when going to battle, we shall find that Terpander and Pindar had reason to say that music and valour were allied. The former says of Lacedæmon:

> The spear and song in her do meet
> And Justice walks about her street;

and Pindar:

> Councils of wise elders here,
> And the young men's conquering spear,
> And dance, and song, and joy appear;

both describing the Spartans as no less musical than war
like; in the words of one of their own poets :

> With the iron stern and sharp
> Comes the playing of the harp.

For, indeed, before they engaged in battle, the king first
sacrificed to the Muses, in all likelihood to put them in mind
of the manner of their education and of the judgment that
would be passed upon their actions, and thereby to animate
them to the performance of exploits that should deserve a
record.' (112 and 113.) We must not forget, too, that
some of the most celebrated lyric poets were Spartans or at
least Dorians.

The music of the Spartans was, however, very limited in
its range. It is said that when the musician Phrynis came
from Lesbos to Sparta with a new-stringed cithara, the ephor
then in power cut off two of the strings. And in the same
way, the eleven-stringed cithara is said to have been taken
by the ephors in Sparta from the pupil of Phrynis, Timotheus
of Miletus, and hung up in the music-hall in the market
place. They remained as constant to the seven-stringed
cithara of Terpander as to the Doric style of melody. All
this contradicts Aristotle's opinion.

The power of music in forming the character was recognised by the ancient Egyptians, and still more by the Greeks,
to an extent which to us moderns is almost unintelligible.
Of this Grote (ii. 190) says: 'The Doric mode created a
settled and deliberate resolution exempt alike from the
desponding and impetuous sentiments. . . . The marked
ethical effects produced by these modes in ancient times are
facts perfectly well attested, however difficult they may be to
explain on any general theory of music.' The tradition
regarding Pythagoras is that he had organised melodies and
harmonies so as to suit different affections and passions of
the soul. Milton's well-known lines in the first book of
'Paradise Lost' naturally occur to us here:

> Anon they move
> In phalanx perfect to the Dorian mood
> Of flutes and soft recorders ; such as raised
> To height of noblest temper heroes old
> Arming to battle, and instead of rage
> Deliberate valour breathed, firm and unmoved
> With dread of death, to flight or foul retreat.

Reading and writing formed, as may be supposed, no necessary part of the Spartan system of education, although no one was forbidden to acquire skill in them, and there were adventure schoolmasters in Sparta for boys. Plutarch says : ' Reading and writing they gave them' just enough to serve their turn : their chief care was to make them good subjects and to teach them to endure pain and to conquer in battle.' (i. 106.) But the boys had to learn by heart the laws and pieces of poetry, which they sang; and also Homer. The majority of boys, we cannot doubt, learned to read and write after manuscripts came into use, but freemen could' find a truly worthy occupation only in gymnastic, war, and hunting. Professor Ussing (p. 78), resting on a passage in Isocrates (' Panathen.' 209), says that many could neither read nor write even in the fourth century B.C. In truth, we find that all states, while engaged in moulding their civic life and holding their own against enemies, necessarily look on literary pursuits with a certain contempt. The mediæval Baron was proud to be able to say that his sons could not write :

> Thanks to St. Bothan, son of mine
> Save Gawain ne'er could pen a line.
>   *Marmion*, vi. 15.

The only literature acceptable in the earliest stages of social life is, first, war-songs and ballads descriptive of personal prowess, and, secondly, hymns to the gods, and, thirdly, songs of lamentation and joy. These, and Homer to boot, the Spartan boy knew although he could not read. We are apt in these days to forget that we may have a highly civilised people without schools of instruction, and, on the other hand that schools may cover a country and the people yet remain uncivilised.

Foreign systems of training and the sciences, were, as might be expected, not admitted, with the exception of mental arithmetic for practical purposes. And, although after the Peloponnesian War (B.C. 431–404) grammarians and rhetoricians are found, yet the statement (whether it be fact or fable) is characteristic, namely, that Cephisophos was banished from the town because he declared that he could speak the whole day long on any given subject. Rhetoric had no home in Sparta. Tragedies and comedies were also forbidden. All purely scientific and learned occupations were held in low esteem.

In brief, the idea of *discipline*, bodily and mental, governed the education of the Spartans; but a certain religious and civic training was obtained through their songs and tales and their rhythmical laws.

3. *The Education of the Young Men*

On entering their eighteenth year, the youths left the public school-houses for boys. It was the practice for grown men to choose boys or youths as favourites, and to be responsible for their training. They were expected to set an example of all manly excellence to their pupils. For their acts, it is said, the man was even punishable. From the eighteenth till their twentieth year they were called *melleirenes* (budding youths), and were allowed to let their hair and beard grow. They were now principally exercised in arms, and occupied with drill and in skirmishing. From the twentieth to the thirtieth year their name was *eirenes*, youths; they lived in separate barracks and were compelled, under superintendence of the *bidiœi* to apply themselves to the prescribed bodily exercises. The more specific military training was now begun. The most distinguished youths were admitted into the troop of 300 knights, who, in peace, were at disposal of the ephors, and in war accompanied each king into the field, by a hundred at a time.

An inscription found in Crete shows that the Cretan and Spartan youth took a public oath to serve the state (probably similar to that which we shall quote in the chapter on Athenian education). At what age they took the oath is not stated — doubtless when they were twenty years of age and were called *Irens*.

'The discipline of the boys,' says Plutarch, 'continued still after they were full-grown men. No one was allowed to live after his own fancy, but the city was a sort of camp in which every man had his share of provisions and business set out, and looked upon himself as not born to serve his own ends but the interest of his country. Therefore, if they were commanded nothing else, they went to see the boys perform their exercises, to teach them something useful, or to learn it themselves of those who knew better. And, indeed, one of the greatest and highest blessings Lycurgus procured his people was the abundance of leisure, which proceeded from his forbidding to them the exercise of any mean or mechanical trade. . . . All their time, except when they were in the field, was taken up by choral dances and festivals, in hunting and in attendance on the exercise grounds and places of public conversation.'

The Spartan youth was not considered a full-grown man and a member of the public assembly till his thirtieth year.

At certain festivals there were public exhibitions of the exercises which the youth had practised in the gymnasium, and of their attainments in music. On the Platanistas (to which I have already referred, an island formed by two small rivulets, and shaded by plane trees) the *melleirenes* annually fought a battle. At the Karneia, the chief festival in honour of Apollo, which the Spartans celebrated in August, the youth in a body had to make a display of the entire round of their musical, orchestric, and gymnastic accomplishments. On a special spot in the market-place they year by year danced the choral dances in honour of Apollo;

here were heard the chants of Thaletas and Alcmæon; here gymnastic games were celebrated in presence of the kings and all the authorities. On such festal days the chorus of old men sang: 'We once were men full of vigour!' and the chorus of the men answered, ' But we are so now; if you care, try it.' Whereupon the chorus of the boys repeated, ' We shall one day be still more vigorous.' This fragment, attributed to Tyrtæus, is preserved in Plutarch (' Lyc.' 21).

The social customs of the free citizens were part of the education of youth from the first, and for a long period the men dined at common tables. On this point Plutarch says, ' They met by companies of fifteen, more or less, and each of them stood bound to bring in monthly a bushel of meal, eight gallons of wine, five pounds of cheese, two and a half pounds of figs, and some very small sum of money to buy flesh or fish with. Besides this, when any of them made sacrifice to the gods, they always sent a dole to the common hall; and likewise, when any of them had been hunting, he sent thither a part of the venison he had killed : for these two occasions were the only excuses allowed for supping at home. The custom of eating together was observed strictly for a great while afterwards, insomuch that King Agis himself, after having vanquished the Athenians, sending for his commons at his return home because he desired to eat privately with his queen, was refused them by the polemarchs, and this refusal he resented so much as to omit next day the sacrifice due for a war happily ended : they then made him pay a fine. They used to send their children to these tables as to a school of temperance ; here they were instructed in state affairs by listening to experienced statesmen ; here they learnt to converse with pleasantry, to make jests without scurrility, and take them without ill-humour.' (i. 97, 98.) He also says: ' After drinking moderately, every man went to his home without lights, for the use of them was, on all occasions, forbid, to the end that they might accustom themselves to march boldly in the dark. Such was the common fashion of their meals.'

16

On the subject of good manners Plutarch says: ' Nor was their instruction in music and verse less carefully attended to than their habits of grace and good-breeding in conversation.'

As regards conversational training, an interesting statement is made by Plutarch (p. 108):

' The *iren*, or under-master, used to stay a little with them after supper, and one of them he bade to sing a song, to another he put a question which required an advised and deliberate answer: for example, who was the best man in the city — what he thought of such an action of such a man. They used them thus early to pass a right judgment upon persons and things, and to inform themselves of the abilities or defects of their countrymen. If they had not an answer ready to the question who was a good, or who an ill-reputed citizen, they were looked upon as of a dull and careless disposition, and to have little or no sense of virtue and honour; besides this, they were to give a good reason for what they said, and in as few words and as comprehensive as might be: he that failed of this or answered not to the purpose, had his thumb bit by his master. Sometimes the *iren* did this in the presence of the old men and magistrates, that they might see whether he punished them justly and in due measure or not; and when he did amiss, they would not reprove him before the boys, but, when they were gone, he was called to account, and underwent correction, if he had run far into either of the extremes of indulgence or severity.'

The brief pointed question and the concise but incisive answer is still known among us as ' laconic ' and specimens are preserved by Plutarch in his ' Apophthegmata.' To give a practical training to the understanding, to have the art of pointed and concise (hence laconic) expression, to grasp the kernel of every affair quickly, to move towards an object with directness — this was the ideal of the intellectual education of the Spartans, and in this the men were expected to train the youths and boys, while they showed them by their conversation how they ought to think of affairs and to treat them.

Education in Sparta, as we see, was a public education, from childhood up to full manhood. Each citizen was concerned in the proper upbringing of his fellow citizens. Every man was a teacher of the boy; every youth had in every man, and in every old man, to give heed to his teacher. Every man, and especially every old man, was authorised and enjoined to chastise the erring boy and youth, not with words only, but with the rod, wherever he found him, in the street or in the exercise grounds. The boy or youth who resisted the warnings of an old man was visited with disgrace and double punishment. Age, indeed, enjoyed in Sparta a respect which is unique in history. The young man stood to the old man in the moral relation of obedience, emulation, and reverence. The younger were required to give way to the old in the streets and to stand up in their presence. 'Only in Sparta is it pleasant to grow old,' could on this account a foreigner once exclaim, when he witnessed this veneration of the youth toward old age. 'The other Greeks know what is becoming — the Spartans alone practise it,' said an old man, who, at Olympia and Athens, was attended to by no one, was mocked by many, and before whose grey head the Spartans reverentially rose up. (Cic. 'de Sen.' 18.)

To conclude: an iron sceptre ruled over the Spartan from his seventh to his thirtieth year. Flogging was the universal punishment; and every boy as well as every youth had to dread the stick of every Spartan, besides the official chastisements of the *pœdonomus*, who, as 'provost-marshal,' went with his whip-bearers through the streets and the exercising grounds. Moreover, the ephors went on circuit every tenth day to inspect the youth, to see whether their clothing, dormitories, and beds were according to the regulations; whether the appearance and growth of the boys was comformable to the required development; and they would even, it is said, whip any one who had grown broader and stouter than he ought to be according to the standard applied. For every offence, for every negligence of the boys, strokes with a cane or lashes with a whip were inflicted; for the Spartans thoroughly believed that the strictest discipline produced the best men.

The Spartan education was public in the ordinary sense of the word. It was public also in the sense that it was open equally to all free-born children. 'There are,' says Aristotle, 'many people who endeavour to describe the Lacedæmonian polity as a democracy because of the many democratical elements in its constitution. We may instance, first, the education of children. The children of the rich are brought up in the same way as those of the poor, and receive an education which would not be beyond the children of poor parents. And the same is true of the years succeeding childhood; and again afterwards, when they reach man's estate, there is no distinction between rich and poor. So, too, they all fare alike in the common meals, and the rich wear a dress which any poor man would be able to procure.' (Arist. 'Pol.' vi. 9.)

4. *The Education of the Women*

The education of the Spartan women was, like that of the men, a public one. To make the young women as fit as possible to be vigorous mothers of robust children, which was considered the most important function of free-born women, a gymnastic course was on the part of the state prescribed for the girls. In separate gymnasia, divided into different classes according to their different ages, they exercised themselves in hopping, dancing the Spartan fling, in running, wrestling, leaping, throwing the quoit and hurling the spear. Like the boys, they also wore the woollen under-garment, although a little longer, yet in their exercises slit up on one, if not both, thighs.[1] They were practised, besides, in melodies

---

[1] On which account the poet Ibycus calls them the 'thigh displayers.'

of many kinds. On particular festivals the young men and maidens danced their choral dances and sang their chants in company. 'Lycurgus ordered,' says Plutarch, 'the maidens to exercise themselves with wrestling, running, throwing the quoit and casting the dart, to the end that the fruit they conceived might, in strong and healthy bodies, take firmer root and find better growth; and withal that they, with this greater vigour, might be the more able to undergo the pains of child-bearing. And to the end he might take away their over-great tenderness and fear of exposure to the air and all acquired womanishness, he ordered that they should go naked [1] in the processions,' &c. They thus grew up, through vigorous exercise of their muscles, exposed to the sun and the free air, so sturdy and strong, that an Athenian woman in Aristophanes was forced to exclaim in regard to one of Sparta: 'How lovely thou art, how blooming thy skin, how rounded thy flesh: what a chest . thou mightest strangle a bull!' In spite of this masculine upbringing, the Spartan women were attached wives and good housekeepers, and there is no evidence, in the opinion of most writers, of a lack of propriety and modesty among the young. On the other hand, Plato in his 'Laws' and Aristotle in his 'Politics' (ii. 9) point very distinctly to a different conclusion.

It is true the Spartan women did not know how to spin and weave well, but they knew how to rule the house well, and at the same time, as members of the state, having a just view of their own position, to speak with freedom in presence of the men. Their dress was simple and unadorned. After their marriage they were veiled when they went from home. They seem to have been thoroughly alive to what the state required from all those who belonged to it, and they exercised upon son and husband a deep and lasting influence. Their opinion was respected, their censure dreaded, their commendation sought. On the great festal days to which we have already referred, the young women used to stand

---

[1] I imagine 'naked' meant destitute of any outer garment, but not positively nude.

round, criticising and encouraging the youth. 'Those who were commended,' says Plutarch, 'went away proud, elated, and gratified with their honour among the maidens; and those who were rallied were as sensibly touched by it as if they had been reprimanded; and so much the more because the kings and the elders, as well as the rest of the city, saw and heard all that passed.' And in later years the husband by the thought of his wife, the son by the remembrance of his mother, were spurred on to all that was esteemed worthy of honour. All have heard of the heroic women of Sparta who offered thanks to the gods in the temples when their husbands and sons had fallen gloriously in battle for their country (as at Leuctra, B.C. 371). One such mother slew her son with her own hand, because he had turned back like a coward from the battle; and another — Gorgo — the wife of Leonidas, delivered to her son his shield with the words, 'Either with this or upon it.' 'If the root is good,' says Plutarch, 'the plant also grows the better,' and puts the question, 'Why should we not in the case of men have as much regard for a good breed as in that of dogs and horses?'

We find two poems in the Greek Anthology illustrative of this feature of the Spartan female character:—

> Eight sons Dæmenata at Sparta's call
> Sent forth to fight : one tomb received them all.
> No tears she shed, but shouted 'Victory !
> Sparta, I bore them but to die for thee.'

Again :

> A Spartan, his companion slain,
> Alone from battle fled :
> His mother, kindling with disdain
> That she had borne him, struck him dead ;
> For courage and not birth alone
> In Sparta testifies a son.

Of the women, then, as of the men, we are entitled to say that the Spartan system demanded the unconditional subjection of the individual will to the will of the community as determined by law. The freedom of the individual had no existence as opposed to the freedom of the whole, or rather in the freedom of the whole the individual had to find his freedom.

Now, what was the result of all this exclusiveness of national life and severity of discipline? Precisely those results which we see flowing from an over-severe system of education in families and schools in these days. So long as the Spartan remained at home, he was all that Lycurgus could have desired him to be — grave, severe, brave, self-controlled, self-sacrificing, long-enduring, full of respect for his elders, full of devotedness to the state. But take the Spartan away from the arbitrary system under which he lived, and we are told that he was lax and licentious, and a prey (curiously enough) to that very vice of avarice against which so many precautions had been taken. How was this? Because his morality was a state-morality, not a personal and individual free growth from within. There was no personal and inner idea of morality up to which he was to live. Instead of this there was a civic, in truth little more than a tribal morality and a tribal virtue, imposed by external authority and maintained by severity. The Hellenic spirit was unquestionably there, but it had forged fetters for itself. When Sparta got the better of Athens and had to lead Greece, it could not do it. (Spartan Supremacy, B.C. 405–371.) Nay, it was disloyal to the Hellenic idea. It wanted that breadth and elasticity of mind, that humanity of spirit, which could alone enable it to understand, and, by understanding, to control, others. How else than by a sympathetic understanding of the rights and feelings of others can justice ever be done among men? And when justice is not done, a state is doomed.

In view of certain modern opinions, it is interesting to note that we have in Sparta as near an approach to state-socialism as the history of mankind has yet exhibited — socialism, moreover, in the most favourable circumstances, because it was the socialism of an aristocracy supported by a slave system. The state regulated the individual life, and, by so doing, crushed out individuality, personal initiation, literary and scientific activity, and ethical freedom. Sparta, as an interesting educational experiment, is a valuable contribution to the history of education, but it is no less instructive to the political philosopher.

CHAPTER IV

ATHENIAN AND IONIC-ATTIC EDUCATION

WE turn now to the chief representative of the Greek spirit — the Athenian. All that we have said of the Hellenic mind and of the Hellenic life-ideals, in introducing the subject of Hellenic education, found its finest and fullest expression in Attica. As in the case of Sparta, we find that with the Athenian, as with all true Greeks, the state or city was the object round which gathered all their interests and all their moral sentiment. Nay, we may even say that the city was the object of their worship, for their very gods were gods to them as protectors and lovers of the beautiful abode which their artistic hands had reared. But the Athenian state, in the narrow sense of the governing body or executive, did not unduly predominate over the lives of the citizen. Their democratic constitution and popular assemblies brought the governing body into perpetual contact with public opinion — variable and fickle, doubtless, but yet full of ever-fresh suggestion. The despotic socialism of Sparta had no place. The state did not impose its abstract conception of life on the citizen, it was rather the citizen in his free activity who voluntarily gave his life to the state. The individual had, it is true, no ultimate rights as against the state organism ; but it was felt that the state itself gained most by the free development of the individual. (See Pericles' speech already quoted.) Accordingly, while up to the fifth century B.C. we might say that even in Athens the morality of the individual was a civic or political morality, the elements of personality and of a free ethics existed even before Socrates, and were powerfully expressed in literature

The Athenian education was in this, as in other respects, a reflex of the Athenian life. ' It is evident,' says Professor Wilkins, ' that a national system of education in the strictest sense of the term would have been wholly foreign to the genius of the Athenian state. To force every citizen from childhood into the same rigid mould, to crush the play of the natural emotions and impulses, and to sacrifice the beauty and joy of the life of the agora or the country home to the claims of military drill, were aims which were happily rendered needless by the position of Attica, as well as distasteful to the Athenian temperament.' At the same time the state, while leaving the education of the citizen by the parents free, prescribed certain general rules. All had to be instructed in gymnastic and music. The Court of the Areopagus, moreover, as *censor morum* and guardian of the ancient constitution, exercised supervision and enforced certain laws, as we may learn from Plato among others. But the main controlling force seems to have been public opinion.

1. INFANCY

Gentle and kindly as the Athenian care of infants was, yet there is no doubt that they were often taken from unwilling mothers to be exposed: the father — not the state, as in Sparta — determined this. But we must note that Sparta exposed none but the physically incapable : the Athenians were more heartless. These exposed infants were sometimes picked up by dwellers outside the walls and brought up ; or sold as slaves. Socrates refers to the grief of a mother deprived of her infant for the first time, and Plato, as we all know, recommends exposure in his ideal state. Aristotle, in his ' Politics,' iv. 16, considers it unnecessary to expose children with a view to keep down the numbers of the population, because other means, such as abortion, &c., can be resorted to, but he maintains 'there should be a law against rearing any cripple.'

On the tenth day after birth, all the friends of the family assembled and brought presents. The child was named by the father. There had been a previous ceremony of sacrifice and of purification on the seventh day. The infant was carried several times round the burning hearth by the nurse, followed by the mother, and hence the ceremony was called Amphidronia or 'running round.' There was much eating and drinking and congratulation, enlivened by music and dancing. On the fortieth day the mother paid the customary devotions at the temple. The child was then formally registered by the father as a member of the city ward.

The first care of the infant fell to the mother and the wet-nurse (*titthe*), and thereafter the ordinary nurse (*tithene*). In the best period of Athens the mother always nursed her own child. Later, wet-nurses were general. As a rule peasant women or female slaves were chosen for this service, as it was long esteemed dishonouring for free women to engage in such occupations; but the slaves when engaged were treated as free, and as members of the family. But free women from the country, and even free Athenian citizens, sometimes undertook the duty; especially after the Peloponnesian War, when, owing to the death of their husbands, they were reduced to great poverty. The noble and the rich Athenians usually preferred to get their wet-nurses from Laconia, that their children might have healthy and vigorous foster-mothers. The cradles consisted of simple trays, or wicker cots, hung like hammocks, but these are now considered to have been of late introduction.[1] When the work of the wet-nurse — it lasted from a year to a year and a half — was ended, she was followed by the ordinary nurse, usually an elderly woman. She gave the child its food, which consisted largely, along with milk, of a kind of broth sweetened with honey. She carried the child out to get the

---

[1] See references in Becker's *Charicles*, p. 24, English edition, 1886.

air, and with it accompanied the mother on her visits, and even to feasts.[1]

To put the child to sleep, cradle-songs and lullabies were sung. Theocritus has preserved or rather given his own idea of one of these, as sung to the twins Herakles and Iphicles:

> Tender she touched their little heads and sang :
> Sleep, baby boys, a sweet and healthful sleep ;
> Sleep on, my darlings, safely through the night,
> Sleep, happy in your baby dreams, and wake
> With joy to greet the morning's dawning light.[2]
>
> THEOC. *Id.* 24, 6.

To pacify and amuse the children, they used a rattle invented by the Pythagorean Archytas, a vessel of metal or wood with small stones in it. Aristotle condescends to refer to the rattle (' Polit.' viii. 6, 2): ' It is also very necessary that children should have some amusing employment: for which purpose the rattle of Archytas seems well-contrived which they give children to play with to prevent their breaking those things which are about the house, for, owing to their youthfulness, they cannot sit still.'

The nurses had the bad habit of many modern nurses and mothers of frightening children by threatening them with bogies. The tales which the children heard from the lips of these uneducated women constituted their earliest education. Plato, Aristotle, and Chrysippus urged that care should be exercised that the tales of the nurses and pedagogues were such as ought to be told to the young.

The ball was a universal plaything. As the children grew older there came the hobby-horse, the game with dice (made of the knuckle-bones of animals cut into square pieces) and spinning-tops both in the house and in the open air. Toys and go-carts and ' mud-pies' engaged the interest of Athe-

---

[1] The child was not allowed to be exposed to the influence of the moon ; and from the day of its public acknowledgment by the father, it was provided with amulets hung round the neck that it might be protected against magical arts and the evil eye.

[2] Hallard's translation, slightly altered.

nian children as of the children of all European nations.
Then followed, at a somewhat more advanced age, a game
which consisted in throwing slantingly into the water small
smooth stones and counting how many leaps they made before
sinking (which we call ' skimming ' or ' ducks and drakes '),
blind man's buff, trundling hoops, and all kinds of games
with the ball, walking on stilts, leap-frog, kite-flying, see-saw-
ing on logs and swinging, &c., &c. Girls had dolls made of
wax or clay, and painted. Blind man's buff was played thus.
The boy with his eyes bandaged moved about calling out ' I
will catch a brazen fly.' The others answered, ' You will
hunt but you won't catch it ' — all the while striking him
with whips till he managed to catch one of them.

At an early age the children wore shoes. Great attention
was paid to their personal appearance generally. Their hair
was twisted into artistic curls and drawn together over the
forehead with a splendid comb, according to the fancy of
mother and nurse. In the case of the girls a slender make
was aimed at by the use of stays, &c.

From all this we see that the early childhood of the
Athenian boy and girl was easy and pleasant. The amusements seem to have been substantially the same as those
which prevail among civilised races at this day. The
mother's influence practically ceased from the day the boy
went to school. Indeed, the want of education among the
Athenian women precluded their exercising much influence
over the boys. But during the first seven years the mother
and the nurse really laid the foundation of the child's education. Nursery rhymes, stories in which animals played a
part, thereafter the rich legendary, heroic, and mythical lore
of the Hellenic races were imparted to the child.[1] A poetic
and dramatic cast of mind was thus given, to be nourished
in future years by the school teaching and by the public
drama and civic festivals.

---

[1] Quintilian says (i. 1. 16) : Chrysippus thinks that no part of a child's life
should be exempt from tuition, and that even the three years which he allows
to the nurses might be turned to good use. There is no evidence that the
Spartan child had nursery stories told to it.

2. CHILDHOOD AND BOYHOOD

The play-time ended with the seventh year. Ussing says, however, that the age at which the boy was handed over to the slave-pedagogue was determined by the age at which he was able to receive instruction, and consequently might be long before seven. The place of the female attendant was now taken by the pedagogue, who did not impart instruction, but had only a moral oversight of his young charge both in and out of the house, and whose business it was to accompany him to the schoolmaster (grammatist) and gymnastic master (pædotribe). For this service they generally employed a slave whom they considered specially adapted for such work, but still oftener one whom on account of age and weakness, or some other defect, they could not profitably employ otherwise. Pericles is reported to have said, when he saw a slave fall from a tree and break his leg, 'Lo, he is now a pedagogue!' The necessary consequence of this pernicious custom was that the free-born boy had but small respect for his pedagogue, and often grew unruly. The pedagogue had charge of the boy at all times. His business was to train him in morality and good manners, and he was granted the power of beating him, if necessary. The rules as to the external bearing of boys in the street and at table were extremely strict in Athens no less than in Sparta. Doubtless the view the pedagogue took of his duties would not always be very lofty. There were, of course, many exceptions. The answer of one pedagogue who had a high conception of his function and was asked what his work precisely was, is worth recording: 'My duty is to make the good pleasant to boys.'

3. STATE SUPERVISION AND SCHOOLS

In what branches of knowledge the father should cause his child to be instructed, stood at his own discretion. By law he was bound only to instruction in gymnastic and music. This is laid down in the laws ascribed to Solon.

The first of these laws, as quoted by Grasberger (i. 2. 215) is: 'Every citizen shall see to it that his son is instructed in gymnastic and music with grammar (*i.e.* literature). Parents who disobey this law are culpable. Only those parents shall be supported (in their old age) by their grown-up sons, who have given them due education.'[1]

The instruction was not provided by the state: the schools were private undertakings. But they were subjected not only to a certain moral control, but also, as I have already stated, to the general superintendence of the public authorities. Although, in obedience to the general order of the state, all Athenian free citizens sent their children to the day-schools, the length of their stay there must have been determined, as it is among all nations, by the social position of the parents. We do not need elaborate archæological inquiries to convince us of this. For the poorer class a little reading, writing, and arithmetic would suffice. But there can be no doubt that whoever wished to be accounted as a truly worthy citizen of Athens must have passed through a certain gymnastic course under the pædotribe (gymnastic master) in the palæstra, the music course in its narrower sense under the citharist (teacher of music), and the literary course under the grammatist. But most of the time seems to have been spent in gymnastic and play.

Nor did the state provide school-buildings any more than it prescribed the details of instruction. But, notwithstanding this, schools (*didaskaleia*) were spread over the various 'wards' of the city and were to be found in all Greek towns. It was not unusual to teach even in the open air in some recess of a street or temple. It is probable that these open air schools were frequented by the poorer classes chiefly or solely. Of the younger Dionysius in Corinth, Justin, xxi. 5, says: *novissime ludi magistrum professus*

---

[1] Monsieur Girard thinks this applied only to instruction in some trade. But if Grasberger's quotation is correct the reference was to education generally.

pueros in trivio docebat. Almost universally, however, there were buildings devoted to school purposes. The misfortune that befel the school in the little Bœotian town of Mycalessus related by Thucydides is well known (vii. 29). The Thracians fell upon a boys' school, which was a large one, and slaughtered all the children. In 500 B.C. the school at Chios fell in, as Herodotus tells us, and killed 119 out of 120 children. Pausanias also tells a story of a Greek who went mad after losing a prize at Olympia, and, returning to his native place, entered a school, and pushing the pillars that sustained the roof, brought it down on the heads of 60 children, burying them under the ruins. But even such schools as were held in buildings did not receive any state-support, and were, strictly speaking, 'adventure schools' supported by fees.

The precise extent of the state supervision of schools, to which I have referred above, is in doubt. The Court of the Areopagus existing before Solon's time but reconstructed by him on a more popular basis, exercised great powers over all questions of morals and conduct; and this power there can be no doubt they exercised, when necessary, in the ordinary schools as they did in the gymnasia of the ephebi or youths. The mere fact that there was no organised school-system would make them all the more ready to exercise their large and undefined powers as occasion presented itself. They were 'superintendents of good order and decency,' and under cover of this it would be hard to say what they might not do. They were a check on the licence of the democracy, and the extent of their power would depend on the prudence with which they exercised it. This Areopagitic Council was shorn of much of its political power in the time of Pericles; but we may presume that there would be little objection to its continued supervision of morals and conduct. Among much that is uncertain we may safely conclude generally that, through the agency of either the Sophronists or Strategi the authorities in Athens kept a watchful eye on schools — especially the gymnastic schools, but without vexatious interference.

Instruction began in the early morning, and by law the schools had to be closed before sunset. The schools of the better class were generally ornamented with statues of the gods, busts of heroes, and pictorial illustrations of incidents in Homer. There is a fragment of such a pictorial table in the Capitoline Museum at Rome — the Tabula Iliaca of Theodorus. On entering, the boy saluted the master and his schoolfellows. The master sat on a high seat from which he taught; the pupils on benches: but whether the teaching was individual or collective (in classes) does not seem quite clear, probably both.

4. EDUCATION OF THE SCHOOL

(a) Primary instruction and methods — literary education

The Music curriculum was divided into two parts, one specially literary, and one specially musical.

In the literary course, under the grammatist, the first elements of reading, writing, and arithmetic were learned.

Reading. — In learning to read, children learned synthetically, *i.e.* they learned the individual letters first by heart,[1] then their sounds, then as combined into meaningless syllables, and then into words. The analytic method of taking words first and analysing the various sounds in them, and teaching these on phonic principles, is held by some to have been practised, but of this there is no sufficient evidence. ' We,' says Dionysius of Halicarnassus, who died about the beginning of the Christian era, ' learn first the names of the elements of speech, what are called grammata: then their shape and functions, then the syllables and their affections : lastly, the parts of speech, and the particular mutations connected with each, as inflexion, number, contraction, accents, position in the sentence ; then we begin to read and to write, at first in syllables and slowly, but when we have attained

[1] Athenæus gives a metrical alphabet, and probably it was chanted (Becker's *Charicles*, p. 232).

the necessary certainty, easily and quickly.[1] 'De Compos. Verb.' c. 25.

Plaques of baked earth on which the alphabet was written or painted were frequently used.

The chief difficulties to be encountered by the child when he began to read were the learning of the proper accents, as these were not indicated by signs, and the separating of one word from another, as words were written continuously without a break.[2] There was moreover no punctuation. It is possible that, inasmuch as good, nay merely intelligible, reading, was in these circumstances, possible only when the sense was fully grasped, the want of separation of words and of punctuation may have contributed largely to mental discipline as well as to good elocution. The manuscripts were either folded or rolled. If the interpretation of Dionysius is correct, parts of speech, &c. were taught orally before beginning to read.[3]

After the pupil was able to read, beautiful reading was practised — special attention being paid to the length and shortness of syllables and to the accentuation. Purity of articulation and accent were specially regarded. The pupils were taught the raising and lowering of the voice, and to bring out the melody and rhythm of the sentences, and all this with distinct enunciation and expression. Homer served as the usual reading-book; then Hesiod, Theognis, Phocylides, and Solon, as well as the fables of Æsop, and generally 'poems in which,' as Protagoras says in Plato, 'were contained many admonitions and illustrations of conduct, also praise and eulogy of distinguished men, that the boys might admiringly imitate them, and strive themselves also to become distinguished.' At an early period collections of the most choice specimens of the poetic art (anthologies)

---

[1] This translation is after comparison of the original with the parallel passage in *De Admir. Vi Dic. in Demosth.* c. 52.

[2] If MSS. were always written as inscriptions were written.

[3] τὰ περὶ ταῦτα πάθη. This must mean either the changes which may be rung on syllables, as when we say *cat, pat, rat,* or the noun-inflexion endings.

were used. These poems, especially Homer, Hesiod, and
Theognis, served at the same time for drill in language and
for recitation, whereby on the one hand the memory was
developed and the imagination strengthened, on the other
the heroic forms of antiquity and healthy primitive utterances regarding morality, and full of homely common sense,
were deeply engraved on the young mind. The poems were
explained to the pupils and questions were asked. Homer
was regarded not merely as a poet, but as an inspired moral
teacher, and great portions of his poems were learned by
heart. The Iliad and the Odyssey were in truth the Bible of
the Greeks. There was also much practice of dictation and
learning by heart of what the pupils wrote down from the
master's dictation — a practice which continued in all schools
and universities till after the invention of printing. In the
Greek schools the master recited and the scholar repeated
after him until he could say the passage by himself. The
scarcity of books had its advantages, as it must have compelled the masters to resort, more than they would otherwise
have done, to oral teaching in which mind meets mind without the interposition of the printed page.[1]

Arithmetic. — In arithmetic only so much was taught
(owing, doubtless, to the cumbrous system of notation) as
was necessary for the reckonings of the market-place. The
Greeks attained great proficiency within these limits. An
abacus or calculating-board was in use (but not the same
as our modern frame), the balls having different values
assigned to them as in the East generally, and to this
day in China. The fingers were freely used to assist in
calculation.

Writing. — For writing they used in earlier times tablets
covered with wax and a stylus or graver, one end of the style
being flattened for rubbing out what was written. These
tablets were often diptychs and triptychs. For the children
who could not yet write, lines were drawn and a copy set
with the stylus; they imitated the copy writing on their

---

[1] See an interesting passage in Plato's *Phœdrus.* Jowett's *Plato*, p. 614.

knees, there being no desks. Some say they began by tracing letters which had been first lightly written by the master (the master guiding the hand); and this is highly probable. Sometimes they carried the stylus over letters cut in wooden tablets. They drew straight lines with a ruler to keep the writing regular. Plato thought very little of writing and considered that not too much time should be given to it. It was enough in his opinion, I presume, to be able to write legibly. When older, the pupils wrote with pen (*calamus*) and ink on papyrus or parchment. Owing to the cost of parchment they practised on the back of leaves already written on on one side.

Drawing. — Drawing was much insisted on by Aristotle ('Polit.' viii. 3). It was not till his time that it began to be taught in the ordinary schools. But in the course of the fourth century B.C. it entered largely, if not always, into the general education, according to Grasberger and others. It was first introduced from Sicyon. The drawing was on smooth boxwood surfaces — white on a black ground, or red and black on a white ground. The instrument used was a pencil.

Geometry. — Highly as both Aristotle and Plato esteemed geometry as a school subject, it would appear that it was not till the later period of Athenian education (end of the fifth century B.C.) that it was introduced into the schools.

Geography was sometimes taught, and maps began to come into use about the time of Plato.

(b) Secondary education

The grammatist was the name of the elementary teacher. (The word didaskalus was used in a generic sense.) Those boys who could afford to continue their education went in Romano-Hellenic times, but not (so far as I can find) during the purely Hellenic period, to a grammaticus; but it must be understood that the line of demarcation between these teachers was by no means, till later times, clear. The 'secondary' instruction, such as it was, was doubtless given by grammatists of more than usual learning, until the two functions were differentiated. In Scotland we have had a similar experience.

In what did the 'secondary' education of the young Athenian consist before secondary schools taught by grammatici took definite form: this probably not till about 350 B.C.?[1] It is difficult to say. It was not till he was about thirteen years of age that a boy began to learn to play a musical instrument, and this, with the lyric poetry with which music was always associated and the continued reading and recitation of poetry, seems to me to have constituted 'secondary' instruction — at least till about 350 B.C. After that date we know that drawing and geometry, and (a little later) grammar as a philological study, began to enter into the curriculum of those who continued at school after the primary period. It would be at this time that the differentiation between primary and secondary schools would naturally arise. We shall see the distinction clearly marked, nay emphasised, in Rome (which followed Greece in all educational matters) certainly not later than 150 B.C. In the secondary school of the grammaticus when it was finally recognised, grammar and literary criticism were leading studies, and the foundations were thus laid for subsequent instruction in rhetoric and oratory, into which studies, indeed, the grammaticus frequently carried his pupils.

The youths after obtaining such secondary instruction as was available went (from about 400 B.C.) to the sophists in order to study rhetoric, &c. These were the highest instructors. I shall speak of them in the sequel.

It is not to be supposed that the system of education above sketched was in any way formally organised. It was a voluntary and natural growth, and doubtless underwent all the fluctuations that are inherent in voluntary institutions.

---

[1] Isocrates assumes a certain amount of what we call secondary instruction in the case of his pupils.

(c) Music in the narrower sense of the word

Music, that is to say the chanting and singing of songs, was, I am disposed to think, the primary basis of all Greek literary education. It was common to the Doric and Ionic races. The music was always subservient to the words. It is not improbable that it was the musician, as being the traditionary channel for ballad and lyrical literature, who first (in the earliest times) added reading and writing to his ordinary instructions. For a considerable time, and until MSS. were accessible, the instruction must have been oral. The functions of the music teacher and the grammatist were afterwards separated. For a considerable period, however, if not always, the music instruction seems to have been given in the same buildings as the literary instruction.

In the special music course, which did not begin, it would appear, till the thirteenth year, the Athenian youth were taught by the citharist to play on musical instruments, especially the lyre, a seven-stringed instrument (originally four strings).[1] For a time, after the Persian wars, instruction was also given on the flute, which became very fashionable, the name being given to any instrument played with the mouth, such for example as our flageolet. It was this instrument which was popular in Bœotia. Plutarch relates that Alcibiades refused to play on the flute, partly on account of the contortions of the face to which it gave rise, partly because he who played it could neither speak nor sing while so doing, and that he also begat in others a most decided aversion to the instrument, which on this account fell at last into contempt. The true cause, however, of its falling into disuse was probably the exciting character of the music it produced and the impossibility of accompanying the music with the voice. The Greek flute had not the soft sentimental tones of the modern flute. The object of the musical instruction was educational,

[1] The cithara was more of a professional instrument, and is discountenanced by Aristotle. It had a sounding-board and was played with a plektron. The most recent authority on Greek music is Dr. Munro, of Oxford, in his book entitled *Modes of Greek Music.*

but also to enable all to take part in religious services and in friendly social entertainments. 'Music,' says Aristotle, Book V., 'was introduced by our forefathers for the rational enjoyment of leisure.'

The boys were instructed in rhythm and melody, and their ear trained to a feeling of the measure. This would be necessary to good elocution. The Greeks believed that by music the spirit of the young was elevated, and that they became rhythmical and harmonious in mind and manners. At the same time table-songs were learned by heart with a view to increasing the pleasure of social meetings. These songs pithily and wittily enforced homely sentiments and the principles of morality, patriotism, and worldly wisdom. The Doric strain (a minor scale) was that usually adopted for such purposes, and they gave it the preference because it was characterised by a dignified repose, and more than any other seemed to give expression to high spirit and to manliness. The soft and voluptuous Lydian measure (a major scale) was denounced as immoral in its tendency, while the Phrygian (also a minor scale) was passionate.[1] In the earliest stage of instruction, the citharist dictated to the children simple songs, which they were required to learn by heart. Then they had to learn the sustained and chant-like airs to which they were set. One of the first poems which they learned, is said to have been :

> Pallas, dread destroyer of cities,
> Thou war-din-raising goddess,
> Holy, enemy-averting daughter of Jove,
> I call on thee,
> Horse-taming, noblest virgin.

The boys were not meant to attain professional skill in singing and playing : their musical ability was only to be so far developed as to enable them, when grown up, to take part in choruses and sing table-songs, &c. This was the direct practical aim of the instruction under the citharist ;

---

[1] The Ionian and Æolian had also their specific characters.

but the main purpose of teaching music was unquestionably to produce harmony and balance of soul, while at the same time introducing the boy to the lyrical literature of his country. The music teaching was never dissociated from verses — lyric poems or hymns. 'The poetry and music together formed a single work of art.' In the 'Protagoras' Plato says: 'They make rhythm and harmony familiar to the souls of boys, that they 'may grow more gentle and graceful and harmonious, and so be of service both in words and deeds; for the whole life of man stands in need of grace and harmony.' And Aristotle and Plutarch utter similar sentiments; and to these we may add Polybius. That the aim of music teaching was ethical is further shown by the stress which both Aristotle and Plato lay on the importance of the state controlling school-music in order to secure sound moral results. In short, the boy was taught music, not that he might be a musician, but that he might be musical.

It was always, indeed, the education of mind and body as a unity which the Athenian kept constantly in view — not technical facility in any art whatsoever. 'To be always in quest of what is useful,' says Aristotle, 'is not becoming to high-minded men and freemen.' Even as regards gymnastic and music the 'professional' was not highly esteemed. Plutarch says that when Alexander played and sang on one occasion with particular skill, his father Philip said, 'Are you not ashamed to play so well?'

Taking the literary and musical education together, we must conclude that 'the mental culture was but plain and simple, yet it took hold of the entire man; and this all the more deeply and thoroughly because the youthful mind was not distracted by a multiplicity of subjects and could therefore more closely devote itself to the mental food and to the materials of culture offered to it.' (Curtius, 'History,' ii. 416.)

The young Greek had a rich literature to draw on. The intellectual and æsthetic education of the children of a nation is necessarily governed by its literature. The Egyptians and

Babylonians, even if they had had an organised system of schools, could have made little of them. The literary materials of Greek national education were on the other hand extraordinarily various and abundant. To Homer is generally assigned the date of about 1,000 years before Christ, and he is closely followed by Hesiod, while the number of unnamed rhapsodists and handers down of national traditions of religion and conduct and of heroism must have been great. In the seventh century before Christ we have in the elegiac and lyrical poets a natural development of the heroic rhapsodist and religious hymn-writer. (Callinus, Archilochus, Tyrtæus, Alcman, and Sappho.) The sixth century again is especially the period of gnomic or ethical poetry — Solon, Theognis, Phocylides, and the sayings of the Wise men. At the end of this century and the beginning of the fifth we have again the lyrical poets Anacreon and Pindar ; and about the same period, tragedy — a combination and evolution of the gnomic, the heroic, and choral lyric — was firmly established by Æschylus. In education, as indeed in public life, the poets, let us remember, were regarded by the Greeks as teachers of wisdom and as moral guides. The end of the seventh and the beginning of the sixth century also saw the rise of speculative philosophy, which reached its highest point in the fifth and the fourth centuries B.C. Oratory also reached its highest and finest development in the fourth. I mention these things because it is impossible for us to understand the literary side of Greek education without realising the immense mass of literary material by means of which the education could be conducted — literary material existing more or less (but always growing from generation to generation in quantity and excellence) for 500 if not 600 years before the birth of Plato in 430 B.C.

(d) Gymnastic

About the eighth year, physical education was begun with gymnastic exercises under the pædotribe (boys' gymnastic master) after preparation had already been made for it by means of easy games in the paternal home. After the age of fourteen or fifteen, gymnastic took precedence of literary instruction. It is doubtful whether the gymnastic instruction of children began at the same time as the literary instruction or after some progress had been made in learning to read and write. The gymnastic exercises had for their object in Athens the discipline of the body with a view to giving it a healthy development and a noble carriage.

The pædotribe, as I have said, was not appointed by the state. Like the teacher of the day-school, he opened a palæstra or wrestling school; but he was in all cases under state supervision, and subject to certain state-regulations which had in view mainly the moral demeanour of the boys. The pædotribe himself gave the gymnastic instruction, but there were present also in the arena the moral superintendent or censor who had the oversight of morals, and the anointers who arranged and superintended the dietetic regimen and anointed or saw to the anointment of the body with oil, which after exercise had to be scraped off.

The palæstra was reserved for boys and the gymnasium for the ephebi (youths of eighteen years) and full-grown men. Plato, and the Athenians generally, looked with most favour on games which gave room for the exhibition of the moral qualities of spirit (or as we should say, pluck) and intelligence — mere animal force being regarded as of comparatively small account.

The exercises were graduated from the easier to the more difficult, and aimed at forming the body in all its stages of development. During the exercises the boys were arranged in two or three divisions. These were united at festivals, especially at the Hermæa. Lively games, especially games with the ball, appear to have been first taken up. Swimming was practised very early.[1] Among the first exercises

---

[1] On this point Professor Mahaffy, I notice, throws doubt. Why he does so I cannot understand, as swimming is especially mentioned in the earliest laws. There was also a common phrase applied to an uneducated man, 'he can neither swim nor say his alphabet.' (See also Krause, p. 100, for an apt authority.)

were: standing on tip-toe, while performing certain active movements of the arms; jumping; hanging and climbing on the rope; holding a weight with extended arms; the simple race; boxing, wrestling, &c. After sufficient training, more advanced exercises were undertaken. There was a contest called the *pentathlon*, in which five exercises performed in succession by the same person were included, viz. leaping, running, throwing the discus, throwing the spear, and wrestling. This had a place even at the Olympic games. The *pancratium*, in which wrestling and boxing together, and the use of feet as well as hands was allowed, seems to have been tolerated, but was reserved for the elder boys; and, always at Athens, under certain regulations which distinguished it from the *pancratium* of the professional athlete. In the palæstra, attention was paid to the deportment of the boys, and the rod was as little spared here as under the citharist.[1] At one time music was associated with gymnastic exercises. Our recently introduced musical drill is consequently only a revival.

Dancing formed part of the physical training; but by dancing was not meant the rhythmical movement of the feet alone but of the whole body: and this to music. But this exercise, admirable as it is, did not form part of the regular training of the young Athenian. Thorough training in dancing was confined to the trained choral bands who performed at festivals and in the temple and theatre. The dances cultivated that grace and delicacy of movement to which the Athenian had already in himself a natural bent. Indeed, it was of common knowledge in the ancient world that even a poor Athenian citizen distinguished himself among all other men by his easy carriage and graceful bearing. The dances were of various kinds, religious, warlike, and Corybantean. Popular dances were also handed down in which all took

---

[1] The proportion of time given to the palæstra and the day-school is not known, nor is it quite certain at what hours of the day the palæstra was chiefly frequented. It is understood, however, that it was visited twice a day — in the morning before breakfast, and again before sunset.

part, but (as I have said above) the training in dancing was not a part of the regular education,[1] though what we now call 'musical drill' was practised.

The ephebi — youths of eighteen years (now of age and capable of bearing arms) — no longer attended the palæstra but the gymnasium, and received there instruction from the gymnast (trainer of professional athletes) and other teachers.[2] Full-grown men also were expected to continue the exercises which as boys and youths they had practised. And on occasion of sacrifices at the *Panathenæa* — special wrestling matches were arranged for them.

(e) Moral education

An ideal aim and a moral purpose ran through the whole of Athenian education. Lucian thus sums up the teaching which the young Athenian received: — 'We commit our children first to the care of mothers, nurses, and schoolmasters, to instruct them properly in their early years; but as soon as they begin to understand what is right and good, when fear, shame, and emulation spring up in their minds, we then employ them in studies of a different kind, and inure their bodies to labour by exercises that will increase their strength and vigour. We do not rest content with that power of mind and body which nature has endowed them with, but endeavour to improve it by education, which renders the good qualities that are born, with us more conspicuous, and changes the bad into better; following the example of the husbandman who shelters and hedges round the plant whilst it is low and tender, but when it has gained strength and thickness takes away the unnecessary support, and by leaving it open to the wind and weather, increases its

[1] Ussing, however, seems to think it was.

[2] The precise distinction between the palæstra and the gymnasium is matter of debate, but I have given the general conclusion. It would appear that in the latter period of Greek history the distinction was not observed as in the earlier. As to the age of the ephebus, some say eighteen and some seventeen. It probably varied.

growth and fertility. We teach them, therefore, first, music and arithmetic, to write letters, and to read aloud clearly and distinctly ; as they grow older, we give the maxims, sayings, and opinions of the wise men, and the work of the ancients, generally in verse, as easier for the memory. When they read of the great and noble actions thus recorded, they are struck with admiration, and a desire of imitating them, ambitious of being themselves distinguished, admired, and celebrated by the poets of future ages as their predecessors were by Homer and Hesiod.' ('Anacharsis.')

Again, in Plato's 'Protagoras' we find a better account of the training of the young Athenian than any that could be constructed by the collation of many passages from Greek authors ; and from it we shall see that in his view the aim throughout was a moral one — an aim to be attained through literature, music, and gymnastic. 'Education,' he says, 'and admonition commence in the very first years of childhood, and last to the very end of life. Mother and nurse and father and tutor are quarrelling about the improvement of the child as soon as ever he is able to understand them ; he cannot say or do anything without their setting forth to him that this is just and that is unjust ; that this is honourable, this is dishonourable ; this is holy, that is unholy ; do this and abstain from that. And if he obeys, well and good, if not, he is straightened by threats and blows, like a piece of warped wood. At a later stage they send him to teachers and enjoin them to see to his manners even more than to his reading and music ; and the teachers do as they are desired. And when the boy has learned his letters and is beginning to understand what is written, as before he understood only what was spoken, they put into his hands the works of great poets, which he reads at school ; in these are contained many admonitions and many tales, and praises and encomia of ancient and famous men, which he is required to learn by heart, in order that he may imitate and emulate them and desire to become like them. Then, again, the teachers of the lyre take similar care that their young disciple is steady and gets into no mischief; and when they have taught him the use of the lyre, they introduce him to the works of other excellent poets, who are the lyric poets; and these they set to music, and make their harmonies and rhythms quite familiar to the children, in order that they may learn to be more gentle and harmonious and rhythmical, and so more fitted for speech and action; for the life of man in every part has need of harmony and rhythm. Then they send them to the master of gymnastics, in order that their bodies may better minister to the virtuous mind and that the weakness of their bodies may not force them to play the coward in war or on any other occasion. This is what is done by those who have the means, and those who have the means are the rich. Their children begin education soonest and leave off latest. When they have done with masters, the state again compels them to learn the laws, and live after the pattern which they furnish, and not after their own fancies; and just as in learning to write, the writing-master first draws lines with a stylus for the use of the young beginner, and gives him the tablet and makes him follow the lines, so the city draws the laws which were the invention of good lawgivers which were of old time; these are given to the young man in order to guide him in his conduct whether as ruler or ruled; and he that transgresses them is to be corrected or called to account, which is a term used not only in your country, but in many others.' [1]

According to Plato and Lucian, then, the moral training of the young Athenian was never lost sight of. The learning by heart of noble passages from the poets and the whole of the music-instruction (in its narrower sense) had the ethical for its aim in the large sense of that term, including æsthetic. Homer, and the poets generally, were (as I have already said) looked upon as text-books of morality and wisdom.

To manners also, which are the outward expression of good feeling, there was much attention paid both in the family, in the street, and in the school. Grace and becom-

[1] Translation taken from Mahaffy on Greek education, p. 37.

ingness of manner was called *eukosmia*, and throughout the whole Hellenic world stood side by side with the other two aims of education — *sophrosyne* and *arete :* — this threefold aim being pursued by means of a training in music and gymnastic. But in the boy the Greeks did not expect to find this harmonious, self-balanced life : he had to be educated to it. The chief virtue of the boy was reverence for his elders, modesty of demeanour, and a keen susceptibility to praise and blame.

As a result of all this, we find that not only a penetrating and active intelligence, but also grace of manner and refinement of speech specially distinguished the Athenian Greek. Cicero (' De Orat.' iii. 11) refers to it, and particularly mentions the sound of the voice and the sweetness of speaking in a genuine Athenian. Even down to the time of Lucian we have evidence of the existence of the same characteristics.

We naturally ask what provision was made for religious education. The answer is that by the worship of the family gods, by the civic recognition of the gods in religious festivals, which were numerous and stately, and by learning and singing religious hymns and choruses religion was inculcated. In truth, it entered in a pleasant and cheerful way into the whole life of the boy and man as part of the æsthetic education on its more serious side.

(f) Advanced education

The ephebi. — The higher education of the Greeks centres in the gymnasium. The gymnasia were state-supported institutions ; and, in addition to a managing president, there was a moral overseer or sophronist and many subordinate officers. The ephebi continued to frequent them regularly and go through more difficult gymnastic than in their earlier years.

Both the moral and gymnastic training may be said to have received their completion in the service in the militia (or state-police) (beginning about the age of eighteen), when among other duties (especially the practice of gymnastic exercises), the youths had to camp out, occupy fortresses and patrol the frontier for two years. There were certain headquarters for the ephebic companies, viz. Eleusis, Sunium, Phyle, &c., besides forts. It was a military service and was at first compulsory. The youths were liable to foreign service only after its completion. It certainly, for manifest social reasons, must have been a great burden on many classes of citizens, and in the later days — those of the Macedonian rule (340 B.C.), it became voluntary, and consequently aristocratic. Hunting also formed part of the occupation of the ephebi.

When they entered on this ephebic training (also as we have seen practised among the Spartans) the Athenian youths, now eighteen years of age, were formally admitted to citizenship before the assembled citizens, and presented with a shield and spear. They took the following oath in the temple of Athene (Grasberger, iii. 61): ' I will not bring dishonour to these holy weapons, and will not desert the comrade who stands side by side with me, whoever he may be. For the holy places and for the laws I will fight singly and with others. I will leave my country not in a worse but in a better condition by sea and land than I have received it. I will willingly and at all times submit to the judges and to the established ordinances, also not allow that anyone should infringe thereon or not give due obedience. I will reverence the ancestral worship. Let the gods be witnesses of this !' [1] Their names were now entered on the citizen-roll of the phratria or ward to which they belonged, and they now in the fullest sense belonged to the state.

The higher education of the Athenian Greek did not end here. All his life long he was instructed by the public

---

[1] There are slight variations both of the words and translation of this oath. I give what seems best. Some put the taking of this oath after and not before the ephebic training. There can be little doubt, I think, that it was taken at about the age of eighteen, even before the word ' ephebus ' as a specific and technical term was in use.

drama, by the contentions and rivalries of civic life, by the great festivals, which were frequent and stimulating, in which the young men took part as members of the choral bands, by the superabounding development of native art, and by the public literary contests which began at an early date in their history and stirred the ambition of youths while moulding the life of maturer men. The civic life, above all, which often stirred questions in which the whole of the Hellenic states were involved, gave a daily education to all citizens. A polity is an education, says Plato.

Whatever might be disregarded, gymnastic was never forgotten. It was indeed in connection with the gymnasia that sophistical and philosophic teaching began, in the later half of the fifth century B.C., as we shall shortly see. As places of common resort they were analogous to the modern club, but they combined with this the freedom of the market-place and the attractions of a public park, adorned with statues of the gods. *Studia sapientiæ*, says Quintilian, speaking of the early imperial times in Rome, XII. ii. 8, . . . *in porticus et gymnasia primum, mox in conventus scholarum recesserunt.* The Athenian gymnasia of the Academy and the Lyceum gave names to the two great schools of Plato and Aristotle. And, later, the philosophic schools were themselves sometimes called gymnasia.[1] In the next chapter we shall speak further of the higher intellectual education.

I have in previous chapters brought into view the meaning of the gymnastic training of boys; as regards young men, the purpose was substantially identical. I may quote with advantage the words of Lucian: 'We teach them likewise to run races, which makes them swift of foot and prevents their being out of breath; the course, moreover, is not on solid ground, but in a deep sand, where the foot can never be firm, but slips away from beneath them; we exercise them likewise in leaping over ditches with leaden weights in their hands, and teach them to throw darts at

---

[1] Hence in modern times in Germany (and occasionally in mediæval times) a gymnasium is the designation of a higher school.

a great distance. You must have seen also in the gymnasium a brass thing like a small shield, round and without a handle or strings; you took one up, I remember, and thought it very heavy, and so smooth that you could not hold it: this they throw up into the air, or straight for-wards, contending who shall cast it farthest; this strengthens the shoulders and gives the limbs their full power and agility. As to the dust and dirt, which seemed to you so ridiculous, I will tell you why we have so much of it; in the first place, we do it that the combatants may not hurt themselves on the ground, but fall soft and without danger; and secondly, because, when they grow wet in the mud and look like so many eels, as you called them, it lubricates the limbs. It is therefore neither useless nor ridiculous, but promotes strength and agility by obliging them to hold one another with all their might, to prevent their slipping away: add to this, that to lift up a man who is anointed with oil and rolled in the mud is not easy. Thus do we exercise our youth, hoping by these means to render them the guardians of our city and supporters of the commonweal, that they will defend our liberties, conquer our enemies, and make us feared and respected by all around us: in peace they become better subjects, are above anything that is base, and do not run into vice and debauchery from idleness, but spend their leisure in these useful employments. Our young men are thus prepared for peace and war.' And again elsewhere: 'Out of the gymnastic struggles another more noble contention springs amongst all the members of the community, and a crown is bestowed, not of pine, of olive, or of parsley, but one with which is wreathed public happiness and private liberty, the ancient rites and ceremonies, the wealth, honour, and glory of our country, the safety of every man's property, with every good and noble gift we wish from the gods. With that crown these are all inwoven, and to this all our toils and labours lead.' We have hitherto been speaking of the period up to about the middle of the fifth century B.C. Up to that date there is

18

no evidence that the higher education involved abstract study of any kind except for a few of a philosophic turn of mind. The higher education was gymnastic, in so far as it was compulsory.

A retrospect will satisfy us that neither in school nor during the ephebic period had the Athenian a hard time. In the school up to the date given above there was not even geometry, geography, or drawing. Music, literature, and gymnastic summed up his education. The life both of the boy and the youth was easy, and by the help of the slave-system which relieved citizens from sordid material claims on their energies, the young were able to live a more unencumbered life than was, perhaps, altogether good for them. It was, however, always life; and owing to the peculiar genius of the people, a life full of interest and freshness, and of intellectual as well as bodily activity.

(g) *School and home-discipline*

The school discipline was severe. The rod was freely used both in the literary, music, and gymnastic training. It is not till the times of Seneca and Quintilian, so far as I know, that we find any protest against corporal chastisement, unless we take the remark of Plato, ' Rep.' vii. 536, as such a protest : — ' In the case of the mind, no study pursued under compulsion remains rooted in the memory. Hence you must train children to their studies in a playful manner and without any air of constraint.' [1] It is not to be supposed that even after Seneca and Quintilian the severity of punishment was lessened. The Greeks and Romans, and after them Christian teachers throughout the middle ages and down to very recent times, associated teaching with flogging as a kind of inevitable necessity.

But I commend this to general attention, that schoolmasters were held of small account. Nor do I believe it possible that, while this class of the community is fitly repre-

---

[1] Locke uses words almost identical.

sented as holding a book in one hand and a cane in the other, it can ever stand high in social estimation. It is only when we find in teachers of youth a high conception of their social function as essentially a spiritual function, that the rod will be regarded as degrading (to the teacher, not to the boy) and the community begin to accord to schoolmasters that respect which then, but only then, will rightfully belong to them. And why? Because then, and only then, will they work for the intellect through the intellect, for the moral nature through the moral nature. A resort to physical force is to be regarded as a sign of weakness in the educator, save in very extreme cases and after much deliberation.

The domestic discipline was more severe than we should have expected from the general character of the Athenians ; but it is an additional confirmation of the importance they attached to moral training. Sandals or slippers were used for personal castigation. Strict attention was paid to the little acts of life, such as the manner of sitting at table and of eating. The manner of taking salt and bread was regulated. Even when the boys had reached their eighteenth year they were held under strict subordination to their parents, and their demeanour in the streets was prescribed. Modesty of demeanour, respect to older men, and a general becomingness of conduct was strictly imposed, not only on boys but young men. Both at home and at school and in the palæstra, the rod was freely used. A verse of Menander is to the effect that a youth who has not been flogged has not been educated.

(h) Education of the women

The women had no school education. It was wholly domestic. The room in which they and their children lived was generally on the upper floor, to which they were mostly confined, except on great festival occasions. There would of course be necessarily more freedom of life among the poorer classes ; but less education. At popular festivals the maidens walked in procession and danced choral dances.[1] On other occasions the girls were confined to the house, and therefore the Athenian women were for the most part slender and pale. The mother gave them instruction in all feminine occupations, in spinning, sewing, weaving, knitting, &c. They sometimes learned a little reading and writing from their mothers, and also singing and playing on the lyre. ' Special emphasis,' says Schmidt, ' was in the case of the girl laid on moral training : propriety of conduct, chastity and purity, were the most beautiful womanly virtues, and domestic thrift, as well as judicious management of the household, the finest womanly qualities.' Woman accordingly had not that social and political influence in Athens which she had in Sparta. Her position was little better than that of an Oriental wife. Marriages were contracts arranged by parents. The wife had no part even in social entertainments. When her husband had guests she was not allowed to be present at the dinner which she had herself prepared.

(i) Method. The schoolmaster. Holidays. School-houses

Method. — Modes of procedure have been occasionally adverted to above in their proper place. As regards method generally, there was none consciously thought out. The teacher pointed to a letter and named it and the boy named it after him. He recited pieces of poetry line by line to the boy, and they were repeated until they had been acquired — later, pieces were written down by the teacher and copied by the pupil. The whole process was essentially a *telling* on one side and learning by heart on the other ; but explanations were always given and asked. When manuscripts became more common the master's work would of course be lightened and the boy's independent activity stimulated.

---

[1] At the so-called bear-festival, says Schmidt (Brauronia) girls between five and ten years of age were every five years consecrated to Artemis, while sacrifices were offered and a passage from the *Iliad* read — a consecration which was meant to be the symbolic commemoration of a pure virginity.

There were no home lessons. Everything was done in school. Any fairly educated Greek could teach on these terms who had the necessary patience. I have already said that, so far as we can learn, the pupils came up in turn to say their lesson to the master. Questions of classification and school organisation had not arisen. It is impossible to doubt, however, that pieces of poetry were learned collectively, as were the alphabet and the multiplication table, to a kind of monotonous chant.

On a vase (about the date of the Peloponnesian War and now in the Berlin Museum) we have an interior view of a schoolroom: and a young man is correcting the written exercise of a boy, another instructs the boys in flute-playing, a third gives instruction in the cithara, while a boy recites poetry to his teacher.

The Schoolmaster. — The day-school master did not take a high position. Demosthenes taunts his great rival with having had to help his father to clean out the school when he was a boy, and evidently regards the work of a primary teacher as a very humble one indeed. 'As a boy,' he says ('De Corona,' 258), 'you were reared in abject poverty, waiting with your father on the school, grinding the ink, sponging the benches, sweeping the room, doing the duty of a menial rather than of a freeman's son.' There was no public qualification for the office of schoolmaster, and hence, chiefly, the low social status. It was the refuge of the distressed. There was a proverbial saying applied to a man who had disappeared: ' he is either dead or become a primary schoolmaster.' Lucian, long after the palmy days of Athenian education, condemns tyrants sent to the nether world to be beggars *or* primary schoolmasters. Dionysius the tyrant taught an elementary school at Corinth, and this is mentioned as an illustration of how low a man might fall. Accordingly, it is absurd to suppose that the aim which the Athenian mind had more or less consciously before it in the education of the young was effectually carried out in the schools. The aim and general method we know — the results were doubtless often disappointing. The family and the state were after all the chief educators.

Fees were paid for instruction, and hence partly the low estimation in which the teacher was held, for the Greek mind looked on paid intellectual work as casting discredit on the recipient; at least till after the time of the sophists.

It is only when the state takes up education as a national concern that teachers receive proper remuneration, and only when they are professionally trained that they have any status whatsoever. It appears from an inscription that at Teos there was an endowment for a staff of teachers in the third century B.C.[1] This endowment provided for girls as well as boys. Only the children of those who fell in battle were educated at the expense of the state.

Holidays. — School holidays and festivals are frequently referred to by the ancients. And when we add to these the public festivals, to which the Athenians were much addicted, we may conclude that the Athenian boy had an easy time of it.

School Houses. — The school-buildings were not of state origin. The literary, musical, and gymnastic teaching of boys was all given in the houses or rooms provided by the adventure teachers. The gymnasia for the ephebi and grown men were, however, provided at the public expense. These were large enclosures planted with trees and adorned with gardens and shrubberies, monuments temples, fountains, &c. All Greek towns were provided with them. In the fifth century B.C. there were three, the Academy, the Cynosarges, and the Lyceum. They served, as I have already said, the purposes of modern clubs as well as exercising grounds, and also in the course of time they were the centres of schools of philosophy and rhetoric.

5. CONTRAST BETWEEN ATHENIAN AND SPARTAN EDUCATION

The education of the Hellene generally was an education, as we have seen, in gymnastic and music — music compre-

---

[1] See Girard, *L'Education Athénienne*, with references.

hending literary and moral training as well as music in its narrower sense. In gymnastic, including the training to physical endurance generally, the Spartan was much more exacting than the Athenian. The Athenian aimed at the perfect development of the body and the maintenance of health; the Spartan at making the body serviceable for the hardest tasks that could be imposed on it. Both, however, had in view the moral control to which good gymnastic training contributes.[1] Neither the Spartan nor Athenian gymnastic, however, is to be compared with our modern British training by means of organised play. In our games both physical and moral ends are gained in a way which was, I believe, quite beyond the reach of the Greek system, and which almost fulfils Plato's conception of gymnastic as an education.

In music, again, the Spartan, as we have seen, was educated, but only in the narrow and modern sense of the word music. Religious and national chants, metrical laws, choral songs, and heroic ballads were, however, taught, and indeed largely practised. The Athenian did all this, but, over and above, he acquired skill on a musical instrument, and he carried out musical education in its larger and literary sense of reading, writing, and arithmetic. The study of the national literature and the cultivation of literary taste by school recitations and by the public drama, were all attended to. The chief instrument in the education of mind among the Athenians, was in brief, literature; and this chiefly in the form of poetry. The Athenian education was (to use a modern expression) wholly humanistic, and yet it had a very direct connection with the intellectual life of the boy when he became a fully-grown man. The Spartan education was ethical (in a very narrow sense) and conservative, resting on law and custom as sacred, and admitting of no development.

The Spartan had a restricted definite and civic aim; the Athenian's aim, though never losing sight of the state, was

---

[1] The Bœotians, again, carried gymnastic into athletics to such an extent as to be hurtful to the bodily growth.

broad as humanity itself. Reading and writing, in so far
as they existed at Sparta, were esteemed only in so far as
they were 'useful.' The Athenian view, on the other hand,
is well expressed in the already cited remark of Aristotle :
' To be always in search of the useful by no means befits
men who are magnanimous and who are freemen.' 'Give
the fellow half a drachma, and let him be gone,' called out
Euclid to his slave, when a pupil asked what advantage he
would gain by mathematical study. To pursue even music
with a view to being an expert and turning it to use, and not
in the interests of a liberal education, was *banausian*. The
Spartan trained the citizen : the Athenian trained the man.
Hence in all the arts which adorn human life the Athenians
were great. They are still the masters of the modern world.
After the school period was over, the education of the citizen
went on, for it was a mere continuation of the work of the
school. The drama, sculpture, architecture, painting, surrounded daily life with the noblest ideals. ' We carry them,'
says Lucian in his ' Anacharsis,' ' to comedies and tragedies at
our theatres, that whilst they behold the virtues and vices of
past times, they may themselves be attached to the one and
avoid the other; permitting our comic writers to expose and
ridicule the citizens; and this we do, as well for their sakes
who may grow better by seeing themselves laughed at, as
for that of the spectators in general who may thus escape
being ridiculed for the like absurdities.' Thus was Athens
throughout the life of each man a perpetual school in the
best sense of that word, and not in the Spartan one. In the
speech of Pericles, part of which we quoted in the first chapter, he is constantly contrasting Athens and Sparta, and the
contrast in their lives we see repeated in their processes of
education.

Note further, that the Athenian system was a free and
voluntary system, the state merely supervising and laying
down general rules, while carefully guarding the morals of
the palæstra and gymnasium. In the laws ascribed to Solon
are found injunctions to all parents to educate their children,

and also certain rules for the schools, but these are all of a merely regulative character. In Sparta, on the other hand, the system was a state system — compulsory and gratuitous. Herein lies, partially, the explanation of its being so hardfast and inelastic. All were cast in one mould. So must it always be with over-centralised administration. This has always to be resisted by a country which prizes freedom and variety of culture.

Sparta, quite consistently with its theory of life and education, took possession of the young citizen at the age of seven;[1] Athens only at the ephebic age of eighteen.

Again, in Athens we have professional schoolmasters ; whereas in Sparta worthy citizens supervise the education of youth.

When we reflect on the past historical survey, we cannot but be deeply impressed by the contrast of East and West. Among the Hellenic races we first find ourselves in the current of a life with higher aims, both national and individual, than any we had previously encountered. Here, first, we find a people living under political conditions which favoured individual culture, intellectual activity, and personal ambition. We breathe the atmosphere of liberty — an atmosphere essential to the life of mind. We also find a religion which, spite of the traditionary popular tales about the gods, was an æsthetic idealism and intensely human. But it is a superficial conclusion that favourable conditions made the Greeks: the political and social conditions were themselves part of the expression of the Hellenic spirit. Let me add that, for the maintenance of this spirit, they relied on the proper upbringing of youth. In nothing were Greek writers more at one than on the necessity of the education of the young with a view to a life worth living and to the security of the state.

I have endeavoured to place before the reader the distinctive characteristics of the education of the two great

[1] Nay, earlier, for it was the elders who determined whether a babe was to live, not the father.

Hellenic types. It has only now to be noted that, after the death of Alexander the Great, Hellenic education all round the Mediterranean had more characteristics in common than in earlier times. The Ionic-Attic idea governed, although at Sparta many of the old customs survived for long after, and into Christian times.

I have been exhibiting the general aim and current of Hellenic education. It is scarcely necessary to guard the reader against concluding that, always and everywhere in the Hellenic cities, this aim was consciously pursued, or that, even in the most favourable circumstances, it was fully realised. Even in the golden age of Socrates, we have complaints of a degeneracy from a level of education which was probably never reached. The well-known *locus classicus* in the 'Clouds' of Aristophanes gives expression to these complaints, but we ought never to attach too much historical importance to the criticisms of professed satirists or humourists.

> 'I prepare,' he says, 'myself to speak
> Of manners primitive and that good time
> Which I have seen, when discipline prevailed,
> And modesty was sanctioned by the laws.
> No babbling then was suffered in the school ;
> The scholar's text was silence. The whole group
> In orderly procession sallied forth
> Right onwards, without straggling, to attend
> Their teacher in harmonics : though the snow
> Fell on them thick as meal, the hardy brood
> Breasted the storm uncloaked. Their harps were strung
> Not to ignoble strains, for they were taught
> A loftier key, whether to chant the name
> Of Pallas terrible amidst the blaze
> Of cities overthrown ; or wide and far to spread,
> As custom was, the echoing peal.'

I shall now speak briefly of the higher education of the few in the fifth century B.C. and thereafter.

CHAPTER V

THE HIGHER EDUCATION IN THE FIFTH CENTURY B.C. AND THEREAFTER

WE have seen that the Athenian youth and boy had, so far as school instruction, primary, secondary, or higher was concerned, an easy time of it up to the middle of the fifth century B.C. And, as historians of education, we have to note the fact that Greece was within sight of the highest pinnacle of its fame in arts and arms before school instruction took a more serious form. In Epic, Elegiac, Lyric, and Tragic Dramatic poetry, all the greatest work had been done before 450 B.C., and in the subsequent sixty years philosophy, history, and even oratory and comedy, had given many, if not most, of their greatest examples to the world.

From, let us say, 460 B.C., we can detect the beginnings of what we call the 'higher' education, and this has of course to be connected with the life of the ephebi. But first we have to consider the historical situation.

As Athens and the other active Hellenic centres progressed in material civilisation and in democratic forms of government, the number of young men of the leisured classes who desired an outlet for their activity in political life and were ready to interest themselves in all sorts of questions, largely increased. Improved facilities of communication among Greek states and the multiplication of political and colonial relations contributed also to the enhancement of public life, especially after the Persian wars, which ended 479 B.C. We had now the beginnings of what is called the Athenian empire. It seemed to have been instinctively felt that the chances of success in public life, now so much enlarged and so much more exacting, demanded more intellectual preparation than heretofore.

The schools of abstract philosophy had as yet engaged the attention of only a select few, and, moreover, did not meet the practical wants of the time.

When we consider the cosmopolitan view of life and politics forced on the Greeks by their warlike encounters with both East﹡ and West and the wide ramification of their commercial relations, the rise of a spirit of inquiry and of criticism of existing institutions and their basis in reason was not surprising. The new intellectual movement sought for satisfaction. And this, quite apart from the growing conviction that, with the increased importance of the democracy came a demand on those who would succeed in﹡political life to study both politics and oratory.[1]

Cotemporaneously with the rise of this new intellectual and political movement, there arose in the Hellenic states teachers who professed to give all the instruction needed for guidance in public life. These men (called sophists, the chief of whom were Protagoras, Gorgias, and Prodicus), taking up their quarters first in one town and then in another, offered their intellectual wares for sale, and thus incurred the contempt of the pure philosophers who held that wisdom was to be neither bought nor sold. They were, however, a necessity of the time. They met the political and educational demands of the age.

The sophists also represented, and to some extent satisfied, the critical needs of the time. As in the case of all other ancient nations, it is difficult to show how the beliefs, religious, ethical, and political, by which the Hellenic communities were held together, grew up. They passed down through the state (sometimes aided by a separate priesthood who consecrated and developed tradition) and the family, not as the product of deliberate scientific investigation, but

---

[1] As long as MSS. were scarce, speaking before public assemblies was the only mode of communication with the people. Rolls were for sale in shops before the time of Plato. There was, however, no public library in Athens till the Emperor Hadrian founded one. The Alexandrian library was founded in 323 B.C. by Ptolemy Soter : an example afterwards imitated by the kings of Pergamus.

as the authoritative voice of a remote antiquity. Nations held fast by their fathers and their gods — who were the gods of their fathers — and clung to these with an unquestioning tenacity as if they alone protected their political life from dissolution. The day of scepticism and reason ultimately arrives for all such authoritative teaching, with what final result to the faith of man and the interpretation of human life, individual and social, we do not even yet know. The Hellenic races, brilliant as they were, formed no exception to this general law of life and progress. The sophistical movement was a revolt against authority and convention, but as a revolt it served its purpose by proclaiming the rights of reason.

The leading sophists had unquestionably studied the systems of philosophy which had come down to them, and were men of culture; but the abstract speculative interest seemed to them to yield little that told on the immediate human interest. They accordingly offered to their eager pupils a kind of philosophy of practical life, superficial it might be, but still having intelligible relations to the world of political activity on which they were entering with all the ardent ambition of youth. Along with this, they also frequently gave scientific instruction in all the knowledge of the time. The more aspiring young men of the upper classes eagerly sought for these instructors because they professed to give, and did, as a matter of fact, give, a rational though doubtless superficial, view of life in all its relations which could be turned to immediate use. They obtained all the general knowledge they wanted from the grammatical, physical, and moral discussions of the peripatetic lecturers; but they prized above all their definite political instruction and their art of rhetoric. Rhetoric had now become a theory as well as an art, and in the course of time unfolded itself as a system so detailed and so encumbered with technical details as to be, to the modern mind, intolerable. Still, with all its superficiality and defects and formalism, the teaching of the sophists supplied a want and gave the only higher education which then existed, or was, perhaps, then practicable.

That the name 'sophist' did not, as time went on and as rhetorical theory was dignified by the more earnest treatment of Isocrates, call forth contempt, is evident from the fact that the designation was almost universally applied to the higher teachers, whether they included philosophy in their course or confined themselves, as was the general rule, to superficial science and a practical oratory.

It was inevitable, under a system of free learning and free teaching such as existed in Athens and the Greek world generally, that evils should arise. Numbers of pretenders offered to give young men a rapid preparation for oratory and consequent success in life. These men gave their pupils the ready-made results of knowledge, and not training. Dialogues and speeches were learned by heart, and youths taught to believe that a superficial acquaintance with the commonplaces of science — political and other — a certain command of the technique of oratory and the attainment of a certain verbal fluency, constituted education. But we know that there were many sophists who took a more serious view of their profession. Thus were brought within the sphere of the higher education all the leisured youth of the country, who aimed at public life in some form or other and for whom abstract philosophy had no attractions. And let us remember that public life under ancient conditions comprised many possible occupations: an advocate in the courts, a political speaker, including in this the whole function of the modern journalist and pamphleteer, and all legislative and administrative employments. Apart, however, from these special practical aims, the higher education under sophists of good reputation had a liberalising character. Speaking 500 years after the death of Isocrates, Lucian in his 'Anacharsis' says, 'We commit our youth to certain good and approved masters, who are called sophists or philosophers' (the designation sophist was frequently used instead of philosopher in Lucian's time, 2nd century A.D.), 'by whom they are taught both to say and to do what is right and just, to attend to and assist the commonweal, to live honestly, never to seek after what is base and unworthy, or to commit violence on any man.' The advanced instruction was indeed ethical and political, in so far as it was not purely rhetorical.

Meanwhile, the philosophical schools which in the fourth century held the tradition of earnest scientific inquiry for the sake of truth alone, gave a profounder discipline: but the youth of the country, down even to the close of classical antiquity, unquestionably regarded rhetoric and oratory as the main end of all their studies, to which philosophy was only contributory. The outcome of the whole was, that in the fourth century the higher or 'university' education comprised, *for those who desired it*, philosophy, which took a wide range, politics, and rhetoric. For the few so disposed, there were teachers of mathematics and astronomy. The higher education continued to maintain this character (speaking generally) in all the towns of the Mediterranean till about 300 A.D.

I have said above that the higher education connected itself closely with the ephebi and their rules of life. They were not always on military duty, and as their athletics were carried on in the gymnasia where philosophers and sophists were in the habit of lecturing and teaching, it gradually became the custom for many of the young men to attend their prelections and to engage in dialogue with them. And indeed, in the preceding generation it had already become a recognised custom for young men, in the intervals of their ephebic training and after it was concluded, to attend one or more teachers of philosophy or politics or rhetoric. The *military* duties of the ephebi were reduced to one year about the time of Philip of Macedon, as I have previously said, and, ere long, ephebic service became altogether voluntary ; and it would appear that the youths were now officially *expected*, though not required, to attend the schools. Thus the ephebic period became virtually a kind of 'university' life — in germ at least. Even then, however, all intellectual pursuits gathered round gymnastic. So that we have this interesting result, that the military and gymnastic training of men above eighteen absorbed into itself what we should in these days call university education — at least in so far as opportunity went — just as the gymnasia themselves became the university headquarters.

It was in the school of Isocrates (393–338 B.C.) that we find the best results of the higher educational activity of the fourth century. His popularity and fame all the world recognises. As Cicero says in ' Brutus,' 32 : 'Isocrates cujus domus cunctæ Græciæ quasi ludus quidam patuit atque officina dicendi.' Plato, in the ' Phædrus,' puts him above all the other teachers of oratory, ' because he has philosophy in him.' Isocrates, however, was not a philosopher in the Platonic or Aristotelian sense ; but rather a man of large general culture and keen political interests who, recognising rhetoric as the greatest of studies, because by means of it one might persuade men to wise political action and to a noble personal life, organised the teaching of this great art. His aim was to make a thoughtful man and a capable citizen ; but a capable citizen was one who could *write* and *speak*, and so influence his fellow-citizens to wise courses. The educational question which Isocrates tried to solve was, ' By what intellectual preparation can this be best attained ? ' He always kept in view the ethical and large political relations of rhetoric. He professed to train for public life and citizenship, not for abstract investigation. The Athenians were by nature an eloquent people ; and, altogether apart from practical considerations, it was to be expected that they would study eloquence, and that it should occupy a supreme place in the higher education. Isocrates at once represented and satisfied the national need. Moreover, he honestly attached supreme importance to style as the servant of justice and virtue — being apparently persuaded that *true* eloquence must always be the reflection of a virtuous and wise mind. Eloquence, he held, has for its aim the development of great truths and is the chief agent in civilisation. And although he saw all round him, to his deep regret, this same eloquence used to tickle the ears of the populace or to advance personal interests or unworthy causes, it did not seem to occur to him that a higher education founded on rhetoric alone must be ultimately doomed to failure. In his view the best form and the best thought were indissolubly allied. Art in speech was the greatest of arts. In training to this, all the faculties, intellectual and moral, were trained. Assuming a good preliminary secondary education in grammar and literature, and recognising mathematics and astronomy as a valuable preparatory discipline, he rested the whole higher education, thereafter, on language as an instrument of thought. His pupils spent two or three years (sometimes even four) under his tuition. We must therefore, I think, look upon this organised school of Isocrates as the mother-university of Europe.

As educationalists the only quarrel we have with Isocrates arises out of his attitude to philosophy in the sense of the pursuit of absolute truth — Science. But having said this, we then become his followers. The fit use of language as the expression of reason in man, and the power of using it eloquently, not for personal aggrandisement, but in the public interest, was unquestionably in those days the mark of the highest culture. Is it not so even now? Given adequate preparation such as Isocrates demanded, and still more such as Quintilian insists upon, there is much to be said for the ancient view, even in these days.

The higher education, said Isocrates, must be (1) Practical — avoiding barren subtleties. (2) Rational, *i.e.* resting on the development of the whole intelligence, not on technicalities. (3) Comprehensive, *i.e.* not limited to the routine of any single profession. He felt that he could carry young men through a curriculum of this kind, which would not, it is true, make them orators if they had no natural genius for eloquence, but would at least make cultured men equipped

19

for the service of the state. If these objects were to be attained, the higher or university education ought to be a school of rhetoric and the sole subject of study should be 'philosophy.' But of philosophy he took a wholly practical view. Denying the possibility of attaining to absolute truth, he regarded philosophy as the application of principles to the actual work and occasions of civic and political life. 'The philosophy of Isocrates,' says Professor Jebb (ii. 41), is the art of speaking and writing on large political subjects considered as a preparation for advising or acting in political affairs.' Philosophy, so regarded, could scarcely fail to mould the character as well as the opinions of youth, while giving them the practical power of using their knowledge for the benefit of society. And this was Isocrates' aim — substantially an ethical one. He defends the better class of sophists in these words: 'Some of their pupils become powerful debaters; others become competent teachers; all become more accomplished members of society.'[1] Instead of the hasty preparation for future life which gave rise to the just criticisms of Aristotle and others on the pretentious character of the vulgar sophists, Isocrates carried the pupils through a carefully organised course. 'I always teach my pupils,' he says, 'that in composing a speech the first thing needful is to define clearly the object which they wish the speech to effect: the next thing is to adapt the means to that end' (Jebb, ii. p. 243); and 'the real essence of his method consisted in developing the learner's own faculty through the learner's own efforts' (Jebb, p. 46). This method was entirely opposed to that of the vulgar sophists, who made their pupils learn by heart speeches and dialogues and then trust to their natural powers of imitation and their own undisciplined use of language; 'as if,' says Aristotle, 'you could teach a man to be a shoemaker by showing him several pairs of shoes.' On the other hand, it must be granted that Aristotle's 'Rhetoric,' while the most philosophical exposition of the subject, could never have made an orator: a long

---

[1] *On the Antidosis*, Jebb's translation (ii. 144, of *Attic Orators*).

course of practical study was indispensable; and the pupils of Isocrates were always carried through a series of exercises in composition and rhetoric which were carefully prepared and revised and corrected by the master.

The death of Isocrates did not affect the position of Athens as the world-centre of all intellectual activity. The ambitious, well-to-do youth of the Mediterranean flocked to Athens to receive their final preparation for life. And this not in the schools of rhetoric alone — for side by side with the rhetorical schools arose the great schools of philosophy, Platonic, Peripatetic, Stoic, and Epicurean, as *organised systems*, each with its teachers and devotees ; and in these the more thoughtful found satisfaction for their philosophical aspirations.

The sophistic and philosophical movements combined told, as might have been expected, on the lower schools. Grammar, drawing, and geometry had been gradually introduced : and thus a formal element was added to the purely literary and musical in the education of the young — especially of those who frequented schools longer than others. Geography, too, found a place in the school curriculum — almost a necessity among a maritime race like the Greeks. Thus the secondary-school curriculum was completed : but for centuries, down, indeed, to the overthrow of the Roman empire, it was only a good secondary school which could boast of embracing a complete course. The result of Hellenic thought on the education of the man was ultimately summed up on the lines of Plato's conceptions, supplemented by Aristotle. And it was this : in the secondary school grammar, literature, music, drawing, geography, arithmetic, and geometry ; in the higher schools, music, arithmetic, geometry, and astronomy (all scientifically treated), these leading to the supreme study, Dialectic in the sense of philosophy.

In the centuries after the birth of Christ, rhetoric and dialectic were regarded as constituting, with grammar, a propædeutic to the higher physical studies. But meanwhile they had altered their character, and were taught only in their formal and barren elements. Together they constituted the *trivium*, the higher studies constituting the *quadrivium*. These names, however, were not in use till the fifth century. All through the middle ages the seven studies taken together constituted the liberal arts. But dialectic as philosophy in the Platonic and Aristotelian sense had vanished from view, and the preparatory 'arts' became restricted in their scope and sterile in their results.

It was to the philosophic schools to which I have above referred that Athens continued to owe its true fame and influence more than to the schools of the rhetoricians. The philosophers pursued truth for its own sake. They represented the scientific spirit. Plato, Aristotle, Epicurus, Zeno, all had their successors.[1] But, while it is true that it was to the philosophic teaching that Athens owed its greatness, it is also true that as a consequence of the great importance assigned to oratory and to style generally, the higher education was always tending to degenerate into the study of rhetoric alone. A short road to oratory was the desire of young men,

[1] The connection of these philosophical schools with certain localities in Athens has been briefly stated by Professor Mahaffy, as follows :

He says : 'There were two gymnasia (in the Greek sense) provided for the youth who had finished their schooling — that in the groves of the suburb called after the hero Academus, and that called the Kynosarges, near Mount Lycabettus. The latter was specially open to the sons of citizens by foreign wives. Thirdly, in Pericles' day was established the Lykeion, near the river Ilissos. They were all provided with water, shady walks, and gardens, and were once among the main beauties of Athens and its neighbourhood. The Academy became so identified with Plato's teaching, that his pupils Antisthenes (the Cynic) and Aristotle settled beside, or in, the Kynosarges and Lykeion respectively and were known by their locality, till the pupils of Antisthenes removed to the frescoed portico (stoa) in Athens and were thence called Stoics. Epicurus taught in his own garden in Athens. All these settlements were copied from Plato's idea. He apparently taught both in the public gymnasium and in a private possession close beside it ; and in his will, preserved by Diogenes Laertius, he bequeaths his two pieces of land to Speusippus, thus designating him as his formal successor. His practice being followed, the title "scholarch" soon grew up for the head of the school and the owner of a life interest in the locality devoted to the purpose. Each master was called the successor (*diadochus*) of his predecessor, and the succession of these heads of schools has been traced with more or less success through all the Hellenistic period.' — *Old Greek Education*, p. 136.

and they more and more tended to gather chiefly round the rhetoricians. The next stage of degeneracy was inevitable. From the moment linguistic art and mere style and oratorical effect became the professed object of study, education was divorced from reality. A man like Isocrates could maintain a living connection between reason, ethical purpose, and speech ; but we cannot imperil education on the expectation of an apostolic succession of men of genius. With the ordinary teacher degeneracy is certain, if we do not hold high the scientific aim of knowledge for the sake of knowledge, living for the sake of life. Form tends to become all in all. Not *what* is said, but *how* it is said, becomes the standard of culture. Education becomes artificial. Art for art's sake passes into artifice. The mind wastes its power over words and niceties of phrase and composition. Originality gives place to imitation. Severe discipline in language, grammar, and logic is lost sight of, and technical forms are got up as if one could be eloquent by rule. Thus rhetoric itself misses its aim — eloquence. Literature and style interest all men, the forms of literature and the technicalities of style are for the arid expert alone. Under the influence of rhetorical rules, the severe, manly, simple, and logical development of a theme in the interests of truth gives place to a weak and insipid but fluent loquacity, not intended to enforce truth or to guide to sound judgment, but merely to tickle the popular ear and to gratify the vanity, or gain the temporary ends, of the speaker. Living oratory disappears. Brilliant language, rhythmical sound, sharp antitheses, metaphors, images, and playing on words had become, even before the Christian era, objects of unfeigned admiration to the youth of the Eastern Mediterranean.

It is usual to speak with a certain sentimental regret of the early decadence of the Athenian higher schools. I can find no ground for holding that they suffered from actual decay till, perhaps, 200 or 250 years after the birth of Christ. Their weakness lay in the commercial rivalry of the teachers and the growing devotion to mere rhetoric. Assuredly, from

430 B.C. to about 300 A.D., Athens, spite of the rise of many
rivals, remained the chief intellectual centre of the civilised
world. Thus for 700 years at least, spite of its great Alexandrian rival, it governed the higher education. Nor was
this education always of so degenerate a kind as satirists
would make us believe. A young man repairing to Athens
had still the best opportunities that had ever existed of discussing the profound questions of philosophy and science,
and of prosecuting an extensive literary and grammatical
course under some approved rhetorician, while entering into
friendly student relations with youths from all parts of the
Roman émpire. What better university education can we
offer now, if the education of young men means the stimula-
tion of intellectual activity in the search for truth, or in the
attainment of professional excellence ? It is true that many
who flocked to Athens and the other university centres of
Rhodes, Pergamon, &c., often idled their time, and that not a
few were content with a very superficial culture, fitted for
mere oratorical display. But may we not, *mutatis mutandis*,
make the same remark now of every university in Europe ?

After all is said that can be said on Hellenic education, I
am disposed to return to my original proposition, viz. that
the Hellenic educational idea, more or less conscious, always
was *Sophrosyne* (self-control, balance, limitation), *Arete*, or
excellence, and *Eukosmia*, or grace and becomingness of
bearing and expression. To say that the Greeks did not
wholly succeed in attaining to this harmonious result is only
another way of saying that they were human beings. None
the less was the tendency always in the direction summed
up by these three words. They always had a more or less
conscious ideal of man, and to this each man was to be educated. The whole of life, it is true, was governed too much
by the idea of the beautiful — the artistic conception of
human life. Hence its charm, its freedom, its want of reverence, and its saucy independence ; hence, too, its failure to
attain, in the case of the great mass even of educated men,

to a profound sense of moral law [1] waiting on all the acts and aims of mortals and relegating all else to a subordinate place. Personal truthfulness, personal purity, and a sense of overawing duty were not to be found in the average citizen, except where an attempt had been made, as in Sparta, to enforce them as part of the state-system of life — an artificial attempt at best. We have in the Greek, I think, a pure exhibition of the finite and æsthetic side of human nature in its most charming and seductive forms. It could not endure; it is not to be imitated, save and in so far as it represents one side of human endeavour. Only where law and duty are supreme, where truth and reality take precedence of form, and these three, Law, Duty, and Truth are recognised as the divine order and the inexorable command, can man attain to the fulness of his own personality, and mould an ideal state composed of citizens harmoniously educated. In the Roman we find some glimpses of this fresh aspect of the problem of national life, and to him we shall now turn.

NOTE ON ARISTOTLE

The history of education is one thing and the theoretical views of philosophers another. And, accordingly, were it not that Aristotle in what he says really speaks in a Greek national sense, and is not merely a theoriser but a representative spokesman, I should not think it necessary to append the following extracts.

ARISTOTLE (pupil of Plato, died 322 B.C.)

GENERAL

' What we have to aim at is the happiness of each citizen, and happiness consists in a complete activity and practice of virtue.' — ' Politics,' iv. 13.

Aristotle refers his reader to the ' Ethics' for this conclusion, and thus shows that with him education as a subject of study had a scientific basis in ethical philosophy.

[1] I am speaking of the Hellenic race, not of individual dramatists or philosophers.

' It is right that the citizens should possess a capacity for affairs and for war, but still more for the enjoyment of peace or leisure. Right that they should be capable of such actions as are indispensable and salutary, but still more of such as are moral *per se.* It is with a view to these objects, then, that they should be educated while they are still children, and at all other ages, till they pass beyond the need of education ' (iv. 14).

The soul consists of two parts — reason in itself, and the lower nature which is capable of receiving the rule of reason. This we find in the ' De Anima ' ; but it is assumed in the educational discussion. In educating we have to train the habits so as to secure the supremacy of reason.

Up to the age of five it is not desirable to make children apply themselves to study of any kind or to compulsory bodily exercises, for fear of injuring their growth. They should be allowed only so much movement as not to fall into a sluggish habit of body. Their amusements should not be of too laborious a sort, nor yet effeminate.

Great care should be taken as to the associates of children, and that all coarseness and foul language be far removed from them, since light talking about foul things is closely followed by doing them.

Education, in the strict sense, begins at seven and may be divided into two periods — seven to fourteen, and fourteen to twenty-one.

(Book V. c. 1.) Education should be regulated by the state for the ends of the state, and each citizen should understand that he is not his own master, but a part of the state.

Also, in the same place, he says : ' As the end proposed to the state as a whole is one, it is clear that the education of all the citizens must be one and the same, and the superintendence of it a public affair rather than in private hands.'

SUBJECTS OF STUDY

Note. — We must bear in mind that Aristotle, like other Greeks, relegated all mechanical occupations to slaves, who were not citizens.

(Book V. 2 of ' Politics.') ' That such useful studies as are absolutely indispensable ought to be taught, is plain enough ; not all useful studies, however, for in face of the distinction which exists between liberal and illiberal occupations, it is evident that our youth should not be allowed to engage in any but such as, being practically useful, will, at the same time, not reduce one who engages in them to the level of a mere mechanic. It may be observed that any occupation, or art, or study, deserves to be regarded as mechanical if it renders the body, or soul, or intellect of free persons unfit for the exercise or practice of virtue.' . . .

'It is the *object* of any action or study which is all-important. There may be nothing illiberal in them if undertaken for one's own sake or the sake of one's friends, or the attainment of virtue ; whereas, the very same action, if done to satisfy others, would in many cases bear a menial or slavish aspect.

'The studies established at the present day are, as has been already remarked, of an ambiguous character. We may say that there are four usual subjects of education, viz. reading, writing, gymnastic, music, and further — although this is not universally admitted — the art of design. Reading and writing and the art of design are taught for their serviceableness in the purposes of life and their various utility, gymnastic as tending to the promotion of valour, but the purpose of music is involved in great uncertainty' (Book V. 2).

MUSIC — THE RELATION OF MUSIC TO LEISURE — ITS LIMITS AS
A SUBJECT OF EDUCATION

Leisure and the noble employment of leisure is the end we must have in view, according to Aristotle.

'There is no consensus of opinion as to the definition of this pleasure [leisure], each individual is guided by his own personality and habit of mind, and he is the perfect man whose pleasure is perfect and derived from the noblest sources.

'It is evident, then, from our consideration of business and leisure, that there are certain things in which instruction and education are necessary with a view to leisure, and that these branches of education and study are ends in themselves, while such as have business for their object are pursued only as being indispensable and as leading to some ulterior object. Accordingly music was introduced into the educational system by our forefathers, not as indispensable — it had no such characteristic — nor as practically useful, in the sense in which reading and writing are useful for pecuniary transactions, domestic economy, scientific study, and a variety of political actions, or as the art of design is, in the general opinion, useful as a means of forming a better judgment of works of art, nor, again, as useful, like gymnastic, in promoting health and vigour. Neither of these two results do we find to be produced by music. It remains, therefore, that music is useful for the rational enjoyment of leisure, and this is evidently the purpose to which it was in fact applied by our forefathers, as it is ranked by them as an element of the rational enjoyment which is considered to be appropriate to free persons' (Book V. 3).

Music, like drawing, is to be followed as a liberal and not as a professional study. Enough should be learned to enable all to enjoy what others do, and for this a certain amount of practical acquaintance with both music and drawing is necessary.

GYMNASTIC AND ITS LIMITS

'As it is evident that the education of the habits must precede that of the reason, and the education of the body must precede that of the intellect, it clearly follows that we must surrender our children in the first instance to gymnastic and the art of the trainer, as the latter imparts a certain character to their physical condition, and the former to the feats they can perform. . . .

'The duty, then, of employing gymnastic and the method of its employment are admitted. Up to the age of puberty gymnastic exercises of a comparatively light kind should be applied, with a prohibition of hard diet and compulsory exercises, so that there may be no impediment to the growth. The fact that these may have the effect of hindering growth may be clearly inferred from the circumstance that in the list of Olympian victors it would not be possible to find more than two or three who have been successful in manhood as well as in boyhood; for the effect of their training in youth is that they lose their physical vigour in consequence of the forced gymnastic exercises they perform. When our youth have devoted three years from the age of puberty to other studies, it is then proper that the succeeding period of life should be occupied with hard exercises and severities of diet. For the intellect and the body should not be subject to severe exertion simultaneously, as the two kinds of exertion naturally produce contrary effects, that of the body being an impediment to the intellect, and that of the intellect to the body' (Book V. 4).

Aristotle then proceeds to discuss the moral effect of different kinds of music, and then seems to get tired of his subject. The whole discussion, though full of good sense, is as a whole inadequate and disappointing.

But gymnastic, though indispensable, is only, like reading and writing, a preliminary ; the true aim of education is the training to do what is virtuous for its own sake and with no ulterior purpose. In this way alone the capable citizen can be produced, and one who will, further, be capable of enjoyment of the noblest kind. This being so, we should read the 'Ethics' as well as the 'Politics' if we are to form a true conception of Aristotle's educational ideal. The process of education is, in brief, instruction and discipline in virtue. From this point of view the 'Ethics' is truly Aristotle's prime educational treatise. What are in the 'Politics' called the subjects of education are in truth only the indispensable subsidiaries or instruments of the true education, which is ethical in its aim.

Aristotle does not, unfortunately, show us how we are to proceed, nor how best to form the noble character whose employment of leisure is noble.

Plato's aim in education is a harmonious man in a harmonious state. This harmonious man is the realisation of 'the good' in the individual, which again is identical with 'the just.' The individual, however, is only a part of a higher harmony, the harmony which is realised in a just state. The individual is thus necessarily subject to the interests of the whole, and must find his particular harmony in and through the larger harmony of which he is merely a part. This Platonic conception is in truth a philosophic rendering and an idealisation of the Doric educational idea.

When we compare the Platonic with the Aristotelian educational aim, we are struck by the more modern spirit of Aristotle. He does not aim at theoretic completeness in his view of man and the state. He takes things as he finds them and keeps his eye fixed on the possible and practicable. The cultured and harmonious man is not an object of concern with him, but only the capable and virtuous citizen. Virtue, in brief, is Aristotle's educational end, the virtue of the individual without regard to an ideal harmony of nature or perfect culture. Let each man be sound in body and virtuous, and Aristotle is content. He demands, however, that he be capable also of enjoyment and that he shall enjoy. He is not to be in such deadly earnest about virtue that he has no vital energy left for enjoyment — enjoyment of a liberal and elevating kind. Where there are such men, the state *as such* may be left out of account we may almost say, although this is to strain Aristotle. Now this I consider to be a practical formulation of the Attic spirit as opposed to the Doric. It is in the spirit of Pericles' address to the Athenians in which he insists on the claims of the individual, whom Plato, on the other hand, would subject entirely, as did the Spartans, to the claims of the state. Aristotle's doctrine is the doctrine of freedom ; Plato's the doctrine of despotism.

Note. — The translations are taken from Welldon's *Politics.*

Authorities. — The more important histories, viz. Ranke, Curtius, Thirlwall ; Encyclopædias ; *Loci classici*, especially from Plato, Aristotle, Xenophon, Plutarch, Lucian ; Krause's *Geschichte der Erziehung, etc., bei den Griechen, Etruskern u. Römern.* Especially, and for details, Grasberger's *Erziehung und Unterricht im classischen Altherthum;* Müller's *Dorians;* Becker's *Charicles;* Professor Wilkins's *National Education in Greece;* Schmidt's *Geschichte der Pädagogik;* [1] Mahaffy's *Old Greek Education;* Capes; Ussing's *Erziehung und Jugendunterricht bei den Griechen und Römern;* Paul Girard's *L'Education Athénienne;* Professor Jebb's *Attic Orators;* Professor Butcher's *Aspects of Greek Life;* Tiele's *Outlines of the History of Religions.* Also references to Cramer, and many others.

---

[1] Sentences, I think, will occasionally be found translated from Schmidt's universal history, especially in the details of Spartan education, but only on subjects and points which are commonplaces.

D. THE ROMANS

At illa laus est magno in genere et in divitiis maximis
Liberos hominem educare, generi monumentum, et sibi.

PLAUT. *Mil.* iii. 108.

CHAPTER I

THE ROMAN PEOPLE AND THEIR GENERAL CHARACTERISTICS

IN passing from the Hellenic races to the Roman people [1] we enter a new phase of life, and yet one which, while different, is, in its deeper relations to the progress of humanity, of equal importance. The human spirit which under the limitations imposed by the Hellenic genius — self-control, virtue, and grace of expression — moves freely in every direction, mobile, subtle, living, joyous, now presents itself to us in a less captivating form; but the personality of man, his self-conscious worth as an individual, his supremacy over the conditions of his own life, are in this new field of educational study, conspicuously exhibited. This personality does not now find a channel for its self-assertion in the creative faculty and the exercise of the imagination. On this side the Roman

---

[1] *Chief dates in Roman History.* — Rome founded 753 B.C. ; expulsion of kings and beginning of republic under consuls, 509 B.C. ; victory of the plebeians in the constitution, 366 B.C. ; Pyrrhus defeated and Rome supreme in Italy, 275 B.C. ; end of.the second Punic war and establishment of Roman supremacy in Spain, 202 B.C. ; Macedonia a Roman province, 148 B.C. ; Spain made into Roman provinces, 123 B.C. ; Rome at this date supreme over the Mediterranean countries. The Gracchi and their attempted reforms, 133–121 B.C. ; Civil war (Marius and Sulla), 88–82 B.C. ; Caius Julius Cæsar puts himself at the head of the government, 48 B.C. ; Cæsar assassinated, 44 B.C. ; Augustus Cæsar emperor, 30 B.C. to 14 A.D. ; the Claudian emperors, then the Flavian emperors, 70–96 A.D. ; Constantine the Great, 306–337 A.D.

mind was essentially imitative. It conquered other nations in arms, and, while doing so, it made conquests also of foreign arts, and it was as acquisitions, not as native products, that it was adorned by them. Much of Roman literature, indeed, suggests vigour of mind and the force of mechanical adaptation of means to ends, rather than the spontaneous outburst of genius. The Roman certainly acquired Greek culture, but it was as a graft on a very homely Roman stock. Their universal masterfulness was even here prominent. Literature was a conquest rather than the inevitable expression of the popular life; and hence it always remained the possession of the cultivated class alone, and was not, as among the Athenians, the atmosphere which all free citizens breathed.

A clear and direct perception of his relation to the outer world, not as a dwelling-place for the gods, but as a world to subdue and reduce to order, was the characteristic of the Roman. His bent of mind was, consequently, essentially practical, and, as practical, prosaic. If the Greek ideal was a beautiful soul in a beautiful body, the Roman ideal was a sound mind in a sound body. Manliness, energy, governing power, intense personality, and that keen perception of the relative rights of men in the matter of property — a perception which is the natural product of an intense personality — formed the basis of the Roman character. It is the Spartan and not the Athenian Greek with whom the Roman has, from the first, certain points of contact; but, in the former case, we have a society in which the individual was largely lost in the community: in the latter, we have a strong and abiding individualism, which yet spontaneously identifies itself with the general good. As can easily be understood in the case of a nation whose genius was so essentially practical, whose life was so wholly a civil life, the chief legacy of thought which they bequeathed to humanity was their moral energy and their jurisprudence. The latter we still study as the basis of all modern law; and this it was which, during a long and critical period, combined with the influence of the Church to hold the civilisation of Europe together, and finally to re-create it. Roman law, indeed, is itself a civilisation.

The origin of this great people as narrated by Livy is now discarded, and many of Hegel's strictures are accordingly now irrelevant. Certain tribes of the Latin race established themselves on the Tiberine hills as elsewhere on the plains of Latium. These Latin tribes developed on the hills which they occupied all the elements of the civic life characteristic of the Latin communities generally, and they did so quickly under the necessities of their position as the advanced guard of Latium, and as masters of the river. They formed a union, and gradually acquired the hegemony of all the Latin race, further extending their dominion to the Volsci on the south, the Sabellian races on the east, and the Etruscans on the north. This, though doubtless the true explanation of the rise of the Roman state, has one defect (if one may venture an opinion against great authorities) : it pushes the theory of Latin unity of race too far, even almost to the ignoring of the mixed elements in the primitive community.[1] All the elements of the Etruscan, the Latin, and the Sabellian were unquestionably mixed in the Roman of history. They did not lie side by side as heterogeneous, but very early constituted a unity.

The transference of power from the kings to the consuls and senate was not only a transference from a monarchical to an aristocratic and oligarchic government, but necessarily gave fresh strength and compactness to the already existing aristocracy. The senators now felt, each in his own person, that he was a king of Rome, and with this accession of dignity there was also an increase of the sense of responsibility which must have told on the gravity and seriousness of individual character and bearing. Hence the senate was truly described as an assemblage of kings. Such a transference of the sovereignty, too, must have made them feel the

---

[1] While we may set aside the Livian predatory origin of Rome, we must yet, I think, regard its mixed elements combined with its position as determining largely its character and its destiny.

necessity of preserving as much as possible the purity and exclusiveness of their order in the interests of the safety of the state, which might have been quickly overwhelmed by the intrusion of the democracy. There can be little doubt that, had the democracy attained to that supremacy which characterised the Athenian Demos, Rome would never have developed into the Roman Empire. A great and noteworthy civic community it would doubtless have been, but little more than this. The Latin communities would have held their own outside the Servian wall, the Samnites and Sabines would have continued to lead an uncontrolled existence, and the already established Etruscan power would probably have permanently overawed the rising state. To create and maintain an empire there must be a continuity of purpose and policy which is alien to a pure democracy. Whether we approve of a hereditary aristocracy or not, there can be no doubt that it conserves a tradition of individual and family life as well as of national policy, and thus contributes powerfully to the stability and permanence of a state in its domestic, and especially in its foreign, relations. At the same time it has its dangers, for it rests the healthy life of the state on one class, and the corruption of this is the corruption of the whole.

The elements of weakness in the Republic which finally made the imperial form of government inevitable it would be irrelevant here to trace. It is not difficult now, after the event, to see that the growth of a city into that unwieldiness of bulk to which Rome attained when it became the centre of the commerce and life of the world, would have made it impossible for even a pure Senate after the mind of Cato himself to hold firmly the reins of power. But with the growth of the Roman Empire the senatorial purity and self-denying patriotism had, as a matter of fact, vanished. The personal aggrandisement for which the tributary wealth of the world gave such opportunities, with the corruptions caused by slavery, the divorce of the Italians from the land as free cultivators, the subversion of religious faith, and the introduction of those larger ideas of personal development and culture which Greece taught, all combined to put an end for ever to the assemblage of kings. The proscriptions of Marius and the reprisals of Sulla had also weeded out the ancient families, and wealthy plebeians, advanced to senatorial rank, had by the time of Augustus almost wholly superseded the ancient nobility. You find now no longer the austere old Roman Senate, but, as an eminent historian has remarked, your eye is arrested by a succession of great individuals who dominated the state. This prominence of individuals, and the impossibility of a city ruling an empire, led to the final organisation of the Imperial Government which, while preserving ancient Republican forms, preserved them as a mere phantom of the past, the lifeless form of a freedom that had been. Assuredly one cause of the corruption of society was the superseding of the traditionary education by unconsidered and unregulated novelties. The old austere domestic system had disappeared, and what had taken its place was not due to any deliberate state-policy, but only to the caprice of individuals — at least till after the empire had been for some time established.

Our chief business, however, is with the Roman people in all their moral greatness and strength as factors in the world-history, taking first of all the period which ends with the fall of Carthage. We find in them great moral qualities — qualities, indeed, which the history of the past shows us to be necessary to the rise of a stable social organisation. The popular idea of the Roman is that of *manly vigour*, and the popular idea is correct. To this it is added by Hegel that he was a creature of the abstract understanding — prosaic, utilitarian, practical. This, also, is true, and hence we may find a key to the Roman character, even in the ideal sphere of his religion.

Religion. — In religion the Roman was unquestionably serious and devout. The community between gods and men was not, however, understood as among the Hellenes. There was no rich mythology to bridge over the space that separated gods and men. The Roman gods were not separate idealised personalities as among the Greeks, who recognised no god to whom they did not give a concrete form. There was, however, with the Roman a deep spiritual side to everything, and *that* the Roman abstracted, assigning to it the name and power of deity. The gods differed in importance only in so far as the abstract thought was more or less generalised. For example, if Jupiter and Juno are the abstractions of manhood and womanhood and Dea-Dia or Ceres the creative power, their position in the Pantheon would necessarily be higher than Fides (fidelity to engagements), Terminus the boundary god, Silvanus the god of the forest, or Vertumnus the god of the circling year. So intense was this spiritual perception and so disposed to fit itself to abstract and yet definite forms, that in the prayer for husbandmen, as Mommsen says, 'there were invoked the spirits of fallowing, of ploughing, of furrowing, sowing, covering in, harrowing, and so forth.' In like manner marriage, birth, and death, and every other natural event, were endowed with a sacred life. This is not to be confounded with element-worship: it was the worship, or at least the abstract and reverential recognition, of the Unseen Power that resided in all things. The feeling of awe with which the Roman regarded the gods, as compared with the joyous friendliness of the Greeks, is well indicated by the fact that the latter when he sacrificed raised his eyes to heaven, the former veiled his head. The *gravitas* of the Roman character was largely due to the seriousness, approaching even sadness, which characterised his religion. The awe with which the Roman contemplated the Unseen is also indicated in the word 'religio,' whether we connect it with 'binding' or 'reflection' (Conscience) — (*religare* or *relegere*). This religion — the early religion of Rome — may be called an organised Animism, but it is very seriously held.

The supreme Roman god was Jupiter Optimus Maximus, not merely as representative of abstract man, but as the reflection of the life of Rome as a civil life, and as the guardian of the state. Doubtless, the position of this god was largely due to Greek influence. Jupiter, as supreme god, was regarded also as father of men and source of all blessings, and preeminently the god of good faith and purity. There was thus a distinct ethical element in the Roman conception; for Jupiter was the god of life and light and purity no less than the divine personification of the Roman State. Next to Jupiter was Mars, as reflecting the military spirit. A deep religious feeling was exhibited not only in the earlier periods of Roman society, but all through its history, spite of Hellenic influences and the introduction among the people of numerous gods. The great Scipio Africanus went daily into the temple of Jupiter to pray, and ascribed all his triumphs to the protecting care of the god of Rome. Even Velleius Paterculus, writing so late as the time of Tiberius, concludes his history with a prayer, part of which only has been preserved, but which begins thus : — 'O Jupiter (Capitolinus)! O Jupiter Stator! O Mars Gradivus, author of the Roman name! O Vesta, guardian of the eternal fire! O all ye deities who have exalted the present magnitude of the Roman Empire, raising it to a position of supremacy over the world! Guard, preserve, and protect, I beseech you, in the name of the Commonwealth, our present State, &c.' Even if this be regarded as a merely conventional conclusion to a history, the fact that it was so would not affect our argument. After all that can be said, however, it is true that just as the cult of Apollo was the true religion of the Greeks, so Rome, as identified with Jupiter, or Jupiter as identified with Rome, was the religion of Romans.

The Hellenic gods, with their accompanying mythical legends, began to enter into the Roman religious system even so early as the time of the kings; but even they, so to speak, became Romans. For, religious as the Romans were, there was little of either the vaguely infinite or the artistic ideal in their objects of worship. The gods all had a practical character, having to do with the civic economy or with social relations or moralities, and religious rites were used to strengthen some of the best habits of the people. Such a system, while promoting the stability of the Commonwealth, could not possibly afford elements for the imagination and for art to work upon. Even Greek sculpture when it entered Rome took the practical form of portraiture and ministered to the pride of family. The finite aims and prosaic character of the Roman were thoroughly interwoven with his religious system, even when the primæval form of it had given way to the worship of Hellenicised deities. Church and State were truly one. In fact religion, as Ihne says (iv. p. 3), 'was with the Romans not a matter of feeling or speculation, but of law;' but, as such, it was a great reality.

In the earlier period of Roman history, the king acted as chief intercessor with the gods, and appointed the priest and priestesses — a power which afterwards passed into the hands of the College of Priests, who nominated a Pontifex Maximus. They were an aristocratic body and constantly abused their office to promote the power of the Senate. Subsequently the tribes elected citizens to the office of president, but during the time of Sulla this privilege was restored to the colleges, and in 63 B.C. it returned to the tribes. The Roman state was thus free from the evils of a hereditary priesthood. The priest never lost his character of being a civil functionary, just as originally the king, as head of the civil power, had been chief priest.

In the last century of the republic, the monotheism which had attached itself to the name of Jupiter Optimus Maximus became more prominent among the cultured few, and in early imperial times we find among the Stoics and Platonists a belief in one overruling God and a devotion to ethical philosophy, which do much to atone for the reckless irreligion or practical idolatry of the many. But when we consider the extinction of ancient tradition and belief and all that constituted the distinctive Roman 'conscience,' we are surprised that society still held together as it did for so many centuries. The Roman seemed still to draw strength from his past history, and an inherited patriotism and concentration of purpose may be said to have survived, in their practical influence, their own death. This Roman religion of patriotism finds expression in the ' De Officiis ' of Cicero, i. 17 : — ' Cari sunt parentes, cari liberi, propinqui familiares ; sed omnes omnium caritates patria una complexa est; pro qua quis bonus dubitet mortem oppetere ei si sit profuturus ? ' We shall see the firm ' basis of this intense feeling in the family and the civic and civil constitution, of which we shall now speak.

Social Life. — The Roman family was the unit of the Roman state. This could not be said either of Athens or Sparta. In the family we find, in its most pronounced form, the absolute authority of the father. "If any one thing,' says Becker in his ' Gallus,' ' more strikingly exhibits the austerity of the Roman character and its propensity to domination, it is the arbitrary power which the father possesses over his children. By the laws of Nature immediate authority over the children belongs to the father only for the time during which they require his providing care, protection, and guidance. The humanity and right feeling of the Grecian legislators led them to look at the matter from this point of view, and they allowed the authority of the father to last only till the son was of a certain age, or till he was married, or was entered on the list of citizens, and they so restricted this power that the utmost a father could do was to eject his son from his house and disinherit him. Not so in Rome. There the child was born the property of his father, who could dispose of it as he thought fit. This power might last, under certain limitations, even till the death of the father.' [1] ' The power we have over our children,' says the jurist Gaius, ' is a right peculiar to the Romans.' In truth we must regard the father of the family as both priest and magistrate. A *patria potestas* so absolute gave unity to the family.

The practice of monogamy was not peculiar to the

[1] *Excursus* ii. to scene 1, p. 179.

Romans, but the· honour paid to the wife as head ·of the household seems to have been first fully recognised by them. The Spartan mother had a high place assigned to her; but, owing to the public system of education, she exercised less personal influence than the Roman. Within the house, woman was not servant but mistress. She exercised a power almost equal to that of her husband. 'Exempted,' says Mommsen,· 'from the tasks of corn-grinding and cooking, which, according to the Roman ideas, belonged to menials, the Roman housewife devoted herself in the main to the superintendence of her maid-servants and to the accompanying labours of the distaff.' She was not relegated to private life in the *gynœceum* like the Athenian wife. She occupied the atrium surrounded by her servants and children. The woman being held in such high honour, and her permanent position as wife being protected by law, she felt that on her largely depended the honour of the family. The high moral character of the Roman matron thus became famous for all time; and her influence on the character and education of her sons was unquestionably great. 'Do not kiss me,' said the mother of the victorious Coriolanus, 'till I know whether you are an enemy or a son,' and when his wife fell on her knees weeping in support of the mother, the haughty conqueror yielded and said, 'Mother, this is a happy victory for you and for Rome, but it is ruin and shame to your son;' and shedding tears, fell back from the city which he had previously doomed. We may, then, confidently accept the remark of Mommsen, that the 'Roman family from the first contained within it the conditions of a high culture in the mere moral adjustment of the mutual relations of its members.' 'As the strictly organised family,' says Ihne (iv. 250), 'forms the basis for the national life of the Roman people and the starting point for the development of the state; so also Roman morality and private economy were determined by the influence which the same family organisation exercised upon every member of society. . . . Labour, frugality, self-sacrifice for the good of the house and state were the active virtues of the old Roman peasant.'

The unity of the family found its centre in the worship of the household gods, the Penates and Lares. The penates were the gods of the hearth, the lares were the 'lords' of the family — the departed spirits of ancestors, who were regarded as still concerned with the well-being of their descendants. The image of the chief lar, clad in a toga, usually stood between two penates in the atrium of the house beside the household hearth. This shrine the ancient Roman saluted daily with a morning prayer and an offering from the table, while three times every month and on all festivities — such as birth-days, assumption of the toga virilis, marriage, or the return of a member of the family after long absence — sacrifices were offered. The father was priest. Though evil spirits among the departed were recognised by the Romans (as among all nations in some form or other) this did not affect their religious trust in the good. The *gens* or clan again was merely an enlarged *familia*, and as each father and mother were priest and priestess in their own house, so the *gentes* had common altars and sacrifices. The state was thus made up of many little states, bound together by mutual interests and religious ceremonies. The authority of the head of each family was the basis of the authority of the central power, and the obedience and military subjection of the members of the families and clan was the basis of that capacity for obedience and discipline which always distinguished the Roman. It was the abstract beliefs in the spirits of 'things' and the domestic worship which constituted the true and effective Roman religion, before the influence of Greece was felt.

The religion of the Roman state, it has been said, was simply the religion of the domestic hearth writ large, for the state, too, had its common hearth where the Vestal Virgins guarded for ever the eternal fire which symbolised at once the sacredness and the purity of the Roman home. But while the goddess of the hearth, Vesta, held her central place of honour in the vaulted temple [supposed to have been

built after the manner of the atrium of a house] between the
Capitoline and Palatine hills, she was worshipped not merely
as a public goddess, as among the Greeks, but at every private hearth. The common meals of the family were taken
round the hearth, and were a daily bond of family union and
a daily act of worship. The penates protected the going out
and coming in of the members of the family, and to them at
every meal libations were offered.

The depth of family feeling among the Romans and the
conservatism of their character are well illustrated by the
practice of carrying masks of their progenitors to funerals, so
that the head of a family might be said to be followed by
his own ancestors to the last funeral rites.

So closely was the Roman life bound up with religion that
we have found it impossible to speak of the one without
the other. The Roman state ultimately rests on Jupiter as
law and order and object of supreme reverence, on Mars as
the arm strong for defence and offence, and on Vesta as sym-
bolising the sacredness and purity of the home.[1]

Civil Relations. — What now was the Roman in his
civil relations, as distinguished from the religious and the
social ?

In the original constitution of Rome the burgesses, or freemen, constituted the state. The elders of the three hundred
clans forming the community were the senate, and co-ordi-
nate with the king. The various members of the family,
however distantly related, constituted the *gens* or clan. The
senators who represented the clans — to the number of three
hundred — were the king's council, but the ultimate appeal
was to the whole body of burgesses or *patricii.* We see from
this that, from the first, the Roman led a public and political
life. The expulsion of the kings and the transference of
power to the consuls and senate (509 B.C.) gave to the

---

[1] The practical disruption of the Roman religion under Hellenic influences
before the end of the Republic, I do not enter into. Spite of all the changes and
the influx of many gods, the old Roman idea seems to me to have survived far
into imperial times.

world the most powerful aristocratic republic the world has ever seen. The burgesses alone had originally the duty of bearing arms, which thus was a privilege. These were the *patres*, and they and their families were called patricians in opposition to the *plebs* — those inhabitants of Rome who had gathered there after the original settlement. It would be out of place here to dwell on the history of Roman civil life, or to speak of the struggles between patricians and plebeians. Even in these struggles a common patriotism was never forgotten. Enough is done for our purposes here if I point out the leading characteristics of life of the Roman generally. It is thus that we get a key to his conceptions of education.

One great event in the development of Roman civil life must, however, be named — the appointment of decemviri to draw up a code of law. This code (the Twelve Tables), approved by the senate and sanctioned by the assemblies of the people, was doubtless largely based on the customary law which had arisen in the preceding centuries. It was more in the interests of the masses of the people than of the aristocratic senate that there should be a code to which all might appeal. The object was the ' equalising of liberty,' for Law, as opposed to the arbitrary decisions of individuals however wise, is liberty. These laws ('fountain of public and private law,' as Livy says) constituted the basis of the great Roman jurisprudence, and in respect of language were concise, lucid, simple, and in all respects admirable. They were cut on bronze tablets and put up in a public place. The date of their publication was 450 B.C., and we may regard this as the second founding of the Roman state. The idea of law and the supremacy of law did not then for the first time enter the Roman mind, but its existence was signalised and confirmed by a public act which was not only the guarantee of Roman liberty but an important factor in the history of European civilisation.

Let us now sum up this brief survey. What have we found? A people with deep religious instincts which lead

us to expect that religious instruction and sentiment will
find a prominent place in the education of children; an
almost sacred family life, with an autocratic father, but
happily also with a true house-mother at its head; a free
and intensely political public life — a life in the forum — at
once cause and effect of a strong sense of that community of
the social organism which is at the root of all true patriotism;
an unquestioned recognition of the supremacy of law, and in
connection with all this a military life reserved as an honourable function for the true citizen.   In Rome the *executive*
authority of the magistrate, whether king, consul, dictator, or
emperor, was never questioned, any more than the authority
of the council of elders.   To the interests of the state as a
whole every individual was prepared to sacrifice himself.
This did not weaken the family idea.   On the contrary, it
was the chief glory of the leading families to have served the
state nobly.   ' Life in the case of the Roman,' says Mommsen
(ii. 4, 8), 'was spent under conditions of austere restraint,
and the nobler he was the less was he a free man.   All-powerful custom restricted him to a narrow range of thought and
action; and to have led a serious and strict life, or, to use a
Latin expression, a grave and severe life, was his glory
Nothing more or less was expected of him than that he
should keep his household in good order, and unflinchingly
bear his part of counsel and action in public affairs.   But
while the individual had neither the wish nor the power to
be aught else than a member of the community, the glory
and the might of that community were felt by every individual burgess as a personal possession to be transmitted
along with his name and his homestead to posterity; and
thus, as one generation after another was laid in the tomb
and each in succession added its fresh contribution to the
stock of ancient honours, the collective sense of dignity in
the noble families of Rome swelled into that mighty pride
of Roman citizenship to which the earth has never, perhaps,
witnessed a parallel, and the traces of which — strange as
they are grand — seem to us whenever we meet them to

belong, as it were, to another world. It was one of the characteristic peculiarities of this mighty pride of citizenship that, while not suppressed, it was yet compelled by the rigid simplicity and equality that prevailed among the citizens to remain locked up within the breast during life, and was only allowed to find expression after death ; but it was displayed in the funeral of the man of distinction so intensely and conspicuously that this ceremonial is better fitted than any other phenomenon of Roman life to give us who live in other times a glimpse of the wonderful spirit of the Romans.'

But the civic and civil life of the Romans could not have sustained itself, even with the help of that respect for ancestry which included a veneration for the forms as well as the life of the past, and for Jupiter as Head of the State, had it not been for the instinctive recognition of law as the basis of true liberty which made Rome an ever-extending and long-enduring power. ' The Romans were distinguished,' says Ihne (iv. 7), ' from all other nations not only by the extreme earnestness and precision with which they conceived their law and worked out the consequences of its fundamental principles, but by the good sense which made them submit to the law, once established, as an absolute necessity of political health and strength. It was this severity in thinking and acting which, more than any other causes, made Rome great and powerful. . . . The divine law, the elder sister of the civil law, was the pattern on which the latter was moulded. Both were characterised by the same severity, systematic order, deference to fixed formulas, and fear of change.'

The Personal Character of the Roman. — The character of the Roman is sufficiently indicated in what we have already said ; but a few more words seem necessary, inasmuch as the tradition of character, no less than that of civic life and duty, was the main source of the education of successive generations for the first 350 years of the city's life.

In the Roman a personality more intense than the Hellenic

is visible. He exists, doubtless, for the state; but in this sense, that the state exists in and through him. From the first a certain self-sufficing Stoic dignity characterises him. Roman personality asserts itself as always subordinate to the state, yet governed by the thought that the state exists through and by virtue of the individual and of the family which the father represents. The state needs the individual, and each citizen proudly bears the burden of the civil life. The feelings of personality, of a regulative will, and of obligation to law and duty, are closely interwoven in their roots in human nature; and where they exist we should expect to find those complex virtues flourish into which personality, will, and a sense of law most largely enter. These virtues are integrity, courage, resolution, persistence, fidelity, and justice, in the sense of law; and the very naming of these ethical characteristics recalls to our minds the ancient Roman of tradition, the founder of an empire. With such a people you expect to find great administrative ability. They are born to govern, and to conquer that they may govern. Their persistency, nay, pertinacity, explains itself. Mark the saying of the proud and overbearing Roman: 'Rome must never conclude a peace, save as victor;' an issue of war only attainable by inflexible hardness, and more, alas, of the external show than the reality of justice to enemies and rebels. With such a people you expect to find a power of subduing nature as well as men to their imperious and imperial will. Their roads, their bridges, their aqueducts, their public buildings, all testify to this.

As the people, *par éminence*, of practical reason, the relations of men as holders of property, which represents to the eye of sense our personalities, are always vividly present to them, and we are not surprised to find a keen perception of relative rights, of practical justice as between members of the same state at least, and subsequently as between nations, and the consequent creation of a sound jurisprudence which, with the extension of the empire, becomes vast and imposing, and from being civic and national becomes imperial and cosmopolitan. To the remark that Greece conquered took Rome captive by its arts, may be aptly opposed this, that Rome fallen took its victors captive by its law, and still, indeed, holds them bound.

The beautiful, however — art and the softer and gentler emotions — are as incompatible with the Roman nature as a joyous delight in life for mere life's sake, and in nature for nature's sake. These things are to be met with, but they are not indigenous : even these Rome must conquer and lay its warlike hands upon and affect to enjoy. In the moral sphere the Roman *virtus* has to be contrasted with the καλοκάγαθία of the Greek.

With all their great qualities, and in perfect consistency with them, it is yet true, as Ihne says (i. 120), 'they were a cold, calculating, selfish people, without enthusiasm or the power of awakening enthusiasm, distinguished by self-control and an iron will rather than by the graces of character. They were proud, overbearing, cruel, and rapacious.'

I may fitly conclude the preceding survey of Roman characteristics in the well-known lines of Vergil (' Æneid,' vi. 847) :

> Others, I ween, with happier grace
> From bronze or stone shall call the face,
> Plead doubtful causes, map the skies,
> And tell when planets set or rise.
> But ye, my Romans, still control
> The nations far and wide ;
> Be this your genius — to impose
> The rule of Heaven on vanquished foes,
> Show pity to the humbled soul,
> And crush the sons of pride.[1]
>
> *Conington's translation.*

[1] Excudent alii spirantia mollius æra,
Credo equidem, vivos ducent de marmore vultus,
Orabunt caussas melius, cælique meatus
Describent radio et surgentia sidera dicent :
Tu regere imperio populos, Romane, memento ;
Hæ tibi erunt artes ; pacisque imponere morem
Parcere subjectis et debellare superbos.

Wealth and the lust and luxury of power ultimately destroyed the distinctively Roman character, although round it there still hovered an imperial magnificence. No nation has yet been found which has been able to resist the insidious inroads of abounding wealth — especially when that is concentrated (as seems to be inevitable), in the hands of a small minority of the citizens. There arises a rivalry in self-indulgence and ostentation among the few and a deep-seated discontent among the, many. The latter are indifferent to the maintenance of the commonwealth; the former are pre-occupied with personal aims and ambitions. In presence of the appetite for self-aggrandisement, civic virtues and public spirit gradually disappear, and the nation is doomed, for it has lost the moral energy that made it. Where each seeks his own things and not also those of another, the community of feeling which constitutes a commonwealth is gone. There exists a veiled internecine war which must make the State an easy prey to external foes, unless it be saved by an internal revolution. We may, in the passing fashion of the hour, talk of a state being an organism, but, after all, it is a mass of individuals; and it is only by the education of these individuals and the maintenance of the sanctity of the individual family that we can hope permanently to sustain public virtue and uphold an empire. Take care of individuals and the family, and the (so-called) ' organism ' will take care of itself.

CHAPTER II

HISTORICAL DEVELOPMENT OF ROMAN EDUCATION

WHAT means now did the Roman take for maintaining his greatness by educating those who were to bear the burden of the state after their fathers had passed away ?

I shall first answer the question very generally in the words of Cicero, who says: ' Among the Greeks some devote themselves with their whole soul to the poets, others to geometers, others to musicians, others again, like the Dialecticians, open up to themselves a new sphere of activity and devote their whole time and life to the arts which mould the mind of youth to humanity and virtue. The children of the Romans, on the other hand, are brought up that they may one day be able to be of service to the fatherland, and one must accordingly instruct them in the customs of the state and in the institutions of their ancestors. The fatherland has produced and brought us up that we may devote to its use the finest capacities of our mind, talent, and understanding. Therefore we must learn those arts whereby we may be of greatest service to the state, for that I hold to be the highest wisdom and virtue.' The humanities and learning, art and the beautiful, these were not the motive forces of Roman education as they had been among the Greeks, but rather those arts which might be of political service. Harmonious development, culture — either of mind or body — for its own sake was an idea alien to the Roman mind. It was only when the seeds of decay had been already sown that Hellenic aims and Hellenic culture found a place ; and then only partially. The practical Roman life was essentially opposed to the Greek æsthetic life.

It is necessary to speak of the education of Rome in successive periods.

First National Period — to 303 B.C.

In his home, in the forum, and in military exercises, the Roman boy for the first four or five centuries of the Republic found his education, and any account of this must necessarily be a mere repetition of what has been already written on the religious, social, and civil life of Rome. Such reading and writing as were necessary for affairs were in some instances acquired from adventure teachers during this period, but it would appear that they were chiefly acquired in the home. The education of the Roman boy was simply the education which home-life, citizenship, and the observance of ancestral tradition gave him. As the fathers and mothers, so the sons and daughters. *Gravitas, honestas, fortitudo, prudentia, justitia* — these were the words which summed up the *vir bonus* and to these the young Roman was trained.

In the Home. — The laws of the Twelve Tables (confirming previous usage) required that a misformed infant should be killed, but the father could decide this question only with the help of a council of his nearest male relatives. There was, however, no law against the exposure of infants, and this was practised under the general rights which the father had ; but it would not appear to have been so much the usage as among the Greeks. In later times, infants whom it was desired to get rid of were often placed before the Temple of Pietas — which thus might be regarded as a kind of *crèche* for foundlings. In 374 A.D. exposure was prohibited by law (Cod. Justin. viii. 52, 2) ; but the law was ineffectual. Ussing points out that Hierocles in the fifth century complains of the continuance of the practice.

Mothers suckled their own children until about the time that Greek customs began to penetrate Roman society. Wet-nurses (almost always slaves, often Greeks) were then employed. On the ninth day after his birth the boy, and on the eighth the girl (Krause, p. 236), received their names (*dies lustricus*) ; this was also the 'naming' day (*dies nominum*), and there was a family feast and dancing. The religious ceremonial, the naming, and the festival, were all at the same time. The child was thereafter registered. A box or ball, with an amulet enclosed, was hung round the child's neck to preserve it from magical arts and the evil eye. This *bulla* was of gold in the case of children of the higher ranks.

The children had their games, to a large extent of the same kind as those common among the Greeks. The amusements of the boys, however, seem to have been chiefly games of various kinds with the ball.

His mother, and afterwards his father, trained the Roman boy and not a slave-pedagogue, and, even when a pedagogue was employed, the maternal supervision was not intermitted, during all the earlier centuries at least; and, in the best houses, not till towards the end of the Republic.

The child, let us remember, was under the influence of a mother who was assigned her true place at the head of the household. The severe discipline and magisterial authority of the father were supplemented by the milder moral influence of the mother, while the reverence shown to the household gods in the various ordinary acts of daily life tended to evoke that feeling of veneration and religiosity which was characteristic of the Roman.

The boy exchanged the *toga prœtexta* for the *toga virilis* about the sixteenth year, when his name was formally confirmed. He entered thus early on the responsibilities of manhood. This change was made with great ceremony, both domestic and public, and accompanied (like other Roman acts) by domestic religious rites, temple sacrifices, and a family festival. The youth's name was now enrolled among the citizens. The education thenceforth was the education of public life, including military exercises; but the home education and influence never ceased.

On festival and religious occasions, and in solemn banquets, the youth was accustomed in the earlier centuries to assist in chanting the national songs, and may be said thereby to have acquired the elements of poetry and music; but they were the barest elements. Later in the history of the Republic, the singing and chanting seem to have been performed by a specially hired class. Music was not, as among the Greeks, a domestic institution and an alleviator of daily life. Nor was the purely practical direction of the Roman training counteracted by their religion as it might have been; for this too, as we have seen, was narrow, always closely connected with the hourly needs of the individual, the family, and the state. Being the growth of the abstract understanding, it did not yield materials for the poetic imagination and the free growth of ideal aims. Youths, after assuming the *toga virilis*, were a great deal in the company of their fathers in the street and forum, and learned in this way the duties

21

of a man and a citizen ; 'virtutis enim,' says Cicero (' De Off.'
i. 6), 'laus omnis in actione consistit.'

The chief education, in brief, which the Roman boy
received was the moral and religious training of home, and
free intercourse with his father and mother. The religion of
the hearth, as I have said, was the centre-point of the religion
of the Roman, and the education was the education of the
hearth. In religion a high standard of observance was maintained. Pietas, the ethical basis of the family, extended to
the gens, and thus a reflected influence on home training was
felt. We see here in operation that family education which
Plutarch,[1] writing 100 years after the birth of Christ,
strongly advocates for all, up to the age at which they are fit
to attend the higher schools. What Sparta aimed at giving
through its public system, and compulsorily, the Roman
aimed at giving through the parents, and freely : that is to
say, he was content with this, because we cannot say that
there was any *conscious* aim. The result was that the
Roman had a more genuine and personal morality than
the Spartan.

Thus during the first centuries of Roman life down to
about 303 B.C. the education was domestic, civic, and military.
In its domestic relations it was profoundly religious. The
sense of duty to moral law, to paternal authority, and to
the state, was ever present to the child and the boy. There
was no element of joy or love in the moral, any more than in
the religious, life. There was, however, a deep sense of
spiritual powers external to man which might be pleased or
displeased by right or wrong conduct in every act of daily
life, and this constituted that 'conscience' of which the old
Roman religion was a formal and habitual recognition.[2]

The literary education of the boys must have been wholly
confined, during the period of which we are speaking, to
religious hymns and national songs — those early lays of
which Cicero mourns the loss, and to which I have adverted

---

[1] Authorship of the essay in Plutarch's works doubtful.
[2] Pater's *Marius the Epicurean*.

above. Schools are indeed mentioned in which the simple arts of reading and writing were acquired. The daughter of Virginius is represented as frequenting one of these, 305 B.C. (Livy, iii. 44), ' Virgini venienti in forum — *ibi namque in tabernis literarum ludi erant* — minister decemviri libidinis manum injecit.' *Tabernæ* were a kind of booths open to the street. Nor is there any reason to doubt that many such schools existed. In the time of Camillus we find mention of a teacher of boys at Falerii (for the *liberi principum*, Livy, v. 27) [1]; and this confirms our conclusion that there was a considerable number of adventure elementary schools (*ludi*) prior to 303 B.C. at Rome, as well as among Sabines and Etruscans. They were generally taught by slaves or freedmen.

But, as we might expect from the domestic character of Roman training, it is probable that when reading and writing were taught, they were taught in the family and by the father. This is the only explanation of the wide diffusion of these elementary arts. In any case, whether by domestic teaching or otherwise, reading and writing, so far as required for purposes of utility, were, at least from the fourth century B.C., widely known among certain classes of Roman citizens — probably as widely known as they were in civilised Europe in the beginning of the eighteenth century. Livy says that Roman boys used to be instructed in Etruscan literature just as in his time they were instructed in Greek (?).

The young men practised gymnastic exercises, but solely with a view to military fitness, in the Campus Martius. Singing, music, and dancing were all alien to the Roman and, indeed, despised by him.

Second National Period. — 303 B.C. to 148 B.C. (Death of Cato).

Till about 250 B.C. Roman education remained *substantially* the same as in the preceding centuries. But during the preceding fifty years a certain development had

---

[1] *Schola* does not occur in the sense of a school till the later imperial times. The word for a school was *ludus* or *ludus literarius*.

taken place. Two historical facts we must take as our guide. First of all, in 260 B.C., Plutarch tells us that Spurius Carvilius, a freedman who had been domestic tutor to the Consul Carvilius, opened a school and was the first to take fixed fees for his instruction. This school Plutarch calls a γραμματο-διδασκαλεῖον. Was he a primary teacher — a grammatist (*literator*), or was he a secondary teacher — a grammaticus ? Without entering into the discussion of this question, I would simply point to the second important historical fact. Prior to the date of Carvilius's school there could be no literary instruction, because there was no literature. It is about this date that we have a sudden development of a national literature, by the help of Italo-Greeks chiefly. Cn. Nævius of Campania was born 273 B.C., and wrote a historical poem on the first Punic War (probably about 240 B.C.), twenty years after Carvilius opened his school. He also wrote dramas and epigrams based on Greek literature. Then Livius Andronicus (a freedman from Tarentum), who died 203 B.C., wrote a translation into Latin of the ' Odyssey '— let us say also about 240 B.C. ; Quintus Ennius, *et sapiens, et fortis*,[1] born 240 B.C. (also like Nævius from Campania), laid the foundation of Roman epic in his ' Annals,' let us say about 200 B.C. ; Pacuvius (born 220 B.C.), a nephew of Ennius, wrote dramas full of Roman national feeling, and he was followed by the great comedian Plautus. Are we to suppose that Nævius and Andronicus, without any literary precursors, all at once gave literary form to the Latin tongue about 240 B.C. ? Is it not more probable that when Carvilius opened his school in 260 B.C. and taught a reformed alphabet and spelling, Latin had taken shape, and that not only traditionary fables were instruments of education but also contemporary Latinity in the form of public records, not to speak of the Twelve Tables, which were in good literary form ?[2]

[1] Horace, *Ep.* ii. 1, where see a list of early writers more or less characterised.
[2] Horace helps us here —

' fœdera regum
Vel Gabiis vel cum rigidis æquata Sabinis,
Pontificum libros, annosa volumina vatum,' &c. *Ep.* II. i. 24.

Carvilius would thus carry his pupils, doubtless a select few, further in the study of Latin than was possible for the ordinary primary schoolmaster. Accordingly, he was a grammaticus. Indeed, if this had not been the case, not only in the school of Carvilius but in other schools, for whom did Nævius and Andronicus write? They must have had an audience. We know, also, that the rude Atellan Fables had before this given place to the higher dramatic form of the *Satura.*

It appears to me that we must conclude that in 260 B.C. and onwards there was gradually growing up in the ordinary ludi a higher linguistic education than had yet been known. Acquaintance with Greek had been common, though not general, before this date, for we know that Postumius, ambassador to Tarentum so early as 282 B.C., addressed an assembly there in the Greek tongue. The frivolous audience laughed at his blunders it is true, but it was no common feat to address a formal oration to Greeks in their own tongue. The increasing intercourse with Magna Græcia and Sicily, and with the Greek colonies of the Mediterranean generally, had, in fact, made Greek familiar as the language both of commerce and diplomacy, and given it an early footing in Rome. Greek slaves and freedmen were employed to teach the language conversationally to the children of the wealthier citizens, and to act as secretaries. Along with conversational Greek, the Roman youth now also had the laws of the Twelve Tables for a text-book, and these as a chant (*carmen necessarium*) had to be learnt by heart. So the Spartan and Cretan boys, it will be remembered, said or chanted their laws. Reading and writing were more widely diffused than in previous generations, and ludi had increased in number. Traditionary songs in praise of heroes also were learnt by heart and chanted, declamation and modulation of tone always receiving great attention.

Education in the true sense, however, was not in the hands of the school-teacher, but was mainly domestic as in the previous centuries. It depended on the character

of the father and mother, and the spirit that animated
public life. Conservative tradition governed it. It has
been well remarked that the less imagination a people
has the more is it governed by tradition; and tradition
governed the unimaginative Roman. The boys were
brought up in the *disciplina vetus,* the manners and customs of ancestors being held in reverence. *Moribus anti-*
quis stat res Romana virisque (Ennius in Cic. 'De Rep.' 5).
There was no suggestion of a state system as in Sparta
whereby to mould the youth into citizens of a certain type,
and yet severity and dignity of life were maintained; but
this wholly through the family and by the power of transmitted custom. This would not have been possible without the existence of a hereditary aristocracy protecting itself
by marriage laws from admixture with plebeians. A native
literature did not exist, except in the form of heroic songs
and public records, rude fables, and satires cast in a rough
dramatic form.

It was now that the Italo-Greek Livius Andronicus, above
referred to, endeavoured to supply the want of a literature
by translating the 'Odyssey' into Latin. He also reproduced Greek dramas in the Latin tongue. The 'Odyssey'
thereupon became a text-book and was studied, and large
portions of it learnt by heart, by the Roman youth. This
change, which was in point of fact the beginning of true
literary education among the Romans, began about 233 B.C.
— Livius Andronicus died before 213 B.C. The school of
Carvilius, already referred to, dates from about 260 B.C.
Mommsen says (iii. 463), 'The place of the Twelve Tables
was taken by the Latin Odyssey' (not for some time after
this, according to Cicero), 'as a sort of improved primer, and
the Roman boy was . . . trained to the knowledge and
delivery of his mother-tongue by means of this translation,
as the Greek by means of the original; noted teachers of
the Greek language and literature, Andronicus and others,
who already probably taught, not children properly so called,
but boys growing up to maturity and young men, did not

disdain to give instruction in the *mother-tongue* along with the Greek.' These were the first steps towards a higher Latin instruction, but they did not yet, properly speaking, constitute such an instruction in any large sense. Instruction in a language cannot manifestly go beyond the elementary stage so long as the language wants a literature. 'Up till that time' (233 B.C.), says Suetonius ('De Gramm.' i.) 'literature, far from being held in honour, was not even known: in fact, the city, rude and absorbed in war, did not yet give much attention to the liberal arts.'

The Latin Odyssey was not only the beginning of Roman literary education but continued to be taught into post-republican times. Horace learned it in the school of Orbilius, and Quintilian favours it.

Literature in education, and with it Hellenism, made steady progress during the whole of the next century, and its dominance in the schools may be fixed at the date of the death of Cato the elder, who had laboured to stem its progress (148 B.C.). At this date, too, Macedonia became a Roman province, and the Second Punic War and the supremacy of the Romans in Spain were already past history.

That the literary education of the young Romans had made remarkable progress during the century that followed the opening of Carvilius's school, is apparent (apart from other ample evidence [1]) from the reception of the Athenian ambassadors, Carneades the Academic and Diogenes the Stoic, by the Roman youth who flocked to hear them discourse in 155 B.C. Already, as Plutarch tells us in his Life of Cato, oratory was much studied in Rome,[2] and the ambitious among the young men were prepared to hear with open ears the philosophic teachings of the Greeks. Polybius, about 167 B.C., refers to the number of capable teachers who resided in Rome. In this year also (167 B.C.) Crates of

---

[1] For example, Scipio and other leading statesmen preferred to write in Greek.

[2] For a sketch of Roman oratory the student will read Cicero's 'Brutus.'

Mallos in Cilicia, a Stoic philosopher and a man of great learning, came to Rome as ambassador of King Attalus. He fell into an open sewer and broke his leg (Suet. ii.), and was consequently compelled to remain in Rome for some time. ' During the whole period of his embassy and convalescence,' says Suetonius, ' he gave frequent lectures, taking great pains to instruct his hearers, and he has left us an example worthy of imitation.'

The date of the death of Cato (148 B.C.) completes the second period of Roman life and education; and a book which he wrote, ' De Liberis educandis,' seems to have illustrated the genuine practical character of Roman educational conceptions in their strictest sense. It doubtless was intended as a protest against Hellenic innovations. The Hellenic idea of culture had not yet indeed taken root, and the words in Cicero (' De Republica,' i. 20) were still applicable: — ' Quid esse igitur censes discendum nobis ? ' To which the answer is: — ' Eas artes quæ efficiant ut usui civitati simus.' The book by Cato was intended to show what a *vir bonus* ought to be as orator, physician, husbandman, warrior, and jurist. So much science only was to be acquired as was necessary for practical purposes. Latin grammar was not included, and this shows that the learned had not yet done much for the grammatical study of the native tongue. Music and the mathematical and physical sciences were excluded. Cato used to say that ' Greek literature should be looked into, but not thoroughly studied.' There seems after this to have been a succession of books of a similar kind; but in all these, knowledge — as such and for its own sake — was not advocated. Cato is spoken of by Quintilian as the first Roman writer on pedagogy.

During this second period, as in that which preceded it, it cannot be said that the masses of the people (and only a portion of them) received any instruction save the rudiments of reading and writing. Those intended for mercantile life continued to acquire these accomplishments, and they were much more widely diffused (as appeared from Cato's book) even among the slaves, than we can now well explain unless it be that these, for the most part, were Greeks or Syro-Greeks. Schools were still what we call 'adventure' schools, and there is no evidence that the differentiation into grammar or secondary schools had yet taken place, although teachers here and there gave advanced or secondary instruction.

On the whole we may say that advanced instruction was chiefly domestic and tutorial, and consequently restricted to the upper classes. Spite, however, of Hellenic influence, the *mores, consuetudines et instituta majorum*, which constituted the *vetus disciplina*, still animated education. The Roman was essentially conservative. The word 'educare' when contrasted with the Greek παιδεύειν is itself instructive. It means to train up a child in the way he should go — the way, viz., of his fathers; whereas, the Greek word has in view all that concerns both the bodily and mental growth of the boy. Education, in this Greek sense, can hardly be said to have existed at the time of Cato's death. Polybius, indeed, writing about this time, remarks on the neglect of education among the Romans, as compared with the attention paid to it among the Greeks.

To sum up. We are justified in saying that literary education cannot be regarded as beginning in Rome till about 233 B.C. After this date, there seems to have been rapid progress, owing to Greek influence. Note also that the Second Punic War ended in 202 B.C., and Rome had now breathing time. Her power was finally established, and she was on her way to empire. Macedon was conquered 168 B.C. The first library was erected at Rome in 167 B.C. Let us put all these facts together and we shall accept readily Mommsen's conclusion that 'even in the time of Pictor and Cato Greek culture was widely diffused at Rome, and there was also a native culture.'

The rapid progress which education made in Rome is partly to be explained by the fact that a recognised scheme of culture already existed in the Hellenic schools of Italy and the Mediterranean cities generally.

Third National Period. — 148 · B.C. onwards (Corinth destroyed 146 B.C.).

We now come to the third period of Roman intellectual life and education. After 148 B.C. it could no longer be said to be specifically Roman at all.[1] It was Greek education as influenced and coloured by the Roman character and aims. It embraced not only the Latin and Greek languages and literature, but music and geometry. After the conquest of Macedonia, twenty years before (167 B.C.), the intellectual traffic between Greece and Rome, already considerable, was greatly augmented, and, from this time forward, Greek language and literature were regarded as indispensable elements in the higher education. Less than fifty years after the death of the great conservative Roman, Hellenism, already dominant in 148 B.C., was now triumphant. Cicero (born 106 B.C.) tells us that at the beginning of his life the ancient education had been wholly overthrown.

The extent to which the cycle of general culture had changed in the Roman world during the course of a century, is shown by a comparison of the Encyclopædia of Cato with the similar treatise of Varro, 'concerning school sciences.'[2] As constituent elements of professional culture there appeared in Cato the art of oratory, the sciences of agriculture, of law, of war, and of medicine ; in Varro, the 'most learned of the Romans' (born 116 B.C.), there appeared grammar, logic or dialectics, rhetoric, geometry, arithmetic, astronomy, music, medicine, and architecture. This scheme of knowledge rests on a wholly Hellenic conception.

And yet we cannot say that secondary schools taught by grammatici existed earlier than 148 years B.C. Before that date, some of the ordinary ludi may have carried boys beyond the limits of a primary education. In all countries we find this transition period. But we are not entitled to go behind the authority of Suetonius, who tells us that Crates introduced the study of grammar at Rome. I speak only of

---

[1] Lucilius, the satirist, was born in 147 B.C.

[2] So far as the contents of these books are now known.

schools: that advanced instruction was given by Greek tutors in families we know. Progress was now, however, very rapid. About 140 B.C. there were, according to Suetonius ('De Gram.' iii.), more than twenty celebrated grammatici at Rome, all, it is presumed, teaching.

The higher education also, which was summed up by the one word Oratory, seems to have begun to flourish about the same time, taught by Greeks in Greek to those who could follow them. It was towards the middle of the seventh century (100 B.C.), that the eminent orators Marcus Antonius and Lucius Crassus flourished, and twenty or thirty years before them the Gracchi. These men must have begun their education as boys about the beginning of the third period. They could speak Greek and hold discussions in it. A decree of the senate (161 B.C.) directed against the rhetoricians and philosophers had failed to arrest the higher education in its beginnings; and the censorial edict against the higher schools so late as 112 B.C. was a *brutum fulmen*. It was, however, the philosophy of the Greeks, and not their literature, that the more conservative among the Romans most dreaded. There was also not a little distrust of the Greek character, and that not without reason. Greek art and artists followed close on the heels of Greek rhetoric. It was about this time also that the women of the higher classes began to participate in the Hellenistic education.

What Cato foresaw had now come. It had been hastened doubtless by the number of Greek scholars who found their way to Rome after the fall of Corinth (146 B.C.); among these there were philosophical and rhetorical teachers of considerable pretensions. The decree of the senate and the edict of the censor above referred to, are so interesting in the history of education generally, that I shall quote fully what Suetonius ('De Rhet.' i.) says:

'Rhetoric also, as well as grammar, was not introduced amongst us till a late period, and with still more difficulty, inasmuch as we find that, at times, the practice of it was even prohibited. In order to leave no doubt of this I will subjoin an ancient decree of the senate as well as an edict of the censors : " In the consulship of Caius Fannius Strabo and Marcus Valerius Messala,[1] the prætor Marcus Pomponius moved the senate that an act be passed respecting philosophers and rhetoricians. In this matter they have decreed as follows : ' It shall be lawful for M. Pomponius, the prætor, to take such measures and make such provisions as the good of the republic and the duty of his office require, that no philosophers or rhetoricians be suffered in Rome.' " After some interval, the censor Cnæus Domitius Ænobarbus and Lucius Licinius Crassus issued the following edict upon the same subject. " It is reported to us that certain persons have instituted a new kind of discipline ; that our youth resort to their schools ; that they have assumed the title of Latin rhetoricians ; and that young men waste their time there, whole days together. Our ancestors have ordained what instruction it is fitting their children should receive, and what schools they should attend. These novelties, contrary to the customs and instructions of our ancestors, we neither approve nor do they appear to us good. Wherefore it appears to be our duty that we should notify our judgment both to those who keep such schools and those who are in the practice of frequenting them, that they meet our disapprobation." However, by slow degrees, rhetoric manifested itself to be a useful and honourable study, and many persons devoted themselves to it both as a means of defence and of acquiring reputation.'

Many native Romans also now began to cultivate the scholastic field, and it became the fashion to study Nævius, Ennius, and Lucilius in the schools, and to comment on these authors critically. The education which had *humanitas,* or culture, in the Roman sense, for its aim was thus finally established, let us say about 625 A.U.C. *at latest,* i. e. 128 B.C. The first formal instruction in Latin rhetoric and oratory *by a Roman* was given (but not for pay) about 128 B.C., the year we have named. His name was Lucius Ælius Præconinus of Lanuvium, commonly called ' The Penman' (Stilo), a

---

[1] This *senatus consultum* was made 161 B.C.

distinguished Roman knight. But it is only as a purely *Latin* rhetor that we can call him the *first*, for Greek rhetoricians taught long before this.[1]

Personal superintendence of the boys of the wealthier classes had been to a large extent and for some time before this handed over to pædagogi — in imitation of the Greek custom. These were also called 'custodes' and 'comites.' They, however, did not instruct the boys but simply acted as guardians and attendants. They were generally Greek or Syro-Greek slaves and freedmen, and were, for the most part, selected with great care. The object the parents had in view was not only a moral one, but conversational fluency in the Greek tongue.

The line which the Hellenistic studies took in Rome was grammatical and philological rather than æsthetic, and in the higher schools it was rhetorical. The more ambitious minds occupied themselves with philosophical questions, especially on the lines of the Academic and Stoic philosophies; but even the study of philosophy always had in view the practical equipment of the orator, except in so far as it afforded material for intellectual fence. The young Roman had at all periods of history to prepare himself for speech in the forum or the senate. Oratory was not only a mark of culture, but also a weapon of offence and defence ('regina rerum oratio,' says Pacuvius). Accordingly, even now when both Latin and Greek literature had become fairly established as part of the ordinary instruction, both in the grammatical and rhetorical schools, the acquisition of oratory still governed those studies which were primarily intended to cultivate the humanity of the pupil *more Græcorum*. Thus true to its own instincts did Rome remain even when the narrow ancient life was beginning to disappear. It is true that the laws of the Twelve Tables

[1] Quintilian tells us (ii. 4. 42) on the authority of Cicero, that the first eminent Latin rhetor who taught by the method of fictitious pleadings in the school was Plotius, towards the end of the life of Licinius Crassus and about the same time as the first school of *Roman literature* was opened by Nicanor Postumus (93 B.C.).

were no longer used as a text-book, that the old domestic
education was maintaining itself with difficulty, and that
Latin and Greek literature now formed the basis of all education; but the chief aim of the literary education was
always oratory, not pure literature. The study of rhetoric,
as constituting the highest education of youth, was regarded
as not merely essential to the formation of a man, 'ingenuus
et liberaliter educatus,' but above all as the road to influence,
power, and public employment.

We now see virtually established in the last period of
the Republic, *i.e.* from 148 B.C., a regular course of instruction having culture or *humanitas* for its object, but always
in subservience to oratory for the uses of public life. The
curriculum might be said to consist of three stages — the
primary, in which reading and writing of Latin and Greek
were taught; then the grammatical and literary instruction
of a higher and philological kind; finally the technical and
elaborate study of rhetoric and the art of forensic orations,
along with such dialectic and philosophy as might be
available.

It was to the Hellenic victory over the old Roman education that we owe Cicero, Vergil, Lucretius, and all that
brilliant crowd of literary men who adorned the last century
of the Republic and the beginnings of the empire. Cicero
was born 106 B.C.; Lucretius 98 B.C.; Vergil 70 B.C. It was
only now that Latin finally took its place side by side with
Greek, if not as an equal, yet as an honourable rival.

Cæsar, and after him Augustus, encouraged and protected
the professors of every art, and many now took to literature
and philosophy as the occupation of men to whom, under an
imperial system, the highest political activity was no longer
open. While, therefore, we may regret with Cato, and at
a later date Tacitus, the decay of the old Roman training,
we must recognise the necessity of the Hellenic invasion if
a larger conception of the ends of education and of life was
ever to animate the Roman mind. The importance of this
in the future history of the world is beyond our power of

estimating, for it was under Roman protection and under Imperial power that all the nobler arts of life were assured of recognition and encouragement in every corner of the civilised world.

And yet it was impossible to turn a Roman into a Greek. He remained to the last prosaic and practical. The Hellenicised few to whom culture pure and simple was an aim, formed a kind of intellectual aristocracy. Even in the time of Augustus we find Horace fully recognising the difference between the Roman and the Greek mind, just as we find the same recognition in the passage we quoted from Cicero. In the 'Ep. ad Pisones,' line 325, Horace [1] contrasts the Greek genius with that of the practical Roman:

'To the Greeks the Muse has given genius, to the Greeks, ambitious of nothing but praise, the power to speak with eloquence. The boys of Rome learn by long calculations to divide a pound into a hundred parts. "Let Albinus' son tell me what remains if from five ounces one is taken." If you have been able to answer "the third of a pound," well done ; you will be able to look after your own estate. Add an ounce, what is the sum? "Half a pound." When we have thus imbued their minds with the canker and care of gain, do we hope that they will compose poems worthy of preservation, worthy of being preserved in cases of cypress?'

---

[1] Graiis ingenium, Graiis dedit ore rotundo
Musa loqui, præter laudem nullius avaris.
Romani pueri longis rationibus assem
Discunt in partes centum diducere.   Dicat
Filius Albini : si de quincunce remota est
Uncia, quid superat ? Poteras dixisse, Triens. Eu !
Rem poteris servare tuam.   Redit uncia, quid fit ?
Semis.   At hæc animos ærugo et cura peculi
Quum semel imbuerit, speramus carmina fingi
Posse linenda cedro et levi servanda cupresso ?

CHAPTER III

CURRICULUM OF STUDY — SCHOOLS, METHODS, AND MASTERS

I SHALL now sum up briefly the course of instruction through which the Roman youth were carried during the third or Romano-Hellenic period, as accurately as it can be ascertained.

Primary Instruction

Up to the sixth or seventh year the child remained at home under his mother and nurse, and under the protection of a *pædagogus*. His elementary instruction then began either at home or in a *ludus publicus* under a *ludimagister* (grammatist, *literator*), where he learnt to read and write. *Ludus* was the word confined to primary schools; *schola*, from the Greek, was applied to higher schools.[1] Horace, in his first book of Satires, I. vi. 72, gives a picture of Italian boys going to school. His father, he says, ' was unwilling to send me to the ludus of Flavius, whither boys the offspring of great centurions were wont to go with their satchels ' (*capsæ calculorum*, says Orelli, *i.e.* bags for holding pebbles to count with) ' and tablets, carrying their fee every Ides, but had the spirit to bring his boy to Rome to be taught.'[2]

In learning their letters, the children first acquired their names and their sequence by heart without regard to their

---

[1] ' Ludus ' was a place for exercise of any kind, *e.g.* ' ludus militaris,' where soldiers were exercised. It thus was naturally used for the place to which children resorted for school exercises. Σχολή (leisure which gave the Latin ' schola,' was originally used by the Greeks to designate a place for the occupation of leisure, and so gradually was applied to a place for philosophical discussions.

[2] ' Noluit in Flavi ludum me mittere magni
Quo pueri magnis e centurionibus orti,
Lævo suspensi loculos tabulamque lacerto,
Ibant octonis referentes Idibus æra ;
Sed puerum est ausus Romam portare docendum,' &c.

form and function, a practice of which Quintilian complains. Writing was begun at the same time with reading, either by copying models or by tracing letters inscribed on waxen tablets or graven in wood — the teacher at first guiding the hand.

The details of the work done in a Roman primary school are not, so far as I can learn, accurately known. Simple reading and writing and very elementary calculation were taught, the last with the free help of the fingers and little stones and thereafter on waxen tablets. I think we can also say for certain that (as in the Greek schools) attention was paid to accentuation and elocution, and that the substance of what was read was always explained. Gnomic verses containing maxims and precepts were taken down and committed to memory. The reading-book was generally the Latin version of the ' Odyssey.' Up to about 80 B.C., the laws of the Twelve Tables were learnt by heart.[1]

Secondary Instruction

About the age of twelve the boy passed into the school of the grammaticus — to whom the epithets ' doctus' and ' eruditus' were usually applied.

There were two classes of grammatical schools — the Greek and the Latin. It was the general custom to go to the former first. This custom was approved of by Quintilian. The pupil, when he entered, usually took with him a certain conversational knowledge of Greek. He was instructed in grammar in the narrower sense, learned portions of Homer and other poets by heart, and was introduced to the critical study of literature and to composition. The fables of Æsop were popular in the earlier stages of instruction. To reading

---

[1] After all that has been written on Roman education, the precise details of work in the primary schools are by no means certain. Doubtless it varied as it has done in our own country and depended on the qualifications of the teacher — at least before the grammatical or secondary schools were fully differentiated.

with purity of diction and good expression much importance was now attached.

Dictation was largely practised with a view to correct spelling, and also because, by means of dictation, select poems could be written down and learnt by heart when the complete works of the poets could not be had. Even when rolls became cheap, this practice of dictation was kept up. The rhetorician even dictated his system of rhetoric.

The Twelve Tables ceased to be learned by heart in the lifetime of Cicero.[1] Music was taught with a view chiefly to rhythm — for music as an *art* was not cultivated at Rome. The employments of leisure were not esteemed there — the Roman was too serious and practical for this. The musicians employed at religious festivals were paid servants.

As to writing, it seems to me doubtful whether in the primary school the pupil advanced beyond writing with the sharp-pointed stylus on waxen tablets; but in the secondary schools they also learned to write on parchment or papyrus with pen (*calamus*) and ink (*atramentum*). In these schools, however, and even in the schools of the rhetoricians, the waxen tablet was constantly in use. With the flat head of the style words could be deleted and corrections made.

Grammatical instruction meant in Rome ordinary grammar as we now understand it, to which all the philology of the time was made contributory; also literature with the explanation of the poets, and criticism. The full explanation of the poets was also the recognised medium for giving general information. Thus, outside the literary text-books, the instruction which the Roman boy received was orally communicated. He was dependent on his master.

The Greek and Latin grammar schools were distinct. As a rule, I have said, the boy went first to the Greek school. Greek was, in fact, the leading study of the secondary schools, and was acquired as if it were a native tongue. The advanced pupils spoke and wrote Greek. But from

[1] Cic. *De Leg.* ii. 23: 'Discebamus enim pueri XII. ut carmen necessarium, quas jam nemo discit.'

about 90 B.C., if not sooner, Latin rhetoric, *i.e.* the adaptation of Greek rhetoric to the Latin language and oratory, began also to be taught. By that time there was a Latin literature and not a few orators, and the language had been moulded into the concise, vigorous, and effective organ of speech which has come down to modern Europe. At the same time it was not unusual for the advanced pupils to declaim in Greek as well as in Latin. If they had not done so, they could not have benefited by the criticism of their Greek teachers who, for the most part, despised Latin.

Geography was taught, as appears from a line of Propertius (IV. iii. 36), ' Cogor et e tabula pictos cognoscere mundos.'

To the course of instruction in the grammar schools we have to add music, with a view to the understanding of metre; not the playing on an instrument, as in Greece. The simple singing or chanting which had been associated with Roman religion and celebration of heroes, was learned from special teachers by a few, but only with a view to proper intonation and rhythm in oratory. By the Roman the horn and the trumpet were preferred to the lyre and cithara which charmed the Greek.

Arithmetic was taught; but neither in the secondary or higher education was it the theoretical arithmetic of Plato, but mere calculation.

Geometry was taught by a specialist, but chiefly in its practical relations to mensuration. As a liberal study it had for the Romans no attraction. So with astronomy.

Dancing was taught, but only privately in the homes of the pupils. It partook very much of the nature of instruction in calisthenics and ' deportment,' and was wholly unlike our modern dancing. The possibility of young men and women waltzing together at a public assembly would have been to the Roman shocking, had it not been inconceivable. Indeed, Cicero says in one of his orations, that no one would dance unless he were either drunk or mad.

Gymnastic had a purely hygienic and military aim, and only those who had assumed the *toga virilis* frequented the Campus Martius. It was with difficulty the Roman ever understood it in the Hellenic sense of a free discipline. The gymnastic of the Romans had, it is true, towards the end of the Republic, borrowed a good deal from the Greeks; but the Campus Martius was never a Greek gymnasium, but essentially a military exercising ground.

The literati or grammatici in the later years of the school curriculum frequently encroached on the work which properly belonged to the rhetoricians, and gave exercises in declamation and disputation, great attention being paid at this stage, and, indeed, at all stages of school-teaching, to pleasing elocution.

In the Roman school of the grammaticus we see only a repetition of the Hellenic school after it was fully developed (let us say in the third century B.C.). The differentiation into primary and secondary schools had now taken place everywhere. It is this developed Hellenic school that is known as the Romano-Hellenic, and it was to be found in all the important towns of the Roman Empire down to the fifth century A.D. But in all things — even in the study of Greek — there was a Roman practical aim, while in all subjects, save literature and what bore directly on the full understanding of the poets, the Roman was superficial and utilitarian. Might we not say, superficial *because* utilitarian?

The further education of the youth after he had assumed the *toga virilis* (generally at sixteen years of age) depended on his future occupation. Those intended for a farmer's life went to live at some farm station; those intended for the army passed very young into the service; those again who were intended for public life or for pleaders and jurists, went to the rhetorical schools and thereafter attended the forum, the comitia, and the senate, attaching themselves to some approved orator or jurist.

The Higher Instruction — Oratory

In the rhetorical schools the young men studied rhetoric and all the arts which could make an effective orator. Cicero ('De Orat.' iv.) tells us that in the last century of the Republic 'no studies were ever pursued with more earnestness than those tending to the acquisition of eloquence.' These studies, as being linguistic and literary in the widest sense, gave a large and liberal cultivation, notwithstanding the practical aim. It was held that to be a 'true orator' a man must study philosophy, mathematics, and, in fact, familiarise himself with the whole encyclopædia. In the schools the youths wrote declamations on prescribed themes (*theses* or *loci communes*) and delivered them with proper accent and articulation. They conducted also fictitious cases, taking sides in the dispute. The analysis of language with a view to mastering all its forms was studied (see Cicero 'De Oratore' and Quintilian). Mathematics, philosophy (at least towards the end of the Republic) and law, as well as literature, entered more or less into this higher curriculum; but the three former seem to have been studied under specialist teachers, and did not form an essential part of the higher instruction with the majority of students. It was only in the closing period of the Republic that native history began to receive attention. In short, we may say that in the higher education of youths who aimed at some form of public life — as all the ambitious among the well-to-do did — the two words 'law' and 'oratory' practically summed up their studies. Philosophy and geometry, which, along with astronomy, included in those days the whole of physical science, were merely touched, save by a few of the more ardent. In a political constitution in which a senate or a popular audience had to be convinced, oratory was the great instrument of the rising politician; while at the bar it was of supreme importance. Even when the Roman began to philosophise seriously, it was always practical *ethical* studies that attracted him. Some substitute had to be found for national tradition and for lost gods. But in its larger scientific aspects, philosophical study was alien to the Roman mind, and took the form, as we see in' Cicero, of literary and academic exercitations. About oratory, however, they were very much in earnest.

Youths of high intellectual ambition did not rest satisfied with the instruction obtainable at Rome, but (at least after 80 B.C.) resorted to Athens and other philosophical and rhetorical centres. In the last decades of the Republic there were many famous schools of this higher class. In addition to Athens, the mother city, we have the great university schools of Rhodes, Apollonia, Mitylene, Alexandria, Tarsus, Pergamus, and afterwards, in imperial times, Smyrnà and Ephesus. In the time of Cicero Marseilles also was already a widely known school.

Women shared in the literary culture of Rome; but only to a restricted extent. That girls occasionally attended day-schools, at least towards the end of the Republic, is certain; but speaking generally, their education was domestic and conducted by private tutors. But many possessed high culture. Referring to the Gracchi Cicero says, *non tam in gremio educatos quam sermone matris.* Much later, similar testimony is borne to the mother of Agricola by Tacitus.

But although the Roman always remained Roman in the midst of Hellenic influences, he had lost, long before the time of Augustus, the old primitive simplicity of life. Probably Cato the elder was the last genuine representative of this, and there is a suspicion of affectation in his intellectual narrowness, frugality, and hardiness. The severe and even stern Roman family life penetrated by a moral and religious spirit had, to a large extent, disappeared owing to contact with other nations and the new liberal education. Wealth, luxury, and Greek scepticism, had begun to weaken the Roman fibre. There were always some, of course, who represented the ancient spirit and who, in the words of Cicero, added Hellenic culture *ad domesticum majorumque morem ;* but the mass of the upper classes, having lost the Roman faith, began to find their life-aim in personal ambition and aggrandisement, save when they adopted a cosmopolitan philosophy and lived apart.

Discipline. Teachers. School-houses

Discipline. — The school discipline was severe. Plautus ('Bacch.' iii. 3. 27), says

> Cum librum legeres si unam peccavisses syllabam
> Fieret corium tam maculosum quam est nutricis pallium.

The rod and strap [1] were freely used both in the elementary and secondary school. All are familiar with Horace's Orbilius plagosus ('Ep.' ii. 1. 70), who transferred to the school the discipline he had learned to suffer and enforce as a soldier. Juvenal refers to school punishments (i. 15), where it would appear that 'to withdraw the hand from the rod' was a phrase for leaving school. Ausonius speaks of the school resounding with many a stroke (*multo verbere*). Martial refers to the 'melancholy rods, sceptres of pedagogues,' 'Ferulæque tristes sceptra pædagogorum' (x. 62). He also speaks of the teacher as 'clamosus,' and it is both to *ludimagistri* and *grammatici* that the epithets 'sævus,' 'acerbus,' 'plagosus,' were justly applied by him. Notwithstanding that Martial in the epigram just quoted appeals to the schoolmaster to be kind to his pupils, if he would have them love learning ; that the stern Cato in his lost book 'De Liberis educandis,' denounced those who strike women and children ; that Quintilian protested against the practice ; that one distinguished teacher was opposed to flogging in the generation preceding Quintilian ; that Verrius Flaccus followed a milder way ; that Seneca advocated lenity, and that Cicero said that virtue was to be instilled, not by menaces, force, and terror, but by instruction and persuasion — notwithstanding all this, the severe discipline continued.

[1] Hor. *Sat. I.* 319, refers to *scutica* as a whip more severe than the *flagellum*, and both were more severe than the ferula, but I am not aware that the two former were used in schools.

Augustine as a boy had to endure severe castigations (370–80 A.D.).

The school hours were long, often beginning before daylight and going on till the evening with an interval for dinner. There appear, however, to have been no home lessons.[1] The pupils seem to have spoken aloud when learning, and the masters out-shouted them. Martial (ix. 69) says:

> Despiteful pedant, why dost me pursue,
> Thou head detested by the younger crew ?
> Before the cock proclaims the day is near
> Thy direful threats and lashes stun my ear, &c.

There were a considerable number of short holidays throughout the year, in addition to every eighth day. But the four months' holiday beginning in the middle of June is now understood to have been confined to rural and elementary schools.

We do not hear of rewards for merit till the time of Augustus. It was Verrius Flaccus who first introduced the custom of giving book prizes; but both in Augustan times and thereafter they were rare.

Position of the Teacher.— The pedagogue who had charge of the boy night and day, and held a paternal relation to him, accompanied his charge to school, sat there with him, and brought him home again. He had considerable powers granted to him with a view to secure obedience, although he was almost always only a slave. The Romans, however, seem to have taken more pains in selecting their pedagogues than the Greeks did. Their reward, when their task was completed, was usually the gift of their freedom.

In the time of the Empire, as well as of the Republic, the position of the elementary teacher was very humble; and before the Empire even the grammaticus, though more esteemed, did not stand high. It was Julius Cæsar who first gave Roman citizenship to the grammatici. Indeed, the occupation of elementary teacher — it could not be called a

---

[1] Ussing says that time was given also for gymnastic.

profession — was looked upon with contempt. Held of low estimation in the best Attic time, it fell still lower in the Roman. I have already quoted from Lucian in the chapters on Greek education, and other references might be given here to Latin writers. Justin, among others, when he refers (xxi. 5) to the story of Dionysius the tyrant of Syracuse having become a primary teacher after his expulsion, uses the following words : ' humillima quæque tutissima existimans, in sordidissimum vitæ genus descendit.' Among Greek fragments there is one which says of a man who had disappeared, ' he is either dead or become a primary teacher.' The teachers were always slaves or freedmen, and had to maintain a daily contest with their unruly pupils. All references to the circumstances of teachers before the time of Cicero represent them as in poverty. The payments to them were for a long period in the form of ' honoraria ' rather than fees. They had to take what they could get.

The grammatici, as I have already indicated, held a higher position and were spoken of with some respect ; but it was only of the rhetoricians (who corresponded to our modern professors), that respectful and laudatory remarks are made by Roman writers.

It was in the first century of our era that the word ' professor' began to be used as applied to experts in some of the ' liberal arts.' Quintilian (xii. 2) says : ' Si geometræ et musici et grammatici ceterarumque artium *professores* omnem suam vitam, quamlibet longa fuerit, in singulis artibus consumpserunt,' &c. In the time of the Emperor Hadrian the title was given to the public, established and paid lecturers in the Athenæum at Rome. The designation ' professores medici ' seems first to have made its appearance in the time of Severus (193 A.D.).[1]

---

[1] Seneca was probably the first to use the designation Professor. He speaks (*Ep.* 89) of ' professores eloquentiæ.' It will probably be found that it was only to rhetorical teachers, and not to philosophers, that the word was applied in the first instance, and then to other specialists. The title ' professor' was in the course of time extended to the grammatici and to the instructors in mathematics and medicine.

Both grammatici and rhetoricians often made large fortunes. As to the social status of all of them we must remember a fact which influenced the ancient mind to an extent which we fail fully to comprehend, viz. that they taught for money. It has also to be noted that they were not held to ' educate,' but only to *teach certain subjects*, and to take their payment like dealers in other articles.

School-houses, &c. — Neither among the Greeks nor Romans were these universal or even common in our modern sense ; nor were they built for educational purposes. Adventure teachers (and all were adventure teachers) naturally provided their own schoolrooms. For a long period any room was good enough for giving elementary instruction. Sometimes schools were held in the open air, in some quiet corner of a street or market place. Horace (' Ep.' I. xx. 17) says :

> Ut pueros elementa docentem
> Occupet extremis in vicis balba senectus.[1]

In the earlier times we read of *tabernæ* — sheds or booths ; and these *tabernæ* in later times were like shops or ' leanto's ' opening on the street, and attached to even fashionable houses. The children for the most part sat on the floor, or, if in the street, on the stones. But the schools of the grammatici seem to have been generally the covered spaces attached to larger buildings, ' giving ' on the street and provided with benches for the children, the master occupying a high seat or *cathedra*.[2] Sometimes they were very much like the verandah of a house. The schoolrooms (*pergulæ magistrales*) were also frequently adorned with works of art — both in sculpture (marble or plaster) and in painting. They were open and accessible to all. Parents and other

---

[1] That this passage is relevant might be doubtful were it not for other confirmatory knowledge. Dion. Chrys. *Or.* 29, is aptly quoted by Orellius.

[2] The assistant (adjutor, or sub-doctor) sat on a stool. The benches had no backs, nor were there desks. The pupils wrote on their knees.

members of the public frequently dropt in to see the boys at their work, and there were great 'speech-days.'

The books were rolls of MS. (*volumina*), which the children carried to school in cylindrical wooden boxes.

The state took no charge of either schools or school-masters; all was left to the parent.

The wealthier families of Rome were not, however, (as I have so often pointed out) dependent solely, or even chiefly, on schools. Both grammatici and rhetoricians were employed in private houses to transcribe MSS. and to educate the children. It is to this form of private education that Quintilian objected.

In early imperial times the number of schools, primary and secondary, began to increase rapidly, and in some cases the teachers were engaged by the municipalities and were paid a fixed salary. We see the beginning of this custom shadowed forth in a letter from Pliny to Tacitus which we shall quote in the sequel.

CHAPTER IV

DETAILS OF INSTRUCTION AND METHOD IN THE GRAMMATICAL AND RHETORICAL SCHOOLS

WE have been speaking generally of the course of instruction in Rome. Let us now endeavour to penetrate into the inside of the Roman grammar and rhetorical schools and see the mode of procedure in more detail, if possible.[1]

The School of the Grammaticus. — The exercises of the grammatical school-boy were (1) Reading, to which, as I have said, great attention was paid. It was a fine art. (2) Reproducing short tales or fables orally, and then writing them as exercises in composition. (3) Paraphrasing. This was graded. The younger pupils were restricted to the employment of the poet's own words when

[1] Following to a considerable extent the guidance of Professor Jullien.

turning his lines into prose order. The more advanced did not mangle the poet (as we moderns do), but were required to expand his lines into prose rhetorical form and might take all sorts of liberties so long as they did not go beyond the meaning of the poet. This was in truth a *rhetorical imitation* of the poet and doubtless a valuable exercise. (4) Short sentences (*sententiæ*) were given on which they rang changes of number, case, and syntactical construction; just as, in our best schools, boys are required to convert direct into indirect in Latin, and *vice versa*. (5) Pithy sentences were also given and the pupil required to explain them, and also to paraphrase them as we have above explained paraphrasing. (6) Prosody and the practice of verse-writing were taught.

Translation from Greek into Latin was not practised in the advanced rhetorical schools until after the time of Augustus. In modern schools we have found this exercise so valuable for boys that we cannot but be surprised that it was not practised from the very first by the practical Romans. Cicero speaks of the great benefit he had obtained from it; but translation, as practised by him, may rather be called imitation.

The above exercises combined with a close critical study of the language and the literary qualities of poems, and the free and elocutionary delivery from memory of numerous passages, constituted the principal work of the grammar school.

But there was a tendency in these schools towards the end of the Republic to retain boys longer than formerly, and to introduce them to exercises in declamation on moral questions of a general kind and in giving descriptions of things and events (the higher forms of oratory — the judiciary and the deliberative — being specially reserved for the advanced schools of the rhetoricians). Quintilian complains of this intrusion of the grammaticus on the rhetor. It was the Latin grammaticus who was chiefly guilty of thus stepping beyond his own sphere, his school being, in the majority of cases, attended after the school of the Greek grammaticus. It is manifest that the practice was of doubtful educational value, inasmuch as it led to premature and showy exhibitions of oratory and thus interfered with the more thorough preparatory linguistic discipline. Especially would this evil be accéntuated by the competition among masters for pupils and the gullibility of the Roman parent, who was doubtless as easily imposed on as the British father.

It is not to be supposed that the Roman boy had thrown on him the impossible task of producing the exercises above referred to without help and guidance. The Greek rhetoricians had reduced thesis-writing and declamation to an art, and the logicians had helped them. 'Topics' (τόποι, places, and in Latin, *loci*) had for their object the fixed development of a subject in a certain form and the art of finding arguments. Without entering into details (which, however, are interesting educationally), I shall borrow from Professor Jullien a statement of the topical hints for an exercise on a *chria*, *i.e.* dictum, or pregnant sentence, ascribed to some distinguished man : *e.g.* Plato says that 'the Muses dwell in the soul of the cultured man.'

1. A laudation of the writer to whom the utterance or deed was ascribed.

2. The paraphrase, in which the thought was expanded.

3. The *motif* or underlying principle which explained and justified the truth of the thought.

4. Comparison, *i.e.* the comparing of the thought with other thoughts like or unlike, just as Plutarch compares characters in his 'Lives.'

5. The example : which was furnished by some distinguished man.

6. Witnesses to confirm the dictum, *i.e.* quotations from authorities who had said the same, or a similar, thing.

7. Conclusion : which often took the form of a practical exhortation.

So guided, and with models of similar exercises before him, often written by his master, the boy could scarcely fail

to produce a fairly good essay or declamation, especially as
the learning by heart of the poets had stored his mind with
words and felicitous expressions.   It was held to be a merit
to borrow from distinguished writers, and not a fault.   Indeed, even in mature authors we find in ancient times and
during the latter half of the middle ages a very free use of
the productions of their predecessors.   It seems to me that
plagiarism may be said to have become a moral offence only
in modern times.

Loci communes (common places) were declamations against
particular vices and in support of virtues in the abstract.
They were thus general in their treatment.   But in these, as
in all other exercises both of the grammatical and rhetorical
schools, there was a recognised development of the theme.
The treatises on rhetoric were intended to help invention, to
practice in the use of correct language, in the nature and use
of tropes and figures of speech and in all the devices whereby
a speaker could influence his fellow men.

The Oratory to which youths were trained, after going
through such preparatory instruction as I have outlined in the
school of the grammaticus, was deliberative and judiciary —
that is to say, eloquence suited to a public assembly or senate,
or to the bar.   As Professor Jullien says, it was *professional*
instruction as opposed to the liberal instruction of the grammatici.   The line of demarcation, however, between the
grammaticus and the rhetorician was never clearly defined.
Much depended on the teacher, as it always does where all
are struggling, each for himself.

That the work of the student of oratory was not narrow,
illiberal, and purely technical may be learned from Cicero,
and from Quintilian *passim*.   As regards the strictly technical training I may with advantage quote from the 'De
Oratore,' i. 31, a passage which admirably sums up the whole
process.

'In the first place I will not deny that, as becomes a man
well born and liberally educated, I learned those trite and

common precepts of teachers in general: first, that it is the
business of an orator to speak in a manner adapted to persuade; next, that every speech is either upon a question concerning a matter in general, without specification of persons
or times, or concerning a matter referring to certain persons
and times; but that, in either case, whatever falls under
controversy, the question with regard to it is usually,
whether such a thing has been done, or, if it has been done,
of what nature it is, or by what name it should be
called; or, as some add, whether it seems to have been done
rightly or not. That controversies arise also on the interpretation of writing, in which anything has been expressed
ambiguously, or contradictorily, or so that what is written is
at variance with the writer's evident intention; and that
there are certain lines of argument adapted to all these cases.
But that of such subjects as are distinct from general questions, part come under the head of judicial proceedings, part
under that of deliberations; and that there is a third kind
which is employed in praising or censuring particular persons. That there are also certain common-places on which
we may insist in judicial proceedings, in which equity is
the object; others, which we may adopt in deliberations, all
which are to be directed to the advantage of those to whom
we give counsel; others in panegyric, in which all must be
referred to the dignity of the persons commended. That
since all the business and art of an orator is divided into
five parts, he ought first to find out what he should say;
next, to dispose and arrange his matter, not only in a certain
order, but with a sort of power and judgment; then to clothe
and deck his thoughts with language; then to secure them
in his memory; and lastly, to deliver them with dignity and
grace. I had learned and understood also, that before we
enter upon the main subject, the minds of the audience
should be conciliated by an exordium; next, that the case
should be clearly stated; then, that the point in controversy
should be established; then, that what we maintain should
be supported by proof, and that whatever was said on the

other side should be refuted; and that, in the conclusion of our speech, whatever was in our favour should be amplified and enforced, and whatever made for our adversaries should be weakened and invalidated.

' I had heard also what is taught about the costume of a speech; in regard to which it is first directed that we should speak correctly and in pure Latin; next, intelligibly and with perspicuity; then gracefully; then suitably to the dignity of the subject, and as it were becomingly; and I had made myself acquainted with the rules relating to every particular. Moreover, I had seen art applied to those things which are properly endowments of nature; for I had gone over some precepts concerning action, and some concerning artificial memory, which were short, indeed, but requiring much exercise; matters on which almost all the learning of those artificial orators is employed; and if I should say that it is of no assistance, I should say what is not true; for it conveys some hints to admonish the orator, as it were, to what he should refer each part of his speech, and to what points he may direct his view, so as not to wander from the object which he has proposed to himself. But I consider that with regard to all precepts the case is this, not that orators by adhering to them have obtained distinction in eloquence, but that certain persons have noticed what men of eloquence practised of their own accord, and formed rules accordingly; so that eloquence has not sprung from art, but art from eloquence; not that, as I said before, I entirely reject art, for it is, though not essentially necessary to oratory, yet proper for a man of liberal education to learn. And by you, my young friends, some preliminary exercise must be undergone; though, indeed, you are already on the course; but those who are to enter upon a race, and those who are preparing for what is to be done in the forum, as their field of battle, may alike previously learn, and try their powers, by practising in sport.'

So far as we know the course of training thus generally sketched by Cicero, it may be concisely summed up thus:

When the Rhetor began from the beginning he carried the youth through the exercises which I have already described as the higher work of the grammaticus, and then gave more advanced work on the same lines while he delivered or dictated lectures on the theory of eloquence. Subsequent exercises consisted of speeches prepared by the pupils, of a demonstrative, deliberative, or judiciary character. The demonstrative consisted very much of the laudation or unfavourable criticism of certain historical, or it might be imaginary, acts and characters; the deliberative was an argument addressing itself to the question whether any act should have been done or not; the judiciary was in the form of a pleading before a judge — attack and defence. These pleadings were often regarding fictitious cases, sometimes regarding cases that had actually been in the courts. The general course of instruction applicable to all forms of oratory embraced Invention, *i.e.* the finding of arguments; Disposition or arrangement; Style or elocution; Memory and its cultivation; and Action or delivery. Disputations were conducted by the students, under the guidance of the rhetor. All sorts of subjects were propounded, but chiefly those having a political or ethical significance. In imperial times, and probably earlier, the rhetors themselves would have public bouts, and people would flock to hear them and encourage them with their plaudits. Divorced, however, as the exercises were from all direct bearing on political action, they tended more and more to become mere declamation.

We now see that the education which took shape to itself under the Roman sway, and which was summed up in the word *humanitas*, was almost wholly a literary education, based, however, on a thorough grammatical study. It is important to note this, and the relative place assigned to other studies, because of its bearing on the history of education even down to our own times.

It is, I think, sufficiently clear that, notwithstanding the literary character of the education, private and public utility governed the Roman practice. Roman education was Greek, but it was Greek translated into Latin. The liberal arts were all cultivated at Rome, but not by Romans. They were to be enjoyed, not pursued. Greek aliens — very often slaves or freedmen — represented all the arts, and were hired. Play-acting, though regarded as a degrading employment, was yet of ' use ' to the orator by teaching him gesture : sculpture was of ' use ' for public monuments and portraiture, and so forth.

Literature, it is true, was in esteem both as a study, an educational instrument, and as a recreation ; but, above all, as necessary to form the orator. Literature for the sake of literature, art for the sake of art, were to the Greek familiar conceptions ; and in his schools it was the *real* of literature, the enriching of the mind with noble utterances and noble forms, which was always prominent. In the case of the Roman we find the discipline of grammar take precedence of the living spirit of literature, without, however, by any means extinguishing it.

Of course there were many individual exceptions to the Roman view of art and the arts among the Romans them-selves ; but the general utilitarian tendency of the Roman mind was always in evidence. The Hellenic ideal of a cultured man — cultured for the sake of culture — was never accepted by the Roman, save in a half-hearted way. Indeed, he had great contempt, and with good reason, for much of the product of the Hellenic system. The lively Greek who frequented the streets of Rome and other Italian towns, and who in his easy self-confidence was ready to talk, and to talk well, on any subject and in favour of any side, was antagonistic to the Roman type of character, and to that serious view of life which had made the Roman and which seemed still to survive in spite of growing luxury, an en-feebled public spirit, and a decaying morality.

I have already said that the loss of the writings of Terentius Varro (died 26 B.C.), the ' most learned of the Romans,' has deprived us of much that would have thrown additional light on the actual state of education and of learning immediately before the birth of Christ. One of his works was entitled 'Libri Disciplinarum.' All the more valuable are the writings of Quintilian which appeared in the last decade of the first century A.D. In him we see the highest type of teacher which the ancient world produced, with, perhaps, the single exception of Isocrates ; and from his writings we can learn both what the Romano-Hellenic education was in its inner working, and also what, in his opinion, it ought to have been. His works, accordingly, are not only of great importance in the history of education as formulating the aims and method of the best kind of Romano-Hellenic school, both grammatical and rhetorical ; but they also contain so much practical instruction for the teacher of all time that I shall now speak of him and his treatise in some detail, confining myself, however, to what is specially instructive to the teacher of the modern school. I am justified in giving this prominence to Quintilian by the further fact that he has governed all modern education since the Renaissance ; and, in truth, we have not even yet advanced so far as wholly to restore the school of Quintilian. The nearest approach to it were the schools of Vittorino da Feltre in the fourteenth and Hegius, Michael Neander, Trotzendorff, and Sturm, in the fifteenth and sixteenth centuries.

CHAPTER V

THE SCHOOL OF QUINTILIAN

MARCUS FABIUS QUINTILIANUS was born at Calagurris (Calahorra) in the upper valley of the Ebro about A.D. 38.[1] He seems to have been taken by his father to Rome

---

[1] Many say 35, and till recently 42 was the accepted date. I give a date between the two as being the most probable. Seneca was born a year or two before the birth of Christ ; Plutarch 48 or 49 A.D. (about the same time as Quintilian), and Tacitus about 61 A.D.

when quite a boy to prosecute his studies. His father was himself a teacher of rhetoric. At the age of about 25 he returned to his native place, where he remained several years in the practice of his profession. At about the age of 30 he again came to Rome in the retinue of Galba (A.D. 68) and began to practise at the bar, attaining some distinction, especially for his clear, exact, and logical statement of cases. Dr. Peterson in his edition of Book X. quotes from Hild as follows: — 'Among the orators of the day, some, ignorant and coarse, had left mean occupations for the bar without any preliminary study, where they made up in audacity for lack of talent, and in noisy conceit for a defective knowledge of law ; others were trained in the practice of delation to every form of trickery and violence ; Quintilian, honest, able, and moderate, stood by himself.'

Later in life he began to give instruction in the oratorical art, including under this, however, a wide range of grammatical and literary culture, which he thought necessary to the education of the true orator. Among his pupils was the younger Pliny. He acquired a great reputation as an instructor, and more honour than was usually conferred on teachers of rhetoric in those days. Domitian gave him permission to wear the insignia of a man of consular rank. It is to this that Juvenal refers in the line (Sat. vii. 186),

If fortune be kind, you will from a rhetor become a consul.[1]

The well-known passage in Suetonius' 'Life of Vespasian' (c. 18) marks the first State action for the maintenance of public schools : 'Vespasianus, who first fixed out of the public treasury a salary of 100 sestertia each to the rhetors, Greek and Latin [2]' (estimated at about 800*l.* a year). As Vespasian reigned from A.D. 71 to A.D. 79, the most active period of Quintilian's scholastic career, we may conclude that he was one of the rhetors endowed by Vespasian, all

---

[1] 'Si fortuna volet, fies de rhetore consul.'

[2] 'Qui primus e fisco Latinis Græcisque rhetoribus annua centena constituit.'

the more that the 'Eusebian Chronicle' (Roth's ' Suetonius,' p. 272) says : 'Quintilian, a Calagurritan from Spain, the first to open a public school in Rome and to receive a salary out of the public treasury, flourished.'[1] Referring to his work as a public instructor, Martial says,[2] 'Quintilian, supreme governor of unstable youth ; Quintilian, glory of the Roman gown !'

After twenty years' teaching he retired from active life at the early age of about fifty, although after his retirement he was employed as a private tutor at court to Domitian's two grand-nephews (A.D. 93).

At the urgent solicitation of many friends and admirers, and also to put a stop to the circulation of notes of his lectures, published with his name but without his authority, he now began to prepare and arrange, with a view to publication, the abundant materials amassed in the course of an active professional life. This occupied him a period of only two years (probably between A.D. 93 and 95). The solicitations of his publisher led him to issue his work sooner than he would otherwise have done. He died before the end of the first century A.D. at the age of about sixty. He himself tells us that he lost his wife when she was only nineteen, and that the two boys she left behind her also died, the younger at five years old and the elder at ten.

The books which he published, sometimes called ' Oratorical Institutions,' are known under the title of ' Twelve Books on the Education of an Orator ': ' De Institutione Oratoria ' are the words which he himself uses in a prefatory letter to his publisher, Trypho.

Quintilian was one of the most Roman of the Roman men of letters. Not only because of the national note in his style as a whole, but for the legal precision and directness of his thought and language, and for the soundness and

[1] ' Quintilianus, ex Hispania, Calagurritanus, qui primus Romæ publicam scholam [aperuit] et salarium e fisco accepit, claruit.'
[2] ' Quintiliane vagæ moderator summe juventæ,
Gloria Romanæ Quintiliane togæ.' — ii. 90.

moderation of his judgments. There is the calmness of
scientific exposition about his reasoning, wholly unlike our
modern style of writing into which we are apt to introduce,
even unconsciously, a certain amount of open or latent
passion. Political and religious bias dominates even our
abstract philosophy and political economy. Every reader
will be disposed to concur in the estimate of Bähr in his
'Geschichte der Römischen Literatur,' where he says: 'We
find in Quintilian a genuinely critical spirit, a sound judgment, and a truly practical sense, a pure refined taste,
a wide literary culture, and an extensive acquaintance
with the whole range of Greek and Roman literature'
(p. 325).

In exposition, Quintilian never uses a single word more
than is necessary to express his thought. He has none of
the amplitude of language which belongs to Cicero. It is
possible that he did not admire copiousness of language as
distinguished from copiousness of argument. It certainly
strikes the reader that while Quintilian was capable of a
far more exact philosophical style than Cicero, richness
and abundance of language were alien to his cast of mind
as well as forbidden by the strictly practical aims of his
book.

But how is it, we are first disposed to ask, that a book
on the education of the orator should in these days concern us as educationalists, except in a very subordinate
way? The answer is already partly given in the preceding
chapter.

Quintilian started with a very enlarged conception of the
training requisite for an orator. This designation, indeed,
as used by him, may be regarded as synonymous with a
completely cultivated man. 'Others,' he says, 'have begun
their treatises on rhetoric as if they were merely putting
the finishing touch of eloquence on pupils already masters
of every kind of learning' (Prœm. 4); 'but I am of opinion
that to make an orator we must begin from the beginning,
and I consequently,' he adds, 'shall begin to shape the

studies of an orator from his infancy just as if he were handed over to me to bring up.' He accordingly proposes to start *ab ipsis discendi velut incunabulis* (as it were from the very cradle of learning). Quintilian does not imagine that education can do everything. On the contrary, he tells us that unless Nature helps, all instructions will be useless. 'Illud tamen in primis testandum est, nihil præcepta atque artes valere nisi adjuvante natura. Quapropter ei, cui deerit ingenium, non magis hæc scripta sunt quam de agrorum cultu sterilibus terris': 'First of all I must bear witness to this, that precepts and arts are of no value without the assistance of nature. Wherefore to him who wants talent these writings are of no more significance than an agricultural treatise to barren lands.' At the same time he held with Isocrates and Cicero that natural powers could be largely augmented and adorned.

Cato the elder, in his lost treatise on education, affirmed it to be the aim of education to produce the *bonus vir*. Quintilian substitutes for this the *bonus orator*, and in doing so he places himself in more direct sympathy with the practical aims of the post-republican Roman life and education. He in fact extends the aim of Cato when in the beginning of the twelfth book he defines the orator to be 'The Good Man skilled in speaking' — *Vir bonus dicendi peritus.* Mere *facultas dicendi* he despises. His idea of an orator is in fact that of a learned, cultivated, virtuous philosopher who, qualified by certain innate or acquired aptitudes, is engaged in the highest practical affairs of life. Practical life for all is always assumed. In the twelfth book, indeed, he talks with some disdain of philosophers, because they withdraw themselves from public occupations. He desires to form a '*Roman* philosopher.'[1] 'The man I educate I should wish to be a *Roman* philosopher who, not

---

[1] 'Illum quem instituo, Romanum quendam velim esse sapientem, qui non secretis disputationibus sed rerum experimentis atque operibus vere civilem virum exhibeat.' — xii. 27.

by disputations apart but by dealing with practical life and by public activity, shows himself to be truly a *vir civilis'* (a man occupied with affairs that concern the commonweal). We manifestly require in such a man, he says, not only the highest ability but also every virtue of the mind. Accordingly, he aims at forming a man who is in the best sense of the word a citizen, adapted for the administration of public and private affairs, who is competent to govern cities by his counsels, to institute them by his laws, and to improve them by his judicial decisions. Then as to the virtues: an orator has to discourse on matters relating to justice, temperance, and fortitude, and how can he do so effectively unless he himself is distinguished by these virtues?

The orator, let us remember, had a large and important function in the public life of the ancients. He was not merely a pleader at the bar, but also before public assemblies. He influenced the whole policy of a country, and among other functions discharged the duty of the modern publicist. At first sight, we may be disposed to question the necessity of goodness and virtue to a good orator; but a little reflection will satisfy us that, when we fully realise the scope of the orator's function as understood by the ancients, we must admit with Quintilian that the truly good orator must himself be good. We all recognise the contrast between learning and wisdom: but it is important to note also that intellectual ability, even the highest, is not necessarily wisdom. The moral element must dominate. Quintilian did not stand alone in his opinion. 'Depravity,' says Aristotle, 'perverts the vision and causes it to be deceived as to the principles of action, so that it is really impossible for a person who is not good to be really wise and prudent.' And how can a bad man give sound counsel in an oration? To the extent to which the counsel, the persuasions, the argument are unsound, it is bad oratory. Coleridge, in his 'Table-talk,' cites from Strabo the opinion, 'to be a good poet one must be a good man.' Carlyle, again, says, 'The real quantity of our insight — how justly and thoroughly we shall comprehend the nature of a thing, especially of· a human thing, depends on our patience, our fairness, lovingness, what strength soever we have ; intellect comes from the whole man as it is the light that enlightens the whole man.' (Vol. v. of ' Miscellanies,' p. 125.) The significant thing for us to note as students of education is that Quintilian, like all competent thinkers on this subject, aimed at a moral result as the supreme end. In our great schools do we consciously do this ? If we do not, then, with all our ' classical' pretensions, we are followers neither of the best Greeks nor Romans. There must be something wrong. Quintilian held that a man could not be engaged in the pursuit of those noble studies of literature and philosophy which were indispensable to the education of an orator, unless he were free from vice. From which may we not conclude that occupation with ennobling studies is the greatest safeguard of youth ? [1]

Mere eloquence in the ordinary sense, fluent faculty of speech, did not constitute an orator in Quintilian's view. He even absorbed the title philosopher into that of orator, as did Isocrates. He wished to produce a man ' optima sentientem, optimeque dicentem ' (xii. 1. 25) 'thinking the best things and expressing them in the very best way,' and not a mere mercenary pleader in the forum, or a claptrap popular talker. By giving to philosophy a practical character and testing it, as it were, by its power of doing practical service to the state, he maintained even for philosophy a higher standard than then existed in many of the schools of Greece and Alexandria. We do not quarrel with Quintilian, then, because, under a very natural tendency, peculiar to his age and nation, to magnify the office of the rhetorician, he used the word orator as a synonym for the perfectly trained and fully equipped citizen : nor yet because he held that the perfect orator was also necessarily the perfect citizen. He admits that no man ever was what he aims at producing; but none

---

[1] ' In eodem pectore nullum est honestorum turpiumque consortium.'

the less ought we all to aim at the ideal,[1] 'none the less, are we to strive after the highest; even if this is not attainable, nevertheless those who strive after it will go higher than those who, having despaired by anticipation of reaching their object, forthwith pull themselves up and halt at the bottom of the hill.'

We see, then, that the analysis of the writings which Quintilian left behind him must furnish us with a knowledge of the best educational conceptions possible in his time, presented in a form thoroughly trustworthy, inasmuch as they come from a man of long experience as a teacher, and of a temper whose ardour was moderated by cool reason and sound judgment. They will also admit us to a knowledge of the kind of training through which the wealthier classes of Roman youth — those who sought to govern their country — were carried at the beginning of the Christian era, when the Hellenic influence was completely established.

I do not pretend to give an exhaustive account of Quintilian, but merely to bring into view his leading principles and methods as these are expounded in his first two books, and only in so far as they may bear on school work in these days. I shall make such reference to his subsequent books as will enable the reader to form an adequate conception of the way in which he discharged the task he imposed on himself.

At the end of his preface, Quintilian gives us a preliminary survey of his plan, as follows:

The first book will contain those things which precede the proper work of the teacher of rhetoric.

The second book will treat of the elements of rhetoric.

The next five will be devoted to *Inventio*, including arrangement (*Dispositio*).

---

[1] 'Non ideo minus nobis ad summa tendendum est . . . quod si non contingat, altius tamen ibunt qui ad summa nitentur quam qui, præsumpta desperatione quo velint evadendi, protinus circa ima substiterint' (i. 19).

The next four will be devoted to Elocution (*i.e.* style), including memory and pronunciation (*i.e.* delivery).

In conclusion will be considered the cultivation of the orator personally, and as a pleader.

First Book

In his first book, Quintilian deals with the instruction of children before the age of seven. After many warnings as to the necessity of providing nurses whose moral character is good, and who have sufficient education to set a good example in speaking, he takes up the intellectual instruction of the child.

He objects to the learning of the alphabet in a memorial way, so that children early acquire the habit of saying the letters, trusting to their memory alone. He advises that the shape and name be always impressed on the child together, and recommends the tracing over of letters which have been cut on a board. He also recommends the use of ivory figures of letters as playthings. When they begin to read words, let the reading be very slow and distinct, he says; otherwise, by hurrying the child, or permitting the child to hurry, you form a bad habit and retard progress.

As to writing, he evidently considers that this art is best begun by tracing the letters on the board referred to above, and thereafter by copying good specimens, according to our modern usage. He thinks that the lines which the pupil is required to imitate should convey moral lessons which he will carry with him to old age. He also thinks that a child, in learning to write, should not be constantly exercised on ordinary words, but on the more unusual words, that he may acquire betimes a knowledge of terms which, at a later period of his studies, may be useful to him. He points out that, as future progress and cultivation depend so much on the art of writing, the pupil should learn to write quickly as well as well, and well as well as quickly.

Memory, he thinks, may be even at this early age cultivated, and passages from the poets and utterances of learned men learned by heart. For this he gives a curious reason, that at this age a teacher can do little for the education of children (as they can produce nothing from themselves) except cultivate their memory.

Above all, he impresses on his readers that children are not stupid; that they are ready in thinking and prompt in learning ('faciles in excogitando et ad discendum promptos'); that it is as natural for the human animal to be so as it is for birds to fly, horses to run, and wild beasts to be savage. 'Characteristic of man is a certain stirring and dexterous movement of mind, and hence the belief in the celestial origin of the soul.'[1] It is the want of proper training which dulls the childish intelligence. Minds naturally stupid and unteachable do certainly exist, but only as monstrosities exist — and they are few in number. Yet some have greater natural aptitude than others.

He objects to Roman boys learning Greek exclusively for too long a period; but he holds that they should begin with Greek (he must mean in the secondary or grammar school), taking to Latin in a year or two, and learning it thereafter *pari passu* with Greek. Greek, let us remember, was at this time, and, indeed, long before, taught to all the upper classes as the source of Roman literature, and it was also known colloquially to the upper classes and to merchants and others through the large number of Greek slaves and pædagogi who frequented Rome, and the universal relations which Rome had with the whole civilised world.

Quintilian now proceeds to discuss the respective merits of public and private education. By public education was, in his time, meant day-schools, such as we are familiar with in Scotland and Germany. Public schools — in the restricted sense of schools in which boys were educated away from the influence of their parents, being boarded at the seat of their education, either in the school buildings or in affiliated houses — are institutions more characteristic

---

[1] 'Nobis propria est mentis agitatio atque sollertia, unde origo animi cœlestis creditur.'

of England than of any other country, though of course known in other countries: in all, indeed, to a certain extent indispensable. Quintilian, accordingly, is contrasting domestic as opposed to school instruction. He argues the question, which in his day was evidently of great importance. Nowadays it has less interest. We are all persuaded that boys, at least, are better instructed in some public fashion, although we may differ as to the desirableness of removing them from the parental roof altogether.

Quintilian draws a very black picture of the domestic life of many Romans — their daily habits of luxury, their sensuality, and their licentious conversation and songs. No day public school could be otherwise than beneficial to the boy of such a family. That is certain. We feel that the 'tone' of a day-school as a whole could not fail, however defective, to be better than the tone of a boy so reared. The school would have to guard against him, not he against the school. In these days we are scarcely, indeed, interested in this question in the form in which it presented itself to Quintilian; education is now for all, and Quintilian assumes that those who prefer private education employ private preceptors and pedagogues, which is possible only to the few wealthy. Public day and public boarding schools are both alike with us simply a necessity. and no amount of argument can now touch the question. The only point which calls for discussion in these days is the relative advantages of these two classes of 'public' schools. We shall find the arguments of Quintilian not altogether inapplicable to this modern question. For he bases his argument for day-schools mainly on the bad influences of the pupil's home, and the consequent luxury, effeminacy, viciousness, and self-conceit which flow from these. So now we may (without formally entering into the discussion here) say that where the domestic atmosphere is bad because of the luxuriousness of homes, the preoccupation of the parents with other things than the bringing up of their children, and the evil influences flowing from the subserviency and flattery of menials, the children should certainly be removed to some other place where they may find that true home which their parents have denied them. For such children a day-school is better, much better, than nothing; but a public *home* school — if I may so designate`it — is best of all.

Quintilian remarks, in connection with school work, on the advantages of emulation, and points out that it is easier for beginners of tender years to imitate their fellow-pupils than their teacher. He refers to a custom which prevailed in the school in which he was himself instructed. The boys were assigned a certain order in speaking or declaiming the passages they had learned — the best being assigned the highest place, and adds (a suggestive fact) that every thirtieth day a fresh arrangement of the order was made according to the results of a fresh exercise. If we would imitate this, adapting it to modern school life, we should have monthly examinations to determine the places of boys in a class — a far sounder system than trusting to the chances of daily 'place-taking,' which, moreover, has many collateral disadvantages.

One other observation Quintilian makes which we may here quote. He counsels masters to moderate their strength so as not to burden the undeveloped powers of the learners, but rather to descend to the level of their understanding — 'ad intellectum audientis descendere.' He compares the ambitious attempt to give boys more than their stage of progress admits of to the pouring of a gush of water into a narrow-necked bottle. The water is lost, whereas a gradual inpouring of it little by little fills the bottle. 'What is greater than the understanding of a boy,' he says, 'will not enter his mind at all; because it is not open to apprehend it.'[1]

He then is led aside to speak of the natural endowments and disposition of boys. He considers that memory — that is to say, that kind of memory which both acquires easily

[1] 'Majora intellectu velut parum apertos ad percipiendum animos non subibunt' (28).

and retains long — is the chief early sign of ability in children. The next indication of talent is the power of imitation; but if this takes the direction of imitating deformities or peculiarities it is a very bad sign. He speaks strongly of this, and says that this mimicking tendency in a boy gives him no hope of his ever having a good disposition. The pupil whom he prefers is he who is capable of receiving what is taught without difficulty and is disposed to ask questions; but inclined to follow rather than to run on ahead. The precocious boy seldom yields good fruit in the long run. He can do little things with great ease, and, instigated by self-confidence, desires to show at once all he can do. Without any signs of bashfulness, he strings words together fluently. There is no *true force*, and what power he shows has not deep roots; and so on.

As to natural disposition; he points out that all boys do not yield to the same motives. 'Some are remiss, unless you urge them on; some resent commands; some are restrained by fear; and others are enfeebled by it; continuity of study shapes some, others get on with more of a rush. Give me the boy,' he says, 'whom praise excites, whom glory urges, who weeps at defeat.'

Quintilian advocates relaxation and play; but he gives us no indication of the amount of daily headwork he expected of a boy. The time-table of a Roman school would be an interesting monument. He considers that boys' dispositions appear more frequently in play than anywhere else: they then reveal themselves unconsciously and we can correct faults while the boy is yet of tender years. (The playground, then, seems to be with Quintilian part of the school.)

As to corporal punishments, Quintilian has very decided opinions. The passage is a celebrated one among educationalists, and I shall give it here.

'I do not at all approve of boys being flogged, although it is an established practice and one approved of by Chrysippus. I object to it, (1) because it is a disgusting practice and fit only for slaves, and indeed if you change the age of your pupil, a personal insult; (2) because if the mind of a boy is so illiberal (ungenerous) as to be inaccessible to reproofs, he will simply be hardened to the infliction of stripes like the worst of slaves ; (3) because there will be no need whatsoever of castigation if the superintendent of his studies (*exactor studiorum*) be persistent.　As things are now, it would seem that the negligence of pædagogi is made amends for, not by requiring boys to do what is right, but by punishing them for doing what is wrong . . . [Not to dwell on these matters,] it is enough to say that to no man ought too much liberty to be allowed in dealing with pupils of tender years and easily injured.' [1]

Secondary Instruction

Quintilian now supposes a boy to be able to read and write Latin, and he considers that the fundamental discipline next necessary for him with a view to his cultivation is grammar. He prefers to begin with the Greek Grammar.　Following the same opinion, it was customary throughout Europe till recently, as we all know, to begin with Latin Grammar, and to trust that boys would see their way through the grammar of their native tongue by means of the Latin.　Hence ' Grammar' schools.　I have already pointed out that there were both Greek and Latin Grammar schools.　Greek Grammar schools preceded Latin ones.　On this point there is an interesting quotation from a lost letter of Cicero's given by Suetonius in his Life of the rhetorician L. Plotius Gallus, which I may here introduce : ' I remember well that when we were boys, one Lucius Plotius first began to teach Latin ; and as great numbers flocked to his school, so that those who were most devoted to study were eager to take lessons from him, it was a great trouble to me that I too was not allowed to do so.　I was prevented, however, by the decided opinion of men of the greatest learning who considered that it was best to cultivate the mind by the study of Greek.'

[1] Plato and Seneca had objected to severity and force before Quintilian. Cicero (' De Orat.' i. 58) is frequently referred to as opposed to coercive means, but he is speaking quite generally and not of schools.

Quintilian lays great stress on the accurate and detailed knowledge of grammar, including what we now call historical grammar, the inquiry into the sounds of letters, the transposition and substitution of vowels and consonants by reference to ancient Latin and Greek forms: then the study of the parts of speech, and inquiry into etymologies, synonyms, &c. The difficulty of fixing the number of the parts of speech and the difference of opinion as regards their origin and proper classification is, Quintilian thinks, no argument against the study. I may be allowed to interpose here that it is an argument *for* the study. These grammatical foundations should be surely and soundly laid according to Quintilian, as the basis of future literary culture. And so far Quintilian was right, if we grant him that the object of all training is to train a man who can speak well and write well. In these days we may follow Quintilian with safety, notwithstanding his apparently limited view of the end of education — because he has already said that only the man trained in all the virtues and in practical philosophy is the true orator. *Mutatis mutandis* we must indeed heartily concur with Quintilian, for a man who would speak well and write well must, first of all, know what he is speaking about, and in the second place he must have been a student of words, of style, and of literary expression. But words alone, considered grammatically, though an important and indispensable discipline, will not give him power of speaking or writing with effect. In modern times, then, we must extend the matter of education if we are to carry out Quintilian's instructions. But while so saying, we must concur with him in thinking that the analysis of language — that is, of words and sentences, and also of mere forms and of etymologies, is productive of much benefit to the intelligence of a boy, and gives a firmness and solidity to the intellect which even logic will fail to give where there has been no such prior grammatical discipline. As to Quintilian's opinion that we should begin with a foreign tongue, we must bear in mind our change of circumstances; the grammar of our own language is now considerably developed and systematised, and the science of comparative philology has thrown great light on origins. Accordingly, English, in the hands of a man of grammatical and philological mind, is now capable of being used as a most valuable instrument both of instruction and discipline. Then, again, the grammatical study of Greek was more advanced than that of Latin in Quintilian's time; and there were other good reasons. A potent argument also which would not suggest itself to Quintilian for beginning with the grammar of our own tongue is that the boy already *knows* it, practically and implicitly. We have only, by pursuing the analytico-synthetic method to raise the indefinite experience to true knowledge — make explicit what is implicit. This is instruction in the grammar of the vernacular.

Quintilian now deals with the *use* of words, inculcating the avoidance of ' barbarisms ' (which are defined to be faults in respect of individual words), solecisms, &c. Quintilian's remarks here contain little of value to us as teachers beyond impressing on all who may read them the importance of employing only such words as are correct in substance and in form. It is not wasted time to direct the attention of scholars to mere words; this is a popular error : the study of words with special reference to their comparative fitness to express a thought, and to their purity of origin, is a valuable discipline. Words carry ideas.

In speaking of correct language generally, Quintilian points out, to begin with, that it rests on *ratio, vetustas, auctoritas*, and *consuetudo* (reason, antiquity, authority, and custom). He then considers each of these sources, or rather guarantees, of correct language in a chapter full of interest for the student of the Latin tongue and of general etymology. After all, in the selection of words we must be guided by the custom of our time, says Quintilian, not the custom of the multitude but the 'consensus eruditorum' (learned or educated men), just as the consensus of good men determines custom as regards manner of living (Horace speaks also of the *usus loquendi*).

He next deals with the *writing* of words as the previous chapter dealt with words *spoken*. The spelling of words is considered here. His general conclusion as to spelling is that words should be written as they are sounded, inasmuch as the very use of written characters is to represent sounds. He makes an exception, however, where custom declares strongly for a spelling though it be inconsistent with the sound.

To the teaching of good reading he attaches, as did all Romans and Greeks, great importance. Reading is to be taught with care, the boy being taught when to read slowly, when with more rapidity, when to speak with vivacity, and when with gentleness of tone. All this depends on practice; and I have, he says, only one thing to enjoin: 'that he may *do* all these things let him understand what he reads.' He adds, and I think the remark as applied to reading is worth our attention, 'Let the reading be manly and grave, but grave with a certain sweetness.' The poets are not to be read like prose writers; at the same time they are not to be read in a sing-song tone, nor 'plasmate effeminata'—that is to say, rendered effeminate by an exaggerated and affected modulation. He tells us that Cæsar once said to a reader of this last kind 'Si cantas, male cantas; si legis, cantas' (if you are singing, you sing vilely; if you are reading, you sing). He objects to speeches in poetry being uttered by the reader as an actor would utter them; but thinks a difference of tone necessary in order to show that they are speeches.

The substance of what is read should be morally good and inspiring, while the literary character of it should be worthy of imitation. Homer and Virgil therefore should be read, and the poets generally, taking care to give to boys only what is morally pure. Those things are to be chiefly perused by boys which most of all nourish the talent and enlarge the mind — books on learning being postponed. Manliness of thought and expression are to be gained from a study of the older writers.

He then refers to the course to be pursued by the teacher in examining on the passages read. The verses should be parsed and scanned. Peculiarities in the use of words should then be brought out and the different senses in which certain words may be taken. But above all, the teacher should point out the beauty of the arrangement, the charm of the subject matter, the appropriateness of the words to the character represented, what is worthy of praise in the substance, what in the words used, and so forth. Historical allusions should be explained; but the pupil should not be overloaded with these, but confined to what is related by authors of mark.

While boys are still young and not yet ready to be handed over to the rhetor, the beginnings of the art of speaking should be taught. Boys should, after they have left behind them nursery stories, be exercised in relating the fables of Æsop, and afterwards writing down the narration. Then they should be required to paraphrase the poets, and to give brief statements regarding events or characters which have a moral significance. (This, I think, was what was known as ' description ').

Quintilian now, leaving the study of language, adverts to those other studies which are necessary to the orator, or completely educated man, taking up specially mathematics and music.

The word music among the ancients, I may here recall to the reader, was a word of varying application. Sometimes it had the limited signification which we attach to it. At other times it was regarded as including also grammar and geometry; and again in its wider sense it included all education, save that which had to do with the discipline and development of the body, which was called gymnastic.

The importance of music, in its restricted sense, for the orator was evident; for he must understand and practise rhythm in his sentences and utterance. Mathematics, which

covered both arithmetic and geometry, can, I think, be shown
to be indispensable only on the presumption that we regard
the orator as our type of an educated man. If we do so, all
that Quintilian says about the importance of musical and
mathematical studies will receive the heartiest support of all
competent persons. The grounds on which he advocates
music are of a practical kind, and the same applies to his
advocacy of geometry. The educational ends of the Romans
had always (as I have frequently said) an objective and
practical character. The recognition of the fact that there
was a certain constitution of mind and the relation of educational instruments to the full development and discipline of
the mind, *as mind*, does not seem to have been entertained
by them. By this I do not mean to convey that the efficacy
of certain studies in sharpening the intelligence, such, for example, as dialectic and mathematics, was not recognised ;
but merely that the development of mind as such was not
the object they had in view. With the Athenian Greeks,
and to some extent even with the Spartans, it was otherwise.
Culture was aimed at — a complete harmony of nature —
mind and body. The object in view with the Romans on the
contrary was to make a man apt for affairs, or, as with
Quintilian, a perfect orator, which included the former.
The practical issue of all education was never lost sight of.

Quintilian, neither in speaking of music or geometry, suggests methods of procedure, but he says much that is pertinent with reference to both. His remarks on the importance
and influence of music are eloquent and recall the Ciceronian
style. When speaking of the importance of musical rhythm
to the orator, he says with epigrammatic force: ' Both by the
tone of voice and the modulation, music sounds forth grand
things in a lofty style, pleasant things sweetly, ordinary
things gently, and in its whole art it is in harmony with the
feelings that are expressed.' [1] The musical education was in
fact instruction in rhythm and intonation.

[1] ' Et voce et modulatione grandia elate, jucunda dulciter, moderata leniter
canit, totaque arte consentit cum eorum quæ dicuntur affectibus ' (24).

As to geometry, Quintilian argues not only for its practical utility, but also for its use as exciting the intelligence, sharpening the wits, and giving greater celerity of perception. Then he shows that geometry is more closely allied to logic than to rhetoric and lauds it as an exercise in deductive reasoning. Note here that in Quintilian's scheme of education, physical science was included, because he finally rests the claims of geometry on its being the engine whereby we rise to a knowledge of the *ratio mundi* and learn that there is nothing which is not ordered, nothing which is fortuitous.

Elsewhere (in the introduction to the eighth book) Quintilian points to the importance of instruction in things: ' Curam verborum, rerum volo esse solicitudinem ' (I desire that there be care for words but a *solicitude* for things); again, ' Sit ergo cura elocutionis quam maxima, dum scimus tamen nihil verborum causa faciendum, quum verba ipsa rerum gratia reperta sint.' (' Let there be the greatest possible care for expression as long as we recognise the fact that nothing is to be done for the sake of words, since words themselves have been invented for the sake of things.')

Quintilian now passes outside general education and proceeds to discuss the training which is peculiar to the future orator only; and although what he says is well deserving of all who hope to distinguish themselves in the pulpit or parliament or at the bar, it bears only very partially on the question of general education. He recommends the student of oratory to take lessons from an actor, but only with a view to *pronuntiatio*, by which he means both the correct and full pronunciation of words, the delivery of passages conveying different kinds of sentiment, and the facial movements to be used, or rather to be avoided. As the pupil gets older, he recommends the recitation of good speeches to his master in the style he would have to adopt in pleading. Gesture should be learned from the masters in the palæstra. But Quintilian draws a strong line between what is becoming in an actor and in an orator respectively.

As to the capacity of the young to study a great many subjects together, Quintilian gives expression to what is characterised by soundness of judgment and freshness, force, and even fervour of style. 'People,' he says, 'who talk of the difficulty of learning many subjects at the same time, forget the nature of the young mind — its facility of movement, its pliancy and its interest in many things. They also forget to remember that the doing of things is not so fatiguing as *cogitatio* or thought; further, that children do not put force on *themselves*, but are guided by others.' He also points out the refreshment which is obtained by varying studies, and even by passing from reading to writing about the *same* subject.

He dwells with force on the importance of early instruction in any department which a man is afterwards thoroughly to know, illustrating this by the case of imported slaves who are very long of overcoming the difficulties of the Latin tongue, whereas children speak freely two years after they have begun to pronounce words. The Greeks called those who excelled in their own special art *pædomatheis* — that is to say, instructed from boyhood. (Plato in his 'Laws' also speaks of this.) In brief, we try to excuse our own sloth by talking of the difficulty which attends the thorough study of many subjects, says Quintilian.

Having now come to the close of the second part of a boy's education, that pursued under the grammaticus, and given him a thorough foundation, Quintilian next hands him over to the rhetor (what we should call university teaching) and the subjects to be pursued under him are considered in the second book.

Second Book

Higher Instruction

After discussing the age at which a young man should pass out of the hands of the grammaticus into the hands of the rhetor, just as we now discuss the age for passing from a High School to an University, in the course of which he remarks that the rhetor had for some time been disposed to leave part of his proper function and do the work of the grammaticus, he dwells with great force on the importance of selecting instructors who will not only afford an example of the strictest virtue themselves, but be prepared to exercise considerable sternness in controlling the morals of those who frequent their schools.

Here, when endeavouring to guide the master, he gives him advice which shows that he has gone straight to the heart of the whole matter. Act, he says, as if you were the father of the pupils. Accept all the responsibilities which a parent feels. Avoid a gloomy austerity lest it give rise to contempt. As a teacher, far removed from heat of temper, but yet not a compounder of faults which ought to be corrected; simple in teaching, patient of labour, persistent and steady rather than immoderate in your demands.[1] Ready with an answer to all who ask questions and asking questions of those who do not seek information. In praising the exercises of your pupils neither grudging nor effusive, because in the former case there arises a weariness of the labour of preparation, and in the latter a disposition towards carelessness. In correcting what is in need of correction, let not the teacher be bitter, and least of all contemptuous, because when the master finds fault as if he had a personal hatred the effect is to drive his pupils from the design of study. Daily let him say many things which his pupils will carry away with them, for the living voice is more potent than precepts which are written, especially if the pupils love and respect their master.

Quintilian objects to allowing the students to applaud each other's exercises, as tending to abuse and as leading the pupil to look away from the right source of judgment which is the master.[2]

---

[1] As a teacher, 'minime iracundus, nec tamen eorum quæ emendanda erunt dissimulator, simplex in docendo, patiens laboris, assiduus potius quam immodicus' (5).

[2] Chapter 3.

He is now led aside for a moment to animadvert on the tendency of parents to think that a second-rate or third-rate master will do well enough for their sons before they reach a certain age and while yet in the elements of a subject, and he points out the fallacy which underlies this view. He also maintains that the ablest man is the best teacher.

I may remark that it is commonly said that men who are profoundly versed in any subject often teach it very indifferently. I am disposed to agree with Quintilian that the ablest and profoundest scholar will teach most simply, most clearly, and most successfully. It certainly is the case that many men of profound attainments in a subject cannot teach it; but it is equally true that more men who have superficial acquaintance with a subject cannot teach it. This is because both alike want the disposition to teach and the faculty of teaching. The question really is : given two men of *equal* teaching disposition and faculty, which of these will teach a subject best, the man of shallow, or the man of profound attainment? I think there can be no doubt of the answer to this, and we must agree with Quintilian; but we must beware of concluding with him that profound knowledge *implies* the fitness to teach. A recent writer in reply to a remark by Dr. Pusey who had said that a man who knew a subject thoroughly could teach it, answered with great point that it should rather be said that 'a man who could teach a subject thoroughly, knew it.' On the other hand, men of known superficiality often seem to teach exceedingly well. This is in the experience of us all; but I believe it to be a delusion. They teach well, though their knowledge be superficial; but it is necessary to note that their teaching also is superficial, and though it may serve well enough the objects of those who desire a smattering and seek display, it is never sound teaching. It cannot possibly be so. The very words used by such an instructor in teaching will want that exactness and precision without which there is no true learning. They will not represent realities either of nature or thought, but confused and loose images of realities only, while all that the subject of the lesson truly suggests will be left outside.

Some of Quintilian's words in this connection are worth quoting: *e.g.* 'He will not count that man among preceptors at all who will not give care to small things. Method, which is of such moment in teaching, is plainest and simplest with the most learned : things taught by the most learned are also so taught that they are more easily understood and more lucid; the less genuine ability a man has, the more does he attempt to raise himself up and stretch himself out : the less he is competent the more obscure he will be.'

Let a preceptor, then, he concludes, be eminent for his eloquence [or, as we should say, his learning] and for his moral character, that so, like Phœnix the tutor of Achilles, ('Il.' ix.), he may train his pupils both to speak and to act [i. e. to know and to do].[1]

Quintilian now passes from general observations and enters more fully on the duties proper to the Rhetorician, and we shall here part company with him. The extent to which the art of oratory was cultivated and the laborious, and (as we now think) vain and futile detail into which it was carried in ancient times has little save a historic interest. In its historical aspects, however, it is for the educationalist worthy of separate study.

There are, however, some good remarks on the training of boys in narrative composition; and also on the nature of boys themselves. He prefers, he says, the boy whose compositions show a certain fecundity, although they may be crude and characterised by want of judgment and taste. This gives hope of future strength. The cure of fertility is easy; but no toil will overcome barrenness. He has little hope of that kind of nature in boys which shows itself in judgment anticipating growth of mind.[2] This is, I think,

---

[1] Chapter 4.

[2] ' Facile remedium est ubertatis ; sterilia nullo labore vincuntur. Illa mihi in pueris natura minimum spei dederit in qua ingenium judicio præsumitur.'

what Goethe calls a matured judgment in an immature mind.
So he objects to a dry master — *magister aridus* — just as
one objects to a dry hard soil for tender plants. Moisture
is needed. Such masters make their boys small and narrow.
In learning merely to avoid faults under such masters, the
pupils fall into the greatest fault of all — that they have no
virtues. The teaching of such a man I may call 'negative'
teaching.

For myself I am persuaded that in the teaching of Latin
and Greek, and still more of our own tongue, the culture of
the whole man which flows from the study of literary expression and art, is seldom yet adequately understood. It is to
this capacity for giving æsthetic and moral culture as well
as a close intellectual discipline, that we must finally rest
the claims of the ancient classics on the continuous attention
of youth. Not that I in any way depreciate the work of the
grammaticus; very far from it, for I hold that there can be
no strict and, therefore, no genuine culture which is not
based on the studies in which it is the special function of
the grammaticus to guide boys. For those who hold these
views, and who desire to give this culture, the study of what
Quintilian now says will be fruitful.[1]

He first lays stress on reading in class from good authors,
preferring to take the best authors at once. At the age at
which boys went to the rhetor there could be little difficulty
in introducing them at once to the best literature of their
country. It is only when good literature is given to minds
as yet unripe for it, that it excites aversion, and rightly does
so. In studying any piece of literature, the teacher, Quintilian says, must direct attention to the circumstances under
which the writing that his pupils are studying was produced,
its logical arrangement and persuasive power, pointing out in
brief all the virtues of language and form. He even thinks
that bad specimens of oratory may be taken, that their vices
of language, style, and arrangement may be pointed out.

[1] Chapter 5.

Such writings, he says, should be commented on to show that notwithstanding their popularity, they are full of obscurities, inappropriateness of language, turgidity, meanness, effeminacy, &c. — the very reason, indeed, why many praise them. For there is a tendency (especially I may add on the part of youth) to think that a direct manner of expression and a natural utterance are destitute of genius, while language out of the ordinary course is held to be in some way more select and worthy of admiration. The preceptor also will test his pupils by asking questions so as to obviate listlessness and inattention, and thereby also to lead to independence of judgment; for we teach in order that teaching may not be always necessary. This kind of literary training Quintilian thinks to be of more value than the study of all the treatises on rhetoric that ever were written.

Quintilian is of opinion that, while the best writers should be read, those should be first studied whose writings are most transparent, postponing, for example, Sallust to Livy. He also thinks that the study of the antique writers of a language should come last, or at least only after the style and judgment are formed, for the reason that while they are weighty with thought, their expression is faulty (though doubtless excellent for its time). The pupils, not being competent to appreciate the thought fully, are apt to run into an imitation of a style alien to their own time, and to imagine that so they resemble these great writers of antiquity. As to contemporary writers, however good they may be, he holds that we ought to postpone the reading of them also, lest imitation should take precedence of the power of sound judgment.[1]

Quintilian, speaking of reproduction, thinks that when a theme is given, the master should for some time at least give instructions how it is to be worked out before the pupil *begins* to work at it; and not content himself with merely finding fault when it is done. He also is of opinion that

[1] Chapter 5.

pupils should rarely be allowed to recite their own compositions, and that the effort of memory necessary to do this will be better expended by learning by heart and reciting the best passages of eminent writers. The memory will be better exercised in this way, and the pupils will also acquire a good stock of phrases and forms of expression.[1]

He now deals with a question often discussed since Quintilian, viz.: whether the peculiar intellectual tendencies of various boys should be specially cultivated, Nature, as it were, giving us a hint in what direction it desires different boys to excel. Quintilian, as aiming at producing the perfect orator, which is his expression for the perfectly educated man, could not of course take this view. While the special talent has to be alone cultivated in those whose general capacity is weak, and who will not yield any return to attempts to educate him all round; yet in all stronger natures we, while promoting the clear purposes of nature in different boys, must yet give general training concurrently. At the same time it would be a waste of time to strive after what *manifestly* cannot be accomplished, and wrong to turn a youth away from that which he can do best to something which he *can* do, but not so well.[2]

Turning now from the teacher to the pupil, he calls on them to love their teachers as well as their studies, and to regard them as *parentes non quidem corporum sed mentium*. They will thus come together with pleasure and alacrity; found fault with, they will not be angry, praised they will be glad, by their zeal they will deserve their teacher's love.[3] It is the duty of teachers to teach, but equally of learners to learn. And then he concludes with an observation which merits to be inscribed on the porch of every school.

---

[1] Chapter 7. [2] Chapter 8.
[3] 'Emendati non irascentur, laudati gaudebunt, ut sint carissimi studio merebuntur.'

As you may sow seeds to no purpose unless the furrows, softened beforehand, nourish them, so eloquence [education] declines to grow and thrive save by the sympathetic concord of giver and receiver.[1]

He next refers to the practice in the ancient schools of encouraging pleadings on imaginary or fictitious cases with a view to the formation of the pleader, and recommends the practice with this precaution, that these should not be vague and turgid but as like as possible to the reality. Even names should be put in to give them a more real character, while at the same time elegance is to be aimed at.[2] And these remarks lead him to a somewhat severe criticism of those who think that no training in oratory is needed and that nature and natural force are to be trusted. The observations made here strike me as applying with great force to those who hold that education is a subject which it is superfluous for educators to study. At the same time, he says that while art is necessary to the study of art, yet the art must be of a general or universal kind and not descend to petty directions, but leave freedom for the adaptation of an orator to the circumstances under which the oration is delivered. In like manner, I would say : — It is not our business to give 'quasdam leges immutabili necessitate constrictas studiosis educandi' (certain laws bound together by an immutable necessity to those desirous of educating), but rather principles and general methods.[3]

In the nineteenth chapter he recurs to the question whether Nature or learning does most for the orator, and comes to the conclusion that if you consider each as subsisting independently of the other, Nature does most; if both co-exist moderately but in equal proportions, Nature

---

[1] 'Sicut . . . frustra sparseris semina nisi illa præmolitus foverit sulcus, sic eloquentia [for which read *educatio*] coalescere [grow and thrive] negat, nisi sociata tradentis accipientisque concordia.'

[2] Chapters 11 and 12.   [3] Chapter 13.

does most; but in the finished or perfect orator learning or art does most.

The next five books of Quintilian deal with invention in oratory and the arranging of what is invented — the logic of an argumentative discourse.

In the introduction to the eighth book he gives a clear and excellent summary of the instructions he has laid down as to the rules of oratory under the various heads of invention and arrangement. In modern times we should consider a young man's time wasted who spent it over these books, and yet it is generally allowed that Quintilian had simplified the subject of rhetoric considerably. In the procemium, Quintilian seems to become half aware of this himself. Many things, he says, should be taught by Nature herself, and precepts should not so much seem to have been invented by teachers as *observed by them as they occurred*. Here we have a hint as to the true method of teaching rhetoric, or the perfect in expression, viz. by reading and criticising excellent models. And what is this but evolving the abstract out of the concrete *along with the pupil:* in brief, proceeding analytically and inductively with a view to the discovery of the general and the abstract? It seems to me that rhetoric ought to be taught as grammar ought to be taught; and by the study of rhetoric I mean (1) the study of the *logical* consecution of an argumentum as uttered; and (2) the study of its æsthetic characteristics.

Quintilian condemns, as strongly as any sense-realist of modern times could, those who 'grow old in the empty pursuit of words' (*quodam inani verborum studio senescunt* (Lib. viii. Procem.)). Our business is to see to things, that is, facts and thoughts, *first*, and thereafter to fit the words closely to these. By 'things' Quintilian meant realities of thought as well as of sense.[1] What, then, would Quin-

---

[1] This passage has often been misapplied.

tilian have said of Latin verses and elegant Latin prose for English youth if he thus discouraged *inane verborum studium* in Latin for a Latin? The only possible defence is that Latin verse-writing cultivates the faculty of expression and the æsthetic perceptions generally in connection with the language in which we think — our vernacular. Does it do so? I do not speak of poets, for they stand apart, it may be held; but are our best prose writers and our best æsthetic critics the men who wrote the best Latin and Greek verses at school and college? Is it not in point of fact generally quite otherwise? Are not such linguistic performances actually hurtful? Does not Nature avenge itself on those who think too much of words instead of things? Do they not belong to the λογοδαίδαλοι, cunning word-artificers of whom Plato speaks? Such linguistic *tours de force* are very clever exercitations — the very highest of clever exercitations, we may admit. But they are no more. If they are to be cultivated at all (beyond the stage of simple translation of English words into Latin verses with a view to quantities), the cultivation of them should be confined to specialists — men who mean to live by Latin and Greek. For them it is the efflorescence of their studies. Why, indeed, do we learn Latin or Greek? For the sake of the literature these tongues enshrine of course, and for the sake of historic culture; but also for the sake of language-discipline and that training in literary perception which is æsthetic discipline. We assuredly cannot attain our end unless we write Latin or Greek prose, and also *do a little* in versification. This may be admitted; but if we keep in view the end proposed — linguistic discipline, the most important of all possible disciplines, because language is the reflex of thought, and, so regarded, covers the whole of life — we shall restrict our exercitations in ancient tongues within narrow limits. In Latin prose, *e.g.* syntactical accuracy we must have, and also Latinity — that is to say, an approach to the Latin cast or mould of expression: in verse, however, we shall confine ourselves to the translation of English *sense* into Latin verse for the sake of quantities and of familiarising the pupil with the poetical idiom of the Romans; but beyond this we shall attempt nothing save as rare and *voluntary* exercises for the few. So with Greek. Words, as Quintilian well says, were invented for the sake of things, not things for the sake of words.

When Quintilian speaks of the art of elocution, by which he means the *speaking forth*, that is to say, the form or style of what has been conceived in the mind, he holds that this requires much teaching and study. At the same time he never loses sight of the fact that thought, reality, truth of conception and aim, lie at the basis of all style. ' The best words,' he says, ' generally attach themselves to our subject and show themselves by their own light; whereas we set ourselves to seek for words as if they were always hidden and trying to keep themselves from being discovered. We never consider that they are to be found close to the subject on which we have to speak, but look for them in strange places, and we do violence to them when we have found them.' Again, in concluding his introduction he says, ' Let the greatest possible care be bestowed on expression, provided we bear in mind that nothing is to be done for the sake of words, since words themselves were invented for the sake of things, and those words are most to be commended which express our thoughts best and produce the impression which we desire.' He also says (xii. 1. 30), ' Nec quidquam non diserte quod honeste dicitur ' (nothing which is honestly and truly expressed is without eloquence). While there is much that is too technical for modern taste in the eighth and ninth books, I doubt if we could not extract from them more sound criticism of style and of the way of teaching ' elocution ' (which is style) than from any modern treatise that I have heard of.

We see that Quintilian, and not only Quintilian but the ancients generally, meant by oratory the utterance of thought on every variety of subject in fit words adorned by such graces as the orator could command. We do not in modern

25

times believe that any instruction in rhetorical forms can give more than an artificial, and therefore a bad, rhetoric or style. And in truth Quintilian sees this clearly enough. At the same time there is such a thing as criticism; and it is to this that Quintilian would introduce the student with a view to self-criticism, and so far there is no doubt that a student so trained would be preserved from many faults. But no amount of such training would make him an orator.

That Quintilian had himself this view of his subject is everywhere manifest, not least in his interpretation of oratory as the general aim of education. It was the general aim only because the utterance of thought (there being first the thought) was the highest manifestation of human reason. Ratio and Oratio summed up the intellectual excellence of man. This was the position of Isocrates also. To reach perfect utterance, according to Quintilian, was impossible, without knowledge of a wide and various kind — philosophy, literature, science; and besides these, personal virtue. Thus the Roman educational aim, like the Greek, was a lofty one. One can easily understand how the common ruck of teachers in the Roman Empire would hasten to their end and attract pupils who hoped by a little study of figures, tropes, and other rhetorical devices to become orators 'in twelve lessons.' The quick degradation of the educational aim of men like Isocrates, Cicero, and Quintilian, was certain, because it was so easy. Lucian's satirical observations on sophists and orators, about 150 years later, were doubtless more than justified.

But oratory, as aim, would have been even in all ages justified, had Quintilian's conception of the qualifications for it been adopted; above all, had men never lost sight of things, not things of sense alone or chiefly, but things of mind, as the main, though not exclusive, object of study. The tendency of forms and formulæ to usurp the place of realities is the characteristic not only of the history of religion in all countries, but also of literature, science, and philosophy. The vestment is more regarded than the body.

It is only the single-minded pursuit of truth in all departments of thought for its own sake that keeps oratory, style, religion, and politics ever living and true.

The ninth and tenth books constitute a treatise on style, and are full of excellent advice; but here again whatever rules Quintilian prescribes, he seems to be always conscious of the small part these play in forming the orator, compared with a knowledge of what has been done by others, and constant practice by the student himself. Write, read, mark, and imitate excellencies of style.

I know nothing likely to be of more value to young men in a modern class of rhetoric and literature than the tenth book. Read for example the third and fourth chapters. How excellent is a saying like this, when Quintilian speaks of polishing the style of any literary production, that 'the file should polish our work but not wear it to nothing.' That this tenth book should be so seldom presented for graduation examinations is evidence that Latin has not been taught with a view to what the literature can teach us, but only for grammatical and examination purposes. Where this can be said the university is, thus and so far, a mere secondary school.

The second chapter of Book XI. contains a very interesting discussion of memory, and is, moreover, historically interesting as summing up all the ancients knew on this subject.

The third chapter affords much instruction to both actors and preachers as well as public speakers, and should be studied by them.

In the twelfth book Quintilian gathers up the threads of his long discourse. He has shown that to be an orator one must be carried through a thorough discipline, and that all literature and science must be studied. Now he concentrates himself on the ethical characteristics of the true orator, the *vir bonus peritus dicendi*, and shows the necessity of high character to genuine success in oratory.

How can a man become an orator who is deficient in discernment, judgment, and prudence? The vicious man is deficient in these qualities. How can he prosecute studies with a single aim to excellence unless he be temperate? How can the unjust man be trusted to speak of justice? Who is most likely to attain the ends of oratory — the persuading of those whom he addresses — the good and truthful man, or the vicious man who has no high moral standard? Quintilian always distinguishes between the merely 'eloquent' man, and the perfect orator. 'What I have in view,' he says, 'is a man who, being possessed of the highest natural genius, stores his mind thoroughly with the most valuable kinds of knowledge, a man sent by the gods to do honour to the world, and such as no preceding age has known, a man in every way eminent and excellent, a thinker of the best thoughts and a speaker of the best words to fit these thoughts.' Even in inferior employments, as in the courts of law, such a man will be great, ' but his powers will shine with the highest lustre on great occasions, when the counsels of the senate are to be directed, and the people to be guided from error into rectitude.' Such a man Vergil depicts in ' Æn.' i. 148. Such an orator plants his feelings in the breasts of others because they are first active in his own breast.

With this high standard in view a man must study philosophy — not that he may be a philosopher who simply discusses and prescribes, but a ' *Romanus sapiens* ' : that is to say, a man who carries his philosophy into civil life. Philosophy is divided into physics, ethics, and dialectics. By physics or natural philosophy Quintilian (curiously enough) understands the general philosophy of life and man, including nature and religion. It is not necessary for a student to attach himself to any sect of philosophers; but only to study philosophy, and get what is noblest and best in it for the formation of his own character. And in saying this, Quintilian, in my opinion, defines the object of philosophic study in an university course even now. In this part of his treatise Quintilian again shows how small a part the mere rules of the rhetorician play in the forming of the orator, as compared with the philosopher, by quoting with approval Cicero as saying 'non tantum se debere scholis rhetorum quantum Academiæ spatiis [gardens]' ('De Orat.' 2, 23).

When we say that Quintilian looked to the study of literature and philosophy as that which was to make the finished orator, let it not be supposed that he ignored the study of nature. Even into the secondary school — the school of the grammaticus — mathematics and science entered, as I have shown in its proper place, and it was taken up in the higher course.

The following chapters of this book deal with the special qualifications of the pleader, such as a knowledge of the civil law, &c. In the tenth chapter we have an interesting survey of Greek painting and sculpture, and a parallelism drawn between the plastic arts and oratory.

The concluding chapter contains a vigorous and eloquent incitement to study and to the pursuit of all excellence.

CHAPTER VI

EDUCATION IN IMPERIAL TIMES

The classical decadence

THROUGHOUT Quintilian's treatise, while rules of composition and of the literary presentation of thought — above all, of oratorical expression — receive ample treatment, the author is always recurring to the substance of knowledge and literature. The discipline, the gravity, and moral earnestness of the Roman are always to the front, and these he would harmonise with Hellenic ideals. Though himself a provincial, he is always the grave conservative Roman: not by any means so Hellenic and anti-Roman as Cicero and his friends had been. His aims are not higher than those attributed to Isocrates, but his mode of attaining them is better, as far as we know; and this because he takes up the whole question of the education of a man. He wrote at a critical time for the ancient world; but he was powerless to arrest the downward progress of the higher education. His book, says Mommsen,[1] 'is one of the most excellent we possess from Roman antiquity, pervaded by fine taste and rare judgment, simple in feeling as in presentation, instructive without weariness, pleasing without effort, contrasting sharply and designedly with the fashionable literature that was so rich in phrases and so empty of ideas.'

The evils of which Tacitus, in the 'De Oratoribus,' complains, and which were to be found in Gaul and Spain as well as at Rome and in the East, were already visible, if not conspicuous, when Quintilian began to teach. The 'De Oratoribus' must have appeared about 74 A.D. (Bähr, ii. 330), and therefore about five or six years after Quintilian opened his school.[2] The language of Tacitus is, however, wholly that of a *laudator temporis acti*, yet we find in his protest so vivid a picture of his own conception of former ages and of contemporary evils, that I may with advantage to the student of education here quote from him.

'It was accordingly usual with our ancestors, when a lad was being prepared for public speaking, as soon as he was fully trained by home discipline and his mind was stored with culture, to have him taken by his father or his relatives to the orator who held the highest rank in the state. The boy used to accompany and attend him and be present at all his speeches, alike in the law-courts and the assembly, and thus he picked up the art of repartee and became habituated to the strife of words, and indeed, I may almost say, learnt how to fight in battle. Thereby young men acquired, from the first, great experience and confidence, and a very large stock of discrimination, for they were studying in broad daylight, in the very thick of the conflict, where no one can say any-

---

[1] Book viii. cap. 2 of *Hist. of Provinces of Roman Empire*.

[2] Tacitus was a man of letters who wrote always with a view to literary and dramatic effect. He had also very strong prejudices and a powerfully satirical vein. We must take all he says *cum grano*, if I may venture to say so.

thing foolish or self-contradictory without its being refuted by the judge or ridiculed by the opponent, or, last of all, repudiated by the very counsel with him. Thus, from the beginning, they were imbued with true and genuine eloquence, and, although they attached themselves to one pleader, still they became acquainted with all advocates of their own standing in a multitude of cases before the courts. They had, too, abundant experience of the popular ear, in all its greatest varieties, and with this they could easily ascertain what was liked or disapproved in each speaker. Thus, they were not in want of a teacher of the very best and choicest kind who could show them eloquence in her true features, not in a mere resemblance; nor did they lack opponents and rivals, who fought with actual steel, not with a wooden sword, and the audience, too, was always crowded, always changing, made up of unfriendly as well as of admiring critics, so that neither success nor failure could be disguised. You know, of course, that eloquence wins its great and enduring fame quite as much from the benches of our opponents as from those of our friends, nay more, its rise from that quarter is steadier and its growth surer. Undoubtedly it was under such teachers that the youth of whom I am speaking, the disciple of orators, the listener in the forum, the student in the law-courts, was trained and practised by the experiences of others. The laws he learnt by daily hearing, the faces of the judges were familiar to him, the ways of popular assemblies were continually before his eyes; he had frequent experience of the ear of the people, and whether he undertook a prosecution or a defence, he was at once singly and alone equal to any case. We still read with admiration the speeches in which Lucius Crassus, in his nineteenth, Cæsar and Asinius Pollio in their twenty-first year, Calvus, when very little older, denounced, respectively, Carbo, Dolabella, Cato, and Vatinius.

' But in these days we have our youths taken to the professor's theatre — the rhetoricians, as we call them. The class made its appearance a little before Cicero's time and was not liked by our ancestors, as is evident from the fact that, when Crassus and Domitius were censors, they were ordered, as Cicero says, to " close the school of impudence." However, as I was just saying, the boys are taken to schools in which it is hard to tell whether the place itself, or their fellow scholars, or the character of their studies, do their minds most harm. As for the place, there is no such thing as reverence, for no one enters it who is not as ignorant as the rest. As for the scholars, there can be no improvement when boys and striplings, with equal assurance, address, and are addressed by, other boys and striplings.

'As for the mental exercises themselves, they are the reverse of beneficial. Two kinds of subject matter are dealt with before the rhetoricians — the persuasive and the controversial. The persuasive, as being comparatively easy and requiring less skill, is given to boys. The controversial is assigned to riper scholars and, good heavens! what strange and astonishing productions are the result! It comes to pass that subjects remote from all reality are actually used for declamation.'

Brodrick's Translation.

Petronius Arbiter, about the same time, laments the decline of the higher education, and satirises the sophists. Confirmatory passages might be added from Juvenal, who died about 120 A.D., but whose satires were probably written in the concluding decade of the first century. Then, about 50 years after Juvenal's death, we can learn from Lucian what the tendency of the 'higher' instruction was — all towards the premature fitting out of youth for success in life, by means of rhetoric and oratory, and a superficial acquaintance with the stock commonplaces of argumentation. There was no careful curriculum of severe study in language, history, dialectic, and literature, as was required by Quintilian, and contemplated, in part at least, by many leading sophist-philosophers, who, long before imperial times, had followed Isocrates. Now, nothing is more certain than this in education, that the moment the vesture of thought becomes an object of worship — whether in the shape of word-cunning, elegance of style, or rules for rhetorical construction and rhythmical effect — the result must be decline and decay. With such an educational end in view, it was not surprising that young men in the second century A.D. should become impatient of the slow processes of disciplinary preparation. They rushed the preparatory grammar, literature, and dialectic in order to get at the sophistics, the declamation and superficial politics of the rhetorical or 'university' schools.

The remarkable devotion to Roman literature and rhetoric in the provinces doubtless helped the decline, while it was a gratifying illustration of the rapid diffusion of the Roman language and literature among the native Gauls and Spaniards.[1] They helped the decline because the native provincials were essentially imitators, though, doubtless, frequently able, and almost always (at least in Gaul) eloquent.

But we are not entitled, even at the bidding of Tacitus, to speak of the decline of education as already accomplished in the first two, or even three, centuries of the empire. On the contrary, there had been great progress. All the countries of the Mediterranean, including Gaul, as far north as Trêves, and Spain as far south as Corduba, were swarming with accomplished men. Some of these were Italians settled in the provinces, but a large number were native Gauls and Spaniards who lived for the acquisition of Roman literature and eloquence, and were as keen in the pursuit of it as the fervent young men of the post-mediæval renaissance. The decline, such as it was, at the time Tacitus wrote, was in the educational *aim;* it was this that contained the seed of decay. True, the old Roman idea was now no longer a living force; but we had in its place the Romano-Hellenic culture — broad, cosmopolitan, and essentially humane. I may here summarise briefly the grounds for refusing to accept the opinion that education as a national movement was retrograding in imperial times.

First; there was the growth of public libraries. From 150 years B.C. onwards, it became usual for the wealthy Roman to collect books, almost wholly Greek. This was following the example of distinguished Greeks 200 years earlier. Æmilius Paullus, moreover, and Sulla conveyed libraries from Greece and Asia Minor as plunder of war. The first *Public* Library in Rome was instituted by Asinius Pollio in the time of Augustus, in the atrium of the Temple

---

[1] Especially after Tiberius shut up the Druidical colleges.

of Liberty on Mt. Aventine. Julius Cæsar had, before this, contemplated a great Greek and Latin Library, but his death cut short his scheme. Augustus himself instituted a library in the temple of Apollo on Mt. Palatine, and a second, the Octavian, in the *Porticus Octavia*. There were other public libraries in Rome, but the greatest was the Ulpian founded by Trajan. All this activity was the fruit of Hellenic example. There had been public libraries in several Greek towns, and in Alexandria, the greatest of them all was founded by Ptolemy Soter in 323 B.C.; before the time of Julius Cæsar, when the greatest part of it was burnt down, it possessed certainly not less than 500,000 volumes. It was soon restored, but only to be totally destroyed during the confusion of the Arab occupation in 640 A.D. At Pergamon also a great library rivalling that of Alexandria had been founded by Eumenes the king.

In later imperial times there were twenty-eight public libraries in Rome. Books (*volumina* or rolls) were cheap, and booksellers' shops numerous. We are assured that in provincial towns this activity was imitated, and that with the large extension of schools under the emperors, and the greater accessibility of books, the facilities for education had been enormously increased.

Secondly; not only in Rome, but throughout Italy and in all the cities of the Empire, grammatical schools had arisen. These were fostered by the municipalities, encouraged by the emperors, and a considerable number of them were endowed with public money. The wide diffusion of grammar (or secondary) schools in all the countries round the Mediterranean may be inferred from the large number of higher or rhetoric schools which grew up in addition to the great schools of Rhodes, Athens, and Pergamos. We learn from Suetonius and other sources that Vespasian, 70–79 A.D., gave salaries from the public treasury to both Latin and Greek rhetoricians at Rome. Quintilian was one of these. This rhetorical school was further developed by Hadrian (117–138 A.D.). The number of professors was largely increased, a noble building was erected, with lecture-halls where orators and poets held forth, and where Greek and Latin grammarians and rhetoricians had numerous students. This institution, called the Athenæum, was the university of Rome for centuries. Antoninus Pius, continued this good work in the provinces, giving both honour and income to the higher teachers. He was the first (it is believed) to make them a privileged class by relieving them of rates and taxes, the obligation to hold municipal offices, to serve in the army, and to have soldiers quartered on them. These immunities were extended to philosophers, rhetoricians, grammarians, and physicians. To prevent abuse of these privileges he restricted the number of each class who were to enjoy them: the smaller towns being allowed five physicians, three sophists,[1] and three grammarians; in large towns (*i.e.* towns in which a court of justice was established) seven physicians, four sophists, and four grammarians were recognised; and in the capital towns of a province, ten physicians, five sophists, and five grammarians. Under Constantine the Great (306–337) these privileges were confirmed and extended, and under Theodosius II. (408) the more distinguished teachers at Constantinople were raised to the rank of counts of the first class. Great schools arose at Marseilles, Trier, Autun, Bourdeaux, and elsewhere.

Meanwhile, at Athens, which still continued to be the home of philosophy, the four philosophical schools had kept up a kind of apostolic succession. Marcus Aurelius had, in 176 A.D., fixed a liberal state salary to be paid to two teachers in each of these schools, besides two teachers of oratory The council of the city appointed to these offices, subject to the approval of the emperor.

Alexander Severus (218) appointed teachers of architecture, mathematics, and mechanics, as well as medicine, rhetoric, and grammar, and even began a system of 'bursaries' at Rome. And in 376, Gratian ordered that in all the capitals of the seventeen Gallic provinces the grammarians

---

[1] This term had become applicable to both rhetoricians and philosophers.

and rhetoricians in both Latin and Greek should receive from the imperial chest a sum equal to their municipal salary.

The higher school or university of Constantinople, which emulated Rome, had its professors increased by Theodosius II. to three Latin rhetoricians, five Greek sophists, ten Latin and ten Greek grammarians, one philosopher, and two jurists. They were accommodated in the Capitolium.

The great school of Berytus was an university of law.

Nor must we omit to mention Alexandria. The Museum of Alexandria, founded by Ptolemy Philadelphus about 280 B.C., was in full activity. Strabo says (xvii. p. 112, Oxford ed.): 'Part of the royal palaces is the Museum, which has cloisters, an exedra (these were semi-circular alcoves at the end of porticoes and fitted with seats where the learned taught their students), and a very large house in which there is a "common-room" for those who are fellows of the Museum and devote themselves to letters: there are public endowments for the College (Synod) and it is presided over by a priest formerly appointed by the kings, now by Cæsar.' The great libraries were accessible to these men and their students. There was an observatory and, it is said also, botanical and zoological gardens. The chief work of this college of learned men was in the departments of mathematics, astronomy, philosophy, and medicine. It is said they chose their own principals: if so they must have corresponded to our Deans of Faculties, as the president was a state nominee. The Emperor Claudius (died 54 A.D.) added a second Museum, in which his own historical works were to be regularly read. Caracalla (died 217 A.D.) confiscated the salaries, and the institution came to an end — that is to say, in so far as it was an endowed system of fellowships — in the third century.

During all these centuries, moreover, numerous grammarians and sophists wandered from town to town and opened private schools.

Nor do the above facts stand alone in the educational history of the time. They indicate the public policy of the

Empire, but they do not reveal that that policy was supported by a wide-spread 'humanity' destined soon to supersede the *humanitas* of mere culture. We find this well
exemplified in a letter (iv. 13), from Pliny the younger (died
about 110 A.D.) addressed to Tacitus :

I am glad [he says] to hear of your safe arrival at Rome. I am
always anxious to see you, and especially just now. I shall stay a
few more days at Tusculum, that I may finish a little work that I
have in hand, for I am afraid that if I break it off when I have all
but completed it, I shall find it difficult to take it up again. Meanwhile, that I may lose no time, I send off this letter, so to speak, in
advance of me, to ask a favour of you which I shall soon ask in
person. First, let me tell you the occasion of it. Being lately at
my native town [Comum, about twenty-eight miles north of Milan]
a young lad, son of one of my neighbours, came to pay me a com-
plimentary call. 'Do you go to school?' I asked him. 'Yes,' he
replied. 'Where?' 'At Milan' [Mediolanum]. 'Why not here?'
'Because,' said his father, who had come with him, 'we have no
teachers here.' 'No teachers! Why surely,' I replied, 'it would
be very much to the interest of all you fathers' (and fortunately
several fathers heard what I said) ' to have your sons educated here
rather than anywhere else. Where can they live more pleasantly
than in their own town? or be bred up more virtuously than under
their parents' eyes, or at less expense than at home? What an
easy matter it would be, by a general contribution, to hire teachers,
and to apply to their salaries the money which you now spend on
lodging, journeys, and all you have to purchase for your sons at a
distance from home. I have no children myself ; I look on my
native town in the light of a child or a parent, and I am ready to
advance a third part of any sum which you think fit to raise for the
purpose. I would even promise the whole amount were I not
afraid that my benefaction might be spoilt by jobbery, as I see
happens in many towns where teachers are engaged at the public
expense. There is only one way of meeting this evil. If the
choice of teachers is left solely to the parents, the obligation to
choose rightly will be enforced by the necessity of having to pay
towards the teachers' salaries. Those who would, perhaps, be
careless in administering another's bounty, will certainly be careful

about their own expenses, and will see that none but those who deserve it receive any of my money, when they must at the same time receive theirs as well. So take counsel together and be encouraged by my example, and be assured that the greater my proportion of the expense shall be, the better shall I be pleased. You can do nothing more for the good of your children, or more acceptable to your native town. Your sons will thus receive their education in the place of their birth, and be accustomed from their infancy to love and cling to their native soil. I trust that you may secure such eminent teachers that the neighbouring towns will be glad to draw their learning from hence ; so that, as you now send your children elsewhere to be educated, other people's children may hereafter flock hither for instruction.'

I thought it advisable to explain the whole affair to you circumstantially, so that you may see more clearly how much obliged I should be if you will undertake what I request. I entreat you, in consideration of the importance of the matter. to look out among the multitude of men of letters whom the reputation of your genius draws around you some teachers to whom we may apply, but without as yet tying ourselves down to any particular man. I leave everything to the parents, I wish them to judge and select as they think fit ; I take on myself nothing but the trouble and expense. If anyone shall be found who has confidence in his own ability, let him go there ; but he must understand that he goes with no assurance but that derived from his own merit. ('Ancient Classics for English Readers — Pliny.')

From this letter we see that two kinds of schools were in existence in Pliny's day: (1) schools, supported by the municipalities, not uncommon (*multis in locis*), and (2) subscription-schools, where sufficient funds could be raised to engage a teacher. When there was a good school in any place, boys came from a distance and seem to have taken lodgings in the place in order to attend it. We also see the importance which Pliny attaches to education, the high value he sets on home training and his opinion as to free education. He sees the danger of bad appointments likely to arise from fixed payments and centralisation, and he also sees the necessity of some subsidy to encourage local effort.

Pliny's letter is itself evidence of the spirit of humanity to which I have already adverted, and which, under the influence of the Stoic philosophy, had already lead to charitable foundations. Large benefactions were made not only by the state but by private individuals, for the maintenance of orphanages ; and successive emperors added to these in many Italian towns.

Nor, as further evidence of educational activity, were writers on education wanting. There were many whose names and books are lost, but some of the most eminent are still household words in the history of education. Omitting the earlier writers, we have Seneca, Quintilian, Tacitus, Pliny the younger, Plutarch, and Musonius the Stoic, who all wrote on the subject of education, and the opinions of any one of whom, in so far as they can be now ascertained, might, in their educational reference, be the subject of an interesting and instructive monograph.

As regards individual life ; it is unhappily true that most of the educated intelligence of the empire sought, under very lax moral conditions, the satisfactions of material wealth or the glory of place and power. The *vetus disciplina*, the *prisca virtus*, was gone from the life even of the senate, now an upstart body of *novi homines*. The religion of Rome was dead, for, as Professor Flint truly says, ' Rome had made the world Roman and become herself cosmopolitan.' [1] And yet we can still find a succession of men of the old Roman type among whom the traditionary dignity of family intercourse and severity of morals survived. The Stoic philosophy, as a noble scheme of life, had established itself in many minds as a motive force, and filled the place no longer occupied by the memories of a great history and an ancestral religion. When we note the humanity and even tenderness conveyed in the letter from Pliny quoted above, and realise also the universal human relations of the Stoic system, we can see that for the cultured men of the empire a noble and beneficent existence was always possible.

[1] *History of Philosophy of History*, p. 56.

In view of all these facts, I repeat that it seems to me absurd to talk of the decline of education in the first two centuries of the Christian era. It never had been so widely extended, and never before had it received so much fostering care. Nor have I found any evidence that the grammar schools were, in their working, seriously defective. The quality of the discipline and instruction of the higher schools, it is true, had degenerated in some quarters because of the large accession to the number of learners and of competing teachers. But an excellent education could still be obtained at all the great centres of the empire.

The ethical element in education was, moreover, making progress, while the intellectual elements of culture were being extended. The Alexandrian philosophy of the time had a religious and mystical tendency, and elsewhere the supremacy of ethics in philosophy and the prevalence of purer and more exalted notions of God have to be noted. These were educative forces of the highest kind. Cicero says much on this subject that might be here quoted. Quintilian, again, advocating the study of ethics by the orator, says: 'If the world is governed by a Providence, the state ought surely to be ruled by the superintendence of good men. If our souls are of divine origin, we ought to devote ourselves to virtue, and not be slaves to a body of terrestrial nature' (xii. 2). Apollonius of Tyana was an itinerant preacher of ethics — a kind of apostle. 'The whole universe which you see around you,' says Seneca, 'comprising all things divine and human, is one. We are members of one great body. Nature has made us relative, when it begat us from the same materials and for the same destinies.' [1]

Depraved superstitions, moral excesses, and brutal pleasures, meanwhile characterised a large proportion of the people, who had not yet found a substitute for their lost gods, while training to civic virtue had become impossible for them under the inevitable imperial despotism.

But I need not dwell on what is a commonplace of moral

[1] Seneca, Ep. xcv., quoted by Mr. Lecky.

history; it will be more to the purpose to give a summary of two writers who exhibit the ethical and humane spirit which was then beginning to permeate society, viz. Plutarch and Musonius.

PLUTARCH [1]

Plutarch, a Greek, wrote his essay on the education of children about 100 A.D. The following is a summary of his wisdom.

The most pregnant and epigrammatic of his utterances is this, ' Nature without education is blind.' In beginning his essay, he says, ' Come, let us consider what is to be said regarding the education of free children, and by what means they may be made virtuous.' But he confines himself within much narrower limits than a purpose so large would have led us to expect. He more than once, as might be expected in a Greek, dwells on the importance of gymnastics for the young and of recreation for adults who are disposed to work hard. Even a bow we have to unbend if it is to do its work properly.

For good agriculture, he says, there must be good soil, a skilful husbandman, and fruitful seed ; so in education, nature is the soil, the master the husbandman, and precepts and instruction the seed. Deficiency in the nature of the child may be supplied by labour and culture. There is a concurrence of three things requisite to virtue — nature, reason, and use. By reason he means instruction, by use he means exercise.

Like all other writers on education Plutarch dwells much on the importance of exercise with a view to habit. Without instruction nature is blind, but even where there is instruction, of what value will it be without constant practice in the good ? He presses the cultivation of the memory in the sphere of intellectual instruction, but beyond this he has little to say on the training of the intellect.

It is on the moral education of the boy and youth that he most strongly insists. Let them be taught, above all, to keep their tempers and to control their tongues. A man never regrets having said too little. That they should be trained to speak the truth is

---

[1] Doubtful whether the essay on education was Plutarch's.

26

essential. Lying is for slaves. He points out that the elements of virtue are love of honour and fear of punishment (τιμωρία), and that the faults of boys are, in truth, trifling in themselves, and easily corrected ; but in youths these faults may grow to vices. 'Childhood is a tender thing, and may easily be wrought into any shape.'

The main instrument of all education is philosophy. By philosophy he means all that bears on the conduct of life. The sole guide of the mind of man is philosophy. By this we are taught what is good and bad, honourable and dishonourable, just and unjust, what we are most to desire and what most to shun, and the duties we owe to the gods, to our parents, friends, strangers, society ; also the regulation of all the passions, &c. In this he repeats Isocrates.

With a view to sound instruction, the writers of antiquity are to be read, confining boys to the good and useful in these.

Parents are enjoined to care for their children's education, and to be careful in their choice of nurses, pædagogi, and masters, not grudging expenditure on so important a matter as education. They are also urged themselves to take an interest in what their children are learning.

On the subject of coercion he says, ' Children are to be won to follow liberal studies by exhortations and rational motives, and on no account to be forced thereto by whipping or any other contumelious punishments. I will not urge that such usage seems to me more agreeable to slaves than to ingenuous (freeborn) citizens! And even slaves when thus handled are dulled and discouraged from the performance of their tasks, partly by reason of the smart of their stripes, partly because of the disgrace thereby inflicted. But praise and reproof are more effectual on free-born children than any such disgraceful handling, the former to incite them to what is good, the latter to restrain them from that which is evil. . . . It is useful not to give them such large commendations as to puff them up with pride.'

As to amount of work to be demanded of the young, Plutarch says that some parents, being over hasty to advance their children in learning beyond their equals, overwork them, and so cause them to be ill-affected to study. For, 'as plants by moderate watering are nourished, but with overmuch moisture are glutted, so is the spirit improved by moderate labours, but overwhelmed by such as are excessive.'

Memory should be cultivated. It is the mother of the Muses. ' Nothing doth so much beget and nourish learning as memory.'

Filthy talk is to be checked, because, as Democritus says, words are the shadows of actions. Children must be brought up to be affable and courteous.

Nothing can be more 'modern' than all this.

Musonius the Stoic, again, is especially interesting, as he discusses the question of the education of women.[1]

' In turning over the pages of the Greek Anthology of Stobæus,'[2] says the late Dr. Muir, ' I found (in the Appendix containing extracts from the collection of John of Damascus, in vol. iv. pp. 212 ff. and 220 ff.) two passages quoted from Musonius, the one headed " On the question whether men's daughters should be educated similar to their sons," and the other affirming that " Women ought to study philosophy." The author, C. Musonius Rufus, was " a celebrated Stoic philosopher," who lived " in the first century of the Christian era " ' (Smith's ' Dictionary of Greek and Roman Biography and Mythology,' s. v.).

The following is a translation of the first of the two passages : —
' The conversation having turned on the question whether people's sons and daughters should receive the same education, the philosopher (after referring to the analogy furnished by the identical training received by both the males and the females of two of the species of animals employed by men to render them active service, horses and dogs) asks whether men ought to receive any special education and training superior to those allowed to women, as if both alike should not acquire the same virtues, or if it is possible for the two sexes to attain to the same virtues otherwise than by the same education. But it is easy to learn that a man has not different virtues from a woman. For, first, the one should have good

[1] The late Dr. J. Muir, founder of the Sanskrit Chair in the university of Edinburgh, and a well-known scholar, printed, or translated, a portion of Musonius about twenty years ago and sent me a copy, from which I now give extracts.

[2] *Joannis Stobœi Florilegium*, edited by Meineke (Teubner's 12mo edition, 1857).

sense as well as the other; for of what use would either a foolish man or a foolish woman be? Then the man could not be a good citizen if he were unjust. And the woman could not carry on the concerns of the household virtuously if not being just, but the contrary, she should first wrong her husband, as they say Eriphyle did.[1] It is also good that the woman as well as the man should be self-controlled [2] (σωφρονεῖν). . . . Perhaps some one would say that courage [literally, manliness, ἀνδρεία] is a quality befitting men alone; but even this is not so, for the best woman also should be courageous, and be free from weakness, so that she may not be overcome either by toil or by fear. Otherwise how can she continue virtuous, if anyone either by terror or by imposing toil can force her to submit to anything disgraceful? Women ought also to repel assaults, for if not they will show themselves weaker than hens, and the females of other birds, which fight for their young against animals much bigger than themselves. How, then, should woman not stand in need of courage? And that they share a certain martial vigour was proved by the race of the Amazons, who subdued many nations by force of arms. So that if other women are deficient in courage, this must be laid to the account of [3] want of training rather than to [weakness of] nature. If, then, the same virtues must pertain to men and women, it follows necessarily that the same training and education must be suitable for both. For in the case of all animals and plants, the application of the proper treatment ought to impart to each the excellence belonging to it. Or, if both men and women should have to possess equal skill in playing the flute, or in performing on the harp, and if this were necessary for their livelihood, we should impart to both equally the requisite instruction. But if both ought to excel in the virtue proper to mankind, and to be in an equal measure wise and temperate, and

---

[1] Eriphyle was the wife of Amphiaraus who was bribed by Polynices with the necklace of Harmonia to betray her husband's lurking place, so that he was forced to join the expedition against Thebes, where he fell.

[2] See Dr. Jowett's introduction to his translation of Plato's *Charmidas*, p. 3, where he calls 'temperance, or σωφροσύνη, a peculiarly Greek notion, which may also be rendered moderation, modesty, discretion, wisdom, without completely exhausting by all these terms the various associations of the word.'

[3] There being a gap in the text here, I have followed the editor Meineke's conjecture as the mode of filling it.

to partake in courage and righteousness the one no less than the
other, shall we not educate them both in the same manner, and
teach both equally the art by which a human being may become
good? Yes, we must act thus and no otherwise. What then?
Some one will perhaps say, Would you think it right to teach men
to spin wool just as you do women? and women equally with men
to addict themselves to gymnastic exercises? No, this I will never
approve. But I say that as in the human race men have a stronger
and women a weaker nature, each of these natures should have
the tasks which are most suited to it, assigned to it, and that the
heavier should be allotted to the stronger, and the lighter to the
weaker. Spinning, as well as housekeeping, would therefore be
more suitable for women than for men, while gymnastics, as well as
out of door work, would be fitter for men than for women: though
sometimes some men might properly undertake some of the lighter
tasks and such as seem to belong to women; and women again
might engage in the harder tasks, and those which appear more
appropriate for men, in cases where either bodily qualities, or
necessity, or particular occasions, might lead to such action. For
perhaps all human tasks are open to all, and common both to men
and women, and nothing is necessarily appointed exclusively for
either; not that[1] some things may not be more suitable for the
one, and others for the other nature; so that some are called men's
and others women's occupations. But whatever things have reference to virtue, these one may rightly affirm to be equally appropriate for both natures, since we say that virtues do not belong
more to the one than to the other. Wherefore I think it is reasonable that both males and females should be similarly instructed in
matters relating to virtue; and they should be taught from their
infancy that such and such a thing is good, and such and such a
thing is bad (the same thing bad for both) and that one thing is
profitable and another injurious, and that this is to be done and
that not; from which wisdom is acquired by those who learn, by
boys and girls equally, and in no way differently by each; then
they are to be inspired with a feeling of shame in regard to everything base. These qualities being implanted in them, it necessarily follows that both men and women will become virtuous.
And those who are rightly instructed, whether males or females,

---

[1] The words of the original (μὴ δὴ δὲ) must apparently bear this sense.

are to be accustomed to endure tòil, not to fear death, not to be crushed by any calamity, so that they may become courageous [or manly]; for it has been shown above that women too should partake in the character of courage [or manliness, ἀνδρία]. Then again, it is an excellent thing to teach them to avoid selfishness [1] and to honour equality, and, as human beings, to seek to benefit and not to injure mankind; and such instruction renders those who receive it just. But why should a man learn these things more than a woman? For if it is fitting that women should be just, then both sexes should be taught these things which are most seasonable and most important. For if the man should know some little matter connected with some artist's department, and the woman not, or conversely, this will not prove the education of each to be different. Only, as regards any of the most important matters let not the one be taught differently from the other. If anyone asks me what science is to preside over this instruction I shall reply that as without philosophy no man can be rightly instructed, so neither can any woman. But I do not mean to say that if women are to philosophise they ought properly to possess fluency and extraordinary cleverness in discussion; for I do not praise this very much even in men; but I mean that women should acquire a virtuous character and nobleness, since philosophy is the pursuit of a noble character, and nothing else.'

The following is a translation of the second passage mentioned above: — 'And when one asked him if women too should study philosophy, he began, somewhat in this way, to teach that they should. Women, he said, have received from the gods the same reason as men, the reason which we use in dealing with each other, and by which we discern, in regard to each act, whether it is good or bad, noble or base. So, too, the female has the same perceptions as the male — seeing, hearing, smelling, and so forth. . . . So, too, not only men, but women also, have by nature the desire and the adaptation for virtue; for the latter, no less than the former, are so formed as to be pleased with noble and righteous actions and to disapprove the contraries of these. This being the case, why should it belong to men principally to inquire and consider how they shall live nobly — which is the province of philosophy — and not principally to women? Is it because it is fitting

---

[1] πλεονέξία.

for men to be good, and not for women? But let us inquire in regard to every particular quality suitable for a woman who shall be good ; for it will appear that she will derive each of these characteristics principally from philosophy. First, a woman ought to be a good housekeeper, and capable of judging what things are expedient for the house, and qualified to rule the domestics. Now, I say that such qualities would belong most to a woman who studied philosophy, since each of these things is a part of life, and the science of matters regarding life is nothing else than philosophy, and the philosopher, as Socrates said, continues inquiring "what things, good or bad, are done in the house." But the woman should further be self-controlled, so as to keep herself pure . . . not to be the slave of desires, nor quarrelsome, nor extravagant, nor fond of dress. These are the works of a virtuous woman; and, in addition, she should control anger, not give way to grief, be superior to all passion. These things philosophy enjoins, and it appears to me that anyone, whether man or woman, who should learn and practise them, would be a most correct person. What then? These things are so. Is not, therefore, a woman justified in studying philosophy, in being a blameless partner of [her husband's] life, a good helpmeet in housekeeping, a careful guardian of her husband and children, and in every way free from the love of gain and from selfishness? And what woman would possess this character more than the student of philosophy, who would be bound, if philosophy is uniform [? in its effects] to esteem the doing worse than the suffering of injustice — insomuch as it is more disgraceful — and to regard being worsted as better than gaining an advantage, and to love her children more than [her own] life? And what woman would be juster than she who possessed such a character? And it befits the educated woman to be more courageous than the uneducated, and the student of philosophy than she who is untrained in it, so that she would neither submit to anything disgraceful from the fear of death, or through shrinking from toil, nor succumb to anyone because he was well-born, or powerful, or rich, or even a tyrant. For it is her fortune to have studied to be high-minded,[1] and to regard death as not an evil and life as not a good, and similarly not to turn away from toil, or at all to indulge in indolence. Whence it is to be expected that such a

---

[1] μέγα φρονεῖν.

woman would work with her own hands, and submit to toil, should be able herself to suckle the infants to whom she gave birth, and minister to her husband with her own hands, and fulfil without reluctance tasks which some consider as work only fit for slaves. Would not, now, such a woman be a great treasure for her husband, an ornament to her relatives, and a good example to those of her own sex who knew her?

'But some will say that the women who visit philosophers must generally become bold and presuming when, leaving their household occupations, they live surrounded by men, and practise discussions, and argue subtly, and analyse syllogisms, while they ought to be sitting at home spinning. But I am so far from approving of women who are studying philosophy leaving their proper avocations and devoting themselves solely to discussions, that I should not even think it fit for men to do this. But I say that they ought to engage in all the reasonings with which they occupy themselves for the sake of their avocations. For as medical speculations are useless unless they conduce to the health of the human body, so if a philosopher holds or inculcates any doctrine, it is of no value unless it promote the virtue of the human soul. But, above all things, we ought to weigh the principles which we think that women studying philosophy should follow, so as to form a judgment whether the doctrine which teaches that modesty is the greatest good can make women bold, or whether that which inculcates the greatest composure can accustom them to live recklessly [or impudently], or that which shows vice to be the greatest evil does not teach virtuous self-restraint, or that which represents housekeeping as a virtue, and exhorts a woman to be satisfied with it and to work with her own hands, does not dispose a woman to practise household occupations.'

I have said enough, I think, to justify me in declining to accept the statements regarding the degeneracy of education in the first or even the second century. The actual facts compel us largely to discount the opinion of stern moralists like Tacitus, or professed satirists like Juvenal or Petronius Arbiter. There is no period of human history which does not afford weaknesses to expose and vices to lash. At the same time, it was the fact that nations

which, like the Greeks and Romans, had lost their traditionary faith, and which regarded rhetoric or oratory —
which at best was only intellectual and æsthetic culture
— as the highest aim of public education, were doomed to
find their mistake. It was easy for ambitious young men —
especially now that oratorical forms and the technique of
rhetoric were settled, and innumerable models were available — to scamp grammatical and literary preparation, and
to mistake glibness of tongue and facility of imitation for
true oratorical power. It was this tendency which Quintilian and Tacitus saw and wished to arrest. It received an
impulse from professed rhetoricians and sophists swarming
from Greece and Asia Minor in search of the means of
support. They could not but compete with each other,
and offer the maximum of accomplishment for the minimum of labour on the part of the student. Lucian, towards
the close of the second century, exposes the evils which by
that time had become conspicuous. The third century, I
consider, was the century of decadence, and also of the rise
of the Christian schools. Let me here note that it is partly
to counteract the tendency to haste and superficiality on
the part of ambitious and active young men that modern
societies have instituted and endowed universities and
schools. Without these, and the conditions of sound attainment which they are authorised to impose as conditions
of graduation and of professional qualifications, we, in these
days, should be flooded with the same evils as overwhelmed
the education of the ancient world. This mode of regulat-
ing education had not altogether escaped the attention of
the imperial administration, as I have shown, but the
measures which were taken were inadequate to counteract
the operation of other causes in a dissolving society.

Meanwhile a new formative force had entered the world
in humble guise, and was steadily making way. It gathered
into a unity and round a sacred personality the Stoic humanity and universalism, the Platonic ethical idealism, and all

the purest conceptions of the Divine which ·the various races of mankind had painfully, and each only partially, elaborated. God immanent in His own world as a God not only of law but of love — Himself seeking man to raise him to sonship — was an overmastering thought. In the presence of this sublime conception, all so-called culture seemed an impertinence, and all philosophy merely subordinate and contributory. In the light of the great idea, citizenship, culture, oratory, all alike, as aims of education disappear. Citizenship of the city of God now transcends while it comprehends the claims of all earthly cities; culture is the mere adornment of the life in Christ, oratory the mere vehicle for proclaiming the Evangel. An organised scheme of guidance for the individual spirit during its transitory passage to an eternal life arose out of the central thought of Christianity; and this superseded all previous conceptions of the education of man. Errors, unfortunately, were made. Philosophy and the products of human genius were, ere long, held to be essentially hostile to the new life. Many centuries had to elapse before Romano-Hellenic culture was found to be compatible with the Christian aim.

To some it may appear that in the past pages, while I have allowed their full educational value to civil laws, and the social organisation of nations, I have yet attached too great an importance to national religious conceptions. I think not. Outside the prosaic and prudential moralities, without which the most elementary society cannot sustain itself for a day, the idea of God and of man as related to Him governs all life, and therefore all education, of the human spirit. It determines all ethics, and consequently all civic and political activity, though it may be silently. For the idea of God is not merely the conception of a world-cause and world-order, but gathers up into itself all the ideal impulses, infinite in their essential character, which place the mind of man on its highest plane of energy — whether in philosophy and art, or in practical politics and the conduct of life. It is the final interpretation of man. That idea, such as it may be from time to time and age to age, lies in the innermost core of consciousness even when its existence is denied. Epicurus has his God as well as Zeno, Plato no less than Paul, the Aztec as well as the Chinese, and above that idea, which also is the ideal, no man and no nation can rise. The educational administrator has to think of these things if he is not, with the best intentions, to leave his country worse than he found it, and sow the seeds of dissolution. 'To govern well,' says Milton, 'is to train up a nation in true wisdom and virtue, and that which springs from thence, magnanimity (take heed of that) ; and that which is our beginning, regeneration and happiest end, likeness to God which we call godliness : and this is the true flourishing of a land. Other things follow, as the shadow does the substance.'[1]

Authorities. — Largely loci classici, especially Suetonius, *De Gramm.* Cicero, *De Orat.* ; Tacitus, *De Orat.* ; Pliny ; Strabo ; Becker's *Gallus ; Erziehung und Jugendunterricht bei den Griechen u. Römern*, von J. L. Ussing ; Ihne's *History of Rome ;* Mommsen's *History of Rome*, also of the *Roman Provinces ;* Hegel's *Philosophy of History ;* Krause's *Geschichte der Erz. etc. bei den Griechen und Römern ;* Bähr's *Geschichte der Römischen Litteratur ;* Emile Jullien, *Sur les Professeurs de la littérature dans l'ancienne Rome ;* Lecky's *History of European Morals.* Also several books mentioned under Greece and references to numerous historians.

[1] *Of Reformation in England*, second book (near beginning).